Advancing Business Ethics Education

Edited by

Diane L. Swanson
Kansas State University

and

Dann G. Fisher
Kansas State University

INFORMATION AGE PUBLISHING, INC.
Charlotte, NC • www.infoagepub.com

Library of Congress Cataloging-in-Publication Data

Advancing business ethics education / edited by Diane L. Swanson and Dann G. Fisher.
  p. cm. – (Ethics in practice)
 Includes bibliographical references.
 ISBN 978-1-59311-543-2 (pbk.) – ISBN 978-1-59311-544-9 (hardcover) 1. Business
ethics. I. Swanson, Diane L. II. Fisher, Dann G.
 HF5387.A35 2008
 174'.40711–dc22

                                                                    2008000854

Printed in the United States of America

*This book is dedicated to all educators who endeavor
to include ethical analysis in the business classroom.*

CONTENTS

FOREWORD

The *Ethics in Practice* series provides a forum for the exploration and discussion of organizational ethics issues that may otherwise be overlooked in the usual venues of academic journals and books. The focus of the series is interdisciplinary, which includes not only a focus on ethical issues in the public, private, and nonprofit sectors, but on the body of knowledge on ethics that can be found in other disciplines as well. The series, therefore, seeks to help readers better understand organizational ethics from a variety of vantage points, including business, public and nonprofit administration, psychology, sociology, anthropology, criminology, and victimology. There is much each discipline can learn from each other, with the common thread being organizational ethics.

As editors, our goal is to provide scholars, instructors, and professionals in ethics and social responsibility with a meaningful collection of books in key areas that will expand thinking on issues of research and pedagogy. We see the series as a consortium where new ideas can be surfaced and explored, future inquiry stimulated, and where old ideas can be seen through different lenses.

An early goal was to establish effective ethics education as a concern within the *Ethics in Practice* series. What role could education play in stemming the tide of seeming widespread unethical decision-making in the work environment? *Advancing Business Ethics Education* by Diane L. Swanson and Dann G. Fisher, provides an excellent inquiry into business ethics education. While there have been many explorations of ethics and social responsibility in numerous scholarly books, the focus on ethics education has more frequently been found in journals and reports. This book is an important contribution to that key aspect of translating ethics research into effective teaching methodologies.

Advancing Business Ethics Education fills a significant void in the area of business ethics education. It takes a holistic approach to the topic, with a

Advancing Business Ethics Education, pages ix–x
Copyright © 2008 by Information Age Publishing

scope that looks within and beyond the confines of the classroom. In it, the editors assemble a series of outstanding papers that focus on the various constituencies of AACSB, Deans, CEOs, faculty, and students, and the critical issues related to reputation, educational design, cognitive and emotional concerns, corporate governance, and global citizenship.

As editors, we believe that you will find the various chapters as thought-provoking and insightful as we have. The ideas articulated in *Advancing Business Ethics Education* will no doubt invigorate the pivotal concerns that confront business ethics education. In these chapters you will find seminal ideas for changing how you think about ethics education and how you teach ethics to your students. The potential impact upon organizations is great indeed.

Finally, we welcome your input and ideas surrounding organizational ethics education and welcome you to contact us with your ideas and comments for future volumes.

Robert A. Giacalone
Carole L. Jurkiewicz
Editors, *Ethics in Practice*

CHAPTER 1

BUSINESS ETHICS EDUCATION

If We Don't Know Where We're Going, Any Road Will Take Us There

Diane L. Swanson
Kansas State University

Dann G. Fisher
Kansas State University

ABSTRACT

The distinguished authors featured in this volume are dedicated to business ethics education. As editors, we are pleased to present their views. Collectively, they point to an exciting roadmap for advancing business ethics education at a critical juncture in the history of corporate America. Unfortunately, such advancements are stymied by the common practice in business schools of marginalizing ethics by scattering ethics topics superficially and incoherently across the curriculum, a habit we find indefensible in a post-Enron climate. This practice signals to students that ethics does not matter as much as other coursework, fails to provide an adequate counterbalance to the amoral

Advancing Business Ethics Education, pages 1–23
Copyright © 2008 by Information Age Publishing
1

subtext that dominates much of business education, lacks the conceptual building blocks needed to make integration effective and life-long learning possible, and renders accurate assessment of learning outcomes difficult if not impossible. Moreover, this scattershot approach fails to prepare students for newly minted and fast-growing careers in ethics compliance, risk management, and corporate social responsibility. The first step toward remedying these problems is to require a stand-alone ethics course in the business school curriculum. In this introductory chapter, we address reasons why business schools resist this remedy and the dangers of maintaining the status quo. Finally, we offer a three part formula for delivering coherent business ethics education as the solution.

INTRODUCTION

Despite the most recent outbreak of corporate scandals, the agency that accredits business schools internationally has not drafted standards that would mandate sound ethics education. Specifically, the Association for the Advancement of Collegiate Schools of Business (AACSB) chose not to require even one stand-alone ethics course in its new standards formulated in 2003. Instead, the agency decided that schools can meet accreditation standards by integrating ethics across the curriculum. As Fred Evans and Earl Weiss observe in their chapter in this volume, this decision was made despite pressure from hundreds of business educators and practitioners who called for a considerably stronger policy. Indeed, the Evans-Weiss survey data (chapter 3) suggest that a majority of AACSB deans actually support stand-alone ethics coursework in the curriculum, even though the accrediting agency rejected this stance in formulating its 2003 standards. Similarly, the National Association of State Boards of Accountancy (NASBA, 2005), while finally poised in the wake of accounting scandals to require ethics education as a qualification to sit for the CPA exam, now appears willing to allow accounting programs to point to coverage broken asunder throughout the curriculum as meeting its ethics requirement. Faced with a tumultuous moral crisis in business, both standard-setting associations have refused to strengthen ethics education by simply requiring a course dedicated to and taught by faculty trained in ethics.

In a post-Enron environment, this status quo is unacceptable. Addressed later, an unfocused scattering of ethics across the curriculum is ineffective. Moreover, the failure to improve business ethics educational standards can easily be perceived by a skeptical public as aiding and abetting recurring corporate scandals. Likewise, the lapse in decisive action in the wake of what many believe to be the worst wave of corporate misconduct in U.S. history reinforces a continued threat of loss of legitimacy for business schools, a dynamic that Deborah Vidaver-Cohen addresses in her chapter on business school reputation. Her clarion call for business schools to meet the reputational challenge (chapter 4) resonates with the views of other authors represented in this volume who are concerned that business schools risk irrelevance. Notably, William Frederick (chapter 2) asserts that the whole curriculum needs to be overhauled to incorporate advancements in the natural and social sciences so that students and practitioners can grasp the natural processes that drive business functions and influence workplace behavior and personal identity within a social milieu. In similar vein, Richard Mason (chapter 7) calls for applications of neuroscience to the non-reasoning emotional level that influences organizational conduct so that business educators can address the emotional maturity and moral development necessary for ethical conduct in business. Sue Ravenscroft and Jesse Dillard (chapter 9) invoke insights from cognitive science to argue that moral imagination is a key component to such moral reasoning, and they advocate incorporating these insights in the ethics classroom. Jerry Calton, Steve Payne, and Sandra Waddock (chapter 8) demonstrate how such goals can be accomplished in a classroom setting where dialogic engagement and reflective practices help develop moral courage and imagination. Diane Swanson and Peter Dahler-Larsen (chapter 10) hold that an imprimatur of self-identity beholden to standard economics poses an impediment to such advancements, and they envision a new sense of self for business ethics education informed by more suitable perspectives.

These authors are calling for no less than a shift in worldview. For such shift to occur, business educators need to transmit a clear signal that ethics matters (Giacalone & Thompson, 2006). This signal must be transmitted to students of general management as well as to those studying more focused or functional areas of business. In terms of the former, O.C. Ferrell and Linda Ferrell (chapter 11) present ethical decision making models that incorporate organizational dimensions and stakeholder considerations relevant to all aspects of management. Donna Wood and Jeanne Logsdon (chapter 13) identify decision parameters that managers questing for corporate citizenship in global environments marked by cultural relativism should consider. Other authors demonstrate the pertinence of ethics to more focused areas. For instance, Archie Carroll and Ann Buchholtz (chapter 14) speak to the ethical implications of corporate governance, showing that it is important for students to understand not only the benefits of good corporate governance but also the tremendous toll that poor governance can take in the aftermath of corporate meltdowns, with billions of dollars in shareholder wealth gone, thousands of jobs lost, and countless lives ruined. Marc Orlitzky (chapter 16) highlights the many ways in which ethics can be part of human resource management coursework, featuring its applicability to staffing, performance appraisal, compensation, and training and development geared toward corporate social responsibility. As

Mike Shaub and Dann Fisher (chapter 15) attest, the relevance of ethics to accounting should be painfully obvious in the wake of accounting scandals. Yet, in their view there is little hope of imparting constructive values to accounting students, as long as the curriculum is tethered to the narrowly self-seeking premises of agency theory, a step child of standard economics. As antidotes, Shaub and Fisher offer three guidelines for ethical decision making that instructors should impart to future accounting professionals. Joseph Petrick (chapter 6) presents data that substantiates the potential for developing such integrity competencies in business students. Even so, he cautions that ethics education is simply a link in a chain of influences on behavior, observing that it is unreasonable to expect that one single link in this chain of inputs can control behavior by itself. We agree. No one is advocating that one ethics course will resolve all ills. The point is that requiring all students to take at least one course dedicated to ethics is the very least that business schools can do in a scandal-ridden corporate environment.

According to the past president of Texas A & M, Robert Gates, the university's responsibility in the wake of unparalleled corporate scandals is obvious. He states:

> All of these liars and cheats and thieves are graduates of our universities. The university community cannot avert its eyes and proclaim that this is not our problem, that there is nothing we can do, or that these behaviors are an aberration from the norm. (Gates, 2002)

Business administrators and faculty must meet this challenge head on. The first step is to place ethics on par with the technical sub-disciplines so that it can serve as a counterbalance to "value free" or amoral economic orthodoxy and its offshoot agency theory that dominates business education (Ravenscroft & Williams, 2004; Swanson & Frederick, 2005). To the point, ethics must be advanced in its own right as part of a comprehensive curriculum. We submit that the cornerstone of this curriculum should be a required, stand-alone ethics course, an assessment underscored by Marc Orlitzky, Joseph Petrick, and Deborah Vidaver-Cohen in the chapters that follow. Indeed, Jim Weber, Virginia Gerde, and David Wasieleski (chapter 5) demonstrate how the business school at Duquesne University delivers ethics in the curriculum based on properly designed, independent ethics coursework. Denis Collins (chapter 12) explains how he has engineered an ethics course to be a vehicle for providing students with service learning projects that accomplish gains in environmental sustainability in practice. These authors' experiences affirm that providing sound ethics education quite simply involves coursework dedicated to the proposition. They also prove that it can be done in academic environments marked by resource constraints and crowded curriculum.[1]

In this introductory chapter, we address reasons why business degree programs resist advancing ethics education, even in the face of successful model programs like Duquesne's. We also delineate the dangers of maintaining the status quo while offering a three part formula for delivering coherent ethics education as the solution. In doing so, we are informed by our previous research in this area as well as insights from our contributing authors who provide important markers on the path toward advancing business ethics education.[2] This collective vision is important because, as the title to this chapter conveys, if we don't know where we are going with business ethics education, any road will take us there. Finally, we point out that ethics in the curriculum can be an opportunity to train students for newly minted careers in compliance, risk management, and corporate social responsibility. To miss this opportunity due to a longstanding habit of sidestepping ethics would be foolhardy for business schools supposedly sensitive to the labor market for their graduates. Moreover, such shortsightedness could also be construed as rubber stamping the damage that ethical myopia in business wrecks on society.

RESISTANCE TO RIGOROUS BUSINESS ETHICS EDUCATION

Although the Academy's acceptance of business ethics as a legitimate area in the curriculum dates back to the 1970s when AACSB standards then plainly pointed business schools to some kind of required course, often labeled "Business and Society" or equivalent nomenclatures, advancements in this area have been marred by backtracking and resistance.[3] This resistance has come from inside and outside business schools. In terms of external impediments, the role of the business school accrediting agency, AACSB, is a particularly troubling stumbling block to long-lasting constructive advancements.

External Impediments

As background, AACSB's previously strong signal that ethics should be part of the business curriculum in its own right was diluted in the early 1990s when that agency adopted more flexible, mission-driven standards.[4] As a result, previous gains in ethics coursework did not last (see Collins & Wartick, 1995; Fisher, Swanson & Schmidt, 2007; Windsor, 2002). Specifically, the new standard allowed stand-alone coursework to be dismantled in favor of flexibility in distributing ethics across the curriculum. We hold this new standard to be woefully shortsighted, as do many others. In approving the 2003 standards that did not require a separate ethics course, AACSB ignored petitions from hundreds of professors and practicing managers as well as two associations—the Washington, DC-based Ethics Resource Officers and the Social Issues in Management Division of the Academy—that at least one ethics course be required as a condition of accreditation.[5] According to Diane Swanson and Bill Frederick (2005) who led the petition campaign in support of Duane Windsor's Open Letter on Business School Responsibility that called for a stand-alone ethics course (Windsor, 2002), AACSB not only ignored the groundswell sentiment for such standard, but also exhibited—unintentionally, no doubt—a cronyism reminiscent of those executives responsible for overseeing gross misconduct in their firms during the last wave of corporate scandals (see Mitroff & Swanson, 2004; Swanson & Frederick, 2005). Here's how. In clandestine circular fashion AACSB is made up of member deans who craft rules that they then apply to their cohorts and themselves. There is no government oversight and hardly any external pressure on this "dean's club" for accountability and transparency in ethics education (Klein, 1998).[6] By all appearances, member deans craft standards flexible enough to retain room to wiggle out of recurring curriculum battles at their own schools. As a result, educational standards can and do yield to political expediency.

Ironically, however, the findings of a 2003 survey of AACSB deans by Evans and Weiss, presented in chapter three, suggest that most business school deans believe that more emphasis should be placed on ethics. Most CEOs surveyed in this study responded similarly. Indeed, between 73% and 81% of the respondents (deans and CEOs) agreed to some extent with the statement, "A concerted effort by business schools to improve the ethical awareness of students eventually will raise the ethical level of actual business practice." *Moreover, an overwhelming majority of the CEOs, deans, and faculty polled agreed or strongly agreed that an ethics course should be required for all undergraduate and MBA students.* We are uncertain how to reconcile these attitudes with AACSB's rejection of requiring even one ethics course in the curriculum, except to repeat our speculation that, in the final analysis, the deans who self-regulate curricular standards settled for flexibility and political expediency instead of sound ethics coverage.

In this wishy-washy accrediting environment of mixed signals, political maneuvering among faculty, discussed next, means that ethics easily gets sacrificed to courses that are sacred cows or currently in vogue (Swanson, 2003). This closed system of self-regulation has failed ethics education (Windsor, 2002). In an article aptly entitled "It's a heckuva time to be dropping ethics courses," *Business Ethics Magazine* gives a troubling account of business schools that have participated in a well recognized past time of downsizing ethics in curriculum, which continues even in the aftermath of the corporate scandals (Kelly, 2002).

To be fair, AACSB officials have included ethics at the top of the list of content areas for accreditation. They also added certain ethics material to AACSB's website, but only after the flood of petitions, mentioned previously, prompted media coverage and heated debate on scholarly discussion lists. In reality, however, AACSB holds fast to the claim that ethics can be integrated across the curriculum absent a foundational ethics course. When asked if ethics can be adequately covered this way, Ray Hilgert, emeritus professor of management and industrial relations at Washington University's Olin School of Business, said: "If you believe it's integrated in all the courses, then I'm willing to offer you the Brooklyn Bridge" (Nicklaus, 2002, p. C10).

Internal Impediments

AACSB's doctrine of curriculum flexibility, which allows each business school to set its own ethics requirements, effectively absolves schools from requiring *any* courses in ethics. Deans and department heads can claim that ethics is incorporated into the curriculum overall, meaning that professors from disciplines such as marketing, finance, operations management, accounting, and strategic management who are not trained in ethics can claim to teach a smattering of it in their courses. In reality, however, these professors find it burdensome to try to integrate well-developed variants of ethics across the curriculum, particularly given their understandable desire to teach their own areas of expertise first and foremost. Not surprisingly, these faculties typically resist championing more ethics coverage. In fact, Evans and Weiss report that when AACSB deans were asked to identify, in an open-ended question, what they believe is the greatest single impediment to increasing the emphasis on ethical education in the business curriculum, approximately 34% of the respondents identified the lack of faculty interest as the greatest impediment. Many deans feel that faculty just aren't interested in teaching ethics, and would rather focus on subjects directly related to their discipline.

The long-term corrosive impact of AACSB's across-the-curriculum doctrine affects faculty strength as well. AACSB's flexibility policy can contribute directly to reducing or eliminating the number of ethics faculty. Always small in numbers, ethics professors face a stacked political deck when curriculum is voted on and courses are reduced or eliminated by faculty fiat (Windsor, 2002). Although a few schools have developed excellent ethics programs in the face of these pressures, these gains are easily lost when professors retire or move to other universities and are not replaced. The

University of Pittsburgh's Katz Graduate School of Business is only one example among several, although surely a uniquely audacious one, where the axe fell on its required ethics curriculum even as the sensational news of corporate scandals was still unfolding (Kelly, 2002).

A core reason for faculty resistance is that most degree programs face a zero-sum curriculum. Therefore, because the AACSB has freed business schools from requiring *any* ethics courses, additional resources are not readily forthcoming. Deans neither have an incentive to champion ethics coursework, nor do they feel any pressure from their faculty to commit resources to this effort. As a result, administrators and faculties are faced with the difficult, if not burdensome, process of attempting to intertwine ethics systematically with technical coverage. The call for increased coverage may prompt departments to debate what areas to omit from the curriculum so that ethics may be added. In many cases, an ethics course is doomed before the debate even begins. As Evans and Weiss report, nearly 32% of the deans they queried responded that there is no room in their core curriculum for another course. Positive results from this scenario are unlikely, since it politicizes ethics coursework, prompting other faculty to protect their turf in a curriculum that lacks space and resources for additional coursework. Indeed, this may be why the majority of accounting faculty in a survey conducted by Blanthorne, Kovar, and Fisher (2007) report contentment with the status quo of integration. The default option is to leave ethics in the hands of individual faculty, resulting in coverage that ranges from sufficient to superficial to nonexistent. In this system of business education, ethics coverage can be up for grabs (Swanson, 2004).

To make matters worse, many faculty members have an inherent bias against ethical concepts due to their academic training in a variant of economics interpreted to be amoral or value-free (Swanson & Frederick, 2005). To their credit, some professors embrace the need for more ethics coverage. Others, products of standard economics education, are much less excited about, if not openly hostile to, the idea. This perception is not without consequences. The homage paid to conventional economics by many business educators justifies promoting narrow self-interest over community goals while ignoring the far-reaching dysfunctional consequences (Orlitzky, Swanson, & Quartermaine, 2006; Ravenscroft & Williams, 2004; Swanson, 1996; Waddock, 2003). Not surprisingly, claims that ethics cannot be taught keep resurfacing among this group, despite convincing evidence that social and behavioral skills can be learned and improved upon through exposure to educational programs that blend theoretical principles and practice (Rest, Narvaez, Bebeau, & Thoma, 1999; Rynes, Trank, Lawson & Ilies, 2003). Indeed, the student data that Petrick details (chapter 6) stands as a testament to the potential to improve student ethics competencies after exposure to just one ethics course.

At any rate, putting ethics on the defensive by the recurring mantra that it cannot be taught is absurd. We know of no other course held to such burden of proof. An accounting professor puts the situation in perspective by asking: "And do we say that financial, auditing, and accounting courses are utter failures when over 500 companies had to restate their financial reports in 2005? Therefore do we stop teaching these courses?" Another professor, formerly a business school dean, observes: "To say ethics education has no influence is equivalent to saying that education has no influence. If we give up on ethics education we might as well give up on all education. Is that what the cynics advocate?" Actually, most business school deans may agree with this sentiment, given Evans and Weiss's report that AACSB deans register general agreement with the statement that undergraduate and MBA "students who take a business ethics course will experience a change in attitude and behavior." Combine this with the deans' overwhelming belief that the recent business scandals will have long-term negative consequences for business, also detailed in chapter three, and the next step of requiring at least one ethics course in the business curriculum would seem to be a no-brainer.

Despite the deans' belief in the efficacy of ethics coursework, it is important to keep in mind that ethics champions have never claimed that one ethics course will resolve all ethical dilemmas. Similarly, one would be hard pressed to find any organizational scholars who would assert that one course in organizational behavior will resolve all questionable organizational dynamics. Obviously, students will find themselves in workplace situations where organizational culture, policies, peer pressure, leadership, laws, stakeholder pressures, and other factors influence the nature of ethical dilemmas and possible responses, a state of affairs that Ferrell and Ferrell explicate in chapter eleven. Given the complexity of these influences, it is modest to propose that at least one course in the curriculum address ethics whole cloth. The very least that business schools can do is to send students into the workforce armed with ethics language and the ability to recognize ethical dilemmas and possible solutions, just as marketing, leadership, and other behaviorally based courses impart specific language and knowledge to students. And do detractors place a similar burden of proof on these courses? For instance, do business faculties demand evidence that all business students who take leadership courses become good leaders? Arguably, universities would need to be shut down if all courses were held to such an impossible standard. Degree programs are designed to impart concepts to students. No faculty can control what happens to graduates after they leave higher education. The hope is that their reasoning processes have improved for the better and that such education is a constructive force in society overall. Such hope is consistent with the mission of the university, which is to facilitate the pursuit of knowledge for its own sake as well as the practical development of personal intellect and character (see Reed, 2004).

The findings from a recent survey of accounting educators by Blanthorne et al. (2007) are representative of obstacles to ethics education in business degree programs overall. This survey reveals that accounting educators believe that ethical development is critical to the profession, necessary to re-establish public trust after recent accounting scandals, and an important step toward making sure that the profession does not lose the right to self-regulate. Although the respondents to this survey assert that more ethics coverage is necessary, they did not favor a stand-alone course, nor did they indicate support for teaching ethical theory. This position seems conflicted but not altogether surprising. It is simply emblematic of the resistance among faculty to changing the curriculum to incorporate ethics. Given this recalcitrance, many deans fail to exert the necessary leadership for change, which is why the mission-driven standards set forth by AACSB are inherently flawed in terms of prompting long lasting advancements in business ethics education.

DANGERS OF THE STATUS QUO: WHY CHANGE IS NECESSARY

Signaling Importance (or Lack Thereof) to Students

The paucity of ethics coverage resulting from the scattershot approach to ethics education poses the obvious risk of graduating students who are not prepared to recognize ethical dilemmas in practice, much less understand, suggest or implement possible solutions. Equally important, the superficial scattershot approach sends an improper signal to students: ethics does not matter as much as technical expertise. For example, accounting programs have settled for an *ad hoc*, disconnected, smattering of ethics coverage across the curriculum. Blanthorne et al. (2007), noting that nearly all (98%) of their respondents favor integration to a stand-alone course, report that less than 5% of accounting faculty surveyed teach a stand-alone course, a 50% decline from two decades ago (Karnes & Sterner, 1988). Moreover, Blanthorne et al. determined that integration of ethics in the average accounting curriculum amounts, at best, to 32 hours of classroom coverage or the equivalent to a 2-credit hour course. These authors note that their findings do not shed light on the depth and quality of coverage but merely indicate that ethics was in some way addressed across the curriculum (see the section on assessment problems below). Thus, their determination probably suggests an upper bound for the amount of integration that is occurring in accounting programs. Nevertheless, weigh that sleight amount of ethics coverage against the 30 credit hours or more that accounting programs commit to developing technical expertise.

Is it any wonder that business schools are at risk for graduating students who believe that technical expertise is more important than ethical integrity?

Ravenscroft and Williams extend the "signaling argument" by contending that indoctrinating students in narrow economic theory well before they are exposed to ethical theory taints their view of the latter. In describing this phenomenon, they state:

> In this world, where maximizing shareholder value is primary and privileged, where firing workers is seen as 'getting rid of the fat' and results in improved stock prices, where minimizing taxes by incorporating in Bermuda, where increasing the minimum wage is seen as anti-business, and where externalizing the costs of pollution is smart because one's competitors are doing it as often as they can, why would students be expected to take ethics courses seriously? (Ravenscroft & Williams, 2004, p. 19)

The problem is not merely an early exposure to a type of economic theory that encourages students to wash their hands of ethics. As Ravenscroft and Williams allude, the dilemma also stems from a lack of curricular balance. Once students have been introduced to the standard version of economics and its elevation of self-interested instead of other-regarding behavior, this view is repeatedly reinforced in the business curriculum by faculties who have little or no background in ethical theory due to their training in value free economics. Hard to fathom that a few hours worth of ethics topics sprinkled indiscriminately across the curriculum can balance the overriding message of indifference or antagonism to ethics that students are receiving. Swanson and Dahler-Larsen (chapter 10) describe the atavistically amoral sense of self conveyed by such education, compared to more justifiable views.

Given this dubious state of affairs, Shaub and Fisher (chapter 15) propose mobilizing influential faculty who believe in and are capable of communicating constructive values to students, rather than trying to force change on faculty who do not wish it. The signal that ethics matters is best given by those educators who believe it.

Lack of Conceptual Building Blocks

Consider how economics is presented. Early in the curriculum, students are exposed to the necessary building blocks. Evidently, the assessment is that economic analysis would be too difficult or cumbersome unless students receive a solid theoretical foundation that they can use to guide analysis. Hence, economic theory and principles are presented early in the curriculum so that the issues that will be examined in the remainder of the students' business education can be placed systematically within an economic paradigm. In short, economics is the theory; business is the application.

Now consider how ethics is presented via the scattershot approach that passes for integration. Students are not exposed to conceptual building blocks in a course dedicated to conveying them. This implies that ethical analysis lacks complexity and/or boils down to application of a few simple rules (e.g., the Golden Rule). In reality, lack of exposure to conceptual building blocks makes application difficult because students (and many of the faculty) lack the theory and principles necessary to channel analysis and dialogue toward constructive ends. This approach is inconsistent with Bloom's taxonomy (1956) because it bypasses or assumes the existence of knowledge, comprehension and application (the first three levels in the taxonomy). Instead, the process moves directly to class discussions and case analyses that require students to be capable of the higher levels in the taxonomy (analysis, synthesis and evaluation) before they are prepared. Lacking solid theoretical underpinnings, this approach easily becomes superficially naive rather than analytically sound. The point is that ethics needs to be delivered whole cloth, not piecemeal.

Students will not take ethics education seriously until it can be viewed as foundational to the application of accepted theories and principles to business. The scattershot approach prevents ethics from reaching the same plane as economics and renders it incapable of serving as a necessary counterbalance to the unrealistic assumptions about human nature parlayed by economic orthodoxy. Before ethics can serve as one of the conceptual and theoretical pillars for business applications, ethical concepts must be introduced at an appropriate time in the curriculum and delivered whole cloth by knowledgeable faculty.

Assessment Problems

The listing of ethics on various syllabi indicating that some topics are covered in some courses does not constitute any particular assessment standard. Instead, it implies that superficial, uninformed coverage can be judged equivalent to an in-depth, consciously designed freestanding course. The so-called "integration approach" just doesn't add up. In many if not most schools, this *ad hoc* approach will fail to yield sound coverage of business ethics, undermining the stated intent of the accrediting agency and setting the stage for inadequate business education for decades to come. For when ethics is scattered across the curriculum, assessing learning outcomes becomes difficult if not impossible. According to Swanson and Frederick, two assessment errors are inevitable:

1. Ethics coverage will be assessed as being sufficient when it is woefully inadequate or even missing in action.
2. Ethics content can be distorted, diluted or trivialized but still pass inspection. (Swanson & Frederick, 2005, pp. 229–230)

The *Chronicle of Higher Education* reports similar skepticism about whether or not professors will devote more than just a cursory nod toward ethics (Mangan, 2003). This suspicion is also reflected in the Evans-Weiss survey, which indicates that 22% of responding deans cite a lack of faculty expertise, especially if the intent is to integrate ethics throughout the curriculum. In the final analysis, the listing of ethics on various syllabi and/or letters from faculty claiming the ethics has been woven into various courses does not necessarily add up to sound ethics education.

It is important to note that assessment failures are but artifacts of how ethics coverage is framed to befit AACSB's mission driven standards devised in the 1990s. This relatively recent shift in policy has prompted business schools questing for accreditation or reaccreditation to engage in a false choice between integrating ethics across the curriculum and offering a standalone course. *But in reality there is absolutely no dichotomy between a stand-alone ethics course and integration, and the issue should not be framed as such* (Armstrong, 1993). Rather, a standalone course is a necessary foundation for attempts to integrate ethics into other courses (Swanson & Frederick, 2005). Because the issue has been artificially framed as either-or, the primary outcome of the more flexible, mission-driven standards adopted by AACSB has been the deterioration of ethics in the curriculum to the point that only one-third of all accredited business schools offer a free-standing ethics course (Derocher, 2004; Willen, 2004), and presumably fewer require one.[7]

This paucity of ethics coursework portends that most business students will graduate without understanding the new public and private initiatives that are changing the landscape against which the business curriculum will inevitably be judged. Their failure to comprehend sweeping reforms in corporate governance, financial market regulations, sentencing guidelines for organizations, rules for prosecuting corporate criminals, and global codes of responsible conduct almost guarantees that business school reputations will be on the defensive indefinitely. Although these reforms are living proof that ethical issues and factual analysis go hand in hand, many business schools will continue to deliver value-free education that rationalizes the behavioral excesses now prosecuted as corporate criminality (Swanson, 2004). Such education can be self-fulfilling (Ghoshal, 2003). It not only encourages students to adopt amorality, but it also teaches them that narrow self-interest should trump collective needs, despite all evidence to the contrary (Ferraro, Pfeffer & Sutton, 2005).

It is high time for business schools to stop functioning as incubators for amoral practitioners who are discouraged from taking collective needs into account. Instead, forward-looking innovations in ethics education are needed, such as that put forth by Collins (chapter 12), who describes how an ethics course can be designed to deliver community-oriented service learning experiences to business students, giving them an opportunity to "walk the ethics talk." As Collins shows, an ethics course in the curriculum does not dampen the potential for creative pedagogy but rather expands it.

Missed Career Opportunities

Although many business schools seem not to have noticed, ethics is a booming, fast-changing area in practice, especially since companies are seeking help in complying with key elements of public policy, including those mandated by the Foreign Corrupt Practices Act of 1977, the Organizational Sentencing Guidelines of 1991 (stiffened in 2004), and the Sarbanes Oxley Act of 2002 (Hyatt, 2005). Today nearly all large U.S. corporations and most businesses of any size have ethics policies or codes, and the number of ethics officers heading companies' ethics programs has increased accordingly (Lawrence & Weber, 2008). Recruiting is vigorous in ethics compliance and accounting controls specifically as well as corporate social responsibility generally (Hyatt, 2005). Currently, the CRO Provider Directory alone lists almost 500 companies offering services in eleven different domains pertaining to corporate responsibility (CRO-E Newsletter, 2007). Furthermore, positions of this type are continuously posted on the CSR and SRI (corporate social responsibility and socially responsible investment) website.[8]

Mirroring these developments in practice, the majority of states now require ethics coursework in continuing education as a condition for CPA license renewal. Specifically, thirty-four of the 54 State Boards of Accountancy have implemented an ethics continuing education requirement (Fisher et al., 2007). In this way, continuing education programs are leading business schools in ethics coverage. Unfortunately, this is like putting the cart before the horse, since continuing education should ideally build upon concepts garnered in accounting degree programs. The danger is that business schools will be viewed as lacking relevance and legitimacy where ethics is concerned. Consider that PricewaterhouseCoopers (2003), critical of the perceived lack of value created by the accounting masters degree, proposes that in-house, extant continuing education be an alternative means to meeting the 150-hour masters requirement. This proposal portends the possibility that ethics education could be taken over by professional constituents by default. If so, the university will be seen as content to abdicate or outsource standards in this critical area of professional education to its detriment.

The bottom line is that business degree programs are lagging both continuing education and the burgeoning demand for ethics practitioners. Moreover, this gap may widen in the future. On this subject Levine (2007) holds that there is bi-partisan support for legislating corporate social responsibility and corporate citizenship programs instead of relying of voluntary efforts. Given this oversight environment, there is every reason to expect corporate social responsibility initiatives to increase, leading to more demand for students trained in the area. And what better training than a course dedicated to ethics and corporate social responsibility, taught by instructors trained in these subjects and willing and able to keep up on research and fast-changing developments? Indeed, the knowledge needed to initiate and implement corporate social responsibility in practice is increasingly specific, requiring knowledge of the law (e.g., Sarbanes–Oxley and the Federal Sentencing Guidelines for Organizations), organizational ethics initiatives (ethics training programs; ethics audits; ethics hot lines; specialized board committees; and the use of ombudspersons, peer review panels, and ethics officers) and participation in company- or industry-specific voluntary codes, often disseminated to stakeholders in separate reports. The point is that business ethics requires specialized training much like auditing is required knowledge for accounting. While it is unthinkable for accounting students to graduate without requisite auditing coursework, business schools can claim that their graduates have ethics knowledge, even though an ethics course is missing in action from the curriculum.

THE SOLUTION: THE BENEFITS OF A THREE PART FORMULA FOR DELIVERING BUSINESS ETHICS EDUCATION

As set forth by Swanson and Frederick, the three-part benchmark standard for business ethic education is quite straightforward.

1. A required foundational ethics course is necessary.
2. Efforts to integrate ethics across curriculum should be a goal.
3. Other initiatives, such as hosting guest speakers, offering service learning projects, and establishing endowed chairs in ethics, are highly desirable. (Swanson & Frederick, 2005, p. 235)

As Swanson and Frederick observe, this formula retains sufficient discretion for individual schools, since it does not dictate the design or placement of individual courses in curriculum. The issue is one of scope. As the Social Issues in Management Governance Committee proposed in 1977, one required threshold course in ethics need not dampen other curricular initiatives (Frederick, 1977). Potentially everyone gains by keeping the material on ethics intact as a required foundational course. By design, this approach encourages cross-fertilization of ideas within other business courses, rendering integration across coursework meaningful. It is an eminently "flexible" base for any and all schools to infuse greater ethical awareness in their students. Moreover, it can serve as a countermeasure to narrowly amoral business education in three ways. First, a stand-alone course sends the proper signal to students: ethics matters. Kultgen (1988, p. 366–367) asserts that if we want our students to embrace the virtues of a professional, steps must be taken to instill them:

> The professions . . . can only invite and equip individuals to become true professionals, that is not just certified . . . , but deeply committed to the professional ideal and incorporating its virtues in their character. This invitation is important. Entry into the profession is a voluntary act and most people who perform it are disposed to learn its ways and take its ideology seriously. They need only be told how.

> Clearly, the professional school plays the critical role. Professional associations and peer groups continue the process of socialization, but these are not likely to be effective if the individual is not aimed in the proper direction at the outset.

Scattering ethics across the curriculum can hardly be seen as aiming students in a clear direction. Instead, it allows schools to perpetuate the prevailing ideology of economic self interest that downplays responsibility to others, as conveyed by a plurality of faculty. There should be no surprise when graduates internalize this ideology and effectively implement it (Ferrarro et al., 2005; Ghoshal, 2003). In contrast, a required, stand-alone ethics course amounts to an unmistakable invitation for students to embrace and earn the public's trust in business.

The second way a stand-alone ethics course mitigates amoral business education is by providing students with the conceptual building blocks that will allow advanced learning to occur throughout the curriculum and beyond. Faculty already integrating ethics coverage into their courses and faculty interested but still apprehensive about introducing ethics in their courses would be able to assume that students have a common body of knowledge upon which to build. Creating ethically sensitive students could have the added benefit of encouraging cross-fertilization of ideas across the curriculum, as mentioned previously. For instance, students engaged in writing assignments and group projects in various courses would have the background to apply ethical concepts effectively to a wide array of cases. This exposure facilitates life-long learning (Mitroff & Swanson, 2004). For instance, Rest (1983; 1986) found that that formal education is the most powerful predictor of moral reasoning ability, and that moral reasoning skills continue to increase as long as formal education is pursued. Moreover, his 56-study meta-analysis (Rest, 1986; 1994) shows that ethical education programs are especially effective in promoting the moral reasoning abilities of graduate and professional school students, which suggests that improving students' ethical reasoning skills through ethics coursework is both relevant and doable (Fisher et al., 2007). It is also called for when continuing education programs, such as those mentioned in the previous section, require ethics coursework that assumes prior knowledge.

Finally, a stand-alone ethics course moves business schools away from the habit of promulgating amorality by providing the opportunity for sound assessment of ethics in the curriculum. Students completing such a course successfully have plainly demonstrated a certain level of achievement in grasping a body of knowledge. That is, they have been evaluated in their proficiency to understand and apply ethics delivered whole cloth in a dedicated course. This method of assessment is simple and time-honored: student performance is reflected in an assigned grade. There is no ambiguity here. Students either pass the course or they do not. In this way, the two assessment errors identified above can be avoided. That is, ethics will not be assessed as sufficient when it is woefully inadequate or even missing from the curriculum. Nor will it pass inspection when its content gets distorted, diluted or trivialized by uninformed inclusion in other courses (Swanson & Frederick, 2005).

Although it is beyond the scope of this chapter to go into the resource implications of staffing faculty in ethics courses, we note that Ph.D. programs specializing in ethics and corporate social responsibility have existed for decades. That there is a supply of trained ethics educators is evidenced by the existence of certain academic associations, including the Society for Business Ethics, International Association of Business and Society, and Social Issues in Management division of the Academy of Management. Conferences and symposia devoted to ethics abound. Even so, if the accrediting agency is serious about advancing business ethics education, then its standards should effectively ensure that a supply of faculty formally trained in the area is maintained in the face of faculty attrition and the habitual axing of ethics coursework encouraged by present policy. To not anticipate and deal with these issues is to ignore realities on the ground.

In terms of other resources, there is no dearth of ethics textbooks and academic journals devoted to or inclusive of ethics. Moreover, corporate resources aimed at ethics practices are growing (Hyatt, 2005) The problem is that most business schools do not take full advantage of the resources that the ethics field has spawned since being recognized as a legitimate area of the Academy decades ago. Of course, the major tradition that informs our understanding of professional ethics is actually some two thousand years old. To deprive business students of this longstanding rich tradition as well as contemporary innovations and applications is worse than shortsighted. It is indefensible.

Business educators need to assume a leadership role for implementing and delivering the three part formula for ethics education. Weber, Gerde, and Wasieleski demonstrate how this can be accomplished in chapter five. Otherwise, allowing business pedagogy to be dominated by a narrowly amoral version of economic theory while providing students with only *ad hoc* glimpses of ethical principles means that business schools can be viewed as complicit in corporate misconduct. Again, Vidaver-Cohen holds that such perception is bound to damage the reputations of business schools. On the other hand, she argues that those schools that deliver strong ethics coverage can be recognized and rewarded for their competitive edge, a possibility that students themselves seem to apprehend. For when Peterson and Albaum (2005, p. 124) sampled 3,034 undergraduate business students from 60 different colleges or universities, they found that a substantial majority believe that "all business students should take a formal course in business ethics." Another survey suggests that students view the current state of business ethics education as substandard in that only 22% of MBA students polled said that business schools are doing a lot to prepare them ethically (Aspen Initiative for Social Innovation through Business [AISIB], 2002), a statistic confirmed by a survey of managers in an executive MBA program signifying that ethical myopia increased with the number of business courses taken (Orlitzky et al., 2006). It appears that business schools are lagging not only continuing education and practice in ethics, but also student expectations and needs.

Given this state of affairs, faculty cannot wait for external agencies to force change in business education. Instead, we must choose to be the change agents, assisting business in rebuilding its sullied reputation by changing our own institutions. The first step is to require a stand-alone foundational ethics course in the core curriculum.

This means discarding the ill-framed, artificial debate about whether a stand-alone course or integration across the curriculum is best. We must do both!

CONCLUSION

Continued reliance on the scattershot approach to ethics education lacks authenticity. It signals that ethics doesn't matter, fails to provide an adequate counterbalance to the amoral economic orthodoxy that dominates business education, lacks the conceptual building blocks needed to make integration effective and life-long learning possible, and makes accurate assessment difficult if not impossible. Moreover, it fails to prepare students for fast-growing careers in ethics compliance, risk management, and corporate social responsibility. The first step toward remedying these problems is to require a stand-alone ethics course. If this is to be achieved, however, university support must be gained and maintained. Because ethics faculty lack curricular voting power, and many other faculty report contentment with the status quo (Blanthorne et al., 2007), the shift toward sound ethics education remains vulnerable to faculty vying for resources for other coursework. Due to this unfortunate politicization of the issue, survival of ethics coursework now depends not only on faculty champions, but also on the interest of university administrators, including presidents, chancellors and provosts who will need to provide budgetary support (Swanson, 2004).

Meanwhile, constructive ideas for advancing ethics in the business curriculum will continue to come from enlightened educators, who, based on direct contact with students and practitioners, are convinced that the status quo must change. Some of these views are set forth in the chapters that follow by notable experts whose support for rigorous ethics education is well informed and longstanding. Overall, these views are organized thematically from broad statements on the need for reform, to best curricular practices, to perspectives that influence the content and scope of ethics education, to more focused applications in disciplinary or functional areas. It is important to consider these visions for advancing business ethics education. Otherwise, if we don't know where we are going, any road will take us there.

NOTES

1. At Kansas State University, our academic home, the College of Business Administration faces the same kind of resource and curricular constraints found at similar institutions. Yet, a standalone ethics course, delivered as "Business, Government, Society," has been required of our undergraduate students since 1967. A similar ethics course has been required in the MBA program since that program's inception in the 1980s, and an elective in Professional Ethics is now offered to MBA and Masters of Accountancy students. The college also features an Ethics Speaker Series and other extracurricular initiatives. We submit that where there is a will to deliver strong

ethics coverage, there is a way. For a description of ethics in the K-State business curriculum, go to http://www.cba.k-state.edu/departments/ethics/
index.htm.

2. Some of our discussion in this chapter is drawn from previously-published
articles by Swanson (2003; 2004), Swanson and Frederick (2002–2003;
2005), Fisher and Swanson (2005), Fisher, Swanson, and Schmidt (2007),
and Mitroff and Swanson (2004).

3. Equivalent nomenclatures for ethics courses include "Corporate Social
Responsibility," "Corporate Social Performance," "Business and Society,"
"Corporate Citizenship," "The Non-Market Environment of Business,"
"Social Issues in Management," "Legal and Social Issues in Business," and
"Professional Ethics," to name a few. While titles vary, the litmus test for a
course dedicated to ethics is that the focus is on delivering ethics literature
in a business and society context. Textbooks for this type of course abound,
replete with case studies.

4. As Swanson and Frederick (2005) note, another policy change occurred
around the same time that AACSB switched to more flexible, mission-driven
standards in the 1990s: The U.S. Department of Higher Education stopped
recognizing AACSB as an accrediting agency. While it is not clear to us why
AACSB lost government recognition (or even what that recognition meant
to begin with), we submit that the trend to "flexify ethics" shortly thereafter
deserves further investigation.

5. Coverage of "Campaign AACSB" included articles in *AFX Global Ethics Monitor Online* (Benner, 2002), *Bloomberg News* (Willen, 2004), *Chronicle of Higher
Education* (Mangan, 2003), *INSIGHT Magazine* (Derocher, 2004), *Pittsburgh
Post-Gazette Online* (Thomas, 2002), *St. Louis Post Dispatch* (Nicklaus, 2002),
and *Topeka Capital Journal Online* (Moline, 2002).

6. Swanson and Frederick (2005) observe that issues of accountability and
transparency in curricular standards are compounded because member
deans of AACSB accrediting teams sometimes have longstanding professional relationships or personal friendships with the deans of the schools
they visit, calling into question the arms-length relationship expected of
accreditation judgments. This raises the specter of cronyism. Yet the sincer-
ity of AACSB deans is not in question. Rather, our point is that organizational bureaucracy can encourage policies and behaviors that narrowly
serve the status quo or, in this case, amoral business education. In such a system, true leadership is rare.

7. This one-third statistic squares roughly with other available data. For
instance, in this volume Evans and Weiss report that only 34% of undergraduate programs and 25% of MBA programs require a course devoted
entirely to ethics, according to their survey of AACSB deans. A narrower
survey of the top thirteen U.S. business schools revealed that only twenty-
three percent require a course in ethics while thirty percent stipulate a
course in which ethics is combined with another subject. The clincher is
that nearly half (46%) of these top schools offer only an ethics elective,
which equates to no requirement at all (see Mac Lean & Litzky, 2003, as
reported in *USA Today*, 2004). This finding is consistent with the Aspen/
World Resources Institute's assessment that most MBAs still graduate without an anchor in social and environmental management. The institute's statistic for schools leading ethics education is particularly dismal. Of the 188

schools surveyed, only six (3%) were identified as cutting-edge in areas of ethics, corporate social responsibility, and sustainability (Schneider, 2003). Given this track record, claims that ethics education is on the rise has to be viewed with some skepticism. Unless schools can point to freestanding ethics coursework taught by knowledgeable faculty dedicated to the enterprise, then it is difficult to know the extent to which students are actually exposed to ethics. As mentioned in this chapter, the listing of some ethics topics on various course syllabi does not constitute any particular standard for whole cloth ethics education (Swanson & Frederick, 2005).

8. To view the CSR and SRI website go to http://www.ethicalperformance .com/recruitment/index.php.

REFERENCES

Armstrong, M. B. (1993). Ethics and professionalism in accounting education: A sample course. *Journal of Accounting Education, 11,* 77–92.

Aspen Initiative for Social Innovation through Business (AISIB) (2002). Where will they lead? MBA student attitudes about business & society. Accessed August 15, 2003, http://www.aspeninstitute.org.

Benner, J. (2002, November 14). MBA accreditation body resists professors' call for required ethics course. *AFX Global Ethics Monitor Online.* Accessed November 16, 2002, www.globalethicmonitor.com/afx-eth/homepage_summary.html.

Blanthorne, C., Kovar, S. E., & Fisher, D. G. (2007). Accounting educators' opinions about ethics in the curriculum: An extensive view. *Issues in Accounting Education, 22,* 355–389.

Bloom, B., (Ed.) (1956) *Taxonomy of education objectives.* NY: David McKay.

Collins, D., & Wartick, S. L. (1995). Business and society/business ethics courses: Twenty years at the crossroads. *Business & Society, 34,* 51–89.

CRO-E Newsletter (2007, May 9). Accessed May 9, 2007, www.thecro.com/ provider_directory.

Derocher, R. (2004, January/February). Knowing right from wrong. *INSIGHT Magazine Online.* Accessed May 17, 2007, www.insight-mag.com/insight.

Ferraro, F., Pfeffer, J., & Sutton, R. (2005). Economics language and assumptions: How theories can become self-fulfilling. *Academy of Management Review. 30*(1), 8–24.

Fisher, D. G., & Swanson, D. L. (2005, August). A call to strengthen proposed NASBA ethics requirements: A three-step formula, *Compliance & Ethics,* 36–38.

Fisher, D. G., Swanson, D. L., & Schmidt J. J. (2007). Accounting education lags CPE requirements: Implications for the profession and a call to action. *Accounting Education, 16,* 345–363.

Frederick, W. C. (1977, Spring). Business and society curriculum: Suggested guidelines for accreditation. *AACSB Bulletin, 13,* 1–5.

Gates, R. M. (2002, October 3). Convocation address by Dr. Robert M. Gates, President Texas A & M University. Accessed November 15, 2002, http:// www.tamu.edu/convocation/convaddress/gates02.html.

Ghoshal, S. (2003, Fall). B schools share the blame for Enron: Teaching brutal theories leads naturally to management brutality. *Business Ethics, 17*(3), 4.

Giacalone, R., & Thompson, K. (2006). Business ethics and social responsibility education: Shifting the worldview. *Academy of Management Learning & Education, 5*, 266–277.

Hyatt, J. C. (2005, Summer). Birth of the ethics industry. *Business Ethics, 19*, 20–27.

Karnes, A., & Sterner, J. (1988). The role of ethics in accounting education. *The Accounting Educators' Journal*, Fall, 18–31.

Kelly, M. (2002, November/December). It's a heckuva time to be dropping business ethics courses. *Business Ethics Magazine, 16*, 17–18.

Klein, W. H. (1998). Recollections on implementing the ideas of *Conceptual Foundations*. In R. F. Duska (Ed.), *Education, leadership and business ethics: Essays on the work of Clarence Walton* (pp. 91–109). Dordrecht: Kluwer Academic Publishers.

Kultgen, J. (1988). *Ethics and professionalism*. Philadelphia, PA: University of Pennsylvania Press.

Lawrence, A. T., & Weber, J. (2008). *Business & society: Stakeholders, ethics, public policy* (12th edition). NY: McGraw-Hill/Irwin.

Levine, M. A. (2007, April 25). Legislating corporate social change. *Corporate Responsibility Officer*. Accessed April 25, 2007, www.thecro.com/node/398.

Mac Lean, T., & Litzky, B. (2003). Task force on integrating ethics and business in society in the U.S. management curriculum. Paper presented at the International Association for Business and Society conference, Rotterdam. Accessed May 17, 2007, http://www.cba.k-state.edu/departments/ethics/docs/priorresearch.htm.

Mangan, K. S. (2003, January 8). Accrediting board endorses stronger focus on ethics in business-school curriculums, *Chronicle of Higher Education*, Accessed January 8, 2003, http://chronicle.com/daily/2003/01/2003010805n.htm.

Mitroff, I., & Swanson, D. L. (2004, June). An open letter to the deans and the faculties of American business schools: A call for action. *Academy of Management News*, 7–8.

Moline, M. (2002, September 30). Professors to focus on ethics. *Topeka Capital Journal*, C1.

National Association of State Boards of Accountancy (NASBA). (2005). *Proposed revisions to the Uniform Accountancy Rules 5–1 and 5–2*. Accessed June 1, 2005, www.nasba.org/NASBAfiles.nsf/Lookup/UAAEducationRulesExposureDraft/$file/UAA%20Education%20Rules%20Exposure%20Draft.pdf.

Nicklaus, D. (2002, December 18). Is a bigger dose of ethics needed in business schools?' *St. Louis Post Dispatch*, C10.

Orlitzky, M., Swanson, D. L., & Quartermaine L. K. (2006). Normative myopia, executives' personality, and preference for pay structure: Toward implications for corporate social performance. *Business & Society, 45*(2), 149–177.

Peterson, R. A. & Albaum, G. (2005). Benchmarking student attitudes regarding ethical issues. In O.C. Ferrell & R. A. Peterson (Eds.). *Business ethics: The new challenge for business schools and corporate leaders* (pp. 115–137). NY: M.E. Sharpe.

PricewaterhouseCoopers (2003). *Educating for the public trust: The PricewaterhouseCoopers position on accounting education*. NY: PricewaterhouseCoopers.

Ravenscroft, S., &. Williams, P. F. (2004). Considering accounting education in the USA post-Enron. *Accounting Education 13*(Supplement 1), 7–23.

Reed, D. (2004). Universities and the promotion of corporate responsibility: Reinterpreting the Liberal Arts tradition. *Journal of Academic Ethics, 2*, 3–41.

Rest, J. R. (1983). Morality. In J. Flavell & E. Markman (Vol. Eds., P. Mussen, Gen. Ed.). *Manual of child psychology: Vol. 3, cognitive development* (pp. 556–629). NY: John Wiley and Sons.

Rest, J. R. (1994). Background: Theory and research. In J. Rest & D. Narvaez (Eds.). *Moral development in the professions* (pp. 1–26). Hillsdale, NJ: Lawrence Erlbaum Associates.

Rest, J. (1986). *Moral development: Advances in research and theory.* NY: Prager Press.

Rest, J. R., Narvaez, D., Bebeau, M. J., & Thoma, S. J. (1999). *Postconventional moral thinking: A neo-Kohlbergian approach.* Mahwah, NJ: Lawrence Erlbaum Associates.

Rynes, S. L., Trank, C. Q., Lawson, A. M., & Ilies, R. (2003). Behavioral coursework in business education: Growing evidence of a legitimacy crisis. *Academy of Management Learning & Education, 2*, 269–283.

Schneider, M. (2003, October 3). B-schools with a broader bottom line. *Business Week Online.* Accessed October 5, 2003, http://www.businessweek.com/print/bschools/content/oct2003/bs2003103_8409_bs001.htm?bs.

Swanson, D. L. (1996). Neoclassical economic theory, executive control, and organizational outcomes. *Human Relations, 49*(6), 735-756.

Swanson, D. L. (2003). Business education puts corporate reputations at risk. *The Corporate Citizen 3*, 34–35

Swanson, D. L. (2004). The buck stops here: Why universities must reclaim business ethics education. In D. Reed & R. Wellen (Eds.), Special Issue on Universities and Corporate Responsibility, *Journal of Academic Ethics, 2*(1), 43–61.

Swanson, D. L., & Frederick, W. C. (2002–2003). Campaign AACSB: Are business schools complicit in corporate corruption? *Journal of Individual Employment Rights, 10*, 151–165.

Swanson, D. L., & W. C. Frederick. (2005). Denial and leadership in business ethics education. In O. C. Ferrell & R. A. Peterson (Eds.), *Business ethics: The new challenge for business schools and corporate leaders* (pp. 222–240). NY: M.E. Sharpe.

Thomas, C. (2002, December 4). Ethics are good business. *Pittsburgh Post-Gazette,* Accessed December 5, 2002, www.post-gazette.com/forum/comm/20021204edclar04pl.asp.

USA Today (2004, March). Bush rebuffed by business schools, 6.

Waddock, S. (2003). A radical agenda for business in society education, presented at the Academy of Management, Social Issues in Management Division, Seattle.

Willen, L. (2004, March 8). Kellogg denies guilt as B-Schools evade alumni lapses. *Bloomberg News Wire.* Accessed May 15, 2004, http://www.cba.k-state.edu/departments/ethics/docs/bloombergpress.htm.

Windsor, D. (2002, October 8). An open letter on business school responsibility. Accessed November 30, 2002, http://info.cba.ksu.edu/swanson/Call/Call.pdf.

CHAPTER 2

THE BUSINESS SCHOOLS' MORAL DILEMMA

William C. Frederick
University of Pittsburgh

SETTING THE SCENE

The half-century struggle to find, and then to secure, a respected niche for teaching ethics and corporate social responsibility in the nation's business schools continues to be contentious and with an uncertain outcome. For some, the torrent of corrupt and fraudulent actions symbolized by Enron seemed to justify greater attention to corporate wrongdoing and misbehavior. This chapter grapples with the way business schools have, and have not, risen to this latest challenge.

The moral dilemma is this: Are business schools complicit in the corporate crimes committed by their graduates a) by inculcating a rationalist mindset in faculty and students that de-centers, or even dismisses, social responsibility and/or, b) by failing to include, or even denigrating, considerations of social responsibility and ethics in their courses of study? Charged with preparing tomorrow's business leaders and professionals, such complicity by the schools would indeed be a serious matter bringing into question the entire role and function of the business schools. A solution to this dilemma is neither readily apparent nor easily discovered, so

Advancing Business Ethics Education, pages 25–42
Copyright 2006 by William C. Frederick. All rights reserved. Adapted from William C. Frederick, *Corporation, Be Good! The Story of Corporate Social Responsibility* (Indianapolis, IN: Dog Ear Publishing, Inc., 2006, pp. 240–256). Used by permission of the author.

this chapter will struggle, as have other observers, to find approximate answers. Only by resolving the dilemma would it be feasible and acceptable for business schools to assume a meaningful role in promoting business's pursuit of corporate social responsibility.

Post-Enron Questions

Following the high-profile corporate corruption cases of the late 1990s and early 2000s, the nation's business schools were criticized for possibly contributing to the widespread fraud and criminal acts by failing to instill a sense of morality and ethical awareness in their students. After all, Enron's Jeff Skilling and Andrew Fastow, two major figures at the center of that company's troubles, held MBA degrees from well-known business schools. But in some circles, the questioning went even deeper, going so far as to cast doubt on the kind and quality of management education itself that was being offered by the business schools. The major target of both criticisms was the MBA degree program, considered to be the schools' premier product and often its major revenue source, not to speak of the continuing reach and influence (and financial advantages) enjoyed by the school from the loyalty of its MBA graduates serving in business, government, and community posts worldwide. Understanding the nature and function of the MBA is therefore key to judging the validity of the attack on the business schools. If the flaw leading to moral compromise or managerial incompetence is located in the MBA program, then the solution to both deficiencies would seem to suggest reform of the MBA curriculum.

Not so fast, some would say, it's not that simple. And they would be correct, of course. But first, it will be useful to take a hard look at what is claimed for the MBA—what is the competence claimed for it—and what in fact it does accomplish for those who hold it, for the school that grants it, and for the companies that hire MBA graduates. There is a world of difference between what might be called "The Official MBA" and "The Real MBA."

The Official MBA

The general promise and expectation of an MBA educational experience is that it produces leaders who will serve in significant posts in business, government, community, and other influential sectors of the economy and society. The language found at the websites of prominent business schools is invariant. Their aim is "to educate leaders" (Harvard Business School); to create "a principled leader of business and society" (Darmouth's Tuck School); to produce "general management leadership" (University of Pennsylvania Wharton School of Business, no date); to provide "leadership" (Stanford Business School). In one way or another, all business schools, whether of elite status or more run-of-the-mill, make the same claims.

For most MBA students, management leadership is to be acquired by taking a two-year course of full-time study on campus, interspersed if possible with an on-the-job training internship between the first and second years of classroom instruction. On this basic theme, many other variations exist: part-time evening courses for working students; executive MBA programs for higher-level managers; weekend courses taken over an extended period of time; distance-learning courses beamed into one or more companies; on-line courses, sometimes paired with occasional campus classes; MBA programs tailored to the needs of a particular company and offered in-house; and other ways of delivering the core elements of an MBA education. The core disciplines and fields are economics, finance, marketing, organizational behavior, operations, controls, information technology, policy, strategy, and the various statistical, mathematical, and analytical techniques that support these functions.

In effect, the business schools are saying, "Take these courses, and you will become a leader. You will be fitted with the skills and knowledge needed to lead and manage an enterprise. Because such leadership competence is in great demand in today's world, you will be financially rewarded in proportion to the importance and contribution you make to your organization's success in the marketplace." As one leading business school states, its MBA students will learn to "refine analytic, decision-making, judgment skills" and gain "lasting knowledge and experience." The Official MBA indeed promises much to students and to the companies who hire them.

The detractors and doubters. The official MBA has come under a withering attack for failing to measure up to its rosy promises. Interestingly enough, the harshest criticisms originate from within the business schools themselves:

1. Stanford's Jeffrey Pfeffer and Christina Fong (2002) cite empirical evidence that the MBA (the "official" one) does not enhance one's professional career, does not exert significant long-term influence on one's salary, and gives too little attention to the kinds of skills important to managers, such as interpersonal relationships, communication abilities, and (ironically) leadership qualities. Taught by faculty members who themselves have no hands-on business or management experience, and whose abstract and highly technical research has little influence on management practice, and who themselves give low priority to classroom teaching, these results are not surprising, though regrettable.

2. Another critic, Lex Donaldson (2002) of the Australian Graduate School of Management, blames contradictions and inconsistencies between the theories produced in management schools and what is required of managers faced with real world problems. Actions based on the core theories learned by MBAs would be self-defeating in the marketplace. That's not the kind of "leadership" any firm would welcome.

3. Two Chinese, one a professor of management, the other a management consultant, analyzed the content of teaching cases widely used in MBA programs in China and the United States. Professor Neng Liang and Jiaqian Wang (2004) discovered a strong managerially-oriented rationalistic bias but strikingly less emphasis on human relations, organizational politics, and symbolic factors such as beliefs, ethics, faith, norms, values, and the social meaning of work. They concluded that MBA instruction through extensive use of cases would produce managers who were likely to be strategy-driven but politically naïve, lacking awareness of human and social factors, and having an exaggerated notion of the power of analytic approaches to complex management problems.

4. Reinforcing this picture of business school failings, USC business professors James O'Toole and Warren Bennis (2005) trace the shortcomings to "a dramatic shift in the culture of business schools" from vocational pragmatics to abstract research. The schools' model of excellence emphasizes "abstract financial and economic analysis, statistical multiple regressions, and laboratory psychology"—at the expense of imparting a practical knowledge of the messy, complex, typically indeterminate world of the practicing manager. Business professors "are at arm's length from actual practice, they often fail to reflect the way business works in real life." MBA instruction fails "to impart useful skills…prepare leaders…instill norms of ethical behavior…(or) lead graduates to good corporate jobs."

5. Another trio of business school faculty members—Diane Swanson of Kansas State University, Dwayne Windsor of Rice University, and I (Swanson & Frederick, 2005)—directly accused business schools of being implicated in the corporate corruption scandals by allowing MBA students to bypass entirely any instruction in the ethics and morality of business practice. Only by requiring MBAs to learn about the ethical impacts of business operations on a wide range of corporate stakeholders, their communities, and the global environment would business education become socially acceptable. Backed by hundreds of business faculty who teach ethics plus some management consultants and business practitioners, this call for new ethics

accreditation standards to be mandated for all business schools offering an MBA degree was first ignored, then rejected by the Association to Advance Collegiate Schools of Business (AACSB) which accredits business schools nationally. Known informally and derisively as "The Deans' Club," whose member deans accredit each other's schools and who are gatekeepers blocking any nonconforming schools that aspire to membership and accreditation, it was charged by Pfeffer and Fong (2002) with acting "to maintain the status quo." That looks suspiciously like a case of the fox guarding the hen house, in this case assuring that the MBA mind is kept free of the clutter of ethics and social responsibility.

6. Yet another charge—that business schools have drifted away from instilling a sense of professionalism in their students—was leveled by University of Iowa professors Christine Quinn Trank and Sara L. Rynes (2003). This loss they attribute to a business disdain for theory and research in favor of a narrow focus on first-job skills; an MBA student culture that commodifies learning into packets of technical information fungible in the job market; a media-sponsored ranking scheme that places undue influence in the hands of corporate recruiters and students to the detriment of a broader professional education; an AACSB accrediting process that fails to provide national and professionally-based educational standards for business education; and business school faculties who yield to pressures from students for easier courses, less theory development, and more practical short-run tools. Missing is a sense of professional excellence that nurtures an awareness of social and ethical responsibility.

7. Other icons of the management teaching world have weighed in with essentially the same critical views of MBA education: Wharton's Russell Ackoff (Ackoff & Detrick, 2002), McGill's Henry Mintzberg (2004; Mintzberg & Gosling, 2002), and USC's Ian Mitroff (Mitroff & Swanson, 2004). Mintzberg particularly has taken the business schools to task for substituting an analytic-technical MBA classroom routine for the richly complex interactive learning that can occur only in and through actual workplace experiences acquired, not in the span of a two-year MBA program, but over a longer arc of time and in varying sociocultural contexts.

The Real MBA

If The Official MBA is essentially a fraud that promises more than it delivers and fails to teach what is most needed by practicing managers, why does it continue to be one of the most popular academic offerings (in spite of a recent decline in MBA enrollments and degrees awarded)? It must be doing *something* to satisfy its supporters. Otherwise, why waste two years and several thousand dollars to attend MBA classes? The answer to this puzzle is found in what might be labeled "The Real MBA."

The Real MBA serves the economic, financial, social, and political interests of the current business order. Students who pass through the MBA system, and the professors who teach them, are part of a wide-ranging, comprehensive business culture that requires the kinds of services that business schools can provide. The MBA program, educationally flawed as it is, may most accurately be seen as carrying out five vital functions that help support and sustain business culture as we know it.

Presumptive business know-how. In spite of known, documented shortcomings summarized above, there is a presumption that MBAs possess a fund of useful knowledge that can be applied to business tasks. The tool kit is thought to be filled with analytic techniques that can support the firm's overall strategy, its marketing aims, its production processes, its financial needs, and the kind of technology and organizational systems capable of achieving these profitable ends. That's what corporate recruiters have been told they will find, so they form long lines to capture the "best and the brightest" of the annual MBA output. They often get just that, particularly management consulting firms, investment banks, auto manufacturers, healthcare organizations, and other highly technologized operations. This kind of technical expertise, though vital to the enterprise, falls well outside the scope of managerial work and does not typically qualify one for membership in the management cadre. John Kenneth Galbraith (1967) once referred to the collective skills of this group as a company's "technostructure," and it is indeed one of the few substantive accomplishments of MBA programs. Another is found in the training of what might be called the "corporate soldiery"—those who find useful places within the lower ranks, performing indispensable though unexciting tasks. Neither leaders, hotshot consultants, nor social climbers, they do not normally enjoy the privileges of The Official MBA and may savor only a few of The Real MBA's benefits. Frequently outsourced, downsized, or out-competed in globalized markets, they lead a more precarious existence than their more well-heeled MBA compatriots.

Pre-screening for the job market. Prospective corporate employers are savvy enough to grasp the advantage of having someone else—in this case, the business school—do the first-level sorting of potential MBA hires. Before being admitted to an MBA program, one must take the Graduate Management Admission Test (GMAT) which is administered and graded by a national testing organization. Scoring high is essential for admission to the top-level business schools. Grade point average (GPA) achieved in prior college or university courses is another marker that can mean success or failure in getting into the program of one's choice. Some schools require applicants to draft essays to demonstrate writing ability and to reveal motives for MBA study. Others interview candidates face-to-face to get a feeling for personality and suitability for MBA study, which can be quite rigorous and time-intensive. Some minimum amount of actual business experience, perhaps from three to five years, is often considered desirable.

Line all of these admissions hurdles up, and you have what corporate recruiters seek—a system that weeds out those who are thought to be not quite suitable for making the MBA run. Pfeffer and Fong (2002) reported that when a partner in a leading management consulting firm was asked why companies recruit at business schools, the reply was, "It is a pre-screened pool."

Affiliative networking. One of the advertised advantages of the MBA degree is joining an exclusive club whose members speak the same language (of business), share knowledge of analytic techniques, and have experienced all of the disciplinary rigors and monetary rewards common to MBA alumni everywhere. As Dartmouth's Tuck School website (www.tuck.dartmouth.edu) tells prospective students, "alumni remain involved long after leaving Tuck, creating an unmatched network for graduates at every stage of their careers." Wharton (www.wharton.upenn.edu) speaks of the "unique bond" formed among its graduates who hold "positions of influence around the world." Here is a professional advantage going far beyond any knowledge found in classroom lectures, case studies, analytic techniques, and between-terms internships. Such affiliative linkages may well pay off as new job opportunities, favored appointments, promotions, board memberships, company-to-company contacts, business deals of one kind or another, and, of course, financial gains for oneself. Quite obviously, these bonds are stronger among the graduates of the elite business schools than the general MBA population. Even in the absence of the affiliative loyalty felt by graduates of a single school, the fact that one has an MBA degree sends a coded signal—almost like the secret signs flashed by urban street gangs—that here is a person of recognized worth, possessing at least the minimum qualifications of membership in the upper echelons of business culture.

Enculturation. Students who first step across the threshold into the business school have already been conditioned to the values, norms, and general viewpoints of business culture—plus a willingness to learn even more about it as a way of finding a job and making a living. They may have been led to the door by family attitudes and parental ambitions, an inspiring teacher, an interesting first-job experience, or simply by living in a society whose political ideology blends easily with the necessities of business and where one hears a constant refrain about the virtues of a free-market economy. In this sense, they are a self-selected group favorably disposed to business. It doesn't take long—only about two years—for this pro-business entering attitude to be strongly reinforced. The Aspen Institute (2002) revealed that entering MBA students who believed that a company's top priorities were customer needs and product quality had decided, by graduation time, that top priority should go to "shareholder value." More strikingly, if they found their personal values to be at odds with job demands, they would seek a job in another company rather than challenge the basic values found in corporate culture. This enculturation process—where one learns to accept (or at least not speak out directly against) the values of business culture—is one of the major accomplishments of an MBA education. One learns to be loyal, not just to classmates now and after graduation but to the company, its goals, and the practices needed to achieve marketplace success.

Social symbolism. Society has many ways to signal social class belongingness: ethnic identity, job type, income, place and size of residence, clothing worn, friends and acquaintances, life style, sports preferences, brand of car, vacations taken, jewelry, hair styles, entertainment favored, preferred leisure activities, household possessions, club or association memberships, even religious affiliations, and on and on. One of the lures of the MBA degree is the unspoken signal that it will open pathways eventually leading into the upper reaches of society's class system. The Big Prize is, of course, climbing to the very apex of corporate success—CEOdom itself. After all, the great majority of case studies that the typical MBA analyzes are written and taught from the perspective of top management. It is the guest CEO who is most frequently invited to give tell-it-like-it-is seminars, and to address the graduating class. One visiting CEO who discovered that not all students in his audience wanted to become CEOs became indignant, demanding "Why not!?" Once there, though, CEOs find themselves surrounded by all the trappings that accompany a position of power and influence. The lavish life style signals membership in society's upper classes.

Quite obviously, not all MBAs attain CEOship although many can be expected to hold high-level executive posts such as chief financial officer, chief operating officer, executive vice president, divisional head, plant manager, etc., and to be compensated accordingly. As a group, MBAs are allowed to put their foot on the middle rungs of the social class ladder, a privilege and opportunity to be exploited. Circumstances then determine how far they will climb. Their MBA badge is a subtle reminder to all that the gates to class privilege are now open to the wearer. As the commencement speaker in a *New Yorker* cartoon once emphatically advised members of a graduating class, "Now, go out there and *get yours!*"

The Real MBA and the socio-economic prizes it holds out to those who win it is a powerful attractant, far more than the (doubtful) educational advantages claimed for The Official MBA. Business schools are not permitted—do not permit themselves—to advertise these unofficial benefits openly, with the occasional exception of the affiliative networking enjoyed by graduates of the elite schools. The business schools' most important purpose is to serve the corporate labor market by screening, disciplining, training, and mentally conditioning its graduates so they may be minimally ready for life within the corporate system. Never mind that most of the knowledge acquired by MBA students is irrelevant to the actual conditions and challenges to be encountered in the workplace, as countless critics have demonstrated. Getting in the corporate door is what it's all about.

All else is peripheral and marginal, including ethics, corporate social responsibility, business history, ecology, personal worth, spiritual aspirations, the downside of technological change, the dark underside of market-induced poverty, the emptiness of a work-routinized life. Only where these can be shown to affect a company's goals or managerial strategies are they permitted to become part of classroom instruction.

The upshot is that MBA graduates in effect hold two degrees: An Official MBA that is managerially irrelevant but symbolically meaningful, and a Real MBA testifying that all has been done to discipline the holder to life in the corporate workplace.

The business schools' moral dilemma would therefore appear to be one of their own making, an outcome of the kind of curriculum offered to students—one that educates narrowly (if at all) and without attention to the many social, non-economic consequences of business operations. Those who would change this situation have argued for a greater focus on organizational ethics (Phillips & Margolis, 1999), corporate social responsibility, stakeholder participation (Phillips, 2003), workplace spirituality (Giacalone, 2004), corporate citizenship (Waddock, 2006), the cultivation of virtuous character (Hartman, 2006), regulatory oversight, social contracts (Donaldson & Dunfee, 1999), global standards of conduct (Calkins & Berman, 2004), and other similar approaches. An unspoken assumption seems to have been that, once in place, these curricular reforms would offset the unethical and socially irresponsible tendencies generated by the rationalist-financial-economic-technical core of MBA instruction. This is tantamount to adding another layer of instruction onto The Official MBA degree, thereby allowing the business school to believe, or at least to claim, that its students are being schooled in ethics and CSR, along with all the rest of the MBA corporate package—and therefore the school is innocent of complicity in corporate wrongdoing.

It is an appealing solution even though unlikely to be accepted by entrenched faculty interests, or supported by AACSB accreditation authorities, or to elicit little more than lip service acknowledgment by corporate recruiters, or to be enthusiastically embraced by students themselves who may wonder how well it suits their immediate ambition and goal of finding a corporate placement. Its salience for coping with the business school's moral dilemma may be questioned on other grounds, as well, this time by stepping away from the pros and cons of business school reform and by stepping into "the natural corporation."

THE NATURAL CORPORATION

Today's business corporations—their actions, organizational systems, decisions, policies, values, and motivational impulses—are an outcome of evolutionary natural processes (Frederick, 2004; 2006) So too are their many links to competitors, customers, suppliers, employees, communities, and the ecological environment a manifestation of natural selection pressures operating over long periods of evolutionary time. The corporation conceals these natural forces from public view, hidden behind a screen of sociocultural practices, habits, and customs, so that the cultural factors seem more substantively real than the underlying natural forces. However, nature's laws and nature's limits condition and channel corporate practice generally. They also contain the firm's normative potentials, i.e., the ability and inclination of the corporation's inhabitants to act in ways judged to be right or wrong, socially responsible or irresponsible, ethical or unethical, morally acceptable or morally corrupt (see especially Frederick, 2006).

Given this natural architecture that defines, sustains, organizes, and motivates the modern corporation, the business school's relationship to the corporation—if such ties are to be at all meaningful—is necessarily mediated through the same set of natural processes. If the corporation's normative potentials are a function of nature's limits and laws, then the ability of the business school—or specifically, its MBA program—to affect the values, ethics, and normative inclinations of its students must also be an expression of those self-same natural limits and laws. For this reason, the business school's normative function—the ability to affect the moral consciousness of its students—devolves from natural laws, not simply from culturally imposed rational rules and regulations. The conclusion is unavoidable: only a concept of ethics and corporate social responsibility that is compatible with nature's laws is relevant to the business school's purpose and teaching function.

The two central nature-mediated purposes of the business corporation—*economizing* and *power-aggrandizing*—are at odds with each other and with the interacting *ecologizing* processes of the firm's environment (Frederick, 1995). Few, if any, of the major ethics/CSR approaches taught in business schools for dealing with the moral issues generated by corporate operations directly embrace, or even accept the existence of, these three natural values lying at the heart of the modern corporation. As pedagogical techniques, *such ethics/CSR courses appear to be, and perhaps are, manageri-*

ally and corporately disengaged from morally meaningful analysis for lack of contact with the natural realm.

Take the much-criticized rationalist mindset found prevalent in MBA programs and said to be at odds with the behavioral realities revealed by the research of social scientists, psychologists, anthropologists, and others. This rationalist notion derives from two sources. One is an economic theory that posits rational self-interest as a basic human trait and then builds analytic models that counsel a rational calculation of benefits and costs as a basis for managerial action. A second source of rationalist thinking is an attitude accompanying and guiding the technology of business operations that calls for pragmatic, instrumental, problem-solving procedures. As presently taught in MBA courses, the resultant rationalist mindset is at odds with the flexible, ever-changing dynamics found in complex adaptive systems like the corporation that operate and try to survive on fitness landscapes (Frederick, 1998). Management simply does not lend itself to a purely rationalist approach because it is a non-linear activity, messy, unpredictable, and largely uncontrollable—*made that way by nature.* Contrary to much criticism leveled at the "rationalist" MBA program, the problem with economic analysis taught there is its disconnection from nature-driven behavioral reality, not that it is rationally analytic. So too with the slings and arrows directed at the technology of business; its shortcoming is not in the analytics and pragmatics it necessarily depends on but in its nonlinearity, its open-endedness, the surprising and unpredictable impacts it has on people and society generally—*also made that way by nature.*

The disengagement of the business school from all of the natural sources that make both management *and* normative understanding possible means that much, if not all, that the schools teach their students is sadly deficient. More alarmingly, it suggests that the blame for ethical failure of the corporations and the schools is misplaced. If a nature-disengaged rationalist/analytic management approach is irrelevant, so too would be an ethics/CSR approach similarly detached from a natural base. The recommended remedies—mandatory ethics courses, stronger accreditation standards, corporate citizenship, transcendent spirituality, virtuous character, global citizenship, social contracts, etc.—would most likely not have their intended effect on the MBA/managerial mind. How could they if both managerially and normatively irrelevant?

In the end, one must ask a fearful question: Would these reforms prevent, or even minimize, future Enrons? The equally fearful answer is "not likely," not because the reforms lack all relevance or intellectual and behavioral bite, but because they do not directly address the natural factors that generate the moral quandaries of corporate operations. Just so long as business schools allow this situation to continue, so by equal measure will they continue to be silent partners in corporate crimes, misbehavior, and wrongdoing.

NATURAL CORPORATE MORALS

A natural system of corporate morals is already firmly in place and need not be imposed by legal or philosophic edict. It exists by virtue of natural selection pressures exerted over tens of thousands of years of human evolution, resulting in behavioral forms and genetically embedded impulses that channel corporate operations into the well known patterns of today's business firm.

The evolved moral framework may be understood as a set of value clusters, or as a corporate black box containing and activating those values, or as the collective behavioral output of ancestral neural algorithms that shape the modern corporate executive mind. The primary natural values, business functions, and algorithmic impulses comprising natural corporate morals are *economizing, power-aggrandizing, ecologizing, symbolizing/technologizing,* and the individualized *X-factors* (Frederick, 1995). Taken together, these naturally evolved values/functions/algorithms create a framework of untold normative significance for the various ways in which business is conducted. Such moral realizations are themselves a part of human evolutionary experience, centered in and made possible by an evolving brain that interacts adaptively with its environment. Eventually recognized as "values" or "ethical/moral principles" long after their behavioral consequences had been accepted and understood as communal adaptive necessities, their original nature-based provenance is often concealed, ignored, and even denied by those who limit their studies to sociocultural explanations of business (and human) behavior. They are indeed an instance of an evolutionary "is" becoming a sociocultural "ought," a possibility and "naturalistic fallacy" forbidden in formal philosophy. They achieved normative status by their perceived effects on human adaptation, survival, and flourishing.

Here within this evolved moral framework, one finds all that is typical of business behavior: the uncompromising drive for profits and growth (*economizing*); the rationalist, calculative impulse to innovate (*technologizing*); the focused, hierarchically controlled managerial power (*power-aggrandizing*); the strategic goal-seeking in competitive markets (*competitive economizing*); the symbiotic linkages of firm and community (*mutualistic economizing*); and the indeterminacy, diversity, and demographic variations found in individualized *X-factors* of workforce members. *These are the natural normative directions, impulses, and behaviors of corporate business. They will be expressed. They will be acted upon as decisions, policies, strategies, and goals. They are the central values, the normative core of the business order.*

Three central normative issues emerge from this corporate moral system, each taking the form of contradictory behavioral impulses:

1. The life-giving, life-sustaining, adaptive benefits flowing from a company's economizing may be offset canceled, or denied by the self-centered power-aggrandizing behaviors of corporate managers.
2. An overzealous, firm-focused economizing drive may disrupt, destroy, and decimate the symbiotic linkages essential to organizational functioning, community life and ecosystem integrity.
3. An obsessive quest for managerial power, when linked to a firm's unlimited expansionist tendencies, can greatly diminish and degrade the life prospects of employees, stakeholders, and host communities.

Any business school curriculum that does not acknowledge and address these behavioral urges, attitudes, and impulses implanted by nature in the business mind, as well as the resultant moral contradictions, cannot hope to provide instruction relevant to the moral issues that arise in the workplace. To affect management behavior, one must come to, and be part of, the manager's place of work and decision making. The managerial mind is a pragmatic, problem-oriented mind, *made that way by nature*. It is only doubtfully open to appeals not consistent with nature's traits. Little wonder that such philosophic nostrums as virtuous character, realizing the good society, attaining social justice, or finding transcendent peace of mind—all worthy ends—are so routinely disregarded by business practitioners.

THE NATURAL MBA

What, then, is to be done? Is there a way out for the business schools, a plan of action to restore business education to a place of integrity and managerial relevance? Must the business schools and their prime MBA credential be handcuffed and taken on a perp walk with the other perpetrators of corporate crimes? Can they instead educate, train, and inspire their students to instill a sense of goodness, a moral mission, a goal of socially responsible professional performance into the business corporation?

To this last question, my answer is yes and takes the form of what might be called "The Natural MBA" whose goal, educational rationale, and major curricular components can be summarized briefly:

1. Teach business school students—undergraduates and MBAs alike— the core elements of natural process that drive business functions and influence workplace behavior. Topics, viewpoints, and perspectives would embrace evolutionary biology, the genetics of human

behavior, the neural basis of decision making and attitude formation as revealed by (f)MRI brain scanning, evolutionary psychology, the dynamics of complex adaptive systems, the natural history of organizational systems, the symbiotic linkages of ecosystems and biotic communities, the parallels and disparities of human and non-human organic life, and the effects—both positive and negative—of all these in forming the business mind and mediating workplace decision making and policy formulation and, ultimately, business practice in general.

2. Require of all entering students a basic background in the natural sciences, the social sciences, and the evolutionary history of *Homo sapiens* to be acquired through prior undergraduate study or pre-admission workshops.

3. Recruit, and train if necessary, a new generation of scholar-teachers knowledgeable about the impacts of natural forces on the business firm, its managers and executives, organizational systems, motives, and functions. Their disciplinary backgrounds and expertise would likely be in one or more of the natural sciences.

4. Design novel computer-assisted delivery systems that can reach directly into the business practitioner's mind *at the virtual point and time of decision making and policy formulation,* presenting an array of natural concepts, analytic techniques, and decision alternatives proven to be relevant to such situations. More than descriptive, these digitized arrays could additionally contain virtual, simulated alternative decision paths derived from different sets of moral assumptions and value commitments held by the involved participants both inside and external to the corporate workplace.

5. Discard all claims of leadership learning and immediate professional advantage currently made for The Official MBA, *as well as the belief that the addition of add-on, marginal courses in ethics/CSR will resolve or dissolve the business school's complicity in corporate corruption and criminality.*

6. Encourage, by funding, the discovery of innovative models of business practice that incorporate and integrate natural processes and sociocultural concepts across the entire range of the business firm's operations—marketing, production, finance, organization, communication, strategy, policy making, information technology, environmental impact, etc. Only those models having a demonstrated impact on actual workplace operations would be supported.

7. Provide reflective insights into the workplace intersections of nature, culture, and personal identity, where the broader societal, metaphysical, and philosophic dimensions of life are realized. These viewpoints might be realized through gifted teachers from the disciplines

of history, social science, humanities and arts, philosophy, and the history of science.

8. In cooperation with business firms, design an on-going "clinical" activity related directly to the operations of the business firm for the purpose of providing hands-on experience in grappling with actual workplace problems and processes, as well as to test and validate the practical relevance of classroom ideas. Comparable in scope and intention to the legal training of "moot courts" and the clinical experiences of post-medical school "residencies" and "grand rounds," these workplace clinics would provide a needed link between theory and practice.

Realizing such an ambitious, even radical agenda might seem most unlikely at best and impossible at worst. When the nation's business schools were challenged in the late 1950s by the Ford Foundation (Gordon & Howell, 1959) and the Carnegie Corporation (Pierson, 1959) to move from narrow vocational training to the broader professional preparation of business leaders, the leading schools adopted and enacted the recommended reforms within a decade, followed by most of the others in relatively short order. Helped out by generous funding from both of the foundations and enthusiastic acceptance by the business establishment, the reforms achieved their general aims in a remarkably short period. But to count on that reform model now is probably unwise and unattainable, given the scale, complexities and global dynamics of corporate operations, plus the vested academic interests of the business schools that are ever more conscious of their "national ranking" (Gioia & Corley, 2002) along with their entrenched and well-paid faculties committed to things as they are. It remains sadly true that it is easier to move a cemetery than to change a university curriculum.

A more likely prospect may be found where least expected: in experimental partnerships between localized but daring business firms and one or more marginalized, out-of-the-way business schools, possibly funded by daredevil high-tech entrepreneurs who seek the sources of innovation underlying their own businesses. Unencumbered by the conventions and shibboleths of both The Official MBA and The Real MBA, these high-tech, nature-inspired, recklessly-naïve educational joint ventures might reach beyond the mere preparation of practitioners and/or leaders to demonstrate the powerfully inspiring creativity and inventiveness hidden within and waiting release from nature's forces—a veritable gusher of ideas and perspectives fungible in intellectual and philosophic fruitfulness for firm, society, and individual—in short, a realization of the natural potentials for life, growth, and opportunity that reside in the practice of business but now securely caged within the stale cultural stereotypes of academia.

THE CONTINUING DILEMMA

Not even a shift of this magnitude, with all of its uncertainty, would entirely resolve the business school's moral dilemma, for all of the natural forces that have laid ethical/CSR problems on business's doorstep will continue to operate on the executive mind and to generate self-serving, uncaring, socially disruptive, environmentally disastrous, morally corrupt workplace practices. Nature tells us that much. No single ethics/CSR course, no mandated ethics requirements, no entire MBA program, no philosophic appeal can entirely deflect those darker, antisocial impulses that surface from time to time in corporate life.

On the brighter side, a nature-informed education—The Natural MBA—can reveal to students and practitioners the natural tendencies and long-embedded ancestral proclivities to build systems of social cooperation and exchange, extend reciprocal justice to strangers, form fair and just social contracts, strengthen the symbiotic bonds of family and community—and to explore ways of bringing these socially humane impulses into the workplace. The business schools' dilemma is resolvable, if at all, by redirecting learning efforts away from The Official MBA and The Real MBA and toward The Natural MBA. Therein lies the prospect of avoiding future corporate Enrons by bringing students and practitioners face-to-face with the ethical potentials and opportunities, as well as the dangers, to be discovered within an evolving nature.

In the end, business schools and the corporations they serve share a common moral fate, one set by nature. Thus linked, they must act in concert to avoid nature's normative downside as they seek and find common cause in the more humane potentials that nature holds out to both.

REFERENCES

Ackoff, R., & Detrick, G. (2002). Russell L. Ackoff interview. *Academy of Management Learning & Education 1*(1), 56–63.

Aspen Institute for Social Innovation through Business. (2002). Where will they lead? MBA student attitudes about business and society. www.aspeninstitute .org/isib/student_att.html

Bennis, W. G., & O'Toole, J. (2005). How business schools lost their way. *Harvard Business Review, 83*(5), 96–104.

Calkins, M., & Berman, S. L. (Eds). (2004). Introduction: Special issue: Business ethics in a global economy. *Business Ethics Quarterly 14*(4), 597–601 and related articles 603–774.

Dartmouth University Tuck School of Business Web site (n.d.). www.tuck.dart-mouth.edu.

Donaldson, L. (2002). Damned by our own theories: Contradictions between theories and management education. *Academy of Management Learning & Education* *1* (1), 96–106.

Donaldson, T., & Dunfee, T. W. (1999). *Ties that bind: A social contracts approach to business ethics.* Boston, MA: Harvard Business School Press.

Frederick, W. C. (1995). *Values, nature, and culture in the American corporation.* New York: Oxford University Press.

Frederick, W. C. (1998). Creatures, corporations, communities, chaos, complexity. *Business & Society 37*(4), 358–389.

Frederick, W. C. (2004). The evolutionary firm and its moral (dis)contents. In R. E. Freeman & P. H. Werhane (Eds.) *Business, science, and ethics,* Ruffin Series No. 4, (pp. 145–176).

Frederick, W. C. (2006). *Corporation, be good! The story of corporate social responsibility.* Indianapolis, IN: Dog Ear Publishing, Inc.

Galbraith, J. K. (1967). *The New Industrial State.* Boston: Houghton Mifflin.

Giacalone, R. A. (2004). A transcendent business education in the 21st century. *Academy of Management Learning & Education 3*(4), 415–420.

Gioia, D. A.,& Corley, K. G. (2002). Being good versus looking good: Business school rankings and the Circean transformation from substance to image. *Academy of Management Learning & Education 1*(1), 107–120.

Gordon, R. A., & Howell, J. E. (1959). *Higher education for business.* New York: Columbia University Press.

Hartman, E. M. (2006). Can we teach character? An Aristotelian answer. *Academy of Management Learning & Education 5*(1), 68–81.

Liang, N., & Wang, J. (2004). Implicit mental models in teaching cases: An empirical study of popular MBA cases in the United States and China. *Academy of Management Learning & Education 3*(4), 397–413.

Mintzberg, H.. (2004). *Managers not MBAs.* Oxford: Oxford University Press.

Mintzberg, H., & Gosling, J. (2002). Educating managers beyond borders. *Academy of Management Learning & Education 1*(1), 64–76.

Mitroff, I. I., & Swanson, D. L. (June 2004). An open letter to the deans and faculties of American business schools: A call for action. *Academy of Management Newsletter.*

Pfeffer, J., & Fong, C. T. (2002). The end of business schools ? Less success than meets the eye. *Academy of Management Learning & Education 1*(1), 78–95.

Phillips, R. (2003). *Stakeholder theory and organizational ethics.* San Francisco, CA: Berrett-Koehler.

Phillips, R., & Margolis, J. (1999). Toward an Ethics of Organizations. *Business Ethics Quarterly 9*(4), 619–638.

Pierson, F. C. (1959). *The education of American businessmen: A study of university-college programs in business administration.* New York: McGraw-Hill.

Swanson, D. L., & Frederick, W. C. (2005). Denial and leadership in business ethics education. In R. A. Petersen & O. C. Ferrell (Eds.), *Business ethics: New challenges for business schools and corporate leaders* (pp. 222–240). Armonk, NY: M. E. Sharpe.

Trank, C. Q., & Rynes, S. L. (2003). Who moved our cheese ? Reclaiming professionalism in business education. *Academy of Management Learning & Education*
2(2), 189–205.

University of Pennsylvania Wharton School of Business (n.d.). www.wharton
.upenn.edu.

Waddock, S. (2006). *Leading corporate citizens: Visions, values, value added* (2nd ed).
New York: McGraw-Hill/Irwin.

CHAPTER 3

VIEWS ON THE IMPORTANCE OF ETHICS IN BUSINESS EDUCATION

Survey Results From AACSB Deans, CEOs, and Faculty

Fred J. Evans
California State University, Northridge

Earl J. Weiss
California State University, Northridge

INTRODUCTION

Recent business ethics scandals have prompted a reconsideration of how ethical issues are presented in the curriculum of university-based business programs. Many business educators believe they are not doing a particularly good job of teaching the importance of character, integrity, ethics, and social responsibility. Swanson and Frederick (2002–2003, p. 151), for instance, argue on behalf of "hundreds of business school professors, plus numerous business managers, several former business school deans, and

Advancing Business Ethics Education, pages 43–66
Copyright © 2008 by Information Age Publishing
All rights of reproduction in any form reserved.

many business school students" that we are in fact doing an increasingly poor job of addressing ethics and social responsibility.

One part of the problem lies in the standards adopted by the Association to Advance Collegiate Schools of Business—International (AACSB) that guide accreditation. Accreditation standards in the 1970s and '80s were relatively prescriptive and encouraged schools to include a course on ethics and social responsibility in the core curriculum. The mission-driven standards adopted in April 1991 were less prescriptive about course content. The core curriculum was allowed to vary according to the mission of the individual program. As a result, the curricular emphasis on ethics and social responsibility declined (Swanson & Frederick, 2002–2003).

In the late 1990s, AACSB began pursuing its vision of becoming the primary accrediting body for business programs internationally. It soon became obvious, however, that the American model of business education implicit in the accreditation standards was not the only formula for high quality. New and even more flexible standards needed to be adopted. A Blue Ribbon Committee was formed on July 1, 2000 to develop the new standards. The initial draft standards circulated by the committee for comment contained no more emphasis on ethics than the existing, mission-driven standards.

The lack of emphasis on ethics and social responsibility in the face of a national crisis of confidence in business concerned not only faculty, but also many deans. At its October 2002 annual meeting, the Western Association of Collegiate Schools of Business (WACSB) passed a resolution stating that greater emphasis should be placed on ethics in the new standards. Evans and Robertson (2003b) conducted a follow-up survey of WACSB deans, finding nearly unanimous support for greater emphasis on ethics in the business curriculum. The results were communicated to the Blue Ribbon Committee and reported at the February 2003 AACSB Dean's Conference in Ft. Lauderdale, Florida.

In early 2003, Evans and Robertson conducted a more comprehensive survey of deans at all AACSB accredited business programs. The summary results of that survey were presented at the AACSB annual meeting in April 2003 (Evans & Robertson, 2003a) and a more in-depth analysis of a portion of the survey was subsequently published (Evans & Marcal, 2005).

As a follow-up to the 2003 survey of deans, we conducted a comparative survey in May 2004 on the ethics of Fortune 500 CEOs and deans and faculty of AACSB member schools in the U.S. The results of the comparative survey have not been published previously.

THE 2003 SURVEY OF DEANS

The 2003 survey of deans was designed to gain a better sense of what is being done about ethics in business education and what those responsible for business education think about the subject.

We received 295 valid returns, for a 36% response rate. Sixty percent of the respondents were from public institutions, 22% were from private secular institutions, and 18% were from private religious institutions. Approximately 10% or 31 respondents were from institutions outside the U.S.

Ethics in the Curriculum: What Business Schools are Doing

We asked a series of questions designed to determine what business schools are doing to teach ethics to undergraduate and MBA students. Table 3.1 displays responses to the question, "Do you require your students to take a course of which at least 25 percent is devoted to ethics?" More than half (56%) of the undergraduate programs and less than half (48%) of the MBA programs require such a course. When asked if students were required to take a course "entirely" devoted to ethics, the response is less favorable. As Table 3.1 indicates, only 34% of the undergraduate programs and 25% of the MBA programs require an ethics course.

TABLE 3.1
Ethics Course Requirements

	Undergraduate		Graduate (MBA)	
	Required	Not required	Required	Not required
A. Do you require your students to take a course of which at least 25 percent is devoted to ethics?				
Dean	56% (132)**	44% (104)**	48% (102)	52% (116)
Public	46% (68)	54% (81)	35% (46)	65% (86)
Private secular	64% (29)*	36% (16)*	50% (24)	50% (24)
Private religious	83% (35)*	17% (7)*	84% (32)*	16% (6)*
B. Do you require your students to take a course entirely devoted to ethics?				
Dean	34% (83)**	66% (153)**	25% (57)	75% (157)
Public	22% (32)	78% (116)	12% (16)	88% (114)
Private secular	49% (22)*	51% (23)*	35% (16)*	65% (30)*
Private religious	67% (29)*	33% (14)*	66% (25)*	34% (13)*

* (**) Indicates the difference in the corresponding measure for public institutions (graduate programs) is statistically significant at the 95% confidence level in a two-tailed test.

The results obtained from responses to both questions varied by the type of institution. Private religious institutions are the most likely to offer significant coverage of ethics in the curriculum, with private secular institutions the next most likely, and public institutions the least likely.

We included an open-ended question that asked the respondents for the titles of the required courses in the undergraduate programs that addressed ethics. Approximately 75% list ethics as the primary topic of the course, including such titles as "Ethics in Business" and "Business Ethics." Fifteen percent link ethics to broader topics such as "Business and Society," "The Environment of Business," and "Business and Social Responsibility." Approximately 10% link ethics to law or the legal environment of business.

Our analysis of MBA course titles finds that only 42% of the titles list ethics as the primary topic, 35% link ethics to a broader topic such as "environment," "government," and "society," and 23% link ethics to law or the legal environment of business.

For those programs requiring an ethics course (defined as a course in which at least 25% is devoted to ethics), we asked if the course was taught in the business school. As Table 3.2 indicates, 57% of the undergraduate ethics courses are taught in the business school, while a much higher proportion of ethics courses in MBA programs (81%) are likely to be taught internally. Virtually all the ethics courses taught by faculty in another discipline are taught in either departments of philosophy or religion.

If the respondents from private religious institutions are removed from the results, only 50% of the undergraduate programs and less than 50% of the MBA programs require as little as 25% of a course to be devoted to the subject of ethics. Why isn't there more coverage? The results from the next section of the survey might offer some answers.

TABLE 3.2
Where Ethics Courses Are Taught

Is your ethics course taught in the school of business?

	Yes	No
Undergraduate	57% (75)	43% (57)
Graduate (MBA)	81% (83)**	19% (19)**

** Indicates the difference in the corresponding measure for graduate programs is statistically significant at the 95% confidence level in a two-tailed test.

Who Should Teach Business Ethics?

Although most of the undergraduate and graduate ethics courses are taught in the school of business, a significant number are taught in departments of philosophy or religion. This raises the question about who should teach business ethics. Should it be taught in the business school by business faculty or outside the business school by non-business faculty with expertise in ethics? Do business faculty who teach ethics need special training? If so, who should provide the training?

To answer such questions, we asked our respondents to indicate their opinion on several statements using a Likert scale ranging from strongly agree to strongly disagree.

As Table 3.3, item A indicates, if a business program requires a course in business ethics, 59% of the deans agree or strongly agree that it should be taught by business faculty, compared with 10% who disagree or strongly disagree. Not surprisingly, over two-thirds of the deans disagree with the statement that "business ethics is best taught outside the school of business by experts in ethics," compared with only 13% of the deans who agree (see Table 3.3, item B).

A difficulty frequently cited by deans in using business faculty to teach ethics is the lack of faculty expertise. As Table 3.3, items C and D indicate, many deans acknowledge this difficulty in their response to the statement, "In most business schools there is an adequate supply of qualified faculty to teach a business ethics course." At the undergraduate level, 46% indicate that there is a shortage of faculty expertise while 37% do not; at the graduate level, the split is 44% to 39%. No statistically significant difference is found between the responses for undergraduate and graduate programs.

It is important to note that the deans are split fairly evenly between those who do and do not believe that their faculty members are qualified to teach ethics. And it is probably fair to say that if the deans have reservations about offering ethics courses in the business school, it is because most faculty have not had specific ethics training. The deans are rightly concerned about the quality of the instruction.

Following up on these concerns, the deans were asked to identify, in an open-ended question, what they believe is the greatest single impediment to increasing the emphasis on ethical education in the business curriculum. Approximately 34% of the respondents identify the lack of faculty interest as the greatest impediment. Many of the deans feel that faculty just aren't interested in teaching ethics, and would rather focus on subjects directly related to their discipline. Nearly as many, 32%, respond that there is no room in the core for another course, making the addition of an ethics course difficult. Another 22% of the respondents cite the lack of faculty expertise, especially if the intent is to integrate ethics throughout the cur-

TABLE 3.3
Attitudes toward Teaching Ethics

	Strongly agree	Agree	Neutral	Disagree	Strongly disagree
A	\multicolumn{5}{l}{If a business program requires a course in business ethics, it should be taught by business faculty.}
	27% (74)	32% (87)	31% (84)	8% (21)	2% (6)
B	\multicolumn{5}{l}{Business ethics is best taught outside the school of business by experts in ethics.}
	4% (11)	9% (24)	20% (54)	24% (66)	43% (118)
C	\multicolumn{5}{l}{In most business schools there is an adequate supply of qualified faculty to teach a business ethics course at the undergraduate level.}
	10% (25)	27% (68)	17% (43)	34% (85)	12% (30)
D	\multicolumn{5}{l}{In most business schools there is an adequate supply of qualified faculty to teach a business ethics course at the MBA level.}
	9% (23)	30% (72)	17% (41)	31% (76)	13% (32)
E	\multicolumn{5}{l}{Doctoral students in business should be required to address ethical issues that apply to their area of specialization.}
	45% (115)	26% (67)	16% (40)	9% (24)	4% (9)
F	\multicolumn{5}{l}{AACSB should provide training for faculty on how to teach business ethics.}
	22% (58)	39% (101)	15% (38)	13% (34)	11% (29)
G	\multicolumn{5}{l}{I believe that business ethics ought to be an important part of the educational mission of AACSB accredited business programs.}
	55% (150)	34% (92)	7% (19)	2% (6)	1% (4)

riculum. Finally, 11% of the respondents see no impediment to implementation and believe that the issue has been addressed.

Response to the statement, "Doctoral students in business should be required to address ethical issues that apply to their area of specialization" is displayed in Table 3.3, item E. The responses demonstrate strong support for ethics education for doctoral students. A remarkable 71% of the respondents agree with the statement compared with only 13% who disagree. But if faculty expertise and interest are perceived as impediments to increasing the emphasis on ethical education, where will doctoral students obtain this education? If doctoral students do not receive the needed training in ethics, won't the problem perpetuate itself when they become faculty? It would seem that this issue must first be resolved before we will see changes in the expertise and interest of faculty.

What can be done to assist faculty in teaching ethics? Table 3.3, item F displays responses to the statement, "AACSB should provide training for faculty on how to teach business ethics." Some 61% of the respondents agree that AACSB should provide ethics training for faculty compared with only 24% who disagree.

When asked if they believe that business ethics ought to be an important part of the educational mission of AACSB accredited business programs, 34% of the deans agree and another 55% strongly agree. Only 3% disagree or strongly disagree (see Table 3.3, item G). Among deans, this represents overwhelming support for a curricular emphasis on ethics.

Additional Survey Questions

The deans responded to an additional series of questions in the 2003 survey that were also contained in a follow-up comparative survey described in the next section. In the accompanying tables, responses by the deans to the same questions contained in the 2003 survey are identified as "Dean (1st survey)" and the follow-up comparative survey as "Dean (2nd survey)."

COMPARATIVE SURVEY

As a follow-up to the survey of deans, we conducted a comparative survey of Fortune 500 CEOs, and deans and faculty of AACSB member schools in the U. S. The surveys were sent out in May 2004. The CEOs were mailed a letter and hard copy survey. The letter was on the stationary of J. D. Power and Associates chairman David Power, and signed jointly by Mr. Power and Fred Evans, dean of the College of Business and Economics at California State University, Northridge. Of the 500 letters mailed, 78 usable responses were received, for a 16% response rate. The dean and faculty list was compiled from publicly available AACSB membership records and sent only to U. S. and Canadian members. Of the 695 educational members in the U.S. and Canada, 95 deans responded, for a response rate of 14%. The survey instructions asked the dean to distribute the survey to his or her faculty. Ninety of the dean respondents did so and from that 1,082 usable faculty responses were received. Unfortunately, the response rate for the deans was relatively low, perhaps because of the large number of ethics surveys being administered at that time.

Our hypothesis was that there would be significant differences of opinion between faculty, deans, and CEOs. We hypothesized that CEOs, having lived through the scandals and prosecutions of recent years and now feeling burdened by Sarbanes-Oxley compliance issues, would be most sensitive to ethical issues and most supportive of increased ethics education in business schools. Faculty, we hypothesized, would be least sensitive to ethical issues, primarily because their focus would be on developing discipline-based substantive expertise. Deans, we hypothesized, would fall somewhere in the middle between CEOs and faculty. As administrators, they are more removed from their discipline and, as fundraisers, more closely in contact with the issues important to business leaders.

Contrary to our hypothesis, the data presented below indicate that there are surprisingly few attitudinal differences between our sample of CEOs, deans, and faculty.

Attitudes About Ethics

Table 3.4, item A, presents responses to the statement, "In general, effective business leaders are ethical." For this statement the differences are statistically significant, with CEOs more likely to agree than either the deans in the first survey or faculty. Perhaps it is not surprising that CEOs are more likely to agree, since the statement can be construed as reflecting on their character. Most CEOs probably believe they are effective and most also believe they are ethical. There is considerably more skepticism about linking the two traits among deans and even more among faculty.

Responses to Table 3.4, item B, "I believe ethical behavior in business has declined in the past decade," also differentiate the respondents. CEOs

---

TABLE 3.4
Perceptions of Ethical Behavior

	Strongly agree	Agree	Neutral	Disagree	Strongly disagree
A. In general, effective business leaders are ethical.**					
Dean (1st survey)	41% (111)	37% (101)	11% (29)	9% (24)	2% (6)
Dean (2nd survey)	31% (29)	61% (58)	5% (5)	2% (2)	1% (1)
Faculty	21% (227)	51% (552)	19% (205)	8% (87)	1% (11)
CEO	42% (33)	51% (40)	5% (4)	1% (1)	0% (0)
B. I believe that ethical behavior in business has declined in the past decade.**					
Dean (1st survey)	18% (48)	38% (104)	21% (58)	17% (47)	5% (14)
Dean (2nd survey)	13% (12)	41% (39)	24% (23)	19% (18)	3% (3)
Faculty	20% (216)	39% (423)	19% (205)	19% (205)	3% (33)
CEO	4% (3)	37% (29)	22% (17)	33% (26)	4% (3)

** Indicates the difference in the corresponding measure is statistically significant at the 95% confidence level in a two-tailed test.

are far less likely to agree with the statement than either deans or faculty. As with item A, the CEOs may be taking this statement as a reflection on their character. If ethical behavior has declined in the past decade, and if many if not most of the CEOs were in their current position for at least a portion of the last decade, agreement with the statement could be construed as a reflection on their integrity.

If the deans and faculty are correct about effective business leaders being ethical while ethics in business is declining, the question that must be answered is what is the proper educational response?

One possible response is to increase the emphasis on ethics in the business curriculum. Table 3.5, item A, indicates agreement across the sample with the statement, "In light of recent high profile business scandals, I personally believe that business schools should place more emphasis on ethics education." More than 80% of the CEOs, deans, and faculty agree that more emphasis should be placed on ethics education, with 1% or less disagreeing. There is no statistically significant difference between the groups. Clearly, all responding groups believe something should be done to improve ethics education in business programs.

This conclusion is also supported by examination of Table 3.5, item B, which indicates a widespread belief that there is a link between ethics education and business practice. Between 73% and 81% of the respondents agree to some extent with the statement, "A concerted effort by business schools to improve the ethical awareness of students eventually will raise the ethical level of actual business practice."

TABLE 3.5
Importance of Ethics Education

	Strongly agree	Agree	Neutral	Disagree	Strongly disagree
A In light of recent high-profile business scandals, I personally believe business schools should place more emphasis on ethics education.					
Dean (1st survey)	43% (111)	37% (95)	13% (34)	6% (15)	1% (3)
Dean (2nd survey)	51% (48)	43% (41)	3% (3)	3% (3)	0% (0)
Faculty	50% (541)	36% (390)	9% (97)	4% (43)	1% (11)
CEO	54% (42)	39% (30)	6% (5)	0% (0)	1% (1)
B A concerted effort by business schools to improve the ethical awareness of students eventually will raise the ethical level of actual business practice.					
Dean (1st survey)	21% (54)	57% (148)	14% (36)	7% (17)	2% (4)
Dean (2nd survey)	18% (17)	63% (60)	14% (13)	4% (4)	1% (1)
Faculty	15% (162)	58% (627)	16% (173)	8% (87)	3% (33)
CEO	14% (11)	64% (50)	18% (14)	4% (3)	0% (0)

TABLE 3.6
Will Attitudes and Behavior Change?

	Strongly agree	Agree	Neutral	Disagree	Strongly disagree
A It is likely that undergraduate students who take a business ethics course will experience a change in attitude and behavior.					
Dean (1st survey)	8% (19)	53% (131)	20% (48)	15% (36)	4% (11)
Dean (2nd survey)	7% (7)	42% (40)	35% (33)	14% (13)	2% (2)
Faculty	5% (54)	41% (444)	31% (335)	17% (184)	6% (65)
CEO	4% (3)	51% (40)	38% (29)	6% (5)	1% (1)
B It is likely that MBA students who take a business ethics course will experience a change in attitude and behavior.					
Dean (1st survey)	7% (17)	53% (126)	21% (51)	15% (35)	4% (10)
Dean (2nd survey)	6% (6)	43% (41)	34% (32)	14% (13)	3% (3)
Faculty	5% (54)	40% (433)	31% (335)	18% (195)	6% (65)
CEO	8% (6)	50% (39)	36% (28)	5% (4)	1% (1)

And additional support comes from general agreement found in the responses to Table 3.6, items A and B, that undergraduate and MBA "students who take a business ethics course will experience a change in attitude and behavior." Although the differences are not statistically significant, faculty appear somewhat more skeptical than CEOs that a course in ethics will lead to more ethical behavior. The deans appear to have the strongest belief that an increased student ethical awareness will eventually lead to raising the ethical level of business practice. Overall, the results demonstrate a firm belief in the efficacy of ethics education in business schools.

Interestingly, there are no statistically significant differences between the MBA and undergraduate responses. In other words, belief that an ethics course will change student attitudes and behavior is the same whether the student is in the undergraduate or MBA program.

When asked whether a business ethics course "should seek" to change undergraduate and MBA students' attitudes and behavior rather than whether it "will" actually change attitudes and behavior, Table 3.7, items A and B, indicate that there is much more agreement. Although not statistically different, the CEOs express the strongest belief, followed by the deans and then faculty. Comparing undergraduate and MBA students, there is no statistically significant difference in the responses.

Although the deans feel that more can be done to educate students in business ethics, they also feel that ethics education is already having an impact. Table 3.8, item A, presents the deans' responses to the statement,

TABLE 3.7
Changing Attitudes and Behavior

	Strongly agree	Agree	Neutral	Disagree	Strongly disagree
A A business ethics course should seek to change (undergraduate) students' attitudes and behavior.					
Dean (1st survey)	21% (52)	46% (113)	20% (48)	9% (22)	4% (9)
Dean (2nd survey)	17% (16)	55% (52)	19% (18)	8% (8)	1% (1)
Faculty	17% (184)	49% (530)	20% (216)	11% (119)	3% (33)
CEO	13% (10)	65% (51)	18% (14)	4% (3)	0% (0)
B A business ethics course should seek to change (MBA) students' attitudes and behavior.					
Dean (1st survey)	19% (46)	46% (109)	21% (50)	10% (24)	4% (9)
Dean (2nd survey)	17% (16)	53% (50)	20% (19)	9% (9)	1% (1)
Faculty	18% (195)	48% (519)	20% (216)	11% (119)	3% (33)
CEO	17% (13)	59% (46)	20% (16)	4% (3)	0% (0)

TABLE 3.8
Impact of Ethics Education

	Strongly agree	Agree	Neutral	Disagree	Strongly disagree
A I believe students are more sensitive to ethical issues in business by the time they complete our program than when they start.					
Dean (1st survey)	25% (66)	53% (138)	15% (39)	5% (13)	2% (4)
Dean (2nd survey)	N/S	N/S	N/S	N/S	N/S
Faculty	N/S	N/S	N/S	N/S	N/S
CEO	N/S	N/S	N/S	N/S	N/S
B The recent heightened concern about ethics in business is of little long-term concern [consequence] for business education.					
Dean (1st survey)	6% (15)	10% (28)	10% (26)	30% (81)	45% (121)
Dean (2nd survey)	1% (1)	5% (5)	7% (7)	54% (51)	33% (31)
Faculty	2% (22)	9% (97)	9% (97)	46% (498)	34% (368)
CEO	4% (3)	6% (5)	8% (6)	51% (40)	31% (24)

Note: N/S = not surveyed

"I believe students are more sensitive to ethical issues in business by the time they complete our program than when they start." Some 78% agree with this statement compared with only 7% who disagree.

All respondents seem to believe that the concern about ethics and any remedies that result should be focused on the long term. Table 3.8, item B, reports responses to the statement, "The recent heightened concern about ethics in business is of little long-term concern [consequence] for business education." The public concern about ethics in business requires a long-term commitment by business educators to better prepare future leadership. There is no statistically significant difference between the respondent groups, where between 75% and 87% of the respondents disagree or disagree strongly with the statement.

As indicated in Table 3.9, items A and B, an overwhelming majority of the CEOs, deans, and faculty agree or strongly agree that an ethics course should be required for all undergraduate and MBA students. The CEOs support this proposition more strongly than the deans or faculty, but only for the MBAs is the difference statistically significant.

In a Zogby International poll of college seniors conducted nationwide in 2002 (commissioned by the National Association of Scholars), 73% of the respondents stated that their professors were more likely to teach them that what is right and wrong depends on differences in individual values and cultural diversity as opposed to clear and uniform standards of right and wrong by which everyone should be judged (Zogby International,

TABLE 3.9
Requiring an Ethics Course

	Strongly agree	Agree	Neutral	Disagree	Strongly disagree
A A business ethics course should be required of all (undergraduate) business graduates.					
Dean (1st survey)	N/S	N/S	N/S	N/S	N/S
Dean (2nd survey)	39% (37)	28% (27)	16% (15)	12% (11)	5% (5)
Faculty	40% (433)	29% (314)	15% (162)	12% (130)	4% (43)
CEO	47% (37)	35% (27)	15% (12)	3% (2)	0% (0)
B A business ethics course should be required of all (MBA) business graduates.**					
Dean (1st survey)	N/S	N/S	N/S	N/S	N/S
Dean (2nd survey)	39% (37)	23% (22)	19% (18)	14% (13)	5% (5)
Faculty	46% (498)	24% (260)	14% (151)	12% (130)	4% (43)
CEO	59% (46)	33% (26)	5% (4)	3% (2)	0% (0)

Note: N/S = not surveyed

** Indicates the difference in the corresponding measure for graduate programs is statistically significant at the 95% confidence level in a two-tailed test.

2002). These results were confirmed in a survey of accounting majors at California State University, Northridge, in 2003 and 2006.

As a follow-up to the Zogby poll, we included two statements intended to assess the basic ethical perspective of the respondents. Table 3.10, item A, states that the professor should communicate to the student that there are "clear and uniform standards for right and wrong" by which everyone should be judged. Table 3.10, item B, states that the professor should communicate that what is right and wrong depends upon "differences in individual values and cultures."

The results indicate that CEOs were considerably more likely to believe that standards for right and wrong are universal than either faculty or deans. For the CEOs, 68% agreed to some extent compared to 48% of the deans and 49% of the faculty. There is a statistically significant difference between the groups.

TABLE 3.10
What to Communicate in an Ethics Course

	Strongly agree	Agree	Neutral	Disagree	Strongly disagree
A In college courses that discuss ethical or moral issues, the professor should communicate to the student that there are clear and uniform standards for right and wrong by which everyone should be judged.**					
Dean (1st survey)	N/S	N/S	N/S	N/S	N/S
Dean (2nd survey)	10% (10)	38% (36)	15% (14)	33% (31)	4% (4)
Faculty	16% (173)	33% (358)	15% (162)	27% (292)	9% (97)
CEO	23% (18)	45% (35)	15% (12)	14% (11)	3% (2)
B In college courses that discuss ethical or moral issues, the professor should communicate to the student that what is right and wrong depends upon differences in individual values and cultures.**					
Dean (1st survey)	N/S	N/S	N/S	N/S	N/S
Dean (2nd survey)	7% (7)	34% (32)	15% (14)	37% (35)	7% (7)
Faculty	8% (87)	37% (400)	15% (162)	27% (292)	13% (141)
CEO	0% (0)	17% (13)	22% (17)	37% (29)	24% (19)

Note: N/S = not surveyed

** Indicates the difference in the corresponding measure is statistically significant at the 95% confidence level in a two-tailed test.

LOG-LINEAR ANALYSIS[1]

To this point, we have only presented responses to the survey questions, but have not looked for relationships between those responses. Log-linear analysis allows us to examine relationships between the statements. For this purpose, we use the results obtained from the 2003 dean survey.

The Deans' Influence

Implicit in our discussion so far is that business school deans have influence over the inclusion of ethics in their own schools' curriculum. Using log-linear analysis, we are able to investigate the influence deans have over the curriculum and what factors shape their views on ethics.

To determine the influence of the deans on ethics course requirements, we examine the associations between three variables: undergraduate students are required to take a course entirely devoted to ethics (E); agreement with the statement "in light of recent high-profile business scandals, I personally believe business schools should place more emphasis on ethics education" (B); and type of institution (I).[2]

The analysis indicates that a dean's support for greater ethics education (B) is not associated with an ethics course requirement (E) *or* with the type of institution (I) where the dean is employed. This result is somewhat surprising since we expected to find an association between the deans' support (B) and ethics course requirements (E).

The independence of the deans' support for greater ethics education (B) and ethics requirements (E) may be explained by the fact that, in general, faculty rather than deans are responsible for curriculum design and implementation. In the case of private religious institutions, an ethics course may derive from a founding premise of the university and be essentially independent of the beliefs of either faculty or administrators.

We find no association between a dean's support for greater ethics education (B) and the type of institution (I) where he or she is employed. This finding is also surprising since we assumed the support for greater ethics education to be an important variable in the selection process for deans at private religious institutions.

We do find a large, positive association between ethics requirements (E) and the type of institution (I), controlling for the dean's support for ethics education (B). Private religious institutions are far more likely to require a course in ethics than public institutions.

Determinants of Support

A second interesting question is what influences the deans' support for increased ethics education. This question is investigated by examining the associations between three variables: agreement with the statements "in light of recent high-profile business scandals, I personally believe business schools should place more emphasis on ethics education" (B); "in general, effective business leaders are ethical" (L); and "it is likely that undergraduate students who take a business ethics course will experience a change in attitude and behavior" (A).

Our analysis indicates that the deans' support for greater emphasis on ethics education (B) is associated with the belief that a business ethics course can change student attitudes and behavior (A).

Interestingly, the results also indicate that the deans' support for greater ethics education (B) is not related to the belief that effective business leaders are ethical (L). This is somewhat surprising since we anticipated that a principal reason for increasing the emphasis on ethics would be to improve business leadership. Apparently the deans believe that students should learn ethical business practice even if it does not always lead to business success.

The results also suggest a small, positive association between the belief that effective leaders are ethical (L) and that business ethics courses can change student attitudes and behavior (A). In other words, deans who believe ethics is a component of effective leadership also tend to believe that ethics can be taught.

Faculty Expertise in Ethics

Another issue that should be explored in greater detail is the concern over a lack of faculty expertise in teaching ethics. That is, do respondents who agree that there is an adequate supply of qualified faculty to teach undergraduate business ethics (C) disagree with requiring doctoral students to address ethical issues (E) and disagree that AACSB should provide training on how to teach ethics (F)?

Our analysis indicates that E and F are associated but that neither statement is associated with C. In other words, agreement with the statement that doctoral students should be required to address ethical issues in their discipline is related to the belief AACSB should provide ethics training, but neither is associated with the belief that there is a lack of faculty expertise to teach ethics.

This result is surprising since we expected to find that respondents who agree that there is an adequate supply of qualified faculty (C) would be more likely to disagree with both the need for doctoral students to address ethics (E) and that AACSB should provide ethics training (F) as hypothesized.

This suggests that the deans' support for greater ethics training among doctoral students and current business faculty is not simply derived from concern over the available supply of faculty who are qualified to teach ethics. Perhaps the deans view business education from a multidisciplinary perspective. As a consequence, they may be especially sensitive to the societal implications of not preparing students to meet the ethical challenges they will face as professionals.

DISCUSSION OF SURVEY RESULTS

The responses from the 2003 deans-only survey, the comparative survey, and the student surveys lead to a number of important observations.

It is significant that ethics is taught more frequently at the undergraduate level than at the graduate level. This finding is important for two reasons. First, many MBA students do not have undergraduate degrees in business and, therefore, have not had exposure to ethical issues in the context of business. Second, MBA programs have traditionally educated the students who become the highest-level business leaders. Based on our findings, these are the students who are least likely to have taken a course in which a substantial part is devoted to business ethics. This suggests that the students who are most likely to face the toughest ethical challenges are least likely to have the appropriate academic preparation.

A second observation is why business programs at public universities are substantially less likely to address ethical issues than private universities, especially private religious institutions. The most obvious reason is that private religious institutions are often founded on explicit, theologically derived ethical principles. Both theology and ethics are an integral part of every student's curriculum. We also see, however, that private secular institutions emphasize ethics more than public institutions, despite not having a specific religious affiliation.

Why, then, do public institutions exhibit even less curricular emphasis on ethics than private secular institutions? Is this a distorted interpretation of the separation of church and state? It may be that in the absence of a professional code of ethics for business, the notion prevails that ethics is related to religion and, therefore, inappropriate for a state-supported institution. This view, of course, is false. Ethics may be based on reason as was true for Plato, religion as was true for St Thomas Aquinas, or natural law as was true for John Locke.

Whatever the theoretical foundation, it is a fact that the judgments people make about what is ethical and what is not are fairly universal within a given society. When we read about egregious insider trading or executives receiving bonuses while asking for concessions from employees, nearly all of us see lapses in ethical judgment. As Bower (1997) points out, such lapses lead to a lack of trust among all important business constituencies. Teaching ethics isn't only about teaching what is right and wrong, it is also about effective leadership. Business programs, public or private, that do not teach ethics do not teach effective leadership (Bennis & Townsend, 1995).

If ethics is to be taught, how is it taught best? Should it be integrated throughout the curriculum, offered as a separate course, or both? Swanson and Frederick (2002–2003) argue that, at a minimum, a separate course is required.

If a course in ethics is required, it must be accommodated in the core curriculum of a business program. That is sometimes difficult, since if a required course is the primary means of introducing the topic, faculty with special expertise in business ethics are needed. If the subject is integrated throughout the curriculum, no such specialized faculty are needed, but the risk is that the students will not develop generalized knowledge of business ethics, since they will have been exposed primarily to anecdotal coverage provided in discipline-focused courses.

Swanson and Frederick quote from a letter Edwin Hartman, director of the Ethics Center at Rutgers University, sent to AACSB, "Business ethics can be successfully taught only by people who have some understanding of moral reasoning. Teaching business ethics without this background is like teaching operations research with no knowledge of mathematics" (Swanson & Frederick, 2002–2003, p. 154). Any business program serious about business ethics should devote core course coverage to the topic and integrate it throughout the curriculum.

If ethics is to be an important component of the business curriculum, should it be taught by business faculty or by faculty outside the business school with expertise in ethics? Most of the deans responding to our survey believe that to have maximum impact ethics should be taught in the context of business. Ethical principles may be universal, but their application is situation specific. We argue that the more a faculty member can get a student to think through ethical situations in a context relevant to business, the more meaningful it will be to the student and the more impact it will have on his or her behavior.

Ultimately, business faculty should develop greater expertise and focus on ethics. Clearly, the deans we surveyed believe that doctoral students need to be better prepared to address ethical issues relevant to their discipline. The deans also support AACSB training for current faculty on how to teach business ethics. Our log-linear analysis suggests that the deans' support for more ethics training is not simply derived from a concern over the available supply of faculty who are qualified to teach ethics. Rather, the deans probably support greater ethics training because they understand its importance in the context of the larger society.

The future of ethics in the business curriculum may ultimately depend upon how AACSB deans interpret the accreditation standards. If the interpretation is generally that ethics is an important part of the curriculum, then business schools will do more because the peer review process will require it. If the standard is ignored in the peer review process, then it is likely that schools will do even less than they are doing now.

In developing its new standards, AACSB's Blue Ribbon Committee (BRC) was responsive to input from faculty and deans. Although the BRC did not meet with a faculty group who supported strengthening the ethics standard, they did consider the group's petition (Swanson & Frederick, 2002–2003). They also considered the resolution and survey of the Western Association of Collegiate Schools of Business (Evans & Robertson, 2003b). The final draft version of the standards published by the BRC on March 10, 2003 included an ethics component in the eligibility section, thus strengthening ethics in the standards as a whole. This version of the standards passed unanimously by the deans of accredited business schools at the 2003 annual meeting.

The standards passed unanimously in part, we suspect, because as our survey shows the deans believe that ethical behavior in business has declined in the past decade and that a concerted effort by business schools is needed to raise the ethical level of business practice. We find, however, only a weak, positive relationship between these two beliefs. Thus the deans' belief that ethical behavior in business has declined is not responsible for their belief in the effectiveness of ethics education.

The deans overwhelmingly believe that the recent business scandals will have long-term negative consequences for business. The deans believe that behaving ethically is a key ingredient in effective leadership; an impressive 78% to 92% of the deans agree or strongly agree that effective business leaders are ethical. Thus an important component of effective business education is introducing students to the ethical ramifications of decision making. The deans also believe that a concerted effort to teach ethics will have a long-term positive impact on the behavior of business executives.

The deans feel efficacious in their ability to teach ethics. They believe not only that business programs should place more emphasis on ethics education, but also that such emphasis "will" change student attitudes and behavior. By a large margin, the deans also believe that ethics education "should seek" to change attitudes and behavior. While the deans believe that more should be done to teach ethics, they are confident that the students in their programs are being exposed to the subject and have increased their ethical awareness by the time they graduate.

Surprisingly, our analysis indicates that the deans' support for ethics education is not related to whether or not a course in ethics was included in the curriculum at their institution. The analysis also indicates that there is no relationship between the deans' support for ethics and the type of institution where he or she is employed. Yet we find a strong positive relationship between ethics course requirements and institutional type.

The finding that deans' support for greater ethics education is unrelated to an ethics course requirement suggests that the dean's influence over the curriculum is fairly limited. This finding comports with the expectation that faculty have primary responsibility for curriculum. Institutional factors also limit the dean's influence. At private religious institutions, for instance, courses in ethics are frequently required of all students, as noted earlier, a requirement that often stems from a doctrinal premise of the university, and exists independently of faculty or administrative preference.

Another factor that may limit the influence of deans is their relatively short tenure, estimated in conversations the authors had with AACSB staff to be approximately four years. Curricular change is a slow process and four years may not be enough time for a dean to exert substantial influence. Still, the influence of deans may be expressed over the long run through other means. The new AACSB accreditation standards were adopted and developed by business school deans, and the increased emphasis on ethics in the new standards was the result of explicit support by the deans.

Finally, the role of academic administration, including that of the dean, is changing. One of the authors, who has been dean at three different institutions for a total of eighteen years, notes that as the expectation for fundraising has increased, the role of the involvement of the dean in academic matters has decreased. The role of the dean as academic first and chief administrator second has shifted to the role of dean as fundraiser first and chief administrator second, with academic leadership barely on the radar screen.

Log-linear analysis also indicates that support for increased ethics education is related to the belief that an ethics course can change student attitudes and behavior. The deans feel that they can change behavior by emphasizing ethics in the curriculum.

There is no association between support for greater ethics education and the belief that effective business leaders are ethical. Thus, the deans apparently believe that ethical behavior is important apart from whatever practical benefit it may have for the student. Perhaps it is because they believe that how their graduates behave ultimately reflects upon the reputation of their business program. Or perhaps it is because they believe that public trust in business leadership has an important influence on the laws and regulations affecting business, with ethical leadership generating greater trust and fewer restrictions.

In the comparative survey, our hypothesis that there would be substantial and consistent differences among CEOs, deans, and faculty for the most part is not borne out. In general, faculty members are as likely to support ethics education as deans and CEOs.[3] The vast majority of respondents in all three groups seem to believe that public concern about ethics will have a significant and lasting impact on business education. There is very strong agreement in all three groups that what is done in business schools will have an eventual effect on business practice. There is overwhelming belief that a business ethics course should be required of all business graduates. With the support of the business community, deans, and faculty, curricular changes necessary to increase the emphasis on ethics should be possible.

On some items, though, the responses of CEOs differ from that of the deans and faculty to a statistically significant extent. The CEOs are considerably more likely than either faculty or deans to agree that a business ethics course should be required of all MBA graduates. One possible explanation for this is CEOs of Fortune 500 companies are more accustomed to dealing with MBA graduates than individuals with only undergraduate degrees.

Two other items where statistically significant differences occur are in response to the statements "In general, effective business leaders are ethical," and "I believe that ethical behavior in business has declined in the last decade." These differences may be explained by the fact that both statements can be construed as reflecting personally on the CEO respondent (e.g., "I am an effective leader, and I am ethical," "I have been an executive for many years, and my ethical behavior has not declined.") We would expect the illustrated thought process to engender a degree of defensiveness and rationalization in CEOs that would not occur in deans and faculty.

CEOs are also somewhat more likely than deans or faculty members to believe that both undergraduate and MBA student attitudes will change as a result of taking an ethics course. Although the differences are not great, it is likely that the dean and faculty respondents have a more realistic assessment of the likely outcome of an ethics course on student attitudes and behavior.

Finally, as Table 3.10 indicates, CEOs are more likely than deans or faculty to believe in universal ethical standards. The Zogby poll (73% of predominantly nonbusiness majors) provides evidence that a universal standard for right and wrong is not what students are being taught.

It is clear that the content of what students are learning about ethical behavior is flawed. Regardless of the philosophical arguments, societies treat ethical norms as universal, even if the content of these norms change over time. As one of the authors (Stout & Weiss, 2003) described previously:

> One could certainly argue that, over time, the moral compass changes within the same society. One also could argue that in different societies at the same point in time, the moral compass varies due to cultural differences. But within the same society at the same point in time, the moral compass that guides the ethics practiced in that society should be calibrated so as to apply clear and uniform standards of right and wrong, not differences in individual values and cultures. (p. 32).

Business leaders are held accountable for their decisions by both the public and politicians. It behooves business leaders to know what the society's prevailing ethical standards are and to act accordingly. In testimony at a legislative hearing or in court, saying that it is okay to break this ethical rule because it is not wrong in Burma, or India, or Germany will not be persuasive.

CONCLUSION

The surveys indicate that while business ethics often is a required part of a student's education, it is not universally required. Given the ethical challenges that seem to befuddle many business leaders, it is easy to make the case that business schools are not doing enough to sensitize business students to potential ethical problems and equip them to make the right decisions. If a high proportion of the organization's leadership has a business degree and ethics is an issue for CEOs, then it is not surprising that they would want the curriculum of business programs to address ethics.

A few critics say that ethics cannot be taught. But if that is true, it is equivalent to saying that finance cannot be taught or marketing cannot be taught. Business schools may not be able to instill or change basic values, but certainly they can make students aware of society's basic values, the consequences of behaving contrary to those values, and how ethics is a component of every major decision. But to do this, faculty must have the expertise to teach it with sophistication and be convinced that ethics is an important dimension of decision making.

The comparative survey demonstrates that there is great support among the primary business school constituencies—CEOs, deans, and faculty—to support greater emphasis on ethics education.

In the short run, AACSB should continue to develop its training program in ethics for faculty and to assure, through the peer review process, that ethical issues are being addressed in the curriculum. In the long run, doctoral programs need to require that their students address the ethical issues systematically so that it will become an ongoing and expected part of research and teaching in all business disciplines.

Individually, business schools should address ethics more aggressively. The professionalization of academic administration has reduced the curricular role of the dean, and our findings confirm that deans have little influence over course development. We feel, however, that the deans should take a more active role in curricular development in their school or college. The deans are uniquely positioned to assess the external pressures from business leaders, politicians, and the public. It is the responsibility of the dean to ensure faculty members are aware of these pressures and the consequences of ignoring them. Most business schools have annual retreats. The dean can bring in business leaders to talk about the educational needs of graduates, including ethics education at the retreat or other faculty meeting. Legislators may also be brought in for the same purpose. While the faculty may not accept the authority of the dean as an arbiter of the curriculum, they may acknowledge his or her role as intermediary between the faculty and external constituencies, and defer to the dean on the relevant issues as a result. In the long run, business leaders, legislators, and the public need to feel confident that "something is being done." If they feel that ethics is not being taught or that students are being taught that ethics in business depends on "differences in individual values and cultural diversity," the door is wide open for government regulation of course content. It is incumbent upon the dean to make sure that each faculty member is aware of the consequences of inaction.

Business schools are remarkably uneven in the attention they give to business ethics. Private religious institutions give the most attention to ethics followed by private secular institutions and then by public institutions.

Responding to this lack of attention, the Ethics Resource Center Fellows issued, in May 2003, a statement expressing the view that business ethics must be made an essential part of the curriculum of schools of business (Ethics Resource Center Fellows, 2003). They pointed out that American business draws many of its leaders, managers, and employees from schools of business. However, if these individuals do not sufficiently appreciate the ethical responsibilities they will assume as business leaders, American business and society as a whole will suffer significant harm.

Business schools have a responsibility to acquaint their students with the ethical challenges they will face in business. Thus, business schools should provide their students with the tools they need to help them meet these challenges in a manner that reflects the highest legal and ethical standards. A solid ethical foundation must be the basis upon which one's business career is built. Accordingly, the Ethics Resource Center Fellows called upon AACSB and all schools of business to ensure that both graduate and undergraduate students develop ethical competency. AACSB has responded, in part, by setting up an ethics education website.

Professions include explicit norms of behavior. Doctors, lawyers, accountants, and psychologists, for example, each have professional ethical codes that define appropriate conduct for their members. The codes are important because, by regulating members' behavior, they generate sufficient public trust to allow professional self-regulation. Absent self-imposed restrictions, public trust will decline and the demand for increased government regulation will increase.

Business places individuals in positions of authority and power who are not constrained by established norms of professional conduct. The result is frequent instances of aberrant behavior, a decline in public trust, and increased government regulation. One way to reverse this trend is to professionalize business management and develop a code of conduct that will effectively regulate the behavior of business professionals and restore public trust. Comprehensive ethics education in university business programs is the first step in establishing these norms of professional conduct. The stakes are high because the only alternative to self-regulation is increasing government regulation.

NOTES

1. Leah Marcal conducted the log linear analysis. The authors gratefully acknowledge her excellent work.
2. To conserve space we have not reprinted the detail of the analysis. For more detail see Evans and Marcal (2005) or contact the authors.
3. One could ask if the response rate for the CEOs is biased with a disproportionate number of ethically concerned CEOs responding. A similar issue was raised regarding the first survey of deans. Our response at the time was that informal conversations with deans revealed a widespread concern about ethics, and the survey results were not counter intuitive. The subsequent and much smaller sample of deans collected in the comparative survey revealed no systematic response differences among the deans in the two surveys, thus confirming our view. We have discussed ethics with a large number of CEOs and business leaders, and find that virtually all think ethics in business is an important issue. We argue that, as is the case with both surveys of deans, there is no systematic response difference resulting in an overrepresentation of ethically sensitive CEOs, and that the results are not counter intuitive.

REFERENCES

Bennis, W., & Townsend, R. (1995). *Reinventing leadership: Strategies to empower the organization.* New York: Quill Books.

Bower, M. (1997). *The will to lead.* New York: Harvard Business School Press.

Ethics Resource Center Fellows (2003). *Proposed standards and business school responsibilities.* Ethics Resource Center. http://www.ethics.org/erc-publications/staff-articles.asp?aid=768.

Evans, F. J., & Marcal, L. E. (2005, Fall). Educating for ethics: Business deans' perspectives. *Business and Society Review, 110* (3), 233–248.

Evans, F. J., & Robertson, J. W. (2003a, April). *Business school deans and business ethics.* New Orleans, Louisiana: AACSB Annual Meeting.

Evans, F. J., & Robertson, J. W. (2003b, February). *Teaching ethics in the business school: Deans' perceptions.* Ft Lauderdale, Florida: AACSB Dean's Conference.

Stout, G. R., & Weiss, E. J. (2003, September). Ethics, Gen Y style. *California CPA,* 32–33.

Swanson, D. L., & Frederick, W. C. (2002–2003). Campaign AACSB: Are business schools complicit in corporate corruption? *Journal of Individual Employment Rights, 10,* 151–165.

Zogby International (2002, April 26). *Survey of college seniors,* from www.nas.org/reports/senior_poll/survey_raw.pdf.

CHAPTER 4

ARCHITECTURES
OF EXCELLENCE

Building Business School Reputation
by Meeting the Ethics Challenge[1]

Deborah Vidaver-Cohen
Florida International University

ABSTRACT

In this chapter, I examine how business schools can strengthen their reputations by taking the lead in efforts to emphasize ethics education. The importance of professional responsibility in today's business climate and the business school's critical role in contributing to this climate are reviewed. The relationship between ethics and excellence is discussed and an agenda is proposed for ways business school deans can build a school's reputation by communicating a strong ethics message to both internal and external constituents. I conclude with suggestions for how business schools can generate visibility for these efforts and make ethics come alive through a process of constituent engagement.

Advancing Business Ethics Education, pages 67–84
Copyright © 2008 by Information Age Publishing
67

INTRODUCTION

Despite considerable investment of corporate resources in a wide-ranging menu of ethics and social responsibility initiatives during the "post-Enron" era, reports of executive misconduct, accounting malfeasance, and systemic corporate corruption continue to make daily headlines in the press. The situation has been variously explained by citing executive greed, legal loopholes, pressure for short term profits, or the wealth of opportunity for misconduct in today's complex business environment. However, another critical element in the equation may be the deeply embedded value system that currently prevails in the majority of American business schools.

In generations past, a formal "business education" was the exception among successful executives rather than the rule. According to Dartmouth's Paul Argenti: "An MBA was not necessary for success, no one paid attention to which school was best (although everyone knew it was Harvard), and a college degree was the psychological equivalent of a PhD today" (Argenti, 2000, p. 171). Today's managers, conversely, enter the business world not only with letters after their names and the principles of finance, marketing and accounting firmly under their belts but also with the unshakable belief—reinforced by their business school professors—that all good things come from maximizing the bottom line.

While this perspective has been uncritically accepted for decades, new pressures are being exerted by business school stakeholders who demand that the lessons of a business education be re-examined and that greater emphasis be placed on building a culture of ethics and professional responsibility within the business school (Vidaver-Cohen, 2007). According to one business school dean, "Schools bear some of the responsibility for the behavior of executives.... If they're making systematic errors in the world, you have to go back to the schools and ask, 'What are you teaching?'" (Stewart, 2004). Schools that fail in this task may find their reputations seriously at risk.

This chapter explores the problem and proposes ways business schools can strengthen their reputations by meeting the ethics challenge. I begin by examining the business school's central role in promoting a professional culture where the ends routinely justify the means—assessing the potential damage this attitude may cause a school's reputation. Next I look at the link between ethics and excellence—showing how business schools can create or enhance a reputation for excellence by emphasizing professional responsibility in both conduct and curriculum. I conclude by discussing ways business schools can create visibility for their ethics initiatives and make ethics come alive through a process of "constituent engagement." The chapter focuses on U.S. business schools where considerable debate has occurred in recent years about how to manage the ethics curriculum. However, the proposed model may also be applicable in other countries where efforts are underway to enhance business school reputation.

CORRUPTION 101

To most business faculty, the early industrial-era notion that surplus revenues should be considered "trust funds" administered by executives "in the manner best calculated to produce the most beneficial results for the community" is as dead as its author, Andrew Carnegie (1889/1962, p. 25). The erosion of this stewardship perspective has not been lost on business students. When asked to speculate about reasons for the epidemic of corporate misconduct in recent years, over 800 respondents in a widely publicized survey of 1700 MBA students cited "priorities communicated during the MBA program" as a key contributing factor. Moreover the majority of study participants also believed that their business education was inadequate with regard to "incorporating issues of social responsibility." In fact, only 22% reported that their schools were doing "a lot" to prepare them to manage potential values conflicts in the workplace (Aspen Institute, 2003, p. 8).

These student observations appear to be shared by the public, and business schools now face heightened media scrutiny as well as the attendant reputational risk this may entail. Most business educators, however, continue to resist making changes that would strengthen their school's ethics culture in a truly meaningful way.

In the Media Spotlight

For the last several years, members of a previously supportive business press have begun to question the foundations of professional socialization communicated in contemporary business schools—highlighting the absence of formal attention to either personal ethics or professional responsibility within the typical business school culture. A *Business Week* correspondent observes:

> B-schools are unlikely to go much beyond the stray ethics courses...when it comes to teaching strong corporate values. And until then, the philosophy MBAs live by is less likely to be "Doing well by doing good" than "Show me the money." (Schneider, 2002)

This perception is echoed in the *Wall Street Journal:* "To some people, M.B.A. graduates are at the root of all the corporate greed and dishonesty.

In a public-opinion survey about how companies can mend their reputa-tions, one respondent declared, "Get rid of the Harvard M.B.A.s" (Alsop, 2003, p. R9). Another observer writes: "Reporters want to know why some of America's corporate elite can't seem to make conscionable decisions on behalf of their employees and shareholders. They also ask whether busi-ness schools are reassessing their approach to educating future business leaders" (Samuelson, 2002, p. 1).

Perhaps one explanation for these observations can be found in the fact that despite recent pressures on business schools to take a stronger stance on ethics and professional responsibility (see AACSB), previously robust ethics programs have recently been diluted or eliminated altogether by school administrators. And in other instances, where ethics requirements have existed for years, the same courses have been downgraded to elective status and combined with "interdisciplinary" coverage of the topic (Swan-son and Frederick, 2003). An article written in the wake of several corpo-rate scandals identified a number of business schools following this pattern. *Business Ethics* Editor Marjorie Kelly writes:

> ...one might imagine that business schools would be deepening their atten-tion to business ethics. But at many schools the reverse is happening. A slow, drip-by-drip erosion of business ethics teaching has been going on in MBA programs throughout the 1990s—and it seems to be getting worse today. (Kelly, 2002, p. 17)

The clearest sign of a problem is when students start to worry. And, as the *New York Times* reports, students are increasingly concerned that the val-ues communicated in business schools are teaching less about good corpo-rate citizenship and more about how to excel in corner-cutting and fraud (Browning, 2003).

The failure of business schools to respond in a timely manner to press critiques and student concerns can have serious drawbacks for a school's reputation, potentially causing even highly regarded programs to lose their competitive edge. For example, in a *Business Week* survey of attitudes toward ethics in the business curriculum, respondents voiced concern over the lack of ethics education offered at most business schools. Only 2% of the 2,700 sampled believed that business schools did *not* need any ethics in the curriculum and a clear majority (64%) believed that ethics should be required as a stand-alone course in the business core (*Business Week Online*, 2003).

Interviewed about the study on PBS Nightly Business Report, *Business Week's* Jennifer Merritt comments: "Right now many corporations are real-izing the pain of not pulling in people with strong ethics as well as strong business skills. So I think it's become part of the skill set that companies are looking for when they're hiring" (Merritt, 2003). If indeed this is the case, schools that fail to provide these skills may watch their reputations erode. And in fact, a *Wall Street Journal* study of corporate recruiters showed weakening reputations among schools that lacked a strong professional responsibility component in the curriculum (Alsop, 2003).

Particularly threatening to a school's reputation is when the failure to give students a strong grounding in ethics creates more objective negative consequences. *Business Ethics* magazine reports one particularly notable example:

> The effects of the lack of ethics training showed up at Morgan State University in Baltimore, MD....when the Maryland Certified Public Accountants examining board challenged May's accounting graduates as unqualified to sit for the exam since none of their required courses emphasized ethics. (Kelly, 2002, p. 17)

Defending the Status Quo

Yet despite the potential reputational costs of failing to pay closer attention to ethics education, many business school deans firmly defend the lack of stand-alone ethics courses in the curriculum. While most deans claim to recognize the value of promoting personal and professional responsibility in a business program, excuses abound for why their schools have failed to make professional responsibility a curricular and cultural priority.

A recent survey of business school deans conducted by the Association to Advance Collegiate Schools of Business (AACSB) clearly illustrates the point. Only 13% of the 239 deans surveyed strongly agreed with the statement that corporate recruiters value non-corporate experience—contrary to what recruiter studies have shown. Less than a third believed that faculty at their own institutions had any interest in "discussing the social impacts of business decision-making." And only 22% saw the value in a stand-alone required course in the ethics area (Woo, 2003).

Off-the-record reasons deans supply for avoiding required courses in ethics or professional responsibility include the need to reduce credit hours in the core curriculum or the need to retain space for courses in the traditional business disciplines. Often, the decision is driven by the simple desire to avoid turf battles with mainstream faculty who see ethics courses as trivial at best, and at worst a threat to the value system conveyed by their own disciplinary training (Vidaver-Cohen, 2004). Many deans also claim that sufficient ethics "coverage" can be obtained by asking these faculty members to "integrate" ethics and professional responsibility topics into their disciplinary syllabi (AACSB, 2004).

Although these approaches make a dean's life easier in the short-term, they may also contain hidden long-term costs for the school. Scholars studying the issue extensively have warned that eliminating ethics courses at business schools could have dire consequences for the reputation of the business profession as a whole:

> That business students can graduate without one ethics course to their credit stands in stark contrast to programs in law and medicine. Clearly, no one wants to be represented by an unethical lawyer or operated on by an immoral doctor. That similar logic is not applied to future managers who will be entrusted with society's scarce resources flies in the face of common sense and calls into question the very integrity of business schools. (Swanson, 2003, p. 35)

The "integration model" fares no better under scrutiny. Although scholars agree that professional responsibility can and should be addressed in the context of traditional business courses, they consider integration alone to be a poor substitute for systematic instruction in the concrete skills required to effectively recognize, respond to, and resolve moral conflicts in the workplace. And, they argue, it is as unreasonable to expect competence in ethics instruction from faculty trained in mainstream business subjects as it would be to expect a philosopher to teach accounting. Swanson and Frederick articulate the case:

> Professors find it burdensome to try to integrate well-developed variants of ethics across the curriculum, particularly given their understandable desire to teach their own areas of expertise first and foremost... The listing of ethics on various syllabi does not qualify as satisfying any particular standard. At best, such *ad hoc* coverage is superficial and uninformed. At worst, it is inaccurate and woefully inadequate. There is simply no substitute for ethics delivered as a dedicated course by knowledgeable faculty. (Swanson & Frederick, 2003, p. 25)

As business students, corporations, the media, and the general public raise the ethics bar for business schools, programs that earn low marks in preparing students for professional responsibility may soon be outdistanced by their competitors. The writing seems to be on the wall for schools with dismissive attitudes towards ethics topics as competitors with vital ethics programs sweep past them at the finish.

ETHICS AND EXCELLENCE:
BUILDING BUSINESS SCHOOL REPUTATION

Although the epidemic of misconduct sweeping through corporate America has created a crisis of confidence in the current system of business education, crisis can present "opportunity" as well as "danger". Crisis management expert Steven Fink defines the term:

> A crisis is an unstable time or state of affairs in which a decisive change is impending—either one with the distinct possibility of a highly undesirable outcome or one with the possibility of a *highly desirable* and *extremely positive* outcome. It is usually a 50–50 proposition, but you can improve the odds. (Fink, 2002, p. 15)

For business schools, impending change takes the form of growing demand from key constituents that schools accept accountability for the moral behavior of their graduates—and that they do something concrete to improve the situation for the future. One way to improve the odds of a positive outcome from this impending change is for business school deans to accept the challenge of making professional responsibility a priority in both curriculum and culture. By meeting this challenge, a business school makes a valuable investment in its own reputation for excellence.

Excellence and the Ethics Connection

In his highly acclaimed book *Ethics and Excellence*, Robert Solomon shows that, contrary to conventional business school wisdom, ethics and excellence *are* fundamentally compatible in the business context. He writes:

> Excellence in business...is a word of great significance...It is a word that suggests "doing well" and also "doing good"...It is a word that synthesizes the demands of the marketplace and the demands of ethics....In business life, the assumption is...that excellence (like quality) sells, that excellence is the key to success. (Solomon, 1992, p. 153)

He also argues that with temptations around every corner, companies can truly distinguish themselves by taking seriously the idea that "the purpose of business is to do what business has always been meant to do—enrich society as well as the pockets of those responsible for the enriching" (Solomon,1992, p. 181).

Solomon's ideas about linking ethics to excellence in the corporate world are equally applicable in the business school context. And with public attention now focused on ways that business schools address ethics topics, those that demonstrate excellence through an unwavering commitment to ethics and professional responsibility can significantly build their own reputational capital.

In their work on corporate citizenship, Vidaver-Cohen and Altman (2000) suggest that attaining excellence involves a process of exceeding expectations, earning admiration, offering inspiration, and creating enduring value. So, for example, a business school that demonstrates a commitment to ethics and professional responsibility through course requirements and culture change *can exceed common expectations that business education focus only on the traditional financial and managerial disciplines.* As a school develops a track record for producing principled graduates who see beyond the bottom line, *it can earn the admiration of key constituents.* Business schools that take the lead in developing a strong program of required ethics-related coursework and that demand high standards of personal responsibility from their students *can inspire other educational institutions to follow suit.* And clearly, given the economic and social costs of recent corporate malfeasance, a stronger focus on professional responsibility in business schools *could help to create enduring value for the American economy as a whole.*

Another central dimension of business school excellence is the degree to which educational programs respond to important developments in the business environment—and the timeliness with which they do so (Garten, 2002). A rapid, comprehensive response can contribute significantly to strengthening a school's image in the corporate eye. And according to studies of factors influencing business school reputation, "a strong image in the corporate sector is among the most important" (Argenti, 2000, p. 177).

Certainly few issues have generated more corporate concern than the rising tide of business misconduct in recent years. Schools that respond by strengthening the breadth and scope of their ethics programs show corporate America they can pay attention to life outside academia and respond in a constructive way. The former Dean of Yale Business School comments:

> September 11, 2001 and the Enron scandal ushered in new and urgent considerations of national security and market integrity.... These developments have combined to radically expand the agenda for business leaders.... future executives will not only need to be technically competent in the basics of finance, marketing, and operations.... They will need to possess a stronger moral compass than so many of today's CEOs have exhibited, not only because it is right, but because public penalties for transgressions in our growing shareholder culture will be severe. (Garten, 2002, p. 1)

Another key foundation of business school reputation, according to Argenti (2000), is *the quality of the students.* Turning again to the *Wall Street Journal* survey, many top companies are now directing campus recruiters to proactively seek out graduates with a steadfast moral anchor rather than the record-breaking finance GPAs previously in high demand. The *Journal's* Ron Alsop reports:

> After all the recent corporate malfeasance, companies are scrutinizing job candidates closely to try to ensure that they're hiring an upstanding individual. In *The Wall Street Journal*/Harris interactive survey, 84% of recruiters said personal ethics and integrity are very important attributes in job candidates. (Alsop 2003, p. R9)

Alsop's observations suggest that a third reputational determinant on Argenti's list—*survey rankings*—can also be positively influenced by the degree to which a business school emphasizes ethics and professional responsibility. In contrast to schools that risk their reputational collateral by continuing to marginalize ethics, those with well-developed ethics programs appear to be strengthening their competitive position. In the *Wall Street Journal's* rankings cited above, schools that "produced principled graduates" received top marks—reflecting "the new era of financial and ethical accountability" (Alsop, 2003, p. R9). A *Business Week* survey of "The Best B-schools" showed similar results (Merritt, 2002).

These two well-known reputational studies, as well as others conducted on a smaller scale, show that along with the usual measures of business school reputation, the way a school handles education for professional responsibility may soon become an important criterion for assessing business school excellence. About the *Business Week* survey Jennifer Merritt reports:

> This year's survey comes at a time of unprecedented upheaval in the business world so schools were naturally subjected to a harsher level of scrutiny.... Recruiters have also returned to their old faithfuls, programs that produce grads with broad abilities, including the soft skills that MBAs had sometimes lacked, and the ethical leadership know-how that is now at a premium. That mentality helped push Dartmouth College's Tuck School of Business up six spots, to No. 10, and Yale University's School of Management up five spots, to No. 14.... To quell the growing disdain for management as a profession, many schools also stepped up and reemphasized business ethics, values, and leadership in an effort to prevent more of their grads from becoming the stuff of sordid headlines. After all, former Enron Corp. Chief Financial Officer Andrew Fastow was a Kellogg grad, and former CEO Jeffrey Skilling earned his MBA from Harvard.... Considering the scandal-plagued state of American business, B-schools' return to fundamentals is good news. Corporate America is in dire need of smart, dynamic, and ethical leaders. The managerial class is also suffering from a lack of new ideas. Business schools are attempting to groom the kind of leaders that can fill the vacuum. (Merritt, 2002)

Given the growing importance of showing a genuine commitment to ethics for solidifying a business school's reputation, the question remains how best to accomplish this goal. Scholars who have studied this issue agree unanimously that the lead must come from the top and that the first step in sending an unequivocal ethics message is to mandate professional responsibility coursework in the core curriculum (Swanson, 2003; Swanson & Frederick 2003; Vidaver-Cohen, 2004).

Although requiring ethics courses of all business graduates cannot by itself accomplish the goal of changing values in corporate America, it is the first place a business school should begin. Curriculum requirements define the parameters of a profession and communicate what is important and necessary for competence in a chosen field. Course requirements also send a strong message about a school's priorities—if a course in a particular subject is not required, the subject simply doesn't "count."

Students, however, are often more cynical about programs that assign three credits to other courses in the business core while offering ethics as a single credit requirement. Many see this as trivializing ethics far more than requiring no ethics course at all. As one student enrolled in a one-credit ethics class observed: "Jeffrey Skilling must have taken one of these: ethics 1/3 as important as laughing all the way to the bank."

Yet despite convincing arguments for requiring an ethics-related course in the business core, many in the business school establishment still believe that "ethics can't be taught in business school" (Swanson, 2003). However, what detractors fail to understand is that the purpose of business school ethics courses is less about teaching students to "be ethical" and more about heightening their sensitivity to ethical issues in the profession—introducing them to a process for recognizing, reasoning about, and resolving ethical dilemmas, as well as providing a new context for understanding their responsibilities as business professionals.

Therefore, although re-socializing business students for greater professional responsibility involves intervention in many areas of business school culture and organizational structure, curriculum must be the first target for change. And business school deans are the ones to take the lead.

The Buck Stops at the Dean's Office

A strong case has been made by several leading scholars that ethics will remain marginalized in business schools without a course requirement edict from the Association to Advance Collegiate Schools of Business (AACSB)—the central accreditation body for business education programs in the U.S, and now branching out worldwide (see Swanson, 2003; Swanson & Frederick, 2003). However, the AACSB has resisted this charge, asking only that accredited schools address "ethical understanding and reasoning abilities" as well as "knowledge of ethical and legal responsibilities in organizations and society" somewhere in the curriculum (AACSB, 2003).

Since AACSB shows no sign of backing off this position any time soon, the next link in the chain is the business school dean. The disturbing results from the 2003 Deans' survey noted earlier (Woo, 2003) indicate that the time has come for deans to smell the coffee—to read the headlines, hear the students, and place concerns of the public above those of self-interested mainstream business faculty. A dean can make or break a school's reputation, and in today's business climate deans who fail to recognize the growing demand for a stronger ethics foundation among business graduates may see their schools left in the dust.

Management scholars have observed that changing organizational ethics climate requires leaders to integrate ethics considerations into all facets of organizational processes. In the absence of such integration, an ethics message cannot be communicated in a meaningful way (Vidaver-Cohen, 1998). Applied to the business school context, ethics must be made an integral part of the school's vision, a mission statement must be designed to support the vision, and formal policies and procedures to reinforce the mission must be put into place (Vidaver-Cohen, 2004).

To integrate ethics language into a school's *vision*, deans must first consider how ethics goals fit with the ideal state targeted for the school and consider how articulating these goals will help the school meet the needs of its constituents. A *mission statement* derived from the vision must then be designed. And whereas a vision asserts what a school *should be*, a mission articulates what a business school *must do* to get there.

Typically, what a school "must do" is manifested most visibly in the curriculum. Although the AACSB accreditation standards contain no list of required courses, the standards do mandate that curriculum be fundamentally mission-driven. And while leeway exists in terms of the areas to be covered in a mission, all mission statements at accredited schools must clearly define the school's educational objectives and fulfill them through curricular coverage (AACSB, 2003).

To provide a solid rationale for ethics or professional responsibility requirements in the curriculum, deans must clearly articulate ethics goals in the school's mission statement. When ethics goals are not stated clearly, efforts to require courses in professional responsibility typically face forceful opposition from faculty in the traditional business disciplines who are either driven by a bottom-line mentality or simply want no interference in a status quo that insures the dominance of their own disciplinary domain.

Once a mission statement is in place, deans must oversee the development of *policies, procedures, and continuous improvement standards* that reinforce the mission's objectives. Once a commitment to ethics is formalized in a mission statement and reinforced by appropriate course requirements, deans will need to implement staffing procedures, reward systems, faculty development policies, and continuous improvement standards to insure a core of faculty able to teach ethics-related courses in a competent and comprehensive way.

Staffing issues can pose a particularly difficult problem for administrators since few schools have sufficient faculty formally trained in ethics-related disciplines to cover an institution-wide requirement. With most schools facing increasing budgetary constraints, deans may need to mobilize external resources to accomplish this goal—tapping into the local business community's interest in hiring more principled and responsible graduates and mobilizing them to fund new faculty lines or sponsor efforts to re-train existing faculty.

Although curriculum may be the most visible manifestation of a school's commitment to professional responsibility, other institutional processes must communicate the ethics message as well—reinforcing required ethics coursework by institutional practice. Academic honesty policies must be introduced, publicized, and protected. University administrators must facilitate the process of reporting misconduct, and they must strictly enforce sanctions against undesirable behavior—on the part of not only students, but instructors, staff, and other administrators as well. A climate of openness should also be encouraged so all members of the business school community feel free to voice their criticisms and concerns.

Although the leadership role in driving an ethics effort belongs to the dean, the AACSB mandates a collaborative model for all phases of a school's strategic planning process. Thus deans must work to build support within the school for ethics initiatives that might be unpopular with faculty. In fact, as noted earlier, faculty resistance is almost guaranteed, so deans must be able to make a powerful case for such change.

Presenting the link between ethics, excellence, and reputation outlined above can provide a useful foundation for obtaining "buy-in" from critical internal constituents. Deans can also actively mobilize support from students, alumni, recruiters, and members of the local business community to help make the ethics case. Most importantly, however, deans should take the time to find common ground with resistant faculty. Even faculty who disagree on principle with the concept of "teaching ethics" would likely see the value of strengthening their own school's competitive position relative to other educational institutions. As Samuelson (2006) and Woo (2003) point out, few schools are adequately preparing students to face ethical challenges in the workplace. And with less than one-third of business schools offering a separate course in the area (Willen, 2004), developing excellence in the ethics and professional responsibility domain can give schools a leading edge over competitors. Nurturing a shared goal of competitive positioning and tying the idea of curriculum change directly to competitive advantage can help deans market the concept of ethics requirements more effectively within their institutions.

Most faculty would also be inclined to support activities clearly shown to enhance the school's standing among local business constituents. As the key source of employment for a school's graduates, and as major financial supporters of business school activities, local companies are critical business school stakeholders. With growing concern among companies about hiring graduates lacking a strong ethical foundation, schools that can demonstrate a genuine commitment to ethics in curriculum and conduct will reap the benefits. Therefore, deans who highlight the importance of meeting local business needs can more effectively motivate faculty to "buy in" to an ethics agenda.

REPUTATION AND VISIBILITY: COMMUNICATING TO STAKEHOLDERS

As reputation researchers have demonstrated, reputations of business schools, like those of private sector organizations, are grounded in the perceptions of key constituents (Argenti, 2000; Corley & Gioia, 2000). When these groups collectively hold a school in high regard, the school earns a strong reputation. To Argenti's "key constituent" list of students, alumni, faculty, recruiters, and the umbrella university, I add the business media, parents of prospective students, and members of the academic community who consider a school's reputation in the level of recognition they extend to its faculty.

In order to capitalize on the reputational benefits of a commitment to ethics and professional responsibility, business schools must insure that efforts in this area are clearly visible to each group. In addition to communicating the school's ethics message through the usual advertising and public relations channels, business schools must walk the walk and carry the ethics banner into other arenas.

Argenti suggests that the key to reputation management in the business school is first to determine each constituency's requirements, then to direct communications about the school's mission and programs strategically to each constituent group. He also notes:

> Today, we must be more aware of how these individual constituencies interact and morph together. For example, recruiters may be alumni, applicants might work for firms that recruit heavily at the school and so on. A careful analysis of these constituencies allows us to determine how they interact and what their individual needs might be. The messages we create for these constituencies... must be direct and strategically positioned for particular constituents to be most effective. Moreover, senior administrators (especially the

dean) need to be intimately involved in managing communications. This is
no longer the domain of PR and publications offices exclusively. (Argenti,
2000, pp. 177–178)

By promoting visibility, such strategic communication can maximize
appreciation of the school's activities within each target group. And it is
not only the school's reputation that would benefit from these activities.
When business schools demonstrate a genuine and proactive commitment
to ethics it can reflect positively on the entire profession itself.

To communicate a school's ethics message across key constituencies for
maximum reputational impact, activities embodying the message can be
designed to meet the needs or spark the interest of each group. Useful
strategies for building ethics visibility include integrating ethics language
into both internal and external communications while simultaneously
eliminating "bottom line" messages, providing support for ethics and social
service engagement among students and faculty alike, honoring business
practitioners who exemplify the type of conduct the school hopes to
encourage among its graduates, and sharing the school's ethics-related
innovations with the academic and local communities.

Table 4.1 outlines a range of visibility activities and suggests specific
stakeholder groups each activity would be expected to target. This model
takes the idea of ethics and professional responsibility to the next level of
commitment—extending beyond the boundaries of academic programming into the arena of real engagement.

CONCLUSION

In this chapter I have discussed how business schools can build reputational capital by demonstrating a strong commitment to ethics and professional responsibility—and by making this commitment visible to important
business school stakeholders. Recent critiques of business education indicate that notions of business school legitimacy may be undergoing an
important transformation (see Alsop, 2006; Ghoshal, 2005; Giacalone &
Thompson, 2006a, 2006b; Mintzberg, 2004; Pfeffer & Fong, 2004; Quelch,
2005). It may no longer be sufficient to simply insure that business schools
produce graduates skilled in the traditional business competencies.
Instead, business educators face growing pressure to demonstrate that
their students understand the social consequences of business decisions
and that they can recognize, reason about, and resolve salient moral conflicts inherent in everyday business activities.

The global business school assessment industry has responded to this
trend with new ranking measures that consider a school's performance in

TABLE 4.1
Ethics Activities and Target Constituents

Visibility activities	Targets
1. *Internal communication*: Introduce ethics language into internal policy and procedure statements, internal meetings, speeches and mottos, and into conversations with students, faculty and administrators. Eliminate language referring to the exclusive importance of bottom line.	1. Students 2. Faculty 3. University
2. *External communication*: Integrate ethics language into media relations and advertising materials, and into public addresses. Eliminate "bottom line" language as with internal communications.	1. Recruiters 2. Parents 3. Alumni 4. Media
3. *Student support*: Sponsor student community service projects. Offer citizenship awards and scholarships for community service. Sponsor student organizations devoted to studying ethics and promoting ethical conduct at the school. Offer public recognition and financial awards for students earning top marks in ethics and related courses.	1. Students 2. Parents 3. Recruiters 4. Alumni 5. University 6. Media
4. *Faculty support*: Offer funding and conference support for faculty research on ethics-related topics. Offer special recognition for ethics-related publications and for activities promoting business responsibility. Offer release time for developing ethics-related instructional materials and for community service.	1. Faculty 2. University 3. Academy 4. Recruiters
5. *Honoring practitioners*: Offer special recognition for members of the business community who have acted with strong moral leadership or have met their economic goals through responsible behavior to all their stakeholders.	1. Alumni 2. University 3. Recruiters 4. Parents 5. Media
6. *Academic outreach*: Sponsor academic conferences and research workshops on ethics-related topics. Invite guest lecturers with an ethics-related research agenda.	1. Faculty 2. University 3. Academy 4. Recruiters 5. Media
7. *Community outreach*: Stay in close contact with business and community leaders, participate in local business activities, and involve community advisors in ethics curriculum planning.	1. Faculty 2. Alumni 3. Recruiters
8. *Boundary spanning*: Invite business professionals to address students about ethics problems in their industries. Invite recruiters to discuss importance of personal responsibility in hiring decisions. Invite representatives from the public-sector to discuss the value of public service. Invite convicted white-collar criminals to address students about the consequences of business misconduct.	1. Faculty 2. University 3. Parents 4. Recruiters 5. Alumni

the domains of ethics and social/environmental responsibility (Aspen Institute, 2005; *Business Week*, 2006; CSR Academy UK, 2005). Many international business school accreditation bodies now also require that these topics be demonstrably covered in the curriculum (AACSB, 2003; CSR Academy UK, 2005; European Foundation for Management Development, 2005; European Quality Improvement System, 2006). Even within academia, traditional resistance to these ideas may be giving way as well. *Academy of Management Learning and Education,* the top scholarly journal in the business education field, recently devoted an entire issue to examining the current states of ethics and corporate social responsibility education in today's business programs. Moreover, the journal's sponsoring organization, the Academy of Management—recognized worldwide as the premier professional association for management scholars—has focused its weeklong annual conference for 2007 on the topic of "Doing Well by Doing Good" (Academy of Management, 2007).

Along with these changing notions of business school legitimacy, new criteria for evaluating business school performance are starting to emerge (Vidaver-Cohen, 2007). The degree to which schools can demonstrate a strong ethics culture may soon become a critical determinant of a program's reputation as educators are increasingly compelled to rethink the nature of business school citizenship.

In *Ethics and Excellence,* Robert Solomon writes:

> The first principle of business ethics is that the corporation itself is a citizen, a member of the larger community and inconceivable without it.... Corporations, like individuals are part and parcel of the communities that created them, and the responsibilities they bear are not the products of arguments or implicit contracts, but intrinsic to their very existence as social entities. (Solomon, 1992, p. 149)

Business schools, like the profession they serve, are also citizens of a larger social collective. And efforts to strengthen reputation are only as meaningful as the underlying values that guide such change. It is only when business educators begin to understand this fundamental citizenship duty that true excellence can be achieved.

NOTE

1.   An earlier version of this paper was presented at the Opening Keynote Session of the 8th International Conference on Corporate Reputation, Image, Identity and Competitiveness and published in the Conference Proceedings on May 20, 2004.

REFERENCES

Academy of Management (2007). Annual meeting, Philadelphia, PA. Aomon-line.org.

Alsop, R. (2003, September 17). Right and wrong: Can business schools teach students to be virtuous? *Wall Street Journal*, R9.

Alsop, R. (2006) Business ethics education in business schools: A commentary. *Journal of Management Education, 30*(1), 11–14.

Argenti, P. (2000). Branding b-schools: Reputation management for MBA programs.
Corporate Reputation Review, 3(2), 171–178.

Aspen Institute (2003). *Where will they lead? 2003 MBA student attitudes about business and society.* Aspen, CO: Aspen Institute.

Aspen Institute (2005). *Beyond grey pinstripes: Preparing MBAs for social and environmental stewardship.* Aspen, CO; Aspen Institute.

Association to Advance Collegiate Schools of Business (AACSB) (2003). *Eligibility procedures and standards for business accreditation.* St. Louis, MO: Author.

Association to Advance Collegiate Schools of Business (AACSB) (2004). *Ethics education in business schools.* St. Louis, MO: Author.

Browning, L. (2003, May 20). Ethics lacking in business school curriculum, students say. *New York Times,* C3.

Business Week (2006, June 6). Best Business Programs by Specialty. http://www.businessweek.com/bschools/06/index.html.

Business Week Online (2003, January 21). MBAs Need More Than Ethics 101. http://www.businessweek.com/bschools/content/jan2003/bs20030121_5068.htm

Carnegie, A. (1962) In E. C. Kirkland (Ed). *The gospel of wealth.* Cambridge, MA: Harvard University Press. (Original work published 1889).

Corley K., & Gioia D. (2000).The rankings game: Managing business school reputation. *Corporate Reputation Review, 3*(4), 319–333.

CSR Academy UK (2005). Competencies in UK business schools. CSRAcademy.org.uk.

European Foundation for Management Development (2005). *Globally Responsible Leadership.* Report of the European Foundation for Management Development. Brussels, Belgium.

European Quality Improvement System (2006). *Equis Accreditation Quality Standards.* Report of the European Foundation for Management Development. Brussels, Belgium.

Fink, S. (2002). Crisis management: Planning for the inevitable. iUniverse publications.

Garten, J. (2002). Time to reassess the education of business leaders. *Association to Advance Collegiate Schools of Business Deans Corner ENewsLine, 1*(12), http://www.aacsb.edu/publications/enewsline/Vol-I/V1Issue12/dc-jeffreygarten.asp.

Ghoshal, S. (2005). Bad management theories are destroying good management practices. *Academy of Management Learning & Education, 4,* 75–91.

Giacalone, R., & Thompson, K. (2006a) Business ethics and social responsibility education: Shifting the worldview. Authors: *Academy of Management Learning & Education, 5*(3), 266–277.

Giacalone, R., & Thompson, K. (2006b) Special issue on ethics and social responsibility. *Academy of Management Learning & Education, 5*(3), 261–265.

Kelly, M. (2002, November/December). It's a heckuva time to be dropping business ethics courses. *Business Ethics Magazine,* 17–18.

Merritt, J. (2002, October 21). The best b-schools. *Business Week,* 84–100.

Merritt, J. (2003, January 20). Whatever happened to Corporate Ethics? *Nightly Business Report.* Community Television Foundation of South Florida, Inc.

Mintzberg, H. (2004). *Managers not MBAs.* San Francisco, CA: Berrett-Koehler.

Pfeffer, J., & Fong, C. (2004). The business school "business": Some lessons from the US experience. *Journal of Management Studies, 4*(8), 1501–1520.

Quelch, J. (2005). A new agenda for business schools. *Chronicle of Higher Education 52*(15), B19.

Samuelson, J. (2002, Summer). Business ethics after Enron. *Ford Foundation Report,* http://www.fordfound.org/publications/ff_report/view_ff_report_detail.cfm?report_index=349.

Samuelson, J. (2006). The new rigor: Beyond the right answer. *Academy of Management Learning & Education, 5*(3), 356–365.

Solomon, R. (1992). *Ethics and excellence.* New York: Oxford University Press.

Stewart, C. (2004, March 21). A question of ethics: How to teach them? *New York Times, 11.*

Swanson, D. (2003). Business education puts corporate reputations at risk, *The Corporate Citizen, 3*(3), 34–35.

Swanson, D., & Frederick, W. (2003). Are business schools silent partners in corporate crime? *Journal of Corporate Citizenship, 9,* 24–27.

Vidaver-Cohen, D. (1998). Moral climate in business firms: A conceptual framework for analysis and change. *Journal of Business Ethics, 17*(11), 1211–1226.

Vidaver-Cohen, D. (2004). Fish starts to rot from head: The role of business school deans in curriculum planning for ethics. *Journal of Business Ethics Education, 1*(2), 213–238.

Vidaver-Cohen, D. (2007). Business school reputation and the impact on legitimacy: How important is ethics? Working paper, Florida International University, Miami, FL.

Vidaver-Cohen, D. & Altman, B. (2000). Corporate citizenship in the new millennium: Foundation for an architecture of excellence. *Business and Society Review, 105*(1), 145–168.

Willen, L., (2004, March). Kellogg denies guilt as B-Schools evade alumni lapses. *Bloomberg News Wire.*

Woo, C. (2003, May/June). Personally responsible. *BizEd,* 22–27.

CHAPTER 5

A BLUEPRINT FOR DESIGNING AN ETHICS PROGRAM IN AN ACADEMIC SETTING

James Weber
Duquesne University

Virginia W. Gerde
Duquesne University

David M. Wasieleski
Duquesne University

INTRODUCTION

This chapter seeks to develop a widely variant blueprint for designing an ethics program within the context of a university or college. Although the authors currently reside in a business school and have undertaken and implemented many of the proposed suggestions contained in this paper (Weber, 2006), our belief is that an ethics program may be developed in any department or school in the university or college and may incorporate any number of the suggestions provided here. What follows are suggestions regarding what one might do, guidelines on how to do it well given our suc-

Advancing Business Ethics Education, pages 85–101
Copyright © 2008 by Information Age Publishing
All rights of reproduction in any form reserved.

cessful and not-so-successful experiences, and warnings of things to avoid or address in implementing an ethics program in an academic setting.

PROGRAM FOUNDATION

Even though it may seem obvious, it is critical to have a clear focus or vision for the program at the outset. Although programs may emerge out of chaos or by accident, having an idea of what the program might look like, even if it does not exactly resemble that vision at the end, will enable the participants of the program to better address critical challenges and focus their energies toward important areas for success. How much can be accomplished? How quickly can things get done? And, most importantly, who are the critical stakeholders in developing the program? These are good questions to answer when building a vision. Some ethics programs focus exclusively on curriculum development, seek outreach to various academic or community stakeholders, develop activities, or some combination of these and other objectives as their focus. On a practical level, it is essential to develop a series of short-term and long-term goals, understand the opportunities and threats within and outside of the university when developing an ethics program, and have a sense of the multi-pronged approach when constructing the ethics program.

Some important stakeholders may play the role of supporters or resisters to an ethics program and may include university administration, benefactors, school or department leadership, senior faculty members, students, alumni, local business or community groups, parents of students, and the faculty entrusted with developing an ethics program. For example, at Duquesne University we have a long-standing tradition, grounded in the university's mission statement, toward ethics education. The university president and provost/vice president for academic affairs are strong supporters of our ethics program. In addition, a business school alumnus is the primary benefactor creating our ethics center through an endowment contribution. Each of these stakeholders is seen as an ally in the quest to create an ethics program. Allies may come from these or other stakeholders. In other situations these stakeholders may initially be seen as resisters to an ethics program in need of conversion before an ethics program is understood and supported as a good idea.

Ultimately, after an assessment of allies and resistors is made and a clear vision of what the ethics program might entail is developed, the critical next step is to sell the blueprint (or plan). As in any organization, promoting a plan or program for action is both an academic and political process. Although the program may be logically sound, there may be numerous political hurdles that must be jumped or alliances that need to be built so that the blueprint can be implemented and the ethics program can take shape.

CURRICULUM: ETHICS COURSE

We believe from our experiences that one of the keys to building an effective ethics program exists at the course level. We argue that a stand-alone ethics course is a necessary, but not sufficient, element of effective ethics education. The mere existence of an independent course does little to encourage ethical behavior if it is not properly designed. There are many rudiments of a core ethics course that need to be in place in order for the entire program to function properly. In this next section, we discuss the structure and content of undergraduate and graduate business ethics courses that serve and complement a model ethics program.

Overall Goals

In designing an ethics course, it is important that the overarching goals of the class are consistent with the grand mission of the university (Pro-cario-Foley & Bean, 2002). Beyond mission statements, we contend that the university must practice what it preaches in its vision rhetoric. This is precisely why the ethics course must be required in the core curriculum. An elective ethics course does not provide the same breadth of student outreach as a required course.

Another issue that profoundly impacts the utility of the required ethics course is when it is offered. Is it more effective to offer an ethics course in a student's freshman or sophomore year, or would ethics education have more of an impact in a student's junior or senior year? Ideally, the best solution is to indoctrinate students in ethics at the start of their college careers. This will provide a critical foundation for ethical recognition and analysis early for the students. This ethical decision framework can be revisited often throughout the curriculum to reinforce the concepts and processes through multiple, discipline-specific courses across the curriculum. But, this rarely can be achieved due to curriculum limitations.

For undergraduates, we believe that students should have exposure to business ethics early in their program so that they can carry the fundamentals with them throughout the rest of their major disciplinary education. At Duquesne University, the business curriculum does not fully begin until students satisfy their core liberal arts requirements at the university level. Thus, we offer the business ethics course in the first semester of the junior year. At this time, real life applications of business cases may be more familiar to students than they would be initially out of high school. Similarly, the graduate business ethics course is offered in the first year of study for the masters of business administration (MBA), masters of accountancy, and masters of taxation students, so the course provides a foundation for future classes.

Learning Objectives

What skills and body of knowledge should students possess to have successfully achieved a virtuous and ethical education? Ultimately, we desire that our students learn how to become ethical leaders once they graduate. Towards this end, the stand-alone ethics course must strive to fulfill the following objectives.

To start, basic survey ethics courses should focus on the individual decision maker in terms of ethical dilemmas, ensuring that the analysis of the dilemmas takes place within a global context. We emphasize that each individual decision certainly will affect multiple stakeholder groups in both the present moment and the long run. It follows that the main overarching objective of the ethics course must be to demonstrate how businesses, government, and society interact to affect stakeholders of a global society (Wicks, 1996).

Secondly, at the individual level of analysis, one of the most critical learning objectives becomes forming an awareness of when an ethical issue exists. This awareness involves self-discovery of the ethical values each person possesses. Certainly, it is critical that students are able to recognize ethical dilemmas in business contexts before any judgments are formulated.

Once that objective is accomplished, the third learning objective should be to enhance and improve the students' ability to reason toward a satisfactory resolution of an ethical dilemma based upon the students' personal value system and reasoning criteria. In concert, the fourth objective is to enable students to identify organizational factors that impact ethical decision making from awareness and reasoning through resolution and implementation. Finally, the student should be able to communicate to others considerations emerging from the decision-making process, and develop resolutions to mitigate shortcomings or potential problems. Although the pedagogy for these objectives may vary based on an instructor's style, the critical concepts and objectives should remain relatively consistent.

Key Concepts

As we alluded to in the previous section, to achieve the learning goals of a stand-alone ethics course, we believe an ethical decision-making model (such as Rest's, 1986) should be presented. Typically, one of the approaches we use to teach this material is a "tool-box" method for evaluating ethical dilemmas. The ethics theories essentially become tools with which cases are reviewed and judgments are made. In choosing the ethics theories that serve as these tools, students understand that there are many different ways of making ethical decisions—for example, a reliance upon consequences, principles, or virtues. These tools can be found in most ethics textbooks (e.g., Velasquez, 2005).

After the ethics theories are introduced, students must become aware of the many influences facing individuals in the workplace that may affect behavior. These influences span different levels of analysis. At the individual level, we teach about personal cognitive biases that affect motivation. Cognitive moral development (Kohlberg, 1981, 1984) is useful in showing students how individuals differ in making decisions based on the breadth of stakeholders considered. Parallels can easily be drawn to the ethics theories discussed in class.

At the organizational level, pressures like socialization, culture, and structure (Schein, 1985) contribute greatly to how decisions are made in the workplace. The organization's culture or climate generated from the company's leadership has a profound effect on how employees perceive ethical issues and make overall judgments (Sims, 1992; Weber, 1995).

Finally, it is useful to highlight how differences in perception of a moral issue's intensity vary across contexts. Moral intensity has been shown to moderate the ethical decision-making model across all cognitive stages (Jones, 1991). Students need to see how in a global environment issues are perceived to varying degrees based on a variety of factors.

Taken together these variables, at different levels of analysis, moderate how ethical resolutions are reached, but all of this needs to be placed in a context of the socially responsible firm. Corporate social responsibility and corporate citizenship are interlinked with ethical decision making and thus should not be separated. Stakeholder relations are deeply affected by how the individual within the firm makes decisions and what action or behavior results. Students should come away from the class seeing how making ethical decisions can ultimately lead to a firm becoming a better corporate citizen, which in turn benefits the organization in the long term.

Pedagogical Approach

In our business school program we use a managerial approach to business ethics, which employs the case method of learning. Thus, we utilize real-life business ethics cases for testing and using the ethical decision-making model. We prefer to use a mix of relevant business cases taken from the news and fictitious cases based on factual elements. If possible, it is desirable to select cases from a variety of disciplines to touch on ethical issues from diverse fields such as accounting, finance, marketing, supply chain, and information technology (among others). This not only shows the application of ethics in a variety of situations, but also builds the expectation that ethics is integrated across the curriculum and any business situation should be evaluated for ethical dimensions.

The course should be writing intensive. Our required stand-alone business ethics course mandates writing assignments throughout the term. Papers requiring students to provide a thoughtful, logical, in-depth analysis of case material are a useful exercise not only for developing writing skills, but also for learning how to form arguments using core concepts in the class. By allowing students the freedom to apply the ethics theories of their choice to resolve ethical dilemmas described in a case, their ability to reason through difficult decisions develops. Instructors are encouraged to provide feedback on writing, allow for revisions so the students can improve their writing skills, and follow established business communication guidelines.

In addition, we encourage instructors to include a public speaking requirement. This can take many forms, but one that we often utilize is the ethics debate. Students are given the opportunity to choose an important business or public policy issue in the current news and are asked to debate the resolution of a contentious issue (e.g., employee surveillance, right to die, etc.). By applying legal, case study, and ethical arguments to both sides of a topic, issues which were previously "black-and-white" to some students will hopefully become grey. The goal is to have students struggle with dilemmas that have multiple "right" perspectives (Badaracco, 1997).

Another public speaking opportunity is for the graduate students to develop an ethics training module for their own organization. Students develop a presentation with several scenarios, present possible responses, and explain the strengths and weaknesses of each response in terms of ethical theory, the ethical decision-making process, and the organization's ethics program. This project requires them to use a variety of tools, communicate ethical reasoning, and demonstrate ethical scenarios across industries, hierarchical levels, and functional areas.

Service learning is becoming an increasingly popular approach across campuses. Service learning allows field service to act as the "textbook" for learning certain topics. By working in the community as a volunteer for a non-profit agency, for example, students can learn key concepts in class more effectively than if they had simply read about it in a book. For the ethics course that integrates discussions of corporate social responsibility and citizenship with dialogues on ethical philosophies, service learning can be usefully employed as a tool to teach the benefits of social responsibility and community service. We recommend that students spend at least ten hours per semester outside of class time in the field volunteering for service agencies. Following this service, they write a paper reflecting on their experience, focusing on how their agency serves the community, how it possibly could be a more effective citizen, and opportunities for the agency to partner with a business organization for a mutually beneficial alliance.

BEYOND THE CURRICULUM

Extracurricular Activities

We have said that effective ethics programs cannot rely on a single required ethics course. Although a stand-alone course serves as a basis and potential anchor for the program, ethics education must be reinforced for knowledge to be retained. In addition to integrating ethics into the core business disciplines (discussed in the next section), extracurricular activities that promote community, ethical leadership, and strong social relations are key in extending the ethics learning process. Student organizations should promote stakeholder outreach and community service in addition to their main charge. If students can witness the mission of the university or business school being constantly reinforced through the actions of each organization or club on campus, then the ethics program will be more effectively promoted and sustained.

One technique that involves students with the community is an ethics award program. Although it can be tailored for the particular school and community, an ethics award program allows the students to see ethics in action in the workplace and to meet leaders and employees who take ethics seriously. For the program to be successful, it should be inclusive and have credibility and legitimacy. For instance, the steering committee should be representative of various stakeholders in the community, including private enterprise, non-profit organizations, and the university. Nominations can be determined in several ways, such as encouraging the general public to nominate an organization, and may include ethical leaders as exemplars. The analysis can be done at the undergraduate or graduate level and should involve students interviewing the stakeholders, collecting and analyzing the information, and making recommendations. The award recipients are then selected and invited to a luncheon or other recognition ceremony. The details can vary, but several schools have adopted a program like this to bring the theory of the classroom to the community and introduce students to ethics in the workplace.

Faculty Development

We chose several strategies for our ethics program that involve faculty development. First, we recruited and developed a core of faculty with a Ph.D. as well as teaching experience and a research publication record in business ethics. This faculty portfolio provides depth for the stand-alone ethics courses and serves as an internal resource for the faculty. The faculty members have varying backgrounds and areas of specialty—decision making and cognitive moral development, psychological components of moral awareness, public affairs, corporate social responsibility and performance, and environmental issues. The faculty members differ in the amount of philosophical or religious training and management scholarship. This variety enables us to be open and comprehensive when developing our ethics program. Had the faculty all been similarly trained with identical research interests, there may have been a tendency to narrowly define the field of business ethics and to be exclusionary in our teaching and research. Instead, we have formal and informal discussions covering a wide range of topics, and there are fewer perceived obstacles in creating a broadly focused ethics program.

A second aspect of our strategy for faculty development is that instructors are expected to integrate ethics into their courses with the intention of maintaining a consistent message to the students and autonomy for the instructors. How can ethics be integrated into functional area courses or across a curriculum? One tactic is to set aside time in each course and have an ethics faculty come in to teach that block of instruction or a specific case that draws on both the functional area of the course and ethics. The appeal of this approach is that the course instructor does not have to be an expert in ethics or field ethics questions raised by the students. The drawback is that it communicates to the students that ethics is something addressed infrequently and requires a specialist when discussed.

A second tactic for incorporating ethics across the curriculum is for the instructor to use textbook or case material to show business ethics applications in a particular functional context. Many functional area textbooks address ethics in a separate chapter or integrate ethics throughout the book. A growing number of business ethics cases are now available for use in this manner. The benefit of this option is that it provides the instructor significant autonomy to choose when to address ethics and in what manner. The drawbacks of this option are that some instructors may feel uncomfortable delving into an area in which they have little expertise and the students may not be receiving a coherent or consistent message about ethics across their courses.

A third, perhaps less formal, tactic is to provide activities outside the classroom that focus on business ethics, such as a speaker or panel discussion. These activities allow for creativity, timeliness of issues, and inclusion of the community that a case in class may not. These programs' shortcomings include that additional resources may be required to fund and advertise the event, voluntary attendance may result in only a select number of students attending the event, and ethics may be understood as outside of the formal learning process often found in the classroom.

Understanding that instructors differ in their levels of comfort discussing business ethics and in their teaching styles, we utilize several techniques to incorporate ethics across the curriculum. Our formal program elements consist of faculty development workshops, guest speakers for classes, co-sponsorship of events, and a speaker series. A faculty development workshop is held at least once a semester, tailored to a specific audience (e.g., those interested in accounting, statistics, and so on). All instructors are provided the ethical decision-making framework used in the stand-alone ethics course as a baseline for what the students bring to the instructor's class. Then instructors can enrich their discussions or assignments by including the ethical aspect of the particular case or issue. Another suggested tool is to include an examination of the functional area's or a related association's code of ethics to show strengths and shortcomings. A discussion of ethical considerations found in cases already taught in the course, as well as a reflection upon the ethical dimensions inherent in current events germane to the course content, is also useful.

Informal elements available when constructing an ethics program include distributing ethics-based resources, building on existing case analyses to include an ethics perspective, using the same articles or cases containing ethical dimensions in different courses, and involving the ethics faculty throughout ad hoc school discussion groups or regularly scheduled committee meetings. As new cases with ethical components become available, we distribute this information to various faculty members. For cases already used in class, the instructor can add questions about the ethical issues, stakeholders and responsibilities, and ethical implications of the recommendations. This encourages students to incorporate knowledge from their other classes and build upon their previous learning. The business school at Duquesne University has a common business magazine available to all students. The same article from this magazine may be covered in different classes evoking different analysis but emphasizing the same ethical issue—such as the decision to produce more hybrid cars, the decision to restructure a firm, a financial scandal, performance reviews, or a new, niche market. Finally, faculty members who are instructors of the stand-alone ethics courses are involved in all aspects of the school, from governance and teaching to research committees. By being an active part of the community, we build connections with the other faculty and develop research projects and class exercises that build on various areas of our ethics expertise.

In addition, faculty can be encouraged to attend outside workshops or conferences on ethics. An institution may allow the flexibility of team-teaching or cohort classes that could allow an even tighter integration of ethics. The tools used will depend on the organization and what fits with the culture and available resources. However, the principle of integration across the curriculum to enhance student learning and communicate a consistent framework is the same.

Ethics Center

Having an ethics center may not be essential for an ethics program, but at Duquesne University we have found that the center provides visibility to the emphasis on ethics, administrative support to those involved in promoting ethics, and a source for program development in the area of ethics.

An ethics center provides visibility for an ethics program. Often an ethics center is a recognizable landmark, bringing contentment to benefactors making contributions to the university for an ethics program and, of course, enabling the benefactor's name to be associated with the ethics program by naming the center in honor of the contributor. Students, parents, alumni, prospective students, and others can see a center as the centralized home for an ethics program. University or school promotional material can emphasize an ethics center as a recognizable focus of the ethics program.

In addition to good public relations, an ethics center can support faculty and others involved in the ethics program. For example, at Duquesne University, the Beard Center for Leadership in Ethics provides faculty members teaching ethics with a library of ethics journals and books. The visibility of the center can provide faculty members with opportunities for professional presentations on ethics or prospects for consulting work with regional businesses. The Beard Center is the administrative home for the school's Integrity Standards Committee, the student-faculty committee that provides oversight to the students' ethics code. The Beard Center assists the committee by publicizing the school's Ethics Advocates program (which includes faculty designated as confidential resources for students seeking to discuss ethics concerns), duplicating and distributing the Code of Ethical Behavior, and documenting and disseminating the work undertaken by the committee.

Finally, an ethics center can support the overall ethics program by developing programs or activities. The Beard Center, for example, offers an ethics speaker program for students and business-oriented luncheon programs on ethics and leadership.[1] These programs add to the public's awareness of the importance of ethics at Duquesne University and its efforts at creating a multi-faceted ethics program.

Outreach to the Business Community

Outreach to the business community is an important aspect of an ethics program. Outreach increases not only the awareness of the university's ethics program, but also support for the continuance of an ethics program through guest speakers, reputation, and attendance at other events. Our outreach to the community is a multi-level approach from local business organizations and regional corporations to international professional associations. A commitment to stakeholder engagement enhances mutually beneficial relationships and generates social capital within the community

At the local level, the faculty serves as speakers for various community and business events. For example, the faculty is involved in the annual Rotary District Ethics Symposium by presenting workshops for the day long event aimed at local high school students. Several faculty members have also spoken on such topics as responsible consumerism and ethical decision making to varied local audiences such as church members and professional association members. Presentations to local groups not only builds the reputation of the university's ethics program, but also adds to a growing network of business people at various levels, organizations, and faculty for future program elements.

The faculty also makes presentations to leadership development groups and business organizations throughout the year. We have given ethics training modules such as ethical decision making and organizational ethics to the Pittsburgh Leadership Development Initiative, corporations, and even our university leadership development program for employees (Foundations for Successful Management). These presentations and workshops are coordinated through several venues—direct contact with faculty members, the continuing education outreach program, and the executive education program. Although requests may come through different sources, we funnel all requests through one coordinator to keep track of what we are asked to do, what we accomplish, and the workload so that no one faculty member is overloaded. This helps to balance the workload and schedules while matching faculty interests and optimizing outreach to the business community.

Besides individual presentations or workshops, we provide other forums for businesses to learn about the latest developments in business ethics and focus on ethics. The Beard Center for Leadership in Ethics publishes a newsletter several times a year highlighting new publications, research cur-

riculum developments, and local business' ethics initiatives. The Beard
Center also hosts a quarterly meeting for the ethics and compliance officers in the area. Called the "Pittsburgh Ethics and Business Conduct Network Luncheon Series," this meeting enables ethics and compliance
personnel in the region to network, share information, and learn about
new developments in business ethics and corporate ethics programs. The
formal 30-minute presentations at the Network luncheons vary in content
from legislation to implementation issues such as ethics training and assessment. Successful luncheons have included an international case study discussion, presentations about the Sarbanes-Oxley Act of 2002, and
interviewing concerns. The benefits from these regular meetings are the
networking for business professionals, the sharing of recent academic
developments to the practitioners, and incorporation of the academic and
practitioner aspects of business ethics. We have been fortunate to work
with some members of our local ethics network who have become adjunct
instructors and guest speakers for our university courses.

Another element of our business outreach is a series of luncheons tar-
geting primarily business and non-profit communities as the audience. We
have three or four of these events a year, focusing on exemplary ethical
leadership and leadership and women in the workplace. The ethical issues
addressed at these luncheons are broader in scope than the ethics network
luncheons. The speaker is usually well known and the topic is one that
draws interest across various industries and functional areas.

Finally, participation in international conferences and practitioner-ori-
ented meetings is another element we use to build and maintain a strong
ethics program. The degree of participation is impacted by budget and
time, but active participation by the faculty in these conferences can
increase the school's network opportunities with ethics and compliance
personnel as well as provide information for the local businesses in our network that may not be able to attend such conferences and meetings.

Although we use a combination of several elements—newsletter, luncheon forums for ethics officers and general ethics luncheons—each ethics program needs to adopt those elements that fit best with its
organization. Not all schools may be able to draw upon a critical mass of
ethics and compliance personnel for a quarterly meeting, but all should be
able to provide presentations and workshops for its business community.
The coordination for business outreach may vary depending on the
school's resources, personnel, and location, but the outcome can be the
same—an integration of academics and practitioners concerned about
business ethics and the development of businesses and students fluent in
business ethics.

Academic Outreach

For an ethics program to be truly effective and for ethics to be fully integrated into the culture of the business school, faculty teaching in the program should ideally conduct research in fields related to ethics or business and society. In order to further knowledge generated in the field, innovative and influential research needs to take place. Classrooms are informed by the research initiated by the faculty. Cutting-edge programs are the ones that utilize faculty who are in the field doing empirical and theoretical research to further knowledge. This implies that the faculty hired to teach various ethics courses must be qualified to actually teach ethics. Thus, ethics scholars are needed to engage students in the classroom. Although instructors with other backgrounds ancillary to ethics and the business environment provide their own unique and oftentimes valuable perspectives to the field, the greatest impetus is achieved by using active researchers in the area.

For instance, research in the corporate social responsibility field has evolved significantly over the last several decades (Frederick, 2006). From philosophical notions of preventing harm and working towards social betterment, corporate social responsibility research has transformed into a more instrumental and practical construct focusing on identifying the most important stakeholders to the firm. Among the most critical questions in the business and society field currently is determining which stakeholders are the most important to a company and how to balance all of their needs (Wood & Logsdon, 2001).

In ethics research, faculty members must remain current. Perhaps in part due to the recent surge in popularity for an ethics agenda within all types of business, the field of business ethics has generated interest across various disciplines. With ethical issues arising in diverse organizational areas (e.g., Information Systems, Accounting, and Finance) in a fast-changing corporate environment, instructors must be aware of the novel ways that ethical behavior is being promoted throughout the firm. Certainly the credibility of instructors will be enhanced if they are investigating emerging ethical issues and new methods of analyzing ethical decision making. For example, in the Information Systems field, Radio Frequency Identification Tags (RFID) are creating a stir in terms of privacy issues related to the database technology being utilized for tracking private information from consumers. An awareness of these new issues facing specific business functions would help relate ethics topics to students from various areas of study.

Ethics research is also driven by examining the influences upon the decision maker when faced with ethical dilemmas at work. These challenges take many forms and operate at various levels of analysis. Managers are influenced not only by their own moral development (Weber, 1990), but also by organizational and contextual factors (Weber & Wasieleski, 2001). The classroom experience would be enhanced by instructors reporting discoveries from their research on these influences to the students.

In the same vein, it is useful to the business public for us to bring in cutting-edge research and perspectives. It is mutually beneficial for the academics and practitioners to share ideas, spread information, and perhaps collaborate on projects. Outreach to the community and faculty development have helped us identify a former ethics officer as a new adjunct faculty with experience in the field and the educational background necessary to teach at the undergraduate and graduate levels.

Just as it is important to incorporate timely research in the business ethics and corporate social responsibility fields, it is also valuable to cross-pollinate and work with faculty in other fields to see the intersections. For instance, those of us who specialize in ethics have worked with professors in statistics, accounting, marketing, leadership, operations, and information technology to produce papers and presentations. These efforts provide the obvious benefits of recognition and co-authorship in strengthening the faculty, but they also provide implicit benefits of bringing the research to the classroom, again communicating to students that ethics is integral in business. Seeing instructors from various fields working together also encourages students to expand and work outside the "silos" of academic disciplines.

WARNINGS AND ASSESSMENT

There may be numerous pitfalls encountered in developing and implementing an ethics program. Thus, the following are only a few possible warnings that may be heeded. First, creating and sustaining a first-rate ethics program is not simple, quick, or easy. Like any program, there are unforeseen complexities, delays, and difficulties. For example, at Duquesne University, the Code of Ethical Behavior took a year to write and another full year to obtain all of the university-required approvals. Initially the members of the code drafting committee thought that writing the Code would be the most difficult and time-consuming element. They did not anticipate or fully appreciate the complexities of the university approval process. Thus, the Code was implemented a year later than expected.

Second, the ethics program requires continuous improvement. Simply, it is never "done," but in constant need of review and enhancements. Consider possible "add-ons" to the program to keep it fresh in the eyes of those you are trying to affect. Consider including different people each year as participants in the program—as supporters to distribute the Code of Ethics, taking the lead in securing an ethics speaker for a student program, or serving on an ethics oversight committee.

Third, communication is critical. The ethics program must be kept at the forefront of all department, school and university communications. Seek to have the ethics program featured in an alumni newsletter and in school promotional material. Find opportunities to make presentations to the University's Board of Trustees, Dean's Council, and other administrative bodies so that they are aware of the program and might assist you in addressing the program's challenges.

Fourth, seeking to coordinate the various elements of the ethics program is a challenge and potential pitfall. This warning points to one advantage of having an ethics center to administratively centralize the various programs and activities. Clearly a strong program is a program that is networked and coordinated, not independent or disjointed and duplicative.

Fifth, pursuing widespread ownership of the program is important. Although a central figure in envisioning and establishing the ethics program may exist, bringing in many others so that "ownership" of the program is widespread is essential. It is important that deans and department chairs feel that they are an integral and leading part of this program, for without them the program might fail. This inclusion is also important with regards to benefactors, alumni, and other key stakeholders.

These are only a few of the warnings that our experience can offer. Undoubtedly the culture of your academic organization and the personalities of those involved will surface additional warnings that must be heeded to protect your ethics program.

Assessment of the effectiveness of the ethics program also may be important. Often human, financial, and other resource allocation decisions are made based on demonstrated outcome performance. Thus measuring how well the ethics program has achieved its goals or objectives may be important for continued support of the program.

Conducting a pre- and post-assessment of the program's impact is ideal to check on improvement (or lack thereof). If a goal is to increase student awareness of the ethical challenges they face as students, then a survey distributed before the program is launched and a year after implementation might enable you to assess how effective the program has been in increasing such awareness. If the objective is to ensure that students are aware of the new Code of Ethics, then a simple questionnaire asking students if they are familiar with the Code or requesting that they mention an item or two from the Code might enlighten you as to the program's effectiveness or highlight areas where the program is in need of attention.

Another assessment technique involves annual exit or year-end interviews or surveys to see how the program is doing from the view of graduating seniors or graduate students. Meanwhile, check each year with faculty members to uncover any new ethical problems they may have encountered. For example, the faculty could be asked about the number and nature of cheating or plagiarism incidents dealt with during the year and whether they were supported by the school's administration as promised in the Code of Ethics. In the first three years of promulgating our Code of Ethical Behavior, the Code was edited each year—slightly changing its language to better address the focus of ethical breeches and the enforcement measures to be taken once violations had been detected.

Surveying external stakeholders could be an important assessment action. Key ethics advocates might check to see if the alumni are aware of the ethics program, if that is a target or objective, and/or how current students view the program. Be sure to keep benefactors in the information loop and check to see if they are satisfied with how their money is being used (often a good approach in seeking additional funding). Undoubtedly other assessment measures are available and whenever possible should be used in conjunction with specific questions that target an understanding of a particular school's ethics program.

CONCLUSION

What we have offered in this chapter is our best effort in sharing our wisdom about developing and implementing an ethics program. Some of our collective experience helped achieve the successes seen in our business school's program, while other knowledge was painfully acquired through our shortcomings or naiveté. Learning from mistakes is often a good way to improve a program. Each program, department or school, and university or college is unique, thus this blueprint was intentionally quite diverse in scope and approach. We hope we have provided some ideas of how to go about developing an ethics program that can fit various organizational cultures, program goals and objectives, and the personnel entrusted with developing the program.

NOTE

1.   For more information on the programs offered by the Beard Center for Leadership in Ethics at Duquesne University, please see the center's website at www.business.duq.edu/Beard. The website also lists other ethics centers.

REFERENCES

Badaracco, J. L. (1997). *Defining moments: When managers must choose between right and right.* Cambridge, MA: Harvard University Press.

Frederick, W. C. (2006). *Corporation, be good!: The story of corporate social responsibility.* Indianapolis, IN: Dog Ear Publishing.

Jones, T. M. (1991). Ethical decision making by individuals in organizations: An issue-contingent model. *Academy of Management Review, 16,* 366–395.

Kohlberg, L. (1981). *Essays in moral development, volume I: The philosophy of moral development.* New York: Harper & Row.

Kohlberg, L. (1984). *Essays in moral development, volume II: The psychology of moral development.* New York: Harper & Row.

Procario-Foley, E. G. & Bean, D. F. (2002). Institutions of higher education: Cornerstones in building ethical organizations. *Teaching Business Ethics, 6,* 101–116.

Rest, J. (1986). *Moral development: Advances in research and theory.* New York: Praeger.

Schein, E. H. (1985). *Organizational culture and leadership.* San Francisco: Jossey-Bass.

Sims, R. R. (1992). The challenge of ethical behavior in organizations. *Journal of Business Ethics, 11,* 505–513.

Velasquez, M. G. (2005). *Business ethics: Concept and cases* (6th Ed.). Upper Saddle River, NJ: Prentice-Hall.

Weber, J. (1990). Manager's moral reasoning: Assessing their responses to three moral dilemmas. *Human Relations, 43*(7), 687–702.

Weber, J. (1995). Influences upon organizational ethical subclimates: A multi-departmental analysis of a single firm. *Organization Science, 6* (5), 509–523.

Weber, J. (2006). Implementing an organizational ethics program in an academic environment: The challenges and opportunities for the Duquesne University Schools of Business, *Journal of Business Ethics, 65,* 23–42.

Weber, J., & Wasieleski, D. M. (2001). Investigating influences on managers' moral reasoning: The impact of personal and organizational factors. *Business and Society, 40*(1), 79–111.

Wicks, A. (1996). Overcoming the separation thesis: A need for reconsideration of SIM research. *Business and Society, 35*(1), 89–118.

Wood, D. J., & Logsdon, J. M. (2001). Theorizing business citizenship. In J. Andriof & M. McIntosh (Eds.), *Perspectives on Corporate Citizenship* (pp. 83–103). Sheffield: Greenleaf Publishing.

CHAPTER 6

USING THE BUSINESS INTEGRITY CAPACITY MODEL TO ADVANCE BUSINESS ETHICS EDUCATION

Joseph A. Petrick
Wright State University

INTRODUCTION

In light of the educational pedigrees of convicted business criminals who have hurt millions of stakeholders, the record of undergraduate business student cheating, and the recently published study documenting that MBA students are the biggest cheats among U.S. graduate students, the public is demanding to know what else business schools are doing besides credentialing more future white-collar business criminals (McCabe, Butterfield & Trevino, 2006; Smith, Davy & Easterling, 2004; Swanson & Frederick, 2005; Trank & Rynes, 2003). Successfully addressing this public challenge and empirically documenting it are front burner concerns of responsible business educators (Hartman & DesJardins, 2007; Sims & Felton, 2006; Swanson, 2004; True, Ferrell & Ferrell, 2005), business professional associations (AACSB Ethics Education Task Force, 2004; Hinings & Greenwood 2002;

Advancing Business Ethics Education, pages 103–124
Copyright © 2008 by Information Age Publishing
All rights of reproduction in any form reserved.

Pritchard, 2006) and business practitioners (Carroll, 2004; Giacalone & Thompson, 2006; Trevino & Brown, 2004).

That is why effectively teaching business ethics in a stand-alone, under-graduate foundational course (Bowie, 2004; Windsor, 2004), framed in a new integrity capacity model, with the goal of improving selected moral competencies, and empirically measuring that success is worth sharing (Beggs, Dean, Gillespie, & Weiner, 2006; Whittier, Williams & Dewett, 2006). The author has empirically tested the business integrity capacity model in the classroom and will present his positive findings which link three moral competency goals to four dimensions of the model in the research section of this chapter.

The structure of this chapter consists of the following aspects: (a) selected competency goals of business ethics teaching, (b) the business integrity capacity model, (c) research methods and findings, (d) limits of research and directions for future research, and (e) a summary.

SELECTED COMPETENCY GOALS OF BUSINESS ETHICS TEACHING

Nearly every business ethics educator wants to prevent unethical conduct, but preventing any and all unethical behavior is an unrealistic goal for either an ethics training program or for a business ethics course (Williams & Dewett, 2006). Ethical behavior is a function of a variety of personal and situational factors including, but not limited to, moral development, enforced norms, opportunity for and punishment of violations, rewards for moral conduct, self-control, and ethics training (Trevino, 1986). It is unreasonable to expect that one single link in this chain of inputs can con-trol behavior by itself. The issue becomes how business ethics education can be a strong link in the chain, rather than searching in vain for ways in which business ethics education alone can eradicate unethical behavior (Williams & Dewett, 2006).

A survey of literature on goals of teaching business ethics reveals at least three targeted competency goals: (a) cognitive decision-making compe-tence; (b) affective prebehavioral disposition competence; and (c) context management competence (Felton & Sims, 2005; Liszka, 2002; O'Fallon & Butterfield, 2005; Rossouw, 2002).

Cognitive Decision-Making Competence

The goal of cognitive decision-making competence in business ethics teaching is to demonstrate the abilities to recognize, understand, analyze and make responsible judgments about moral matters in business (Rossouw, 2002; Sims, 2002a, 2002b). Although there are a variety of ethical decision-making models (Ford & Richardson, 1994; Kelley & Elm, 2003; Loe, Ferrell, & Mansfield, 2000), the following cognitive competencies are essential to them:

1. *Moral awareness*—demonstrating the ability to perceive and discern the ethical dimensions of a business issue as distinct from its economic, legal, or cultural dimensions. This entails an awareness of the multiple stakeholders inside and outside of the firm that may be adversely impacted by business decisions and the commensurate moral responsibilities associated with those impacts (Anderson, 1997; Rossouw, 2002).

2. *Moral understanding*—acquiring the conceptual foundation to understand the moral roots of business ethics conflicts and dilemmas. Moral understanding permits the process of cognitive decision-making in business ethics to move forward with the use of all the relevant theoretical resources necessary for initial moral discourse and preliminary moral judgment formation (Mahoney, 1999; Trevino & Brown, 2004).

3. *Moral reasoning and dialogue*—engaging in moral argumentation and dialogue rather than relying exclusively on legal precedent, emotional intensity, or politico-economic expediency to justify resolutions of business ethics issues. Taking a reasoned stance on an ethical issue develops intellectual independence and allows individuals to actively participate in sustained, respectful, critical moral discourse (Brown, 2005; Trevino, 1992).

4. *Moral complexity resolution*—analyzing challenging ethical issues by acknowledging moral tradeoffs by inclusively balancing arguments for moral results, rules, character and context and engaging in moral dialogue about the factual observations, value priorities, evaluation assumptions, and reasonable responses to opposing views before arriving at sound moral resolutions and enacting them (Brown, 2005; Petrick & Quinn, 1997).

Affective Prebehavioral Disposition Competence

The goal of developing affective prebehavioral dispositions in business ethics teaching is to shape and internalize the inclinations, motivations and expectations to be ready to act ethically at individual and collective levels (Hartman, 1996; Hill & Stewart, 1999; Paine, 1991). A person with superior cognitive decision-making competence does not automatically demonstrate a strong character disposed and ready to behave ethically in a business setting. What is needed besides cognitive competence is attention to the internalized affective, volitional, relational, and imaginative dimensions of character development (Brown, 2005; Chen & Wang, 2002; Solomon, 1999a, 2006; Whetstone, 1998). Strengthening character presupposes the possibility of intra-personal improvement and increasing degrees of internalized congruence between words and deeds, so that virtue cultivation at the emotional, moral, social, political, and intellectual levels can enhance the repeated readiness to act ethically and to spontaneously demonstrate behavioral disposition competence (Doris, 2005; Paine, 1991; Petrick & Quinn, 1997; Solomon, 2006). The following competencies are essential to achieving this goal:

1. *Moral sensitivity/emotional virtue*—empathizing, caring about and sympathizing with past, current and future victims (or potential victims) of business actions while intuiting the appropriate category of moral concern (Paine, 1991; Solomon, 1993, 1999b). Along with cultivating other emotional virtues (e.g., honesty and love) that consist of feeling and expressing joy when acting ethically or experiencing "moral" passions (as opposed to "immoral" passions such as arrogance, greed, envy, apathy, gluttony, lust, jealousy, sloth, or hate), morally sensitive business leaders restore humane caring to the emotional standards of expected rapport in business stakeholder relationships (Gilligan, Ward & Taylor, 1989; Goleman, Boyatzis & McKee, 2004; Noddings, 1984; Solomon, 1992, 2006).

2. *Moral courage/moral virtue*—exhibiting the strength of one's convictions by resolutely persevering and overcoming adversity (Chaleff, 1998; Keyes, 1998; Mahoney, 1999). Along with cultivating other moral virtues (e.g., trustworthiness and resilience) that consist of resolutely heeding the call of an examined conscience, morally courageous business leaders are determined to persevere in continually improving the morality of business practices and challenging others to do likewise (Brown, Trevino & Harrison, 2005; Chaleff, 1998; Solomon, 1992, 2006).

3. *Moral tolerance/socio-political virtue*—exhibiting the willingness to allow others to express views and lead lives based on a set of beliefs contrary to one's own as long as mutuality of respect and restraint from violence prevail (Heyd, 1996). Along with other social and political virtues (e.g., respect and justice) that consist of the spontaneous fondness for the company of good people and the responsible use of power, morally tolerant business leaders instill respect for diversity and dialogue in business decision making (Brown, 2005; Walzer, 1997).

4. *Moral imagination/intellectual virtue*—disengaging from and mentally critiquing the situation at hand, projecting preferred alternatives, and evaluating newly formulated possibilities in terms of their moral worth (Cuilla & Burns, 2004; Johnson, 1993; Kekes, 1993). Along with cultivating other intellectual virtues (e.g., wisdom and prudence) that consist of knowing and appreciating what is ethically desirable, morally imaginative business leaders do not callously settle for narrowly, manipulative work environments, but stimulate themselves and others by imagined yet actualizable visions of more morally worthy work settings (Kupperman, 1989; Werhane, 1999).

Context Management Competence

The goal of developing context management competence in business ethics teaching is to enable individuals to acknowledge responsibility for skills in designing, building and/or shaping supportive moral environments within and outside organizations that sustain cognitive and behavioral moral competence (Petrick & Quinn, 1997; Trevino, Hartman & Brown, 2000; Trevino & Weaver, 2003). Context management competence focuses on improving the "moral barrels" (organizations and other environments) into which the "moral apples" (good people) are placed organizationally and extra-organizationally, domestically, and globally. If fully implemented, context management competence should create and/or enhance a morally supportive environment that facilitates stakeholder ethical actions (Fudge & Schlacter, 1999; Petrick & Quinn, 2000; Wood, Logsdon, Lewellyn, & Davenport, 2006).

The following context management competencies are essential to achieving this goal:

1. *Responsible management of the organizational compliance and ethics context*—knowing how to design, implement, control, and continually improve the organizational compliance and ethics system to ensure an ethically supportive environment in the workplace (Schoorman, Mayer, & Davis, 2007; Trevino & Weaver, 2003). The moral manager must understand and be able to use the formal and informal systems within the organization to construct a network of processes to rapidly control and justly punish immoral conduct (Trevino, Hartman & Brown, 2000). In addition, that manager must be able to recognize and reward morally commendable conduct in the firm (Paine, 1994). Although the organizational compliance orientation prevents criminal activity (in terms of the U.S. Federal Sentencing Guidelines and the Sarbanes-Oxley Act of 2002, for instance), the organiza-

tional ethics orientation enables responsible moral conduct based on moral culture development, moral infrastructure processes, and transparent moral accountability (Brown, 2005; Cameron, Bright & Caza, 2004).

2. *Responsible management of the corporate governance context*—knowing how the system by which corporations are strategically directed and controlled through the distribution of rights and responsibilities among the board, managers, investors, and other stakeholders so that accountability for managing business integrity capacity as a strategic asset is assumed and the system continually improved (Colley, Doyle, Logan, & Stettinius, 2003; Monks & Minnow, 2004). Exposure to different types of corporate governance systems and how they handle CEO compensation, audit engagements, level of investor activism, and level of stakeholder voting and non-voting participation enlarges the framework of choice so that the responsible enactment of an ethically supportive corporate governance context is possible (Cameron, Quinn, Degraff, & Thakor, 2006; Luo, 2007; Waddock, Bodwell, Leigh, 2006).

3. *Exercising business citizenship to influence the institutionalization of ethically supportive, extra-organizational contexts in the domestic and global environments*—knowing how to exercise domestic and global business citizenship in a systematic manner that demonstrates and institutionalizes commitment to triple bottom line (i.e., economic, social and ecological performance) accountability and intergenerational sustainability (Fort & Schipani, 2004; Wood, Logsdon, Lewellyn & Davenport, 2006). Business citizenship context management competence goes beyond domestic and global compliance to proactively partnering with private, public, and non-profit institutions to strengthen the network of human and natural sustainability agreements and standards that advance the national and international external moral contexts of business (DesJardins, 2007; Dunphy, Benveniste, Griffiths & Sutton, 2000; Leipziger, 2003).

Now that the targeted competency goals for teaching business ethics in a stand-alone undergraduate business ethics course have been identified, it is time to explicate the theoretical model of business integrity capacity that was successfully used as a framework for improving those business student moral competencies.

THE BUSINESS INTEGRITY CAPACITY MODEL

The business integrity capacity model is based on an expanded definition of the multiple dimensions of the concept of integrity and framed as a key strategic capacity for which business leadership can be held accountable (Petrick & Quinn, 2000, 2001). There is a definite need for greater specificity regarding the facets of integrity so that the substantive personal, organizational, and extra-organizational dimensions of integrity capacity can add clarity and force to moral discourse, guidance, and conduct (Audi & Murphy, 2006; Paine, 1997).

As a strategic capacity, integrity entails both personal (e.g., integrity as a specific and/or general virtue for an individual) and impersonal (e.g., organizational and system structural integrity) components. The latter is often ignored in the business ethics literature (Audi & Murphy, 2006; Carter, 1996; Halfon, 1989). Just as structural integrity is a precise measure of the quality of architectural/engineering construction and the ability of the structure to function as required, so also organizational and system integrity can be measured qualities of conceptual architecture and the ability of the structures of companies and other moral contexts to function as morally supportive environments. To demonstrate business integrity capacity today, the business leader must not only model a specific range of virtues to demonstrate process moral alignment between word and deed, but also be able to manage organizational and system structural components to create, sustain, and continually improve the morally supportive contexts within which business operates (Petrick & Quinn, 2001; Petrick, 2004; Trevino, Hartman & Brown, 2000). The positive effects of perceived managerial integrity on employee attitudes are one of many strategic benefits of business integrity capacity (Davis & Rothstein, 2006). This moral challenge is a daunting one, but one that is no less central to business leadership competency.

According to the abbreviated version of the business integrity capacity model, the net outcome of leveraging this strategic asset at the organizational level is the production of reputational capital that eventually leads to sustainable global competitive advantage, as indicated in Figure 6.1 (Jackson, 2004; Petrick, Scherer, Brodzinski, Quinn & Ainina, 1999).

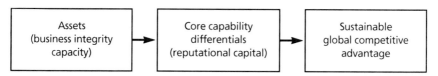

Figure 6.1. Business integrity capacity model of strategic advantage. Adapted from Petrick, J., Scherer, R.F., Brodzinski, J.D., Quinn, J.F., & Ainina, M.F. (1999).

Figure 6.1 is based on the resource-based view of the firm, in which firm-specific assets and core capabilities are critical to success (Barney, 1991; Peteraf, 1993). These assets and capabilities are inherently complex and difficult to replicate (Barney & Hesterly, 2007). Inevitably, some students misinterpret this abbreviated external perspective of the value of business integrity capacity as meaning that the latter is *only* marginally, instrumentally valuable, so alternative shortcuts to competitive advantage ought to be taken. Indeed, some leaders and companies attempt to obtain competitive advantage by neglecting to develop business integrity and simply use public relations ploys to enhance the image of reputability rather than cultivating the substantive dimensions of business integrity capacity (Jackson, 2004).

Although business integrity capacity may have instrumental external value, it is its intrinsic value to persons, organizations and systems that is paramount in business ethics (Koehn, 2005; Petrick & Quinn, 1997). It is the sincere and sustained moral commitment to business integrity capacity that shapes corporate character and builds a sense of honor and pride in responsible business leaders and their stakeholders. Over time, those corporations are often rewarded financially and non-financially as people discern the difference between a well-deserved good reputation and one generated from clever but disingenuous public relations/image management motives.

Business integrity capacity, therefore, is defined as a personal, collective, and system ability that has both intrinsic and instrumental value, and which is demonstrated in four measurable, activity dimensions that involve: (a) coherently *processing* moral awareness, deliberation, character and conduct; (b) regularly rendering balanced and inclusive *judgments* regarding moral results, rules, character and context; (c) routinely demonstrating moral maturity through *developed* moral reasoning and relationships; and (d) designing, sustaining, and improving morally supportive intra-organizational and extra-organizational *systems*. The four dimensions of business integrity capacity are process, judgment, development, and system factors; they both enable and reflect the different facets of integrity capacity implicit in moral coherence, moral soundness, moral maturity, and moral wholeness (Brown, 2005; Petrick, & Quinn, 1997, 2000, 2001).

First Dimension: Process Integrity Capacity and Moral Coherence

Process integrity capacity is the coherent alignment of individual and collective moral awareness, deliberation, character, and conduct (Rest, 1986). The need to address lapses in process integrity capacity is evident by the frequent disconnect between business moral rhetoric and actual behavior that provokes stakeholder criticism of moral hypocrisy, e.g., multinational corporations that tout their public relations images as responsible corporate citizens while engaging in morally objectionable practices that pollute the natural environment and exploit indigenous workers.

Ordinary language definitions of personal integrity as embodying cohesive and sincere adherence to moral principles and commitments refer to process integrity capacity. A person of integrity is commonly understood to be one who is morally aware (i.e., perceives, discerns and is sensitive to moral issues, demonstrates both autonomous reflection and interdependent moral deliberation in the analysis and resolution of moral problems), is ready to act ethically (i.e., exercises intellectual, social, moral, emotional, and political virtues that build strong character and motivation to act ethically), and engages in responsible, aligned and sustainable conduct (i.e., takes action that is consistent with personal moral resolutions on a regular basis, even at great personal sacrifice, and can publicly prize the moral justifications for doing so). Moral coherence between belief and expression, awareness and deliberation, word and deed, and among moral judgments, commitments, and actions is a hallmark of authentic personal integrity.

Moral coherence also entails social process integrity. Teams, firms, cities, and institutions, for example, with high process integrity capacity are more likely than competitors to be aware of and more rapidly respond to multiple stakeholder moral concerns, arrive at balanced decisions that form sound policies, and build supportive moral systems that sustain business and social excellence. They exhibit a coherent unity of purpose and action in the face of moral complexity rather than succumb to collective inertia or biased decision making (Brown, 2005).

Second Dimension: Judgment Integrity Capacity and Moral Soundness

Integrity also entails moral soundness that is enabled by and reflected in judgment integrity capacity. Judgment integrity capacity is the balanced and inclusive use of key ethics theories and dialogic resources in multiple stakeholder relationships to analyze and resolve individual and/or collective moral issues (Petrick & Quinn, 1997; Quinn, Faerman, Thompson, McGrath, & St. Clair, 2006). Ethics theories can be organized into four categories: teleological ethics theories (emphasizing moral results/purposes), deontological ethics theories (emphasizing moral rules), virtue ethics theories (emphasizing moral character), and system development ethics theories (emphasizing moral contexts). Morally sound judgment is determined by the degree to which an individual in interaction with multiple stakeholder relations achieves good results, follows the right rules, cultivates virtuous character, and sustains morally supportive contexts throughout life without underemphasizing or overemphasizing any of these factors. On the other hand, ruthless individuals who overemphasize the achievement of good short-term financial results while violating moral and legal rules, forging vicious character traits like callous insensitivity to others, and destroying morally supportive contexts demonstrate a lack of sound moral judgment and dishonor the diversity of stakeholder relationships.

At the social level, exhibiting moral soundness and judgment integrity capacity for teams, organizations, cities, and institutions means optimally achieving good results (profits in the private sector, votes in the public sector, and donations in the nonprofit sector), by adhering to standards of right conduct and following the right rules, while habitually developing virtuous character traits in moral work climates, and creating and/or sustaining morally supportive intra-organizational and extra-organizational contexts. All four theories and their arguments communicated in a dialogic relationship, with appropriate emphases for each issue, are necessary for inclusive and balanced analysis and resolution of moral issues. Business leaders who refuse to engage in the moral dialogue process and unilaterally insistent upon overemphasizing or underemphasizing good results, right means, virtuous character and/or morally supportive contexts incur the same adverse consequences as business leaders who cannot handle behavioral complexity, which can lead to neglected opportunities, eroded trust, and corrupted environments due to a failure to deal with offending individuals.

The moral soundness of social judgment integrity capacity is also demonstrated by the extent to which specific moral principles guide role relationship decisions in the private, public, nonprofit, and corporate domains. In the private domain of shared interests (e.g., role relationships between doctors and patients, producer and consumer, teacher and student), moral soundness is demonstrated by the extent to which the moral principles of equality, decency, reciprocity, and honesty are included in and guide transactional and participatory ethics decisions. In the private domain of conflicting interests, moral soundness is demonstrated by the extent to which the moral principles of justice, honoring diversity and beneficence are included in and guide recognitional ethics decisions. At times morally sound judgment gives precedence to the rights of others over self-interest out of respect for retributive justice, the inherent value of relationship diversity, and beneficence (i.e., the avoidance of doing harm, repairing or compensating the harm done, preventing harm being done by others, avoiding bringing about conditions that generate harm, and doing good wherever and whenever you can to sustain trustworthy relationships).

In the public domain (e.g., role relationships between elected officials and citizens, public employees and government authorities, public administrators and natural resources), moral soundness is demonstrated by the extent to which the moral principles of public deliberation, fairness, civic cooperation, concern for the common good, and public trust, attention to civic reciprocity and responsible natural stewardship are included in and guide representative and ecological ethics decisions. In the nonprofit domain (e.g., role relationships between donors and recipients, volunteers and NGO administrators, needy populations and international aid agencies), moral soundness is demonstrated by the extent to which moral principles of cultural openness, transparency, respecting resource boundaries, compassionate sensitivity, accountable generosity, planetary citizenship, and emancipation are included in and guide civil society and philanthropic ethics decisions. In the corporate domain (e.g., role relationships between employees and employers, suppliers and distributors, investors and managers), moral soundness is demonstrated by the extent to which the moral principles of meritocratic justice, respect for ownership rights and multiple stakeholder interests, legal growth and responsible property management, corporate citizenship, and triple bottom line accountability are included in and guide market ethics decisions (van Luijk, 2004).

Third Dimension: Developmental Integrity Capacity and Moral Maturity

Developmental integrity capacity is the cognitive and affective final improvement stage of individual and collective moral reasoning and caring relationship formation capabilities from an initial stage of preconventional self-interested concern (morally immature, selfish connivance) through a stage of conforming to external conventional standards (partially morally mature, external-governing compliance), and to a final stage of postconventional commitment to universal ethical principles and responsive caring relationships (morally mature, self-governing civic integrity). Postconventional principled moral reasoning and caring relationship prioritization demonstrate moral maturity (Kohlberg, 1984). Morally mature leaders are living examples of developmental integrity capacity who have internalized their identity-conferring commitment to universal principles like justice and responsive caring relationships, are emotionally attuned to their stakeholders, and elevate the moral expectations and performance of stakeholders to the level of social integrity. Erik Erikson, for example, regarded integrity as the highest stage of personal ethical and psychological development (Erikson, 1994; see also Cohen, 2006).

In comparison, individual and collective connivance is the lowest stage of moral development characterized by the use of direct force and/or indirect manipulation to determine moral standards. Business leaders and work climates that sustain this stage of moral immaturity are either issuing threats of force (e.g., "Get it done now or else") or developing exclusively exploitative relationships based on mutual manipulation (e.g., "I'll lie for you if you lie for me") to enact a moral jungle. Firms and societies that abuse their members perpetuate this moral immaturity.

Individual and collective compliance is the intermediate stage of moral development characterized by either conforming to popular work norms or adherence to externally imposed standards. Business leaders and work climates that sustain this stage of partial moral maturity abandon the moral jungle and are either admonishing employees to secure peer approval (e.g., "Everyone in your work group must follow these traditional standard operating procedures") or commanding them to comply with organizational hierarchy and/or externally imposed regulations (e.g., "You must conform to government regulatory standards or you will be imprisoned"). Corporate external compliance efforts prevent criminal misconduct and limit corporate legal liability, but they do not enable responsible internally governed moral behavior. Compliant business leaders whose highest moral aspirations are to stay out of jail are not operating at the level of commitment to developmental integrity.

Individual and collective commitment to integrity is the highest stage of moral development characterized by the use of substantive democratic participation and/or internalized respect for universal moral principles and caring stakeholder relationships as a basis for determining moral standards. Business leaders and work climates that sustain this stage of moral maturity are either identifying and satisfying the wishes of the majority (e.g., "Everyone should participate in public deliberations and vote but the majority opinion will prevail in policy formation") or eliciting commitment to universal moral standards (e.g., "Whatever policies we adopt by consensus must meet universal standards of justice, care, and global citizenship"). Firms and societies committed to developmental integrity standards act like morally mature citizens on behalf of other internal and external stakeholders – domestically and globally.

Fourth Dimension: System Integrity Capacity and Moral Wholeness

System integrity capacity is the demonstrable capability to design and/or sustain organizational moral infrastructures and extra-organizational relationships that provide a whole supportive moral environment for ethical conduct. The system contexts within an organization and outside it can either partially or wholly support or inhibit ethical action (e.g., the morally impoverished environment of a corrupt organization located in a crime-infested city in a bribery-riddled nation on a heavily polluted planet wholly inhibits viable institutionalization of system integrity capacity). Individuals and collectives that design and/or sustain supportive moral environments at the intra-organizational and extra-organizational levels demonstrate system integrity capacity (Brenkert, 2004; Brown, 2005).

At the intra-organizational level, system integrity leaders design and/or sustain purposes, policies, processes, and procedures that not only meet legal compliance standards (e.g., conformity to the revised U.S. Federal Sentencing Guidelines and the Sarbanes-Oxley Act), but also support relational integrity (Goodpaster, 2006). Relational integrity entails respecting individual employees as citizens, securing trustworthy, reciprocal interpersonal work relations, empowering and justly compensating collaborative teams, implementing organizational ethics needs assessments and system moral performance improvement measurements, and using reward/reporting systems that hold all employees accountable to ethical standards (Brown, 2005).

At the extra-organizational level, sub-national entities like cities, states, or regions, national socio-political cultures, and international human and nonhuman standards create moral environments that enhance or inhibit process, judgment, and developmental integrity capacities. For example, since business leaders and firms are a part of the system of domestic civil society, the extent to which they form cooperative partnerships with city, state, regional, and national socio-political leaders to co-sponsor projects that mutually support human flourishing and intergenerational co-prosperity indicates their capacity for designing and/or sustaining domestic system integrity. In addition, since business leaders and firms are a part of the system of global civil society, the extent to which they promote responsible industry standards globally, support international laws, treaties and standards for free and fair trade, endorse global human and natural sustainability standards (e.g., the Global Compact principles of respect for human rights, fair labor standards, natural environment stewardship, anti-corruption, the Earth Charter provisions of caring for the community of life, ecological system integrity, socio-economic intergenerational justice, democracy, nonviolence and peace) indicates their capacity for designing and/or sustaining global system integrity (DesJardins, 2007; Mulgan, 2006; Newton, 2003; Waddock, 2004).

Given the stated business ethics competencies and the description of the business integrity capacity model, the results of business ethics teaching using a competency-focused, theoretically justified approach can now be reported.

RESEARCH METHODS AND FINDINGS

Undergraduate business students who were enrolled in thirteen sections of a required undergraduate course entitled "Business Integrity" were given pretests on the first class meeting and posttests on the last class meeting in an academic quarter system to measure any moral competency improvements using the business integrity capacity theoretical dimensions as the foundational structure for course content. The tests were numbered so that each student's progress could be tracked with anonymity. The aggregate difference between the posttest and pretest results was recorded as the mean improvement in ethics competencies. Business ethics students were asked to indicate the extent to which they agreed or disagreed with each of the eleven statements in Table 6.1 using a seven-point Likert scale that ranges from strongly agree to strongly disagree. The results were then analyzed by the University Statistical Consulting Center and a subset of its analysis is contained in Table 6.1.

Specifically, the sample consisted of 400 undergraduate students enrolled in thirteen sections of a junior-level undergraduate "Business Integrity" course over a period of three years. The sample consists of 53% females and 47% males. The mean age of the sample was 23.2 years (SD = 4.7), with a mode of 21 years. The ages ranged from 18 years to 49 years. In terms of academic majors, the sample included 91 for Accountancy (22.8% of the sample), 86 for Management of Information Systems (21.6%), 54 for Marketing (13.5%), and 42 for Management (10.5%). The remainder of the sample consisted of 126 individuals with various other business-related majors (31.5%).

The improvements were calculated for each survey-taker and for each statement. The means were calculated for each statement, and t-tests were used to see if any of these means were significantly different from zero. All 11 of the statements showed significant improvement between the pretest and posttest responses in Table 6.1. After using a Bonferroni correction for multiple tests (see Tabachnick & Fidell, 2006), the results of the t-tests for all eleven statements were significant at $p < 0.0001$.

With regard to the process dimension of business integrity capacity, students were better able to recognize ethical issues in business that affect multiple stakeholders inside and outside the firm after completing the stand-alone course. They better understood how regularly engaging in ethical business practices strengthens their character and sustains their humanity. In the affective, prebehavioral area of ethics competencies, students improved their positive attitudes toward moral toleration and moral imagination, their caring about the impact of business actions on others, and their determination to continually improve the morality of business practices.

TABLE 6.1
Business Integrity Capacity (BIC) Model and Improvements in Business Ethics Competencies

Ethics statements (n = 400)	BIC model dimensions	Ethics competencies	Mean improvement	t value*
1. I recognize (perceive) ethical issues (as distinct from economic and legal issues) in business that affect multiple stakeholders inside and outside the firm.	Process	Cognitive	1.867	41.45
2. I understand how regularly engaging in ethical business practices strengthens my character (readiness to act ethically) and sustains my humanity	Process	Cognitive	1.910	83.89
3. It is important to tolerate diverse and even opposing moral perspectives and to creatively imagine ways to morally improve situations at work.	Process	Affective prebehavioral	.922	41.10
4. I care about the impact of business actions on those affected by it and I am determined to continually improve the morality of business practices.	Process	Affective prebehavioral	1.067	27.81
5. I understand the multiple factors (results, rules, character and context) to be considered in making responsible ethical judgments through moral reasoning.	Judgment	Cognitive	3.397	83.89
6. I understand how my business philosophy and management/work style influence and reflect my value priorities with regard to expected business behavior.	Judgment	Cognitive	3.862	95.07
7. Ethical business leaders are expected to elevate the moral development of their followers and their work culture/climate.	Developmental	Affective prebehavioral	1.727	40.03
8. Corporate governance leaders are morally accountable for managing business integrity capacity as a strategic asset to enhance or protect organizational reputation.	Developmental	Managerial	1.945	40.24
9. Business should be held to triple bottom line accountability (for economic, social and ecological performance) to respect current and future generations of multiple stakeholders.	System	Managerial	2.032	40.98
10. Ethical business leaders should develop their organizational compliance and ethics systems to sustain a morally supportive work context.	System	Managerial	1.307	31.60
11. Ethical business leaders should exercise positive influence in their firms' external socio-political-legal-ecological environments, both domestically and globally, to sustain a morally supportive external context for responsible business citizenship.	System	Managerial	1.170	28.96

* The results for each statement are significant at $p < .0001$.

With regard to the judgment dimension of business integrity capacity, students strongly improved their cognitive understanding of the multiple factors (results, rules, character and context) that need to be balanced and included in making responsible ethical judgments. They also improved their understanding of how their business philosophy and management style influenced and reflected their moral value priorities for judging expected business behavior.

With regard to the developmental dimension of business integrity capacity, the students raised their expectations that ethical business leaders should elevate the moral development of their followers and their work culture and climate. In addition, students raised their organizational context moral expectations regarding the accountability of corporate governance leaders to manage business integrity capacity as a strategic asset in order to embrace or protect organizational reputational capital.

Finally, with regard to system integrity capacity, students increased their moral context management competencies by increasingly specifying triple bottom line accountability and multiple stakeholder respect for current and future generations, the necessity to implement an organizational compliance and ethics system to institutionalize a morally supportive work context, and the importance of exercising responsible business citizenship, domestically and globally, to positively influence the extra-organizational context to be as morally supportive as possible.

In effect, the findings of the pretests and posttests demonstrate that it is possible to document statistically significant improvements in business ethics competencies using the integrity capacity theoretical model within a stand-alone, required, foundational course that provides a systematic, focused grounding for undergraduate business students in business ethics. In the absence of endorsement from the accrediting agency, the Association to Advance Collegiate Schools of Business (AACSB) that such a foundational course in business ethics be required, however, the course can become vulnerable to relegation to elective status or conversion to a business law emphasis that merely conditions students to fear legal penalties (Sims & Felton, 2006; Swanson & Frederick, 2005).

LIMITS OF RESEARCH AND FUTURE RESEARCH DIRECTIONS

There are a number of research limits that need to be acknowledged. First, since some pretest and posttest ethics statements contained two variables (e.g., question 3 contained both moral tolerance and moral imagination variables; question 4 contained both moral caring and moral resolution variables), the extent of statistically measured improvement on each factor cannot be determined. Separating the factors would have diminished that issue. Second, the face validity of the survey items administered in a business ethics course may well have generated social desirability bias on both pretests and posttests. Students may well have wanted to "put their best foot forward" on the pretests in an ethics course and then rationalize their investment of time and energy in the course by doing the same on the posttests. To some extent, it is important to acknowledge that this cannot be completely controlled for given the type of survey methodology employed. Third, the business ethics survey items did not measure actual moral behavior during the course or on the job subsequent to the course, but only cognitive, affective prebehavioral and managerial moral competencies. The research limit, of course, is that students may "talk a good game" but not actually "walk the talk" at college or later at work. The limited scope of the targeted business ethics competencies must be acknowledged.

Nevertheless, the research results indicate that systematic, stand-alone, foundational business ethics education that is competency-focused and theoretically sound can become a strong link in the chain of inputs that impact business undergraduate moral behavior.

There are a number of future research directions to take. Future business integrity capacity research could include: (a) longitudinal follow-up research on all the business ethics students in all the sections over a two, five, or ten year period; (b) employer reports on responsible work conduct of employees prior to and subsequent to taking a stand-alone foundation course on business integrity capacity; and (c) cross-cultural research on the differential impacts of a stand-alone business integrity capacity course in other countries with other business students and/or business practitioners.

SUMMARY

This chapter has empirically documented improvements in business ethics' competencies in 400 undergraduate business students in an AACSB-accredited business college in a U.S. public university using the business integrity capacity model to teach business ethics in a stand-alone, foundational, undergraduate course. The author has reported statistically significant improvements in three business ethics' competencies that are linked to the four dimensions of the business integrity capacity model: process, judgment, development and system. Finally, the author acknowledged research limits and provided recommendations for future research.

REFERENCES

AACSB Ethics Education Task Force (2004). Ethics education in business schools. *Ethics Education Task Force of AACSB International, 1*(1), 1–8.

Anderson, J. (1997). What cognitive science tells us about ethics and the teaching of ethics. *Journal of Business Ethics, 16*(3), 279–291.

Audi, R., & Murphy, P. E. (2006). The many faces of integrity. *Business Ethics Quarterly, 16*(1), 3–21.

Barney, J. (1991). Firm resources and sustained competitive advantage. *Journal of Management, 17*, 99–120.

Barney, J. & Hesterly, W. (2007) *Strategic management and competitive advantage: Concepts and cases.* Second Edition. Upper Saddle River, NJ: Prentice Hall.

Beggs, J., Dean, K., Gillespie, J., & Weiner, J. (2006). The unique challenges of ethics instruction. *Journal of Management Education, 30*(1), 5–10.

Bowie, N. E. (2004). Special Issue: The stand alone course in business ethics. *Journal of Business Ethics Education, 1*(2), 3–9.

Brenkert, G. (Ed.). (2004). *Corporate integrity & accountability.* Thousand Oaks, CA: Sage.

Brown, M. E., Trevino, L. R., & Harrison, D. A. (2005). Ethical leadership: A social learning perspective for construct development and testing. *Organizational Behavior and Human Decision Processes, 97*, 117–134.

Brown, M. T. (2005). *Corporate integrity: Rethinking organizational ethics and leadership.* New York: Cambridge University Press.

Cameron, K. S., Bright, D., & Caza, A. (2004). Exploring the relatedness between organizational virtuousness and performance. *American Behavioral Scientist, 47*, 766–790.

Cameron, K. S., Quinn, R. E., Degraff, J., & Thakor, A. V. (2006). *Competing values leadership: Creating value in organization.* Northampton, MA: Edward Elgar Publishing.

Carroll, A. (2004). Managing ethically with global stakeholders: A present and future challenge. *Academy of Management Executive, 18*, 114–120.

Carter, S. L. (1996). *Integrity.* New York: Basic Books.

Chaleff, I. (1998). *The courageous follower: Standing up to and for our leaders.* San Francisco: Berrett-Koehler Publishers.

Chen, L., & Wang, C. (2002). The concept of integrity in China and western countries: Its difference and implications. *Journal of Philosophy Research, 8*, 35–40.

Cohen, E. D. (2006). *The new rational therapy: Thinking your way to serenity, success, and profound happiness.* Lanham, MD: Rowman & Littlefield Publishers.

Colley, J., Doyle, J., Logan, G., & Stettinius, W. (2003). *Corporate governance.* New York: McGraw-Hill.

Cuilla, J., & Burns, J. M. (2004). *Ethics—the heart of leadership.* Second Edition. Westport, CT: Greenwood Publishing.

Davis, A., & Rothstein, H. (2006). The effects of perceived behavioral integrity of managers on employee attitudes: A meta-analysis. *Journal of Business Ethics, 67*(4), 407–419.

DesJardins, J. R. (2007). *Business, ethics, and the environment: Imagining a sustainable future.* Upper Saddle River, NJ: Pearson-Prentice Hall.

Doris, J. (2005). *Lack of character: Personality and moral behavior.* New York: Cambridge University Press.

Dunphy, D., Benveniste, J., Griffiths, A., & Sutton, P. (2000). *Sustainability: The corporate challenge of the 21ˢᵗ century.* Sydney: Allen & Unwin.

Erikson, E. (1994). *Identity and the life cycle.* New York: Norton.

Felton, E. Jr., & Sims, R. R. (2005). Teaching business ethics: Targeted outputs. *Journal of Business Ethics, 60,* 377–391.

Ford, R. C., & Richardson, W. D. (1994). Ethical decision making: A review of the empirical literature. *Journal of Business Ethics, 13,* 205–221.

Fort, T. L., & Schipani, C. A. (2004). *The role of business in fostering peaceful societies.* Cambridge, UK: Cambridge University Press.

Fudge, R., & Schlacter, J. L. (1999). Motivating employees to act ethically: An expectancy theory approach. *Journal of Business Ethics, 18,* 295–304.

Giacalone, R., & Thompson, K. (2006). Business ethics and social responsibility education: Shifting the worldview. *Academy of Management Learning & Education, 5,* 266–277.

Gilligan, C., Ward, J., & Taylor, J. (Eds.) (1989). *Mapping the moral domain.* Cambridge, MA: Harvard University Press.

Goleman, D., Boyatzis, R., & McKee, A. (2004). *Primal leadership: Learning to lead with emotional intelligence.* Boston: Harvard University Press.

Goodpaster, K. (2006). *Conscience and corporate culture.* London: Blackwell.

Halfon, M. S. (1989). *Integrity: A philosophical inquiry.* Philadelphia: Temple University Press.

Hartman, E. (1996). *Organizational ethics and the good life.* New York: Oxford University Press.

Hartman, L. P., & DesJardins, J. (2007). *Business ethics: Decision-making for personal integrity & social responsibility.* Boston: McGraw-Hill Irwin.

Heyd, D. (1996). *Toleration: An elusive virtue.* Princeton, NJ: Princeton University Press.

Hill, A., & Stewart, I. (1999). Character education in business schools: Pedagogical strategies. *Teaching Business Ethics, 3,* 179–193.

Hinings, C. R., & Greenwood, R. (2002). Disconnects and consequences in organization theory. *Administrative Science Quarterly, 47,* 411–421.

Jackson, K. T. (2004). *Building reputational capital: Strategies for integrity and fair play that improve the bottom line.* New York: Oxford University Press.

Johnson, M. (1993). *Moral imagination.* Chicago: University of Chicago Press.

Kekes, J. (1993). *The morality of pluralism.* Princeton, NJ: Princeton University Press.

Kelley, P., & Elm, D. (2003). The effect of context on moral intensity of ethical issues: Revising Jones's issue-contingent model. *Journal of Business Ethics, 48,* 139–154.

Keyes, C. (1998). Social well-being. *Social Psychology Quarterly, 61,* 121–140.

Koehn, D. (2005). Integrity as a business asset. *Journal of Business Ethics, 58,* 125–136.

Kohlberg, L. (1984). *The psychology of moral development: The nature and validity of moral stages.* New York: Harper & Row.

Kupperman, J. (1989). Character and ethical theory. *Midwest Studies in Philosophy, 13,* 98–111.

Leipziger, D. (2003). *The corporate responsibility code book.* Sheffield, UK: Greenleaf Publishers.

Liszka, J. J. (2002). *Moral competence: An integrated approach to the study of ethics.* Upper Saddle River, NJ: Prentice Hall.

Loe, T. W., Ferrell, L., & Mansfield, P. (2000). A review of empirical studies assessing ethical decision making in business. *Journal of Business Ethics, 25,* 185–204.

Luo, Y. (2007). *Global dimensions of corporate governance.* Malden, MA: Blackwell Publishing.

Mahoney, J. (1999). Cultivating moral courage in business. In G. Enderle (Ed.), *International Business Ethics: Challenges and Approaches* (pp. 249–259). Notre Dame: University of Notre Dame Press.

McCabe, D., Butterfield, K., & Trevino, L. (2006). Academic dishonesty in graduate business programs: Prevalence, causes, and proposed action. *Academy of Management Learning & Education, 5*(3), 294–306.

Monks, A., & Minow, N. (2004). *Corporate governance* (Third Edition). Malden, MA: Blackwell Publishing.

Mulgan, T. (2006). *Future people.* New York: Oxford University Press.

Newton, L. H. (2003). *Ethics and sustainability: Sustainable development and the moral life.* Upper Saddle River, NJ: Pearson-Prentice Hall.

Noddings, N. (1984). *Caring.* Los Angeles: University of California Press.

O'Fallon, M. J., & Butterfield, K. D. (2005). A review of the empirical ethical decision-making literature: 1996–2003. *Journal of Business Ethics, 59*(4), 375–413.

Paine, L. S. (1991). Ethics as character development: Reflections on the objective of ethics education. In R. Edward Freeman (Ed.), *Business Ethics: The State of the Art* (pp. 78–90). New York: Oxford University Press.

Paine, L. S. (1994, March/April). Managing for organizational integrity. *Harvard Business Review,* 106–117.

Paine, L.S. (1997). Integrity. In P. H. Werhane & R. E. Freeman (Eds.), *The Blackwell Encyclopedia Dictionary of Business Ethics* (pp. 335–336). Oxford: Blackwell Publishers.

Peteraf, M. (1993). The cornerstones of competitive advantage: A resource-based view. *Strategic Management Journal, 14,* 179–191.

Petrick, J. (2004). Sustainability, democracy and three challenges to global judgment integrity capacity. *Innovation: Management, Policy & Practice, 6*(2), 156–166.

Petrick, J., & Quinn, J. (1997). *Management ethics: Integrity at work.* Thousand Oaks, CA: Sage Publications.

Petrick, J., & Quinn, J. (2000). The integrity capacity construct and moral progress in business. *Journal of Business Ethics, 23,* 3–18.

Petrick, J., & Quinn, J. (2001). The challenge of leadership accountability for integrity capacity as a strategic asset. *Journal of Business Ethics, 34,* 331–343.

Petrick, J., Scherer, R. F., Brodzinski, J. D., Quinn, J. F., & Ainina, M. F. (1999). Global leadership skills and reputational capital: Intangible resources for sustainable competitive advantage. *Academy of Management Executive, 13*(1), 58–69

Pritchard, M. (2006). *Professional integrity: Thinking ethically.* Lawrence, KS: University Press of Kansas.

Quinn, R. E., Faerman, S., Thompson, M., McGrath, M., & St. Clair, L. (2006). *Becoming a master manager: A competency based framework*. Fourth Edition. New York: John Wiley.

Rest, J. (1986). *Moral development: Advances in research and theory*. New York: Praeger.

Rossouw, G. J. (2002). Three approaches to teaching business ethics. *Teaching Business Ethics, 6,* 411–433.

Schoorman, F. D., Mayer, R. C., & Davis, J. H. (2007). An integrative model of organizational trust: Past, present, and future. *Academy of Management Review, 32*(2), 344–354.

Sims, R. (2002b). Business ethics teaching for effective learning. *Teaching Business Ethics, 6,* 393–410.

Sims, R., & Felton, E. (2006). Designing and delivering business ethics teaching and learning. *Journal of Business Ethics, 63*(3), 297–312.

Sims, R. R. (2002a). *Teaching business ethics for effective learning*. Westport, CT: Quorum Books.

Smith, K. J., Davy, J. A., & Eastering, D. (2004). An examination of cheating and its antecedents among marketing and management majors. *Journal of Business Ethics, 50,* 63–80.

Solomon, R. C. (1992). *Ethics and excellence: Cooperation and integrity in business*. New York: Oxford University Press.

Solomon, R. C. (1993). *The passions: Emotions and the meaning of life*. Indianapolis: Hackett Publishing Company.

Solomon, R. C. (1999a). Business ethics and virtue. In R. E. Frederick (Ed.), *A Companion to Business Ethics* (pp. 30–37). Malden, MA.: Blackwell Publishers.

Solomon, R. C. (1999b). *A better way to think about business: How personal integrity leads to corporate success*. New York: Oxford University Press.

Solomon, R. C. (2006). *True to our feelings: What our emotions are really telling us*. New York: Oxford University Press.

Swanson, D. L. (2004). The buck stops here: Why universities must reclaim business ethics education. *Journal of Academic Ethics, 1,* 43–61.

Swanson, D. L., & Frederick, W. C. (2005). Denial and leadership in business ethics education. In O. C. Ferrell & R. A. Peterson (Eds.), *Business ethics: The new challenge for business schools and corporate leaders* (pp. 222–240). New York: M.E. Sharpe.

Tabachnick, B., & Fidell, L. (2006). *Using multivariate statistics*. Fifth Edition. New York: HarperCollins.

Trank, C., & Rynes, S. (2003). Who moved our cheese? Reclaiming professionalism in business education. *Academy of Management Learning and Education, 2*(2), 189–205.

Trevino, L. (1986). Ethical decision making in organizations: A person-situation interactionist model. *Academy of Management Review, 11,* 601–617.

Trevino, L. (1992). Moral reasoning and business ethics. *Journal of Business Ethics, 11,* 445–459.

Trevino, L., & Brown, M. (2004). Managing to be ethical: Debunking five business ethics myths. *Academy of Management Executive, 18*(2), 69–81.

Trevino, L. K., Hartman, L.P., & Brown, M. (2000). Moral person and moral manager: How executives develop a reputation for ethical leadership. *California Management review, 42*(4), 128- 142.

Trevino, L., & Weaver, G. (2003). *Managing ethics in business organizations.* Stanford, CA: Stanford University Press.

True, S. L., Ferrell, L., & Ferrell, O. C. (2005). *Fulfilling our obligation: Perspectives on teaching business ethics.* Kennesaw, GA: Kennesaw University Press.

van Luijk, H. (2004). Integrity in the private, the public, and the corporate domain. In G. Brenkert (Ed.), *Corporate Integrity and Accountability* (pp. 38–54). Thousand Oaks, CA: Sage

Waddock, S. (2004). Creating corporate accountability: Foundational principles to make corporate citizenship real. *Journal of Business Ethics, 50,* 313–327.

Waddock, S., Bodwell, C., & Leigh, J. (2006). *Total responsibility management.* Sheffield, UK: Greenleaf Publishers.

Walzer, M. (1997). *On toleration.* Haven, CT: Yale University Press.

Werhane, P. (1999). *Moral imagination and management decision-making.* New York: Oxford University Press.

Whetstone, J. T. (1998). Teaching ethics to managers: Contemporary problems and a traditional solution. In C. Cowton & R. Crisp (Eds.), *Business ethics: Perspectives on the practice of theory* (pp. 177–206). Oxford: Oxford University Press.

Whittier, N. C., Williams, S. D., & Dewett, T. C. (2006). Evaluating ethical decision making models: A review and application. *Society and Business Review, 4,* 94–112.

Williams, S. D., & Dewett, T. C. (2006). Yes, you can teach business ethics: A review and research agenda. *Journal of Leadership and Organizational Studies, 12,* 109–120.

Windsor, D. (2004). A required foundation course for moral, legal and political education. *Journal of Business Ethics Education, 1*(2), 10–26.

Wood, D. J., Logsdon, J. M., Lewellyn, P. G., & Davenport, K. (2006). *Global business citizenship: A transformative framework for ethics and sustainable capitalism.* Armonk, NY: M.E. Sharp.

CHAPTER 7

CONSIDERING THE EMOTIONAL SIDE OF BUSINESS ETHICS

Richard O. Mason
Southern Methodist University (emeritus)

THE CORE OF THE ISSUE

I have asked my family, my friends, and my community for forgiveness. I've agreed to pay a terrible penalty for it. It's an awful thing that I did, and it's shameful.
But I wasn't thinking that at the time.

—Barrionuevo, 2006, p. C1, (emphasis added)

Daniel Petrocelli, the defense lawyer for former Enron CEO Jeffery Skilling, wrenched this mea culpa out of Andrew Fastow, Enron's disgraced former CFO, as he cross-examined him in the trial of Skilling and Kenneth L. Lay, Fastows's former bosses. Fastow's attempt at repentance is not unlike that many miscreants make when the magnitude of their misdeeds finally reaches their conscience. Before that time, however, they were running largely on emotion, driven by greed and power seeking, and, to a large extent, they were unmindful of the potential for shame or guilt their actions carried. It is human nature to be self-centered. But when self-cen-

Advancing Business Ethics Education, pages 125–145
Copyright © 2008 by Information Age Publishing

teredness spills over into greed impelled by hubris it becomes socially destructive. Overcoming this predisposition among our students is the major problem confronting education for business ethics.

A Personal Perspective

I served as the Director of the Cary M. Maguire Center for Ethics and Public Responsibility at SMU in Dallas, Texas, a campus wide ethics support facility, when Enron and other business scandals occurred. The disgrace was felt deeply among many members of our constituency as, in general, these events punctuated the entire public's conscience. People from all walks of life were outraged. And, some of them shared their concerns with me and the faculty and staff at our school, often in very excitable terms. "Why don't you teach more business ethics in your classes?" "What are you doing to prevent this from happening again?" "Why can't your school do a better job of imparting ethics?" These are just a few of the many questions that were tossed at me repeatedly during meetings, conferences and at formal and informal receptions.

I have to admit now that my responses to these legitimate questions were rather weak. Yes, we teach business ethics in a course in our undergraduate program. Almost every course in the business curriculum has some ethics content. Our Ethics Center has determined that over 100 courses offered by the university contain more than a modest amount of ethics content. Since all undergraduates must take several of what our university refers to as "Cultural Formation" courses, it is well nigh impossible to graduate from SMU (and, I strongly suspect most other universities) without some exposure to ethics. So, I had some feeble answers for my inquisitors, just enough to get me past the most uncomfortable moments of these encounters. Nevertheless, something deeper continued to gnaw at me. The more I thought about what I was telling people the more dissatisfied I became. I suspect my questioners were not very satisfied either. Since then I have been mulling over the sources of my dissatisfaction and have tried to discover for myself what education for business ethics can do about it. The public can, and often does, expect too much from collegiate business ethics courses and materials. There is a limit as to what can be accomplished at this educational level at this time in our students' lives with the resources that can reasonably be made available. But, the public can also expect too little. This means that those of us who are responsible for imparting business ethics to our students and to the community need to think carefully about what the nature of the problem that we face really is and what we can realistically do about it.

What follows is a kind of prolegomenon, a preliminary discussion about some things that should be taken into account before a full blown program of education for business ethics can be developed.

Examining the Problem

One of my inquisitors—a seasoned executive and a vocal advocate for ethics, asked me "Can't you just impress on them how important it is to be honest, tell the truth, and respect your fellow man?" He's right, of course; but, would that it be so simple. I dare say that every single student in our classes would agree with him. Our students, for the most part, know and can recite back to you the importance of these virtues. Most can espouse them readily. *Exposure isn't the issue. Internalization is.*

Like Fastow at his infamous peak, the people responsible for the business scandals let their emotions take over and they did not *think*. We need to answer a fundamental question: How do people overcome some of their natural emotional tendencies, reflect on what they are doing and begin to adopt and act on the common values they espouse?

To address this and related questions, among other things, I began to read some of the biographical material on key characters in the Enron and other recent sagas including Kenneth Lay, Jeffery Skilling, and Andrew Fastow. (Among the sources consulted were Bryce, 2002; Eichenwald, 2005; McLean & Elkind, 2003; Seay, 2002; Smith & Emshwiller, 2003, and Swartz & Watkins, 2003) It quickly became clear to me that these people did not grow up in a moral vacuum. It would be hard to argue that during their life time they were not exposed to basic moral ideas such as right and wrong, good and bad, truth telling, following the rules (including rules for accounting), fairness, and respect for others. Lay, for example, famously wrote and had promulgated widely a mission and values statement for Enron. Its four pillars are laudatory: respect, integrity, communication, and excellence. Lay also argued Enron's business should be conducted in an environment that is open and fair. Enron's 2000 annual report contained a statement of values that expressed his espoused philosophy:

> We treat others as we would like to be treated ourselves. We do not tolerate abusive or disrespectful treatment.... We work with customers and prospects openly, honestly and sincerely. (Enron Annual Report 2000, p. 55)

So, Lay could talk a good game, as in other contexts could Skilling and Fastow. It is just that their behavior was not predicated on these espoused values.

Herein lies the fundamental problem. While a course in business ethics can reinforce prevailing ethical values—and I am all for that!—and while, moreover, such a course can show how these values are related to fundamental business processes and functions, that's about as far as they currently go. The curriculum at the universities my protagonists attended— Missouri, University of Houston, SMU, Harvard Business School, Tufts, Northwestern,—surely contained ethics content. Somehow, when push came to shove in their business lives, however, this exposure did not take, at least fully. When "the rubber met the road" on crucial business decisions they let their self-centeredness overwhelm their stated values. I arrived at the personal conclusion that common morality and typical business experience—just being a participant in the global business community—is usually enough to expose business people to the norms of society and prevailing ethical requirements of doing business. In short, I concluded, these people who became miscreants knew, or should have known, what ethically acceptable behavior in their business dealings was; but, they chose not to act on it. In the terms of ethics they succumbed to *temptations*. Temptations consume us when a person's emotions overpower his or her ethical leanings.

How Well are Temptations Dealt With in our Classes?

I asked myself: How well do I handle this problem in my classes?

As I reviewed what I teach in my business ethics course and what I know about other instructors' course approaches, it became clear to me that I was not really very effective in preparing my students to cope with temptations. The prevailing approach in my classes, and I believe many others', is to confront students with moral *quandaries* or dilemmas. Also included in many courses are cases and materials referring to a moral agent's responsibility for offering *criticism* with respect to others' discretions and for *systems regulation*. Resolving these three types of ethical issues—quandaries, criticism, and systems regulation—requires rational analysis and reasoning. This, of course, is an essential skill for our students to develop. But it is not enough.

Consider a typical case taught in many ethics classes: the Ford Pinto calamity of the 1970s. Drivers and passengers died or were seriously injured in fiery crashes as a result of rear-end collisions exacerbated by imprudently placing the auto's gas tank directly behind the rear axel. In class discussions I try to place each student in the role of a key decision maker at Ford and confront them with moral quandary type issues: how do you make a trade-off between the cost of refitting the car and the cost of insurance liability? How does a responsible executive place a value on human life when approving a model design? How safe is "safe" and at what cost? Or, was the cost/ benefit analysis used by Ford's analysts ethically defensible?

A discussion of criticism is also appropriate. An early test revealed that when the Pinto was struck from the rear at 20 miles per hour the tank was likely to rupture and spray out gasoline; so, I ask the whistleblower question of who knew about the danger and Ford's considerable exposure and, therefore, should have spoken up. I explore how information flows, incentive systems and the company's decision making structure might be changed so that this kind of ethical shortfall would not occur in the future. Finally, we conclude with a systems regulation discussion of the role of national safety regulation and other legal tools for addressing the broader social policy issues raised by the Pinto experience.

Similar issues can be brought up when teaching the Enron case. It is productive to do a reasoned moral analysis of the decisions Enron's executives made to create partnerships, form special purpose entities, manipulate prices in California, sell broadband capacity, and adopt mark-to-market accounting. The willingness of Sherron Watkins to finally step forward and why so many others in the know did not criticize Enron's policies offers a good opportunity for discussion on employee responsibilities in situations in which they feel the company is operating unethically. The broader social systems regulation concerns that eventually led to reforms of board of directors' practices and the Sarbanes-Oxley bill are also excellent topics for discussion. Yet, other than a wave of the hand at power grabbing, status seeking and greed, I have made little attempt to pin down the emotional energy that must have driven the likes of Lay, Skilling and Fastow. Despite the fact that Lay went to his grave claiming that he had done nothing wrong—as *New York Times* columnist Joe Nocera opined "Even at the End, Ken Lay Didn't Get It" (Nocera, 2006) and Skilling still protests that he is innocent of the 19 counts for which he was convicted, it seems to me they, too, as Fastow admitted in his testimony, succumbed to temptations. They were not thinking—ethically—at that time. In sum, they were not employing a personal moral analysis to the quandaries, systems critiques, and regulation problems they faced because, simply, they did not want to. That is, they were not bridling in their temptations.

Much the same problem occurs with the teaching of the Pinto case. During the discussion we touch on the executives' motivation, including, for example, Ford's president Lee Iaccoca's edict to produce a car that weighed no more that 2000 lbs. and would cost no more that $2000 within two years and what it means when a hard-charging executive like Iaccoca puts pressure on employees to cut costs and meet deadlines.

The typical approach to teaching these two cases, in my opinion, provides valuable discussion and learning. It addresses directly the *cognitive* reasoning side of being human and operating in business and opens the door to a discussion of some of the underlying emotions that influenced that reasoning. Nevertheless this type of teaching plan seldom penetrates the deeper *conative* forces—impulses, desires, volition, striving—that underlie an executive's or employee's actions. In summary, it is apparent to me that the coverage of a considerable amount of business ethics material, such as the Ford Pinto and Enron cases, serves to improve a student's capacity to *reason* about ethical issues—no small feat and a vital undertaking. But, there is little evidence that it does much, if anything, to change a business student's underlying emotional structure so that he or she is less likely to act out of narcissism, greed, hubris or to let other emotions dominate. In particular, it does little to thwart his or her inclination to place short-term personal preservation and job security ahead of the rightful claims of all other stakeholders in society. That is, as educators of business ethics we know and practice quite a bit about how to lead students to ethical waters. Nevertheless, a question remains: how well do we know how to make them drink?

The drinking of ethics,—or more specifically to application of ethics drunk, it turns out, must take place at a specific time in the brain's mental processing. As the brain encounters a problem, there is a relatively short time period during which one's emotions have been aroused but before a decision is made and acted upon. During this period the internalization of ethics can be most effective.

THE BRAIN EVOLVES FROM EMOTION TO REASON: A SKETCH

The human brain developed as Homo erectus evolved into Homo sapiens. It started off as just a cluster of fast snapping neurons located in the hindbrain which is connected directly to the spinal cord, a mid brain, and a part of the forebrain which is connected directly to sensatory organs including the eyes, ears, nose and mouth. This primitive brain was reactive and geared for survival. In time more complex behaviors were needed and the front part of the brain expanded and became more complex. In particular three areas emerged: the hypothalamus which coordinates basic drives and human motivations, the hippocampus which houses memory, and the amygdale which is the seat of emotion, emotional learning, emotional evaluation and responding. These three areas are often referred to as the limbic system and are mostly located in the orbitofrontal cortex. As primates developed, diversified their behavior and became more social they developed an additional layer of neural tissue that surrounded the limbic system. Called the neocortex, it is the seat of most reasoning, thinking, planning, decision-making and other deliberative processes that allow humans to reflect and free them from responding to only an immediate situation. When an event of interest occurs in a human's environment the basic path of response begins with the sensatory organs that send neural messages to the limbic system that in turn informs the neocortex. To over-simplify the basic pathway is: sensation→emotion→reason→behavior.

The Magical 100+ Milliseconds

Neuroscientists have discovered that this basic pathway has a timing and awareness pattern. In response to an eliciting event, one that has some valence for the individual, the brain's processing unfolds in three basic time phases. First is a "readiness potential" phase during which the uncon-scious firing of neurons is stimulated. Next, is a "signal" phase during which a neural signal is sent to the appropriate motor or activation areas of the person. Finally, there is a deliberative or "veto" period before the act is actually taken during which the brain is made consciously aware of the act it is about to perform or the decision it is about to make. During this final phase the conscious self can either continue with the unconscious decision it has made or it can *veto* it. It is during this last phase when one's moral development and ethical training most prominently come into play.

For example, neuroscientists have determined that for the human brain to perform a straight forward task, such as making a fundamental volun-tary hand movement, it takes between 500 to 1000 milliseconds, starting from the initial point-in-time the brain is first aroused to the point the task is actually begun. Of this total time the first 300 ms are spent in the "readi-ness potential" phase. It then takes between 50 to 100 ms for the brain to send a neural signal to the motor mechanisms of the hand so that the actual movement can be initiated. This leaves 100 ms, or up to about 600 ms, during which the brain is consciously aware of the act it is about to per-form. During this "magical" 100+ ms time frame it is possible for the con-scious self to assume control. According to neuroscientist Benjamin Libet who started performing experiments on this phenomenon in the early 1980s, this is when human beings are able to exercise their free will (Libet, 1999, p. 45). Moreover, it is during these 100+ ms when one's moral devel-opment and ethical training can be exercised.

A pioneer cognitive neuroscientist, Michael Gazzaniga, explains:

Neuroscience also tells us that by the time any of us consciously experience something, the brain has already done its work. When we become con-sciously aware of making a decision, the brain has already made it happen. This raises the question, Are we out of the loop? It is one thing to worry about diminished responsibility due to insanity or brain disease, but now the normal person appears to be on the deterministic hook as well. Should we abandon the concept of personal responsibility? I don't think so. We need to distinguish among brains, minds, and personhood. People are free and

> therefore responsible for their actions; brains are not responsible.... Brains
> are automatic, rule-governed, determined devices, while people are person-
> ally responsible agents, free to make their own decisions.... responsibility is
> what happens when people interact. (Gazzaniga, 2005 p. 89)

To a large extent ethics happens during those final magical 100+ ms of
agency freedom. Our conscious minds may not have free will, Vilayanur
Ramachandran argues, but rather "free won't" (Ramachandran, 1998, p.
22). That is, before an untoward or morally questionable act is executed
human beings are capable of vetoing it. This finding has several important
implications for education for ethics. The obvious implication is that people need to acquire the ethical evaluation tools and the will power necessary to react efficiently and ethically during those last 100+ ms. This
requires an ability to recognize and cope with one's emotional reactions to
temptations. Human nature dictates that both generally negative emotions
like anger, fear, jealousy, greed and hubris and the more morally positive
emotions such as empathy, love, joy, gratitude, and a sense of fairness will
well up in a person's unconsciousness almost instantaneously in reaction to
a decision stimulus (de Waal, 1996). Emotions, therefore, play a key role in
formulating the act to be taken or decision to be made. That act can be
checked, however, or reformulated during the last 100+ ms. A temptation
to do something one desires but knows is wrong, consequently, can be
overridden during this time. Thus, a moral individual must display
strength of will and moral courage to overcome the temptations that he or
she will inevitably encounter during the last 100+ ms.

The role of ethics exposure during the "readiness potential" phase
should also be considered. It is natural for human beings to instinctively
call forth survival responses to events they meet in their environment. That
is, our experiences evoke emotional responses and most of this evocation
takes place in special compartments of the brain, primarily the orbitofrontal cortex—the lower third of the prefrontal cortex including, in particular,
the medial prefrontal cortex, posterior cingulate/precuneus, and superior
temporal sulcus/temperoparietal junction. Research has shown that orbitofrontal cortex or limbic system is among the most consistently active
areas of the brain when an individual's emotions are stirred up. Psychologist Jonathan Haidt explains:

> The orbitofrontal cortex plays a central role when you size up the reward and
> punishment possibilities of a situation; the neurons in this part of the cortex
> fire wildly when there is an immediate possibility of pleasure or pain, loss or
> gain. When you feel yourself drawn to a meal, a landscape, or an attractive
> person, or repelled by a dead animal, a bad song, or a blind date, your orb-
> itofrontal cortex is working hard to give you an emotional feeling of *wanting*
> to approach or to get away. (Haidt, 2006, pp. 11–12)

In essence, in order for a person to act ethically, mental processes activated during the last 100+ ms of mental processing must cope effectively with the powerful emotional forces that have been generated during the first 300 ms. Haidt offers a useful metaphor for conceptualizing this problem: the emotional *elephant* is at work during the first 300 ms and the beast must be reined in by a reasoning *rider* during the last 100+ ms.

Elephants and Riders

Haidt is noted for his studies of the emotional basis of morality and the ways moral values vary across cultures. The human mind, he believes, is best understood as a huge craving elephant guided tenuously by a tiny rider. In this captivating metaphor the elephant represents a human's fundamental instincts, drives, desires and emotions—all forces that have been inculcated instinctively by needs to survive. In contrast, the rider represents reason. In the course of human evolution the elephant evolved first as an almost automatic reaction mechanism directed toward bodily survival. "*The rider evolved [later] to serve the elephant*" (Haidt, 2006, p.18). In addition, "The mind is divided into parts that sometimes conflict. Like a rider on the back of an elephant, the conscious, reasoning part of the mind has only limited control of what the elephant does" (Haidt, 2006, p. xi). In summary Haidt alludes to a famous analogy drawn by the Buddha:

> In days gone by this mind of mine used to stray wherever selfish desire or lust or pleasure would lead it. Today this mind does not stray and is under the harmony of control, even as a wild elephant is controlled by the trainer. (Mascaro, 1973, verse 326)

In sum, Haidt concludes:

> ...the rider is an advisor or servant; not a king, president, or charioteer with a firm grip on the reins....The elephant, in contrast, is everything else. The elephant includes the gut feelings, visceral reactions, emotions, and intuitions that comprise the automatic system. The elephant and the rider each have their own intelligence, and when they work together well they enable the unique brilliance of human beings. But they don't always work together well. (Haidt, 2006, p. 17)

Haidt is reminding us that human beings have many failings. They lose control, get misdirected in achieving their goals, succumb to temptations, and tend to rationalize or "confabulate"—fabricate socially acceptable reasons to explain their behavior.

What Does the Elephant/Rider Metaphor Mean for Business Ethics?

Today, it appears, the elephant is in control. Many business executives ignore or fritter away that precious 100+ ms. To my way of thinking, the Enron debacle serves as a lighting rod, a negative exemplar, shedding light on the many ethical lapses in which reason has been overpowered by stronger, more primitive forces. As we wax into the 21st century numerous scandals—corporate, government and personal—have alerted us all to the fragileness of many business leaders' moral underpinnings and the limits of their ability to channel their emotions.

The daily news is full of examples of people who recently have lost their ability to control the elephant that rages inside them. The elephant and rider metaphor reminds us that at the outset of any moral investigation we must acknowledge a fundamental principle of human nature: a person's desires and needs, fears and wants can overpower his or her rational thinking in many different situations and that, as a consequence, unethical acts may result. The elephant is always active.

Andrew Fastow is a case in point. This shamed Chief Financial Officer came from a good family background and was educated at leading schools, including an MBA from Northwestern's top ranked Kellogg School. But, from the beginning he was a man in a hurry to become wealthy and gain social status. According to an article posted on *Time's* website Fastow became a key cog in turning Enron into a "swaggering, rule-breaking, deal-making cult" (*Time Magazine Online Edition*, 2006). Yet, pursuant his own personal goals (and with Lay's support) he convinced Enron's board to make an exception to its conflict of interest policy so that he could control a number of special purpose entities (SPEs). He used this ploy reputedly to pocket $60.6 million in total for himself and his family while, at the same time, he was developing some elaborate structured finance scams that were instrumental in pushing Enron into bankruptcy. The acts Fastow took out of greed contributed immeasurably to the harm—corporate failure, lost retirement, lost jobs, etc.—that thousands of people suffered as a result of Enron's downfall (Bryce, 2002).

Author Jack Beatty offers us an insight into how Fastow used bribery as well as deception to do his deals:

> You are Andrew Fastow, Enron's CFO, and you have this problem. You have set up more than 3,000 partnerships to hide Enron's losses of more than $500,000,000. An Enron controller is pressing you on the unsavory details of your scheme. You get him transferred. His replacement you cut into the deal. He gives you $5,000 to invest in one of the partnerships and two months later gets a $1,000,000 return. Your problem has disappeared. You have snared him in what we might call an Enron. You yourself are mega-Enroned, as over-

seer and beneficiary of partnerships for which you have gained 30 million dollars. (Beatty, 2002, p. 1).

Among other things being "Enroned" means that one has given up control of his or her emotions and let a greedy culture dictate or condone one's behavior. That is, the Enron elephant is in charge.

Psychologists and neuroscientists are beginning to study the role the elephant plays in moral decision-making and under what conditions it can be reined in. Studies in ethics and moral psychology have heretofore focused primarily on reasoning. Recent evidence, however, suggests that moral judgment is more a matter of emotion and affective intuition than of deliberative reasoning. At least two lines of inquiry are potentially relevant to education for business ethics.

TWO RELEVANT RESULTS
FROM PSYCHOLOGICAL RESEARCH

The Trolley and Footbridge Experiments

Judy Garland sang:
I went to lose a jolly
Hour on the trolley
And lost my heart instead. (Gottlieb & Kimball, 2000, p. 489)

Ethics, working through neuroscience, may have found it.

Joshua Greene, a philosopher cum moral psychologist, studies moral decision-making by subjecting his subjects to neuroimaging (fMRI) while they are contemplating moral quandaries. Included among his 60 some odd dilemmas are the famous "trolley" problem and the "footbridge" problem, a conundrum that has been proposed and analyzed by philosophers such as Judith Jarvis Thomson (Thomson, 1986, pp. 94–116). These problems are presented as follows:

1. A runaway trolley is careening down the tracks toward five people who will certainly be killed if the trolley proceeds on its present course. But there is a switch on the line. You can save these five people by diverting the trolley onto a different set of tracks. However, an unwitting individual is standing on the spur. This person surely will be killed if you flip the switch. Is it morally permissible to redirect the trolley and thus prevent five deaths at the cost of one?

2. A runaway trolley is careening down the tracks toward five people who will certainly be killed if the trolley proceeds on its present

course. There is no switch. You are standing on a footbridge over the tracks next to a very large person. The only way to save the five people is to push this person off the bridge and onto the path of the trolley. In the process this person will surely be killed. Is it morally permissible to push the person onto the tracks and thus prevent five deaths at the cost of one?

Greene, Sommerville, Nystrom, Darley and Cohen (2001) confronted their participants with three types of problems: moral-personal, moral-impersonal and non-moral. The researchers point out, importantly, that problem 1, as stated above, is "impersonal," whereas problem 2 is best described as "personal," because in problem 2 the agent has to intentionally and directly push another person to his death. The team applies three criteria in order to classify a problem as "personal": (a) the act is likely to cause serious bodily harm, (b) the harm will be done to a particular person, and (c) the harm will occur in such a way that it does not result from the deflection of an existing threat onto a different party. The footbridge problem 2, therefore, is "personal" because it satisfies these criteria.

Studies show that most people say "yes" or "appropriate" to the trolley/switch/spur version 1—the impersonal version. That is, they would throw the switch. In contrast, most people say "no" or "inappropriate" to the footbridge version 2—the personal version. These participants would not intentionally push another person to his certain death. Why?

What makes it permissible to sacrifice one person to save five in the first case but not in the second? Their findings have important neurological as well as psychological implications. The two problems, it turns out, engage different psychological processes, different parts of the brain. Specifically, the researchers found "that brain areas associated with emotion and social cognition (medial prefrontal cortex, posterior cingulate/precuneus, and superior temporal sulcus/temperoparietal junction) exhibited increased activity while participants considered personal moral dilemmas such as problem 2, while 'cognitive' brain areas associated with abstract reasoning and problem solving exhibited increased activity while participants considered impersonal moral dilemmas such as problem 1 (Greene, et. al. 2001, pp. 2105–2107). At the same time, areas of the brain associated with working memory, which has been linked to ordinary manipulation of information and reasoning, were considerably less active during the personal moral questions than during others.

Greene and his associates also measured how long it took subjects to respond to the problems. Their theory of emotional interference predicted that the participants' reaction times would be longer if they made emotionally incongruent decisions—those which occur when a participant responds "appropriate" in the moral-personal condition (e. g. saying "yes" or judging it "appropriate" to push a human being off the footbridge in dilemma 2). As predicted, in responding to problems that were classified as moral-personal it took significantly longer for participants to arrive at an emotionally incongruent response of "appropriate" than that to arrive at an emotionally congruent response of "inappropriate." Specifically, for moral personal problems on average it took participants about 5000 ms to give an "inappropriate" answer, that is, it was unacceptable to push the person off the footbridge. Whereas, those who decided it was "appropriate" to do so took closer to 6750 ms, about 35 percent longer. These delays suggest that these subjects' brains were working harder to overcome their instinctive negative emotional response when they were approving a personal moral violation. There were no significant differences in the reaction times between responses of "appropriate" and "inappropriate" in the other two conditions: moral-impersonal and non-moral.

These studies and others conclude that emotion is a significant driving force in moral judgment. Moreover they show that "reasoning can play an important role in the production of impersonal moral judgments and in personal moral judgments in which reasoned considerations and emotional intuitions conflict. These results also suggest that much, although not necessarily all, moral judgment makes use of processes [of the brain] specifically dedicated to social cognition and, more specifically, the representation of others' mental states" (Greene & Haidt, 2002, pp. 517–523).

MISCHEL EXPERIMENTS ON SELF-CONTROL AND DELAYED SATISFACTION

In 1970 Walter Mischel at Stanford University conducted a set of experiments with 4 year olds (Metcalfe & Mischel, 1999; Shoda, Mischel, & Peake, 1990). He first established that the children he was going to work with liked marshmallows and that, moreover, they liked two marshmallows much better than they did one. The children then were ushered into a room containing a table upon which two plates had been placed. One plate had just one marshmallow on it; the other two. Also on the table was a bell. Mischel told his young subjects that he was going to leave the room for a little while. He instructed them: "If you wait until I came back, you can have the two marshmallows. But, if you can not wait, ring the bell. I will return and you can have the plate with just one marshmallow." Then he left.

Columnist David Brooks portrays the scene:

> In videos of the experiment, you can see the children squirming, kicking, hiding their eyes—desperately trying to exercise self-control so they can wait and get two marshmallows. Their performance varied widely. Some broke

down and rang the bell within a minute. Others lasted 15 minutes." (Brooks, 2006, p.4a)

A few of the subjects held out until Mischel returned and were rewarded with the two marshmallows. As an integral part of the research the experimenter recorded the number of seconds each child waited until he rang the bell.

Subsequently in 1985—the subjects are now about 19 years old—Mischel mailed the children's parents a questionnaire asking about their child's personality, performance on college entrance exams (SAT), and ability to delay gratification and deal with frustration. Mischel discovered a direct correlation: the number of seconds a child waited to ring the bell in 1970 predicted both what parents in 1985 reported about that child's personality and the likelihood that the child was admitted to a top university.

Brooks continues:

> The children who waited longer went on to get higher SAT scores. They got into better colleges and had, on average, better adult outcomes. The children who rang the bell quickest were more likely to become bullies. They received worse teacher and parental evaluations 10 years on and were more likely to have drug problems at age 32. (Brooks, 2006, op. cit)

Haidt summarizes:

> Children who were able to overcome stimulus control and delay gratification for a few extra minutes in 1970 were better able to resist temptation as teenagers, to focus on their studies, and to control themselves when things didn't go the way they wanted.

> What was their secret? A large part of it was strategy—ways that children use their limited mental control to shift attention. In latter studies, Mischel discovered that the successful children were those who looked away from temptation or were able to think about other enjoyable activities. These thinking skills are an aspect of emotional intelligence—an ability to understand and regulate one's own feelings and desires. An emotionally intelligent person has a skilled rider who knows how to distract and coax the elephant without having to engage in a direct contest of wills. (Haidt, 2006, p. 18)

Trolley and marshmallow studies confirm the central role that emotions play in human behavior and moral judgment. They also provide some clues as to how moral reasoning approaches can be used by a rider to harness his elephant. Mischel's marshmallow studies indicate that by encouraging the development of emotional intelligence capacity in individuals they can learn to thwart a temptation by examining its opportunity costs. The long-term pay-off seems to be a more successful life. People who became "Enroned" were unable to do this. Many innocent people suffered as a consequence. The trolley studies indicate, among other things, that if you want people to reflect more deeply on a problem, "personalize" it. The participant's in these studies either didn't want to inflict harm on an innocent bystander or they agonized about sending him to his death.

Both of these studies, as valuable and insightful as they are, deal with "toy" problems—contrived issues constructed specifically to examine stark differences in a hypothetical environment. Real world problems are never encountered in such a rarified environment. Emotions that affect moral judgments are evoked in a context. How might that context be studied?

MITROFF'S ONION MODEL APPLIED TO ETHICS

Human behavior—untoward, unethical or moral—can be analyzed as the result of several different forces that are at work. In his studies of human caused crises Ian Mitroff has developed what he colloquially calls an "onion model" (Figure 7.1) which has proven to be extraordinarily useful for identifying the forces affecting human behavior (see Mitroff & Pearson, 1993, p. 56).

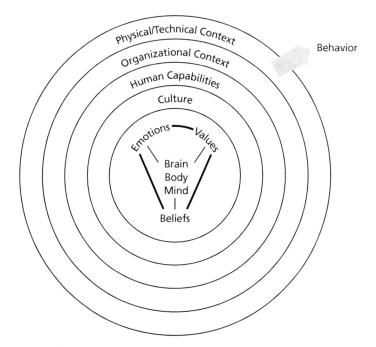

Figure 7.1. Mitroff's onion model applied to ethics. Adapted from Mitroff and Pearson (1993).

Application of the model begins with the behavior to be examined and then peels it back layer by layer to its root causes. Say, an automobile is rear-ended and explodes. That's an untoward or undesirable behavior to be investigated. Mitroff says that the first step is to identify the proximate technical or physical cause of the event. In the case of the Pinto, for example, it was the regrettable placement of its gasoline tank. Mitroff notes that there is a very strong lure in most situations for those in power to simply correct the technical cause and be done with it. Move the gas tank, fix the O-ring on *Challenger*, patch the foam on *Columbia*, pay compensation to the families of dead tobacco smokers or women made ill from leaking breast implants. Pay a fine to Californians harmed by Enron's manipulating energy prices. These corrective acts, however, are just palliatives. Perhaps they are necessary, but they deal only with the immediate symptoms of the underlying problem. They do nothing to prevent similar deviant behavior from happening again. In Mitroff's experience organizations that focus only on palliative corrections are prone to future crises. Hence, they are acting unethically now and likely to continue to do so. Consequently, this is just the surface area—the more tangible and visible—of the onion in his model. One needs to peel away more.

Below the surface of the technical is the organizational. The technical aspects of a business' behavior are orchestrated through the matrix of an organization. Decision structures, patterns of power and authority, and information flow all contribute to the outcome. The shape of technology and how it is used is determined in part by the organizational context in which it evolves. In the case of the Pinto Iaccoca's edict, the manner in which it was diffused and carried out throughout the various units of the organization, and the incentive and reward structures that accompanied it had a substantial impact on the cost/benefit analysis that ultimately influenced the design of the car. Enron's chaotic "free-for-all" organizational design and its personnel policies like "rank and yank" also contributed to its ethical downfall.

At the next lower level, occupying positions and roles in an organization, are human beings who have skills, capabilities, limitations and fragilities. Mitroff argues that an effective crisis or moral analysis should also examine the personal strengths and weakness and quirks of the actual individuals who occupied crucial roles at the time decisions were made and actions were taken. Ask how did their skills and idiosyncrasies affect the outcome? Ken Lay was an effective smoozer but remote and distant from daily affairs, genial but clueless. Skilling was an accomplished strategic consultant and a model builder who also believed that his view was the only acceptable view of things. Fastow was a well- trained financial engineer who was ambitious, impatient and greedy yet deeply insecure.

Moving a level deeper, in addition to their personal attributes people are influenced considerably by the matrix of cultures they inhabit. A culture, for social psychologist Edgar Shein, is a "pattern of shared basic assumptions that a group learned as it solved problems of external adaptation and internal integration, that has worked well enough to be considered valid and, therefore, to be taught to new members as the correct way to perceive, think, and feel in relation to those problems" (Schein, 1992, p. 12). This pattern of shared assumptions shapes the way people will behave. It forms the context for the decisions they make and the actions they take and influences the way they will employ their capabilities. When people became "Enroned" they had bought into a culture of narcissism that was exciting for a while but in the end highly dysfunctional. McLean and Elkin provide two brief insights:

> Lay had hired lots of his old cronies. They had ill-defined jobs and a line straight to the man who had hired them. Morale was terrible. Backbiting had become part of the Enron culture. Power plays were a daily occurrence. And it was nearly impossible for the company to act decisively, because executives felt they could always get Lay to reverse a management decision. All the politicking had practically paralyzed the company. (McLean & Elkind, 2003, pp. 25–26)

> But what brought Enron down was something more complex—and more tragic—than simple thievery. The tale of Enron is a story of human weakness, of hubris and greed and rampant self-delusion; of ambition run amok; of a grand experiment in the deregulated world; of a business model that didn't work; and of smart people who believed their next gamble would cover their last disaster—and who couldn't admit they were wrong. (McLean & Elkind, 2003, p. xxv)

Giving rise to the cultural dimension is the emotional center of each individual who comprises the group, the fears and hopes that each human being carries with them all of the time. Cultures are created to cope with their members' emotional concerns. How people use their capabilities, reason through problems, and succumb to their fragilities always reflects their emotions as was discussed above. How humans act in organizations, and even the kinds of organizations they create stems, in part, from their emotional concerns. Included in the complex of an individual's overall emotional makeup are three related things:

1. Emotions—immediate visceral reactions to external stimuli examples of which are anger, love and fear. Emotions involve certain bodily changes, such as an accelerated or depressed pulse rate and result in some momentary bodily changes or distortions.
2. Values—assumptions people make about what they care about most.
3. Beliefs—assumptions they make about the world in which they live.

These attributes are experienced first in one's brain and are promulgated to his or her mind and body. At the brain, mind, body level emotional reactions occur either as an immediate response to external stimuli or are the result of an indirect subjective process, such as one's memory, association, or introspection. Studies have shown, however, that the force of external stimuli diminishes in importance as a direct cause of a person's emotional reaction, in proportion to that person's maturity and level of moral development.

Mitroff argues, and the neuroscientific studies cited above support, that this non-reasoning emotional level influences significantly all actions that human beings take and that, hence, all behaviors organizations exhibit. He says that in order to understand and to influence an organization's behavior we must peel back "the onion" and reveal its origins in order to identify, examine, deal with and, if necessary, change the underlying emotions. It occurs to me that despite the plethora of literature on Enron and about the likes of Lay, Skilling and Fastow we still know little about the emotions, values and beliefs that drove these men to do what they did. Nevertheless, I am convinced that their emotional makeup had every bit as much to do with precipitating the scandal as was any potential lack of exposure to business ethics on their part. The next major challenge to education for business ethics is to address this emotional level and to develop methods for imparting the emotional maturity and moral development necessary for people to act ethically in business. Somehow we have to learn how to infuse our students with the moral courage and moral will they need to manage their emotions and act ethically.

Moral courage derives, in large part, from an ability to understand and manage people, beginning with one's self. It relies on a different type of intelligence. Peter Salovey and John Mayer call this ability "emotional intelligence" and they define it as: "the ability to monitor one's own and others' feelings and emotions, to discriminate among them and to use this information to guide one's thinking and actions" (Salovey & Mayer, 1990, p. 185).

Drawing on Salovey and Mayer's earlier article, Daniel Goleman (1995) developed and popularized a view of human emotional intelligence. Specifically, Goleman argues that Emotional Intelligence requires the development of five emotional competencies:

1. The ability to identify and name one's emotional states and to understand the link between sensations, emotions, thought and action.
2. The capacity to manage one's emotional states, to control one's emotions and to shift undesirable emotional states to more acceptable ones.

3. The ability proactively to enter into emotion states that are associated with drives to achieve and be successful.
4. The capacity to be empathic, to read, be sensitive to, and to influence other people's emotions.
5. The ability to enter into and to sustain satisfactory interpersonal relationships.

Developing and testing programs that develop these emotional competencies is a task for further research. A good place to start, however, is to have students complete the "Personal Values and Life Goal Inventory" developed by Gerald Cavanagh (Cavanagh, 1998, pp.33–36). This is an excellent tool for helping students understand—and talk about—their personal values and goals. Another helpful instrument is the "VIA Inventory of Strengths" a 240-item self-report questionnaire that measures the degree to which students endorse each of 24 strengths of character, classified into six virtues: wisdom, courage, justice, humanity, temperance, and spirituality. This inventory was developed by psychologists Martin Seligman and Christopher Peterson (Peterson & Seligman, 2004). These two educational tools help students become more self-aware and help them personalize the virtues. Once they have this self-knowledge it is somewhat easier for them to discuss their emotional reaction to a case or issue and how they might channel it.

CONCLUSION

This chapter has argued that emotions are as fundamental to ethics and ethical behavior as is reason. The elephant is always active. The most challenging task facing education for business ethics is to develop competent riders, people who can consciously practice ethics during last 100+ ms. The trolley and footbridge studies suggest that an ability to make situations more "personal" will help. The marshmallow studies establish a need to develop a capacity among our students to delay gratification. Mayer, Salovey's and Goleman's works on emotional intelligence offer a theory and some approaches for developing methods to impart emotional intelligence as it relates to ethics to our students. If the Enrons of the future are to be avoided and personalities with exceptional business skills like Lay, Skilling and Fastow are to be encouraged to adopt more morally desirable behaviors and goals then business ethics curriculum must deal more effectively with its students' underlying emotions. Advancing business ethics education requires it.

REFERENCES

The American Heritage Dictionary. (2000). Boston: Houghton Mifflin.

Barrionuevo, A. (2006, March 12). The courtroom showdown, played as Greek tragedy. *New York Times*, C1, 3.

Beatty, J. (2002, March 13). The Enron Ponzi scheme. *Atlantic Unbound*, 1.

Brooks, D. (2006). Focusing on the core questions of America's human capital. *Durango Herald*, 4a

Bryce, R. (2002). *Pipe dreams.* New York: Public Affairs.

Cavanagh, G. (1998). *American business values: With international perspectives.* Upper Saddle River: Prentice-Hall.

de Waal, F. (1996). *Good natured: The origins of right and wrong in humans and other animals.* Cambridge MA: Harvard University Press.

Eichenwald, K. (2005). *Conspiracy of fools.* New York: Broadway Books.

Enron annual report 2000, 55. Retrieved February 4, 2008 from http://www.tcpipelineslp.com/investor/reports.2005_annual_report.pdf.

Gazzaniga, M. (2005). *The ethical brain.* New York: Dana Press.

Goleman, D. (1995). *Emotional intelligence: Why it can matter more than IQ.* New York: Bantam Books.

Gottlieb, R., & Kimball, R. (2000). *Reading lyrics.* New York: Pantheon Books, 485, from The Trolley Song lyrics by Hugh Martin, in the 1944 film *Meet Me in St. Louis* , staring Judy Garland.

Greene, J. D., Sommerville, R. B., Nystrom, L.E., Darley, J. H., & Cohen, J. D. (2001, September 14). An fMRI investigation of emotional engagement in moral judgment. *Science, 293,* 2105–2107.

Greene, J., & Haidt, J. (2002, December). How (and where) does moral judgment work? *Trends in Cognitive Sciences, 6*(12), 517–523.

Haidt, J. (2006). *The happiness hypothesis.* New York: Basic Books.

Libet, B (1999). Do we have free will? *Journal of Consciousness Studies 6*(8–9), 45.

Mascaro, J. (1973). *Dhammapanda*, verse 326. USA: Penguin Group.

McLean, B., & Elkind, P. (2003). *The smartest guys in the room.* New York: Portfolio.

Metcalfe, J., & Mischel, W. (1999). A hot/cold-system analysis of delay of gratification: Dynamics of willpower. *Psychological Review, 106*, 3–19.

Mitroff, I. I., & Pearson, C. M. (1993). *Crisis management: A diagnostic guide for improving your organization's crisis-preparedness.* San Francisco, CA: Jossey Bass, Inc. Publishers.

Nocera, J. (July 6, 2006). Even at the end, Ken Lay didn't get it. *New York Times*, C1.

Peterson, C., & Seligman, Martin, E. P. (2004). *Character strengths and virtues: A handbook and classification.* New York: Oxford Press, American Psychological Association.

Ramachandran, V. (1998, September 5). Quoted in The zombie within. *New Scientist,* 22.

Salovey, P., & Mayer, J. (1990). Emotional intelligence. *Imagination, Cognition, and Personality, 9,* 185–211.

Schein, E. H. (1992). *Organizational culture and leadership* (2nd edition). San Francisco: Jossey-Bass.

Seay, C. (2002). *The Tao of Enron.* Colorado Springs, CO: Navpress

Shoda, Y., Mischel, W., & Peake, P. K. (1990). Predicting adolescent cognitive and self-regulatory competencies from preschool delay of gratification: Identifying diagnostic conditions. *Developmental Psychology, 26*, 978–986.

Smith, R., & Emshwiller, J. (2003). *24 Days*, New York: HarperBusiness.

Swartz, M., & Watkins, S. (2003). *Power failure*, New York: Doubleday.

Thomson, J. J. (1986). *Rights, restitution and risk*, Cambridge: Harvard University Press.

Time Magazine Online Edition (2006, September 28). Retrieved September 28, 2006 from http://www.time.com/time/business/article/0.8599.201871.00html

CHAPTER 8

LEARNING TO TEACH ETHICS FROM THE HEART

A Journey of Discovery From the Inside Out

Jerry Calton
University of Hawaii–Hilo

Steve Payne
Georgia College and State University

Sandra Waddock
Boston College

ABSTRACT

This chapter explores teaching and learning approaches that enable both faculty and students to speak from the heart and better connect as co-learners in a process for building more ethical leaders and managers. In particular, we introduce our experiences with wisdom circles involving faculty in our field. We then explore several related forms of dialogic engagement and reflective practices that share many similar learning assumptions as wisdom circles and that can help participants find their authentic voice as a basis for developing moral courage and imagination. We believe that these emerging

Advancing Business Ethics Education, pages 147–166

forms of dialogic engagement will have increasing application for faculty development and as a teaching/learning approach for business ethics and related courses in business schools.

INTRODUCTION

Some time ago, Bird and Waters (1989) argued that "good conversation," that is, authentic conversation that allows real and ethically charged issues to be surfaced, was at the heart of creating ethical organizations. Claiming that many managers were morally mute, Bird and Waters noted that such good conversations were very difficult for many organizations to hold. Similarly, in the management/business classroom, finding the courage to teach from the heart and thereby having the potential to reach the hearts of learners can require courage and a stepping away from traditional teaching methods toward methods that allow for authentic voice and for personal stories and insights to be generated (Denton & Ashton, 2004).

Mostly, as professors we are conditioned by our own classroom experiences and professional norms to attempt to keep ourselves, our own points of view, and our personal lives out of our work—out of the classroom and out of professional meetings. Yet, as Kolb and Kolb (2005, p. 207) point out, despite the fact that one of the key ways that human beings make meaning from their experiences is through conversation, "genuine conversations in the traditional lecture classroom can be extremely restricted or nonexistent". If we make a link between what Bird and Waters (1989) tell us about the need for good conversations that allow ethical issues to be surfaced in organizations and what Kolb and Kolb note about the relative paucity of such good conversations in the classroom where learning about organizations is taking place, perhaps we might take seriously the need to create more space in the management classroom itself for such good conversations.

As Kolb and Kolb (2005) suggest, real learning based in experience means making space not only for knowledge acquisition from external sources of authority, but also for learning "from the inside out" based on personal exploration and reflection, often in dialogic interactions with others. We feel that this quest for self-knowledge about ethical ground rules needed to build and sustain both personal and public relationships must arise not only from the cool calculations of the head, but also from the warm workings of the heart. This paper will explore some methods that we have been experimenting with, as self-confessed novices, both in workshops with management faculty at conferences and to some extent in our own classes, in learning how to teach from the heart. Very much a work-in-progress, these ideas represent our tentative reaching out to explore a few of presumably multiple means that we believe can help not only our students but also ourselves as instructors to use our authentic voices in teaching and in learning together within a shared co-learning environment.

Our hope is that we can suggest ways by which our students can become more "reflective" (Schön, 1987) or "mindful" (Kabat-Zinn, 1995) business practitioners. We thereby hope to find a space for our students to learn more about how ethical obligations and judgments are involved throughout their business, professional, and personal lives. We have explored Native American-style wisdom circles, self-reflective practices like modified vision quests and meditation with subsequent sharing, as well as interactive dialogic encounters to encourage both critical student self-reflection and opportunities for co-learning.

THE WISDOM CIRCLE AS REFLECTIVE PRACTICE

Justification for creating these types of conversational spaces for co-learning is offered by the noted educator, Parker J. Palmer (1998). He argues that to grasp fully the miracle of teaching as a co-learning process, we need to get past the more typically asked questions of *what, how,* and *why.* We need to explore the *"who"* of teaching. We began exploring the possibilities of wisdom circles and guided meditation as a vehicle for authentic conversation at professional meetings of the International Association of Business in Society (IABS) in 2005 and 2006. We built on the experiences of others with wisdom circles (Garfield, Spring, & Cahill, 1998) and of one of the authors, Sandra Waddock, in leading similar dialogue- and experience-based sessions on mindfulness with Larry Lad and Judy Clair in previous years. Below we explore the process and outcomes of the wisdom circle session that we held in March 2006 in Merida, Mexico.

The wisdom circle format is an especially well-crafted vessel for inviting participants to undertake a voyage of personal discovery. As co-conveners, we used the bus excursion to Mayan ruins, the opening reception, and serendipitous encounters while breaking bread to recruit willing pathfinders for our wisdom circle journey. A common response to our invitation, in effect, was, "Won't this risky encounter, which asks us to reveal something of our inner selves to our students or colleagues as a way to forge a stronger learning connection, actually make us more vulnerable and undermine our authority as professional teachers and scholars?" This question often was posed by women, who tend to feel that they must remain on guard to preserve their professional stature in the gender wars, which, sadly, have not entirely by-passed the groves of academe. Indeed, Palmer has identified a "culture of fear" which permeates the "disconnected" lives of many educators, not only women, but all of us. He opens his second chapter of *The Courage to Teach* (1998) with an evocative poem, which Jerry Calton

read to begin the process of establishing a sense of connection within the
safe and, potentially, sacred space of our wisdom circle:

—"Lit Instructor"—
Day after day up there beating my wings
With all of the softness truth requires
I feel them shrug whenever I pause:
They class my voice among tentative things,
And they credit fact, force, battering.
I dance my way toward the family of knowing,
Embracing stray error as a long-lost boy
And bringing him home with my fluttering.
Every quick feather asserts a just claim;
It bites like a saw into white pine.
I communicate right; but explain to the dean—
Well, Right has a long and intricate name.
And the saying of it is a lonely thing.
By: William Stafford; quoted by Palmer (1998, p. 35)

Our workshop session asked those who chose to join the wisdom circle
to explore together the inner landscape of what it means to "teach from
the heart." Almost all participants brought to the circle a story of a previous
peak teaching experience. Sharing this story required an act of courage.
Before one's authentic voice can explain why a story is meaningful, it is
necessary to reflect upon and reveal something of one's inner self. Such
cycles of self-reflection and engagement with others through dialogue are
critical for the process of learning together. It was in this spirit that we gath-
ered within the wisdom circle.

The wisdom circle, modeled on the discourse practices of Native American tribal councils, has been widely employed as an exploratory counseling
method for encouraging personal reflection and participant sharing of
insights to achieve shared developmental objectives, such as improving
cross-cultural understanding, or coping with substance abuse or marital
discord (Garfield et al., 1998). However, the wisdom circle format (Wisdom Circles, n.d.) has not been applied, in our knowledge, to help educators explore ways to reflect upon the connection between their inner selves
or values and assumptions and their out-reaching teaching choices and
methods. A wisdom circle provides a welcoming and safe space for participants to look within themselves to find their "authentic voice," so that
many can find the courage to speak from the heart and listen respectfully
and empathetically until the real "talk" begins. The dialogic rules and rituals, or "constants," of the wisdom circle help to convene this sacred space
in a remarkably short time, if each who enters the circle is prepared to
open his or her heart to the learning possibilities therein.

The first constant is "*Honor the circle as sacred time and space.*" The ritual of reducing overhead illumination and lighting candles on a prayer cloth to mark a break with normal or "profane" time invites heightened awareness of the potential for learning and speaking from the heart. Conveners invited joiners to place meaningful tokens of their lives near the candles— wedding rings, pictures of loved ones, other tokens of affection, regard, and connection. Sandra Waddock shared that she had been studying shamanic teachings for several years, seeking both personal spiritual growth and a way to encourage her students at Boston College to think and act more "mindfully." She then led the circle in a short meditation based on the writings of Kabat-Zinn (1995), instructing participants to close their eyes, sit quietly, and "become the mountain" or go to a mountain to ask it what it had to say about learning and teaching. By entering into this meditative state, each joiner sought to slough off distractions and center their self within the circle. The short debrief also allowed people to express some of their own personal insights, which, of course, varied widely depending on the individual, but focused on insights related to the strength of the mountain, climbing and striving, and centeredness.

The second constant is "*Create a collective center*" by agreeing upon a topic or intention. Using a method similar to appreciative inquiry (Watkins & Cooperrider, 2000; Cooperrider & Srivastava, 2001; Cooperrider, Sorensen, Yaeger, & Whitney, 2001), we then asked members of the circle to recall and consider the nature and significance of a peak event in their teaching lives that had been a truly extraordinary and exciting learning encounter, and to reflect on what had been the characteristics of the situation, the learners, and the learning leader. This led into constants three and four—"*asking to be informed by our highest human values,*" such as compassion and truth, and "*expressing gratitude for the blessings and teachings of life*" by honoring our interdependence with others in the web of life. By sharing with respect to these end goals each participant can make the link to leading an ethical life—and learning to manage in a way that is deeply linked to ethics.

In this way, we prepared the way to the fifth constant, "*creating a container for full participation and deep truth telling.*" Within the circle, each person is empowered to speak without interruption or cross talk. Rather than a "talking stick" to confer the right to speak, we used a ceremonial heart-shaped rock, symbolizing the capacity to speak from the heart. It is remarkable how quickly this conferral of the stone deepened the conversation, adding weight to the speaker's contribution, while sharpening the respectful attention of those listening.

This experience led naturally to the sixth and seventh constants: "*listen from the heart*" and "*speak from the heart.*" To serve as a compassionate witness, listeners must not judge or try to interpret someone else's story. Nor should the listener try to "fix" the speaker by offering external advice. The story can only serve as a basis for reflection on one's own experience and as a contribution to the group's learning. While speaking from the heart, participants should draw upon direct experience, avoid abstract conceptual language, and stay in touch with their feelings. If moved to share those feelings, the speaker should express difficult things without self-judgment and without blaming others.

Constant eight "*makes room for silence to enter the circle*," allowing time for reflection, for meditation, and for a sense of the sacred to emerge as the group proceeds. In retrospect, the silences were powerful generators of meaning, sharpening the dialogic tension and eventually calling forth a new contribution from someone's inner experience. The requirement that only the holder of the stone could speak respected those not yet ready to speak, while inviting them to share a story that was meaningful, not only to self, but also to others. Each story was a gift, gratefully received as a contribution to shared insight. Constants nine and ten forged a stronger circle by "*empowering each member to be a co-facilitator of the process*" and "*committing each person in the circle to an ongoing relationship*" so as to build commitment to a spirit of trust and caring.

The wisdom circle rules and practices or "constants" discussed above mesh closely with the conditions of "paradoxical tension" that Palmer (1998, p. 74) associates with the electrically charged dialogic space of a genuine learning encounter: (a) The space should be bounded and open, (b) The space should be hospitable and "charged", (c) The space should invite the voice of the individual and the voice of the group, (d) The space should honor the "little" stories of the students and the "big" stories of the disciplines and tradition, (e) The space should support solitude and surround it with the resources of community and, (f) The space should welcome both silence and speech.

LEARNING FROM PEAK EXPERIENCES

In a very profound sense, the medium was the message for those who participated in our wisdom circle. The process, as it unfolded, is virtually impossible to disentangle from individual or group learning outcomes. The exploratory telling of stories opened the way to an integrative experience within each person, as well as to exploring and valuing his/her own experience of learning in relation to others. The stories of peak teaching and learning experiences shared many common elements. Many of these insights emerged from the reflective inquiry led by Steve Payne toward the end of the workshop:

1. Peak learning experiences often arise spontaneously from an apparent breakdown in regularly scheduled class activities, and in response to shared frustrations over difficulties in promoting higher-level learning engagement. This is not to say that such learning experiences cannot be planned in advance. However, preparation must be geared toward calling attention to complex, open-ended opportunities for learning together, where paradoxical tensions can be explored via self-reflection, empathetic sharing, respectful listening, and interactive dialogue (Calton & Payne, 2003).

2. Sometimes a peak learning experience can be triggered by a private, personal reaction to the issue by the instructor, thereby demonstrating his or her vulnerability and relinquishing a distancing role of the teacher as impartial "expert."

3. Student initiative and leadership often emerge from such classroom experiences, as arguments are raised, alternative perspectives are expressed and challenged, and rules of engagement are clarified and renegotiated.

4. New insights on the learning challenge tend to arise organically from an emergent, self-organizing, interactive learning process, rather than from a formally, "rational" inquiry process.

5. Class "buy-in" of learning outcomes is greater because of increased participant engagement, as reflected in more shared leadership of the inquiry process, and more shared ownership of learning outcomes.

6. These peak learning experiences are usually associated with personal insights or discoveries by instructors that influence their future instructional repertoire.

7. Some stories of peak teaching experiences captured smaller, personal moments of insight. However, all such experiences countered traditional role assumptions of teachers and students as transmitters and receivers of given knowledge and called forth broader perspectives that arose from both heads and hearts of co-learners.

Many examples of the best teaching/learning experiences had to do with a process of letting go of preconceived ideas about what should happen in the class and allowing an emergent process to take place. In such peak learning experiences, the instructor often provided a focal point for the conversation and means for learners to channel their thoughts, but she or he did not control nor get in the way of the learners' own learning process or particular destinations. This "getting out of the way" of learning by trying to put ego aside is advised by educational theorists, such as Finkel (2000) in his book *Teaching with Your Mouth Shut*, and helps accomplish what others such as Vella (2002) insist is critical to dialogue and enhanced learning—closing the distance between students and the teacher. In addition, these experiences involved the instructor showing his or her authentic self in a new way to learners, thus, allowing for an authentic response by learners. Typically, these stories illustrated experiences in which real excitement and engagement occurred both with the material and with others in the learning situation. The instructor's role became, in a sense, one of creating a space—a physical, intellectual, emotional, and even spiritual space—where actual learning and caring connections could occur. This type of learning is what Cunliffe (2002) calls fully embodied and also arguably builds a strong ethical core in learners, whether in students or their instructor as a co-learner, because it helps "us move from being morally-neutral technicians to considering the morality and responsiveness of our practices" (Cunliffe, 2002, pp. 41–42).

In the sense that wisdom circles and similar dialogic approaches help embody learning more fully and create a grounded sense of morality, they arguably have the potential to create a greater sense of integrity with more richness of meaning among learners. Rather than dissociating learning from the rest of one's life, embodied experiences that tap the mental, physical, emotional, and even spiritual resources of the learner repair some of the rift between knowing and doing, and between theory and practice, that has plagued management education in general and ethics education in particular.

One question that arose during our workshop debriefing was whether certain types of content (e.g., finance or management science) lend themselves to the types of peak experiences described by participants in the wisdom circle. Because emotional engagement and real expressions of individuality and personal meaning typically are displayed in such interactive encounters, there are opportunities for deeper connection to the material by students. Since dialogic formats and rules of engagement provide a safe space for students, topics involving ethics and social responsibilities, as introduced in textbook readings and through ethics-related cases or vignettes, seem especially appropriate for encouraging much deeper student reflection and richer conversations about their own ethics-related experiences, questions, or concerns. To the extent that integrative learning encounters are desirable within "content" classes such as finance, we are not prepared to rule out the use of wisdom circles or other related methods for encouraging self-reflection and dialogue throughout the business curriculum.

These relatively abstract ruminations on the learning outcomes of our Merida workshop do not do justice to the remarkable sense of intimacy and trust engendered by the voluntary decision of participants to share their stories and, thereby, reveal something of their inner selves. By blending our authentic voices, we became, for a short time, a small learning community capable of touching each other's hearts. This is a rare event for an academic conference. One measure of our impact on each other is the quiet smiles of recognition and appreciation among circle participants in subsequent sessions. Another is the even quieter thanks to conveners from those few in the circle who said nothing at all during the workshop. Several confided that they were so moved by the new experience that they had not quite found the courage to speak, though they looked forward to a future opportunity to do so.

Imagine the opportunities for exploring shared concerns and gaining deeper personal insights concerning ethics-related teaching, if such face-to-face engagement were readily available on a more frequent or continuing basis. College courses in organization behavior and social responsibility/ethics offer a unique potential for setting time aside, beyond other course activities, for learning dialogues that continue over several months. These learning activities would allow students to develop more trust in each other, while also exploring ethical issues from the "inside out." Rather than seek to indoctrinate students and future managers to apply externally derived standards of ethical conduct, these co-learning exercises would encourage students to reflect inwardly on who they are and where they stand before looking outwardly and empathetically for imaginative insights on how the impact of potential actions might be perceived by others. These experiences would also encourage students, as future managers, to speak with their authentic voices while reaching out to others in a joint search for behavioral guidelines to govern interactions that would be fair and beneficial to all concerned. We embrace Palmer's (2004) insight that inner reflection gives rise to mindful action, since each individual must seek and forge a "hidden wholeness" that binds his or her private self (i.e. "soul") with their public responsibilities and actions. Learning ethics from the inside out requires accepting a commitment to speak with an authentic voice within a dialogic search for an "undivided life" that is true to the self, while also embracing responsibility toward others.

OTHER FORMS OF DIALOGUE FOR THE CLASSROOM AND FACULTY DEVELOPMENT

Other learning approaches share similar dialogic assumptions as wisdom circles, and might help students and faculty create the capacity for speaking with a more authentic voice and for deeper exploration of personal experience and meaning. These dialogic learning experiences appear to produce similar effects with respect to helping learners explore their own, often implicit, assumptions and the moral basis for their decision-making and actions. While these teaching/learning approaches have, as yet, not been linked formally to teaching managerial ethics and responsibility, we would argue that such approaches, conducted over time and with effective facilitation, could create more morally conscious and grounded managers and leaders. Among specific types of learning dialogues that appear to us to have potential for business ethics faculty are those described briefly below.

Circles of Trust

Palmer (2004) introduces what he refers to as "circles of trust" for learning purposes. Palmer's concern is that too many people have fragmented lives in which their personal values do not match what they perceive is necessary conduct in this world to be successful. Among the key assumptions (Palmer, 2004, pp. 116,182) for these types of circles, based somewhat on Quaker learning traditions, are the following:

1. A special form of community and caring through dialogue is created which is informed, less by traditional reasoning, and more through personal stories, metaphors, and questions that allow situations to be viewed in different lights;
2. Discourse is not intended to persuade, dissuade, or "fix" someone else. Each person can speak from his/her center to others in the circle though words and images that take them to a deeper level as they hold, rather than suppress or ignore, learning tensions;
3. Truth exists in the circle, not through external authority or short-term convictions of individuals, but through conversation in which "the voice of truth that we think that we are hearing from within can be checked and balanced by the voices of truth others think that they are hearing;" and
4. Occasional use of honest, open questions helps a participant clarify his or her own viewpoint, instead of speech either to affirm or disconfirm these views or to give counsel.

Palmer (2004) recommends that participants in circles of trust listen respectfully and expand from what has been said by others to reveal their own truths. Sharing one's views honestly, without trying to gain favor or support and by overcoming the fear to speak one's truth, is a key goal of these circles of trust.

Palmer's dialogic approach through these circles of trust is associated with an organization known as The Center for Courage and Renewal (2006). This is an educational non-profit organization that has offered programs over the last decade for educators, groups, and communities to "renew their spirits and reconnect who we are, with what we do." Retreats are scheduled around the country, as well as training programs for those who are interested in learning facilitator skills for creating circles of trust. This organization gets its funding, along with other "social change" programs, from the Fetzer Foundation. Another facet of this teacher formation program is a more specific focus on community colleges (The Center for Formation in the Community College, 2006).

Learning Circles

Other educational theorists employ the term "learning circles" to describe somewhat similar dialogic teaching and learning practices. For example, Educators for Community Engagement (ECE), formerly known as "The Invisible College" (2006), is a non-profit organization that seeks to foster more democratic education and community experiences through learning circles, service-learning, and dialogue. Their goal is to encourage college faculty, students, staff and community partners to integrate learning and service within the diverse communities in which they work and live. ECE relies upon cooperative and democratic learning methods, and particularly learning circles that draw upon the stories and experiences of community partners, to try to discover more creative approaches for addressing community and social problems. By emphasizing personal experience over existing theory or experts, and through open dialogue and careful listening over the course of several days, participants work together to improve their understanding and skills.

Such learning processes, as taught through ECE workshops and facilitator certification programs, derive from a tradition of concern for social justice through democratizing education and spurring community development and from the ideas of well-known leaders in that movement such as Myles Horton, Septima Clark, and Paulo Freire. Descriptions of how to plan for and integrate learning circles into various teaching and learning contexts, such as for a college courses in philosophy or ethics, are available (Collay, Dunlap, Enloe, & Gagnon, 1998; Bonner Curriculum, n.d.). The guidelines or format for learning circles, although similar in many ways to those for wisdom circles and circles of trust, differ in a more directive role for the facilitator of the circle and more focus on a specific community or social challenge.

Horizontal Evaluation

A dialogic approach that also shares many assumptions of previously described circles and that might be applied for certain faculty development purposes by those teaching business ethics courses is what Gitlin (1990) calls "horizontal evaluation." It is a dialogue in which faculty start collaboratively by analyzing the relationship between their teaching intentions and their actual practices in order to unearth possible "living contradictions" or gaps between what they intend to do in their teaching and what they actually accomplish (Gitlin, 1990, p. 542). Learning intentions or goals are sometimes proposed in advance. A fuller understanding of these intentions can also emerge gradually, through the dialogue of participating faculty. Ethics and management theories suggest the possibility that dialogic exploration of one's own teaching experiences as a faculty member or of one's own experiences in confronting tough ethical dilemmas might be useful pursuits. Rest (1986) points to the linkage between ethical reasoning, formation of intent, and actual conduct in certain models of ethical development. Ansoff (1965) advocates "gap analysis" of differences between plans and results in management theory. A more authentic approach to ethical learning might even involve faculty sharing with students an occasional experience in which the faculty did not live up to his or her own moral intention in a personal, business, or professional setting, followed by personal reflection and sharing of feelings aroused by this decision.

TEACHING CHALLENGES ASSOCIATED WITH RELATED FORMS OF CIRCLES AND DIALOGUES

A number of challenges arise, no doubt, in trying to create wisdom circles, circles of trust, and learning circles in classes involving business students. Significant advance planning and facilitation skills appear to be necessary to engender more student openness and authenticity as well as to maintain a very safe space for all students involved in these circles. Taking responsibility for such student learning goals requires considerable "up-front" guidance for students concerning dialogue guidelines or constants, and perhaps some contracting ritual or process in which students commit to reading and trying to follow these guidelines. Explanations and rationales for learning circles probably need to be cast in "student-friendly" or less stilted language than the vocabulary and concepts used by some educational theorists assuming critical theory or workplace spirituality perspectives. Opportunities should also be provided for students who have further questions to meet with the instructor/facilitator and pursue these issues, or even other means made available in a few special cases for students to complete alternative learning activities.

Cognitive and affective dissonance is often associated with change and learning activities, and such circles hold the potential to become learning interventions that could touch students more deeply than typical classroom experiences. Although circles of trust are described by Palmer (2004, p. 183) as being designed to be neither invasive nor evasive for participants, there is a potential for certain students unearthing rather intense personal problems for which they have initially, at least, unpleasant affective states. Can the instructor anticipate these possibilities, determine these student difficulties when these occur, and be prepared to assist students through referrals to student counseling or otherwise? In required student reading prior to starting such circles, examples might be given of several anticipated and possibly problematic types of student attitudes or reactions to the circle.

Suggestions on ways to cope with such initial responses in order to protect the safety and values/constants of the learning circle might also be provided. In *The Courage to Teach,* Palmer (1998, pp. 89–95) provides some useful guidelines on the purposes of learning communities. He warns against adopting the assumptions of a "therapeutic community," which insists upon intimacy as a prerequisite for communal intervention to "fix" a participant who has joined the circle. Forced intimacy can drive the private self further into hiding, preventing the personal reflection that must precede respectful engagement with others. When intimacy becomes the norm, we lose our capacity to discover a connection to the strange and to strangers, which Palmer contends is the essence of education. For Palmer, the hallmark of a learning community is acceptance of the claim that "*reality is a web of communal relationships, and we can know reality only by being in community with it*" (Palmer, 1998, p. 95; emphasis in original). Thus, reality unfolds from reflection on what rings true to the inner self, followed by construction of a meaningful connection between the self and others. Palmer (2004: 90–111) also recommends that the learning circle focus its attention "at the slant" via considering metaphoric "third things," such as provocative poems, rather than the intimate details of a participant's own story. Such indirection can provide a buffer of safety, so that each participant can reflect on what the poem says about his or her inner meaning, while gaining courage to speak, thereby opening up the possibility of learning together. Palmer recommends that each participant in the circle keep notes on his or her own personal reflections, rather than on the general outline of the conversation. Thus, ethical understandings and feelings are built inside out by each person who inhabits a co-learning community.

For these circles to have some of the potentials described by Palmer, Vella, Cunliffe, and others, special consideration concerning the issue of their grading or evaluation appears warranted. With little grading weight or extrinsic motivation for these circles, would some less mature students be motivated to engage in active listening or participation? Associated with student learning circles and dialogic engagement in the literature by some (e.g., Cunliffe, 2004; Ho, 2005; Hughes, Kooy, & Kanevsky 1997) is the recommendation for the use of student journals. Comments that arise in these dialogues can spur reflection by those listening that might lead to their efforts to explore personal questions and issues in written form. Should such journals be encouraged or required, and if so, should these journals be graded and assigned academic credit? Cunliffe (2004) draws a distinction between journaling and subsequent critical reflection on journal entries, which she requires students to incorporate into a graded integrative essay that addresses the student's personal insights into an ethical situation, why these insights are important to that student, and what the student plans to do now.

Another teaching design issue is whether to include a few key student roles within the circle, such as a student facilitator for each circle who would pay special attention to reminding others of the policies or constants of the circle. A recorder might briefly summarize major topics/concerns that the group has covered in that week and those class members who were actually present for their circles. Issues of the degree of facilitating structure in these circles and the type of controls or assessment for learning outcomes occurring through these circles also deserve thought and planning. Learning circles and dialogic encounters can touch multiple levels on each of three dimensions, cognitive, affective, and psycho-motor skills, found in common learning outcome taxonomies (Bloom, 1956; Krathwohl, Bloom, & Bertram, 1973; Simpson, 1972) and could be so assessed.

THE ROLE OF REFLECTIVE PRACTICES IN FOSTERING ETHICAL LEARNING

The types of dialogic processes described in earlier sections are critically important to fostering a sense of "other," which is a core element of ethical behaviors. Extrapolating from Bauman (1993) and Rorty (2006), we suggest that the key to learning to behave ethically is to find ways to help students reflect inwardly first and begin to appreciate what Palmer (2004) called the "undivided self," which serves as the basis for developing empathetic understanding of others. Thus, the moral imagination must arise from within and in relation to particular others, rather than from a modernist attempt to rationally and autonomously deduce and apply universal ethical principles. This perspective suggests that to become fully aware of the impacts of their own actions on others and society, students need exercises both to help them look within the self, as well as interactive, dialogic exchanges. Such inward-looking reflective exercises might include meditation, personal histories and vision statements, and even Native American style vision quests. Below we will briefly explore some of our experimentation with these different methodologies.

Meditation and Reflection on Practice

In the spring of 2006, one of us was given the opportunity to teach a capstone seminar for college seniors, about half of whom were management students. Called "Leadership and Mindfulness," this seminar incorporated periodic meditation exercises to help students become aware of how mindlessly many of them were going through their days. Initially resistant to the concept of mindfulness ("I *like* multi-tasking." "Won't paying full attention to what I'm doing, if it's something simple like brushing my teeth or eating, just waste precious time that could be used more productively?"), the students nonetheless were willing experimenters. To their surprise, many of them found that by slowing down and focusing on what was happening now, or taking time out of their hectic schedules for even five minutes of reflection, they were able to become more aware of the influence of their own pre-dispositions and behaviors on situations they faced. When the students then were asked to reflect on a situation in which they had exerted some leadership and write up the incident, many of them found that they were able to step away from their emotional engagement in a typically stressful, conflictual situation, and with this distance to assess their own behaviors in a more realistic light.

Personal Histories and Vision Statements

For some years, one of the authors has been asking students in strategic management and social issues in management classes to write personal and, sometimes, social vision statements as one of their first written assignments. This assignment asks the student to reflect seriously about what she or he would like to have accomplished in, say, 20 or 30 years, or at the time of retirement. For many students, it is the first time they have been asked to think seriously about this issue, and particularly about what they would like to see as their contribution to the world and what their real passion in life might be. Not as a by-product, but as a central element of the assignment, they need to deal with the issue of whether their current path is placing them on the road to making a contribution or whether they are living what Henry David Thoreau called "lives of quiet desperation." Although certainly not the case for all students, for quite a few, the process of thinking mindfully proves to be quite compelling, forcing them to think about why they are pursuing their current path and whether or not it is a productive one, even in light of their own goals. More than one student has changed careers dramatically as a result of this type of reflection, frequently choosing a path of service. Those who maintain current career paths, too, have clearly begun to think more seriously about their role(s) in the home and family, the community, and the broader society, and whether there is consistency and integration between their words and their actions, as well as their inner and outer selves.

Vision Quests

One other type of activity involving inner search and reflection that proved fruitful, again in the capstone course, was a highly modified Native American style vision quest, which was the final exam/project in the course. Students were told to go out for a minimum of two hours in nature, by themselves, with a fundamental question: what is my purpose in life? They were to seek in nature what answers might be there for them and then write up a short description of their experiences. Several students had truly amazing experiences, although others were more ordinary, but almost all seemed to gain personal insight. Perhaps the students' words speak best for themselves.[1] One student, probably the most visionary in the class, who had a remarkable vision about the energy connecting beings on earth, wrote the following:

> If music is my vocation, or if it is my [a]vocation, I do not know. But what I have now come to realize, which has surely passed my mind before, but only briefly, is that my dedication to service, my yearning to help others, and to assist them in whatever way necessary, may be able to be fulfilled through giving them music, through teaching, performing, and showing people the ineffable energy which is universally drawn out of music, and has been for all time.

Another student gained profound personal insight with long-term implications for the ethics of how he lives his life: "In my vision quest, it's not that I could see what I was doing, but it was more of a feeling, or a calling, to do something different than what most people do. It was a calling to create something, to do something that has a lasting impact on people. This is the part of my vision quest that has had the most profound impact on me."

Still another student experienced a profound new sense of self: "In a world where people are forced to pack as much into a day as possible, I felt I must serve another purpose. I must be a calming presence emotionally and practically for people. I must be a restorative influence rather than a draining one." The student further reflected, "Though this initially seemed like a very passive approach to service, it began to take true form in my mind. I must not merely be a place where people can go to avoid their problems and be safe from acquiring a greater burden. No. I must be a force that alleviates existing pressure. I must have meaningful conversations with people when I can sense this buildup."

None of these experiments in reflective practice derive from traditional approaches to the teaching or learning of ethics. However, the strength of the writing and conviction with which students articulated their personal visions suggest that they are genuinely and passionately engaged in a search for a pathway to a more ethical life. Without necessarily discarding traditional approaches to teaching ethics, we invite others to experiment with teaching methods that call forth personal reflection and interpersonal dialogue as a way to learn ethics from the inside out.

CONCLUDING REMARKS

A key development in the business ethics and society literature has been study of approaches taken by corporate managers for improved stakeholder engagement and dialogue (Andriof, Waddock, Husted, & Rahman, 2002; Calton & Payne, 2003). Certain forms of dialogue have been recommended for their potential to set the stage for possible resolution of complex, messy problems through their emphasis on stakeholder learning and relationship building. Opportunities for students to explore multi-stakeholder dialogues and engagement processes exist through an educational package such as *The Clayoquot Controversy: A Stakeholder Dialogue Simulation* (Lawrence & Svendsen, 2002). Such dialogic learning experiences might be enhanced in certain ways, however, if students were confronted with an ethical dilemma or social problem that actually existed in their own surrounding community and it involved collaborative study and dialogue by students who were encouraged to bring their own identities and interests to the challenge. For example, business students are occasionally given service learning projects in which they interact with and try to assist officials from third-sector organizations in their community. Such service learning projects might be enhanced through student learning circles initially that lead to students better appreciating community social needs, their actually selecting an appropriate service client and project, and then their participating in dialogues with key stakeholders of that non-profit organization.

Several of the authors are currently experimenting in their business ethics and related courses with dialogic assumptions and formats that share similarities with, and most of the constants of, wisdom circles. Creating a special space for this unique type of learning appears to be an art and involves certain communication skills (silence, active listening, etc.) that we as academicians can discuss, but don't always, or even often, practice ourselves. Palmer (2004, p. 116) stresses that such circles or ways of being are quite countercultural for many of us and these require "clear explanation, steady practice and gentle but firm enforcement by a facilitator" who helps participants to avoid falling into unhelpful communication habits. Creating a classroom co-learning environment with a culture that includes and respects reflection and dialogue about matters of heart or spirituality can be challenging in a business school academic climate steeped in a scholarly tradition that insists on separating facts from values, empirical "truth" from mere normative opinion. A pervasive culture of fear that promotes a defensive concern for preserving a safe distance between personal "feelings" and professional status renders it difficult to open up a reflective dialogue with teaching colleagues, as well as students. There can also be a "Catch 22" dilemma of recognizing our need for more integration or wholeness, when we are so caught up in our "fractured" world that we can hardly find the time or space to achieve the experience of balance and healing in our work or personal lives.

However, our memory of the warm and respectful meeting of minds and spirits in our recent wisdom circle at the 2006 IABS meeting in Merida, Mexico, reminds us that ethical understandings and feelings arise within communities of meaning from the telling of stories that reflect our aspirations to achieve the good life. When we share our stories, inviting our students to reflect on what they mean in their personal lives and in their unfolding relationships with and responsibilities to others, we are convening a communal meeting around the conversational campfire. Within this circle, strangers are welcome, so long as they accept the commitment to learn how to live together, talking and talking until the "talk" begins. As we exercise our imaginative sympathy with the plight of others (See Rorty, 2006), we learn that our fates are intertwined and that our collective moral imagination is needed to reveal the hidden wholeness that makes us human and connects us all. We invite other teachers, students, and practitioners of business ethics to join us around the fire, sharing vision quests, talking story, and learning how to teach and learn from the heart.

NOTE

1.   Students gave permission to use their words anonymously.

REFERENCES

Andriof, J., Waddock, S. Husted, B., & Rahman, S., Eds. (2002). *Unfolding stakeholder thinking: Theory, responsibility, and engagement.* Sheffield, UK: Greenleaf Publishing.

Ansoff, H. I., (1965). *Corporate strategy: An analytic approach to business policy for growth and expansion.* New York: McGraw-Hill.

Bauman, Z. (1993). *Postmodern ethics.* Oxford: Blackwell.

Bird, F. B., & Waters, J. A. (1989). The moral muteness of managers. *California Management Review, 32*(1), 73–88.

Bloom B. S. (1956). *Taxonomy of educational objectives, Handbook I: The cognitive domain.* New York: David McKay.

Bonner Curriculum: Learning Circles. (n.d). Retrieved July 8, 2006, http://www.bonner .org/resources/modules/modules_pdf/BonCurFacilLearnCircles.pdf

Calton, J., & Payne, S. 2003. Coping with paradox: Multistakeholder learning dialogue as a pluralist sensemaking process for coping with messy problems. *Business & Society, 42,* 7–42.

Collay, M., Dunlap, D., Enloe, W., & Gagnon, G. W. (1998). *Learning circles: Creating conditions for professional development.* Thousand Oaks, CA: Corwin Press, Sage Publications.

Cooperrider, D. L., Sorensen, P. F., Yaeger, T. F., & Whitney, D. (Eds.), (2001). *Appreciative inquiry: An emerging direction for organization development.* Champaign, IL: Stipes Publishing, LLC.

Cooperrider, D. L., & Srivastva, S. (2001). Appreciative Inquiry in Organizational Life. In David L. Cooperrider, F. Peter, Sorensen, Jr., Therese F. Yaeger, & Diana Whitney (Eds.), *Appreciative inquiry: An emerging direction for organization development* (pp. 57–100). Champaign, IL: Stipes Publishing, LLC.

Cunliffe, A. L. (2002). Reflexic dialogical practice in management learning. *Management Learning, 33*(1), 35–60.

Cunliffe, A, L. (2004). On becoming a critically reflective practitioner. *Journal of Management Education, 28*(4), 407–426.

Denton, D., & Ashton, W. (Eds.). (2004). *Spirituality, action, and pedagogy: Teaching from the heart.* New York: Peter Lang Publishing Inc.

Educators for Community Engagement. (2006). Retrieved July 6, 2006, http://www.e4ce.org/LearningCircles/LearningCircles.htm

Finkel, D. L. (2000). *Teaching with your mouth shut.* Portsmouth, NH: Boynton/Cook Publishers.

Garfield, C., Spring, C., & Cahill, S. (1998). *Wisdom circles: A guide to self-discovery and community building in small groups.* New York: Hyperion Press.

Gitlin, A. (1990). Understanding teaching dialogically. *Teachers College Record, 91*(4), 537–563.

Ho, P. L. (2005). *Reflective learning through learning journals: Can business students do it?* Paper presented at the Higher Education Research and Development Society of Australasia Conference, Sydney. Retrieved July, 8, 2006, http://conference.herdsa.org.au/2005/pdf/refereed/paper_076.pdf

Hughes, H. W., Kooy, M., & Kanevsky, L. (1997). Dialogic reflection and journaling. *Clearing House, 70*(4), 187–190.

Kabat-Zinn, J. (1995). *Wherever you go there you are: Mindfulness meditation in everyday life*. New York: Hyperion.

Kolb, A. Y., & Kolb, D. C. (2005). Learning styles and learning spaces: Enhancing experiential learning in higher education. *Academy of Management Learning and Education, 4*(2), 193–212.

Krathwohl, D. R., Bloom, B. S., & Bertram, B. M. (1973). *Taxonomy of educational objectives,the classification of educational goals. Handbook II: Affective domain*. New York: David McKay Co., Inc.

Lawrence, A. T., & Svendsen, A. (2002). *The Clayoquot controversy: A stakeholder dialogue simulation*. [CD-ROM-based simulation and teaching note]

Palmer, P. J. (1998). *The courage to teach: Exploring the inner landscape of a teacher's life*. San Francisco: Jossey-Bass Inc., Publishers.

Palmer, P. J. (2004). *A hidden wholeness: The journey toward an undivided life*. San Francisco: Jossey-Bass Inc., Publishers.

Rest, J. (1986). *Moral development: Advances in research and theory*. New York: Praeger.

Rorty, R. (2006). Is philosophy relevant to applied ethics? *Business Ethics Quarterly, 16*(3), 369–380.

Schön, D. A. (1987). *Educating the reflective practitioner: Toward a new design for teaching and learning in the professions*. San Francisco: Jossey-Bass.

Simpson E. J. (1972). *The classification of educational objectives in the psychomotor domain*. Washington, DC: Gryphon House.

The Center for Courage and Renewal. (2006). Retrieved July 6, 2006, http://www.teacherformation.org.

The Center for Formation in the Community College. (2006). Retrieved July 6, 2006, http://www.league.org/league/projects/formation/index.htm

Vella, J. (2002). *Learning to listen, learning to teach: The power of dialogue in educating adults*, revised edition. San Francisco: Jossey-Bass.

Watkins, J. M., & Cooperrider, D. L. (2000). Appreciative inquiry: A transformative paradigm. *Journal of the Organization Development Network, 32*(1), 6–12.

Wisdom Circles (n.d.). Retrieved September 19, 2005, http://wisdomcircle.org/format.html.

CHAPTER 9

MORAL IMAGINING

Toward Using Cognitive Science in Teaching Business Ethics

Sue Ravenscroft
Iowa State University

Jesse Dillard
Portland State University

ABSTRACT

In this chapter we briefly describe and criticize traditional philosophical approaches to teaching moral reasoning and propose developing moral imagination as a way to enrich traditional ethics instruction. Because our minds are embodied in and constrained by our physical properties and because human reasoning is linguistically structured, we rely on devices such as prototype, metaphor, frames, and narrative. We consider the role and implications of these devices on moral reasoning. Next, we look at how business faculty have begun to introduce the concept of moral imagination and how this undertaking might be advanced. While we do not offer specific pedagogical recommendations, we argue that the insights gained from cognitive science can make ethics education more powerful and relevant.

Advancing Business Ethics Education, pages 167–189
Copyright © 2008 by Information Age Publishing
All rights of reproduction in any form reserved.

INTRODUCTION

Imagination is central to human meaning and rationality for the simple reason that what we can experience and cognize as meaningful, and how we can reason about it, are both dependent upon structures of imagination that make our experience what it is.

—Johnson, 1987. p. 172)

Despite recent increased clamorings for more ethics in the classroom, faculty teaching business ethics face formidable challenges. First, they face the unreasonable expectation that the purpose of a business ethics course is to make students more ethical. Although it is unusual for any such characterological objective to be imposed on faculty teaching traditional business disciplines, those who oppose the teaching of ethics argue that students do not emerge from ethics courses notably more ethical in their behavior. Secondly, faculty, including those who may not be thoroughly versed in philosophical ethics, often assume that traditional philosophy offers the only conceptual foundations for moral reasoning and therefore feel obligated to provide an overview of these philosophical approaches to ethics. Such an overview, which usually consists of a look at the dichotomy of deontological (duty-oriented) versus teleological (goal-oriented) ethical principles, allegedly provides the foundation from which students and faculty may begin to consider cases and do applied ethics. We argue that faculty and students will all be short-changed by relying on such an overview.

We begin our deliberations by recounting some personal experiences teaching ethics. We have used an approach that begins with descriptions of traditional summaries of ethical schools of thought—deontological ethics, teleological ethics, and virtue (character-based) ethics. After we describe differing overarching principles, we present students with a case. The American Accounting Association's Seven-Step model for teaching ethics (cf. Langenderfer & Rockness, 1989) requires that students work through several clarifying and amplifying steps, such as listing the parties affected and how they might be affected, and then select an action for the character in the case who is facing the ethical issue (often misleadingly referred to as a "dilemma"). More than once, after we have had a fairly lively discussion about these issues and have provided strong, clearly differentiated examples of the various philosophical approaches to ethics, the class has come to an embarrassing, awkward spot. Once students are asked to apply the broad philosophical principles they have just learned and processed, they seem adrift, unable to go in a neat syllogistic way from the various premises to a clear and certain conclusion. Students have even complained that although the discussion preceding this question was interesting and engaging, it did not unambiguously lead them to the "right" answer. We felt a sense of disconnect that reflected the frustration and sense of puzzlement that the students were experiencing.

CRITICISMS OF THE STATUS QUO

We are not alone in our discontent. Derry and Green (1989) provided an early critique of the integration of ethical theory in twenty-five business ethics textbooks. Derry and Green found that these texts tended to introduce formal philosophical theories, acknowledge the difficulties of reconciling tensions among such theories, and then ignore the gulf between the theories and actual ethical decision making. Macdonald and Beck-Dudley (1994, p. 616) say that the standard approach of providing students a "brief exposure to moral philosophy often leaves them worse off than they were before." Bartlett (2003) criticizes the literature of business ethics because it is focused on the wrong unit of analysis; business ethics either ignores social contexts and focuses only on isolated individual behavior and judgments, or it ascribes social context too much influence and ignores individuals. He concludes that:

> ...although theoretical bases for the study of business ethics have been offered in the form of both moral philosophies and the psychology of moral development, these approaches are only of limited value when it comes to attempting to apply ethical theory to real-life situations. (Bartlett, 2003, p. 233)

Whitbeck (1998) argues that asking students to choose among a foundationalist school of philosophical ethics has at least two negative consequences.[1] First, it alienates students who realize that in addition to their contemplation of abstract ethical principles, their experience, religion, family, and their society have done a great deal to shape their understanding of ethical issues. Second, the underlying pedagogical assumption is clearly that if a student understands the philosophical positions, the student will be able to more easily respond to ethically difficult situations. Yet students, and faculty, who may comprehend the abstract principles with some sophistication and clarity still struggle when cases are not clear unambiguous instances of the general principles, and when abstract principles conflict. Whitbeck argues strongly that "top down" reasoning from philosophical principles is not how people routinely make ethical decisions. Ethics does not reduce to Logic 101.

Jonsen and Toulmin (1988) state that the top-down approach of moving from general principles to specific cases fails in the two common situations described above and in a third, less common situation. Ethical principles fail when "historical changes in our social relations, technical resources, and psychological understanding undercut the factual presuppositions of our earlier moral concepts" (Jonsen & Toulmin,1988, p. 326). Jonsen and Toulmin ask, for example, whether a married person who undergoes a sex change is still married in a state that has not legalized same-sex unions. This particular issue would not have arisen prior to transgender surgery procedures.

Most recently and most unrestrainedly, Rorty (2006) provides the focus of a forum on the basic question of whether ethics, as a branch of formal philosophy, or any other sub-field within formal philosophy has a role in applied ethics. Rorty, who does not shy from controversy, says, "God has provided no algorithms for resolving tough moral dilemmas, and neither have the great secular philosophers. Urging that there is something that *makes* actions wrong or moral beliefs true is an empty-gesture." Rorty (2006, p. 371) goes on to argue that collectively people are now morally superior to people in the past because we have a broader definition of and extend more rights to more people. Women can now vote; slavery is outlawed; torture is officially forbidden by international conventions. These signs of progress arose because people could envision alternatives to their current behavior, and the "source of these new alternatives is the human imagination" (Rorty, 2006, p. 373). Although Rorty's argument is passionate and colorfully presented, Rorty is trained as a philosopher. And as Whitbeck (1998, p. 7) notes, "philosophers usually do not even raise the question of how moral agents reason."

So questions remain regarding whether and how traditional moral philosophy fails to lead us to satisfactory answers to ethically framed questions, especially with respect to business and accounting related questions. What are the lacunae in the moral reasoning laid out by traditional philosophical models? We believe that tentative answers to these questions are being reformed and reshaped by an increasingly clearer understanding of how people reason about and create ethical structures. For an overview of how cognitive science relates to ethics, we rely primarily on Johnson and Lakoff's work (Johnson, 1993; Lakoff, 1996; Lakoff & Johnson, 1999). Johnson proposes that recent findings by cognitive scientists, psychologists, and linguists can help to map a course that reflects how people respond to ethical questions, how we formulate and frame our reactions, and what might be reasonably expected to occur in a course devoted to ethics.

OVERVIEW OF THE TRADITIONAL ETHICAL MODEL

Those educated in the US/Western European tradition share a view of morality, according to Johnson (1993), even if we do not consciously articulate the underlying tenets of that view. Our beliefs, which Johnson calls the "Moral Law Folk Theory," presume that universal moral principles apply, people need insight to comprehend and apply those principles, and people have a binary nature such that they need to exercise and impose their reasoned conclusions to rein in their baser, more impulsive emotive nature which can prevent the rational and consistent application of moral principles.[2] Such a portrayal of morality and moral reasoning fails in two ways. First, it does not account for the role of our non-foundational mental activity, i.e. it fails to account for moral imagination, and secondly, it inaccurately describes human nature.

The Moral Law Folk Theory

Moral Law Folk Theory represents the intuitions and implicit assumptions that undergird the standard philosophical approaches to ethics. To understand the power and prevalence of the Moral Law Folk Theory, we must elaborate on its assumptions, which Johnson (1993, p. 5) says are based on flawed philosophy, "bad metaphysics, bad epistemology and bad theories of language." The Moral Law Folk Theory assumes that we have a rational nature, which places us above other creatures, and that we also have an emotional, baser, more physical aspect. Passions and desires tend to derive from the physical and can be kept in check, restrained, and governed only by the exercise of reason; our lower nature is balanced and ruled by our higher nature.

The Moral Law Folk Theory assumes that reason structures and determines ethical behavior thusly:

1. There is one and only one conceptualization for any situation;
2. Literal concepts with unambiguous meanings are used to state moral laws and apply them to situations; and
3. Moral situations are defined/characterized by a set of necessary and sufficient conditions (Johnson, 1993).

If Moral Law Folk Theory were valid, then we should be surprised to ever experience or observe moral uncertainty, and we should never struggle with conflicting ethical obligations. Rules would define the appropriate behavior for each situation (and all situations would be well defined). When facing conditions Q1 through Q4 Person X must do Action Y because of Ethical Principle P.

Johnson states unequivocally that modern cognitive science negates all the implicit claims underlying Moral Law Folk Theory. We do not have such clearly defined, clearly demarcated, distinct situations, concepts, or rules; ethical situations are not defined by a set of necessary and sufficient conditions. Our use of ethical concepts is defined in terms related to larger frames and schemas, which are shaped by past experience and which we continue to re-shape via our current behaviors. We rely on radial categories with prototypes, salient highly typical members or instances, and many other members with more distant resemblances to the prototypes. Before elaborating on current findings from cognitive science, we look more closely at the two primary philosophical approaches to traditional ethics—deontology and teleology.

Immanuel Kant—Exemplar of Deontological Formalism

Kant, who epitomizes deontological ethics, stated his Categorical Imperative as a purely formal rule that is derived from pure reason alone and is free of empirical content. The difficulty with that type of rule is its lack of connection to lived experience or to the circumstances in which the rule must be applied. How, using what rule or guidance, does a person know whether the situation she is currently facing is one in which this purely formal rule applies? Realizing that people face great difficulty in applying the Categorical Imperative to concrete situations, Kant introduced a "figurative substitute." In other words, people are to apply a more practical law to the concrete situations they find themselves in and ask if, should their immediate planned actions be taken, they would behave consistently with the Categorical Imperative. However, the situations in which the rule applies are not delimited or described exhaustively. Some theorists note that even in morally neutral settings, "every attempt at a context-free definition of an action, that is a definition based on abstract rules or laws, will not necessarily accord with the pragmatic way an action is defined by the actors in a concrete social situation" (Flyvbjerg, 2001, p. 42). Ethically laden situations and rules are even more fraught.

To comply with Kant's explicit moral imperative, we must, in essence, map the purely formal, logical Categorical Imperative to a related, but physically concrete situation. Logic and reason do not suffice to guide action; we must use metaphorical reasoning to create and apply a rule in *concreto* that exemplifies the rule arrived at by pure reason. Because people face many situations in which the "necessary and sufficient" conditions of the Categorical Imperative do not unambiguously apply, people must rely on "an imaginative envisioning of situations that do not actually exist in our present world" (Johnson, 1993, p. 75), i.e. the use of both imagination and metaphor.

The question regarding *how* people go about applying general formally derived ethical principles or duties to specific, concrete cases is critical to the argument against foundationalist ethics. To illustrate, Johnson turned to the case of a rule prohibiting wheeled vehicles from being taken into a public park (Hart, 1958). We immediately interpret the rule to mean that automobiles, trucks, SUVs, and motorcycles are not allowed.[3] But do we immediately conclude that bicycles, tricycles, scooters and even roller skates are disallowed as well? And what do we think of baby strollers, little red wagons, wheel barrows, or wheeled luggage? They all fit the definition of 'vehicle' and they all have wheels; thus they must be wheeled vehicles and are therefore prohibited. Hart (1958, pp. 607–8) concludes that:

> If a penumbra of uncertainty must surround all legal rules, then their appli-
> cation to specific cases in the penumbral area cannot be a matter of logical
> deduction, and so deductive reasoning, which for generations has been cher-
> ished as the very perfection of human reasoning, cannot serve as a model for
> what judges, or indeed anyone, do.

Hart argues that in the process of applying laws, even those as simple and direct as the proscription of wheeled vehicles from public parks, we interpret and by our interpretation, which is normative, we determine and continue to re-shape the law. We do not simply deduce from a set of neces-sary and sufficient conditions whether a particular vehicle with wheels is prohibited under the law. Instead, we decide normatively whether we should include baby strollers, for instance, within the rule or not:

> Once we move far enough away from the simple paradigmatic cases to which
> the chosen generalizations were tailored, it becomes clear that no rule can
> be entirely self-interpreting. The considerations that weigh with us in resolv-
> ing the ambiguities that arise in marginal cases, like those that weigh with us
> in balancing the claims of conflicting principles, are never written into the
> rules themselves. (Jonsen & Toulmin, 1988, p. 8)

In comparison to ethical principles, laws are written far more con-sciously and explicitly and should presumably be more clear-cut and well defined. Ethical notions and rules are even less likely than laws to be clearly-defined sets or principles with necessary and sufficient conditions from which we deduce instances (Johnson, 1993). Instead, relying on research from cognitive linguistics, Johnson argues that ethical notions and rules rely on prototypes. We have a fuzzy-edged core of prototypical instances that clearly fall within the parameters of the rule, but there are many penumbral instances that require moral imagination to decide and resolve.

A claim that moral concepts are not governed by well-defined philo-sophical rules does not mean one must accept relativism. People from shared cultures have many stable, core concepts arising out of common experiential conditions. By their nature, prototypes have a core exemplar on which people agree. To use a non-ethically-laden example, in North America we tend to see robins as prototypical birds, while penguins and emus and other flightless species are less likely to be a core exemplar. Similarly, we would probably all agree cars, motorcycles, trucks and SUVs are wheeled vehicles for applying the law forbidding their presence in public parks. We would probably all agree that roller skates and baby strollers are not. But we might debate about skateboards. Whether that debate is normative, reflecting and shaping ethical issues about the appropriate use of public parks, or deductive, dependent for resolution solely on definitional criteria of "wheeled vehicle," is crucial to the argument Johnson is making against foundationalist philosophies.

Utilitarianism—Formalism of Imaginary Calculations

A second foundational approach to ethics is teleology, with an emphasis on desirable outcomes rather than on formally derived principles. Utilitarianism is the best-known teleological ethics and represents an extreme effort to make ethics scientific. The result is reductionism in its severest form; morality becomes a sort of hedonic calculus. An overemphasis on calculations as a way to describe and explain all of human behavior was perhaps best exemplified and derogated by Charles Dickens in his creation of Mr. Gradgrind, the anti-hero of *Hard Times*. The theory of utilitarianism, even in its ostensibly more acceptable forms such as rule-utilitarianism, requires extraordinary knowledge. It requires that people have:

> ...complete knowledge of their ends, which are regarded as completely determinate, fixed, and given in advance of their moral deliberations about the means to these ends. They have all the relevant knowledge, both of themselves (their instincts, motivations, wants) and of the mechanisms of causality in the external world. (Johnson, 1993, p. 123)

Furthermore, it is assumed that people can amass all of this extraordinarily complex and diverse knowledge into an algorithmic, calculative process ending in a solution that allows comparisons among alternatives. One might have thought that Kenneth Arrow's (1950) argument against the possibility of inter-personal utility comparisons would have been the death knoll for utilitarianism, but it is still presented as a possible approach to ethics in textbooks.

In summary, both deontological and teleological approaches assume Universal Reason. Traditionally, Universal Reason characterizes the unique category structure of an objective world that is independent of human beings (disembodied) and human perceptual and reasoning capabilities. Human beings are thought to be unique in our capacity to reason using some portion of Universal Reason, the structure of which is defined externally and independently of experience. Through this disembodied reasoning process, people can gain objective knowledge of the world. Objective knowledge and objective truth require a correspondence between concepts and objective features of the world. The conceptual systems of Universal Reason must be monolithic, i.e., univocal and internally consistent. According to this theory, people have the ability to maximize their self interest because Universal Reason facilitates the literal calculation of self interest. Our will is free of bodily constraints; our desires, feelings, and emotions can be overcome by acts of will. Reasoning must be conscious for one to be wholly free. Finally, a universal morality that is objective, rational, and knowable comprises a system of universal principles that arise from a universal notion of what is good, which yields an absolute right or wrong in any given situation.

Such foundationalist views grounded in Moral Law Folk Theory are rejected by cognitive scientists who argue we have an embodied moral reasoning structure which continues to construct, and be reshaped by, our subjective moral imagination. Next, we examine a cognitive-science-based rendering of morality.

MORAL IMAGINATION AS THE BASIS FOR MORAL REASONING

Traditionally, a person is morally rational when she applies a set of universal laws to a specific situation in order to discern what it would mean to act morally.[4] Johnson rejects this position and proposes that moral rationality occurs when an individual uses her moral imagination to define and shape and respond to a situation.

Background and Terminology

In this context "moral" pertains to the "ongoing imaginative exploration of possibilities for dealing with our problems, enhancing the quality of our communal relationships, and forming significant personal attachments that grow" (Johnson, 1993, p. 209). By "imagination" we mean:

> ...that capacity which allows us both to experience present situations as significant and to transform them in light of our quest for well-being...the means for going beyond ourselves as presently formed, moving transforma-

tively toward imagined ideals of what we might become, how we might relate to others, and how we might address problematic situations. (Johnson, 1993, p. 209)

By extension, moral imagination is the:

...capacity to see and to realize in some actual and contemplated experience possibilities for enhancing the quality of experience, both for ourselves and for the communities of which we are a part, both for the present and for future generations, both for our existing practices and institutions as well as for those we can imagine as potentially realizable. (Johnson, 1993, p. 209)

Moral imagination occurs through the use of metaphorical reasoning. Metaphorical reasoning is embodied reasoning. Embodied reasoning occurs within the enabling and constraining parameters of human physical make up, including our sensory and neurological capabilities and our past experiences. Metaphorical reasoning is different from traditional philosophical reasoning because it is embodied, whereas the traditional view separates rational analysis and ethical reasoning from our physical make up. By "embodied" we mean that our physical make up enables and constrains our reasoning capabilities. In other words, our embodied cognitive capabilities provide the context for our individual moral reasoning. Within, and as a result of, this context, reasoning occurs primarily through the application of metaphor, the use of a word or phrase that is not meant literally but rather to make a comparison. A metaphor assigns the attributes of one entity to the object of the comparison (Lakoff & Johnson, 1999).[5] To teach ethical reasoning, we must understand the dominant metaphors used in framing moral reasoning. The dominant metaphors channel our ethical reasoning and become manifest in our decisions and actions.

The new findings emerging from cognitive science and linguistic philosophy (Johnson, 1993; Lakoff & Johnson, 1999) could have a major impact on the way we understand how ethics are experienced, practiced and taught. Central in legitimating this perspective is the Socratic imperative to "know thy self." Lakoff and Johnson argue that until we can move beyond the limitations of traditional philosophy we will be significantly constrained in understanding ethics and in developing the teaching of ethics. They describe their ideas as grounded in the cognitive science of the "embodied mind."

Before we proceed, it will be useful to specify several other terms. Cognitive science is the empirical study of the mind based on the neural modeling of cognitive operations (Churchland, 1989) and offers a new understanding of how human beings conceptualize experience, reflect on it, and come to new understandings. The term "cognitive" can refer to any kind of mental operation and structure involved in language, meaning, perception, conceptual systems, and reason. We recognize that aspects of our sensorimotor system contribute to our ability to conceptualize and reason. Lakoff and Johnson (1999) assume a decidedly materialist ontology that obviates any possibility of a body–mind duality. The possibility of a Kantian-type universal reason that is known via a disembodied purely formal process does not exist.[6] Instead, the mind is "embodied" and is therefore situated in and circumscribed as to its capabilities and possibilities by the body's perceptual and sensorimotor systems. "The architecture of your brain's neural networks determines what concepts you have and hence the kind of reasoning you can do" (Lakoff & Johnson, 1999, p. 16). Neural networks, which are learned, are the source of rational thought. In order to understand rational thought, we must understand these neural configurations and the principles of their computation.

A person's reality is the culmination of the sensory body, peculiarities of the brain, and environmental interactions. Lakoff and Johnson (1999) argue that because human processing capability is limited, people must rely on categories to organize and process inputs/stimuli. People form categories automatically and unconsciously in day-to-day life. Concepts are defined as neural structures that allow us to characterize and reason about categories. Making inferences with respect to a category is facilitated by neural structures such as prototypes, metaphors or scripts. In the absence of specific contextual information, typical prototypes are used to make inferences about category members and to evaluate category members relative to some conceptual standard.

The structure and the types of categories are determined by the characteristics of our bodies, brains, and experiences. A hierarchy of categories exists, with base level categories being the ones that we primarily rely on to reason, understand and organize our knowledge.[7] Base level categories are an intermediate level in the categorical hierarchy and represent an easily accessed prototype. For example, within the categorical hierarchy of vehicle—car—sports car—Corvette, the base-level category of car, is cognitively basic. We have already (in a slightly different context) looked at the difficulty of clearly delimiting the category of vehicle. The base level category represents the highest level at which the category members have *similarly perceived overall* shapes that allow us to rely on a *single mental image* or prototype to represent the entire category. For example, we have a mental image of a car, and we can differentiate it from the image of a wagon or truck or airplane, but there is no single mental image of a vehicle for which we can conjure up a representation. Base-level categories provide the highest level of generality at which people use physiologically similar motor actions to interact with category members. For example, we have sensorimotor programs for interacting with a car but we do not have such programs for acting with the higher-level category of vehicle. We "know more" about the base-level categories because this is the way our knowledge is organized; base levels tend to be the default or neutral contexts at which people reason if they do not have access to a more explicit category identification.

If these premises are correct, then we see that our reason (in the form of our mental categories) is mediated by and through the body and is not and cannot be derived solely from an independent, universal reality. Given our physical characteristics, the base level is the level at which human beings optimally interact with their environments. The categories by which we differentiate and reason about our world are both enabled and constrained by our neural and bodily capacities, our sensorimotor experiences, and our evolved and developed ability for base level categorization.

Metaphorical Morality

Given the connection between our sensorimotor experience and our subjective understanding, we need to explore the mechanism by which sensorimotor experiences are translated into, applied toward, and circumscribe the boundaries of our ethical reasoning. Lakoff and Johnson (1999) claim that metaphor is the cognitive mechanism by which our mental imagery associated with sensory experience allows us to conceptualize subjective experience. Metaphors are constructed when sensorimotor experience is linked with certain subjective experiences.

For example, people associate intimacy, a subjective experience, with the metaphor "close" because of the sensorimotor experience of being physically close to people with whom one is intimate. For instance, we may say of a friend "She and I are very close" even though the friend lives at a great distance from us; but we probably do not realize we are speaking metaphorically. Primary metaphors arise naturally, automatically, and unconsciously from everyday experiences and provide the building blocks of complex metaphors. Primary metaphors provide an inferential structure to our literal subjective experience. Metaphors represent "cross-domain mappings, from a *source domain* (the sensorimotor domain) to a *target domain* (the domain of subjective experience), preserving inference" (Lakoff & Johnson, 1999, p. 58). The connections between sensorimotor experience and subjective experience are reinforced through neural activation over time. Lakoff and Johnson claim that there are no innate universal metaphors. However, because so many sensorimotor experiences are common across all or most people, there will be corresponding universal primary metaphors that are learned.[8] We combine primary metaphors with cultural models, folk theories, or widely accepted beliefs to create complex metaphors.

Morality is a complex metaphor and moral reasoning is, thus, both enabled and constrained. Moral reasoning is constrained because it is embodied; moral reasoning is enabled because it is imaginative and goes beyond direct sensorimotor experience. At this point, we need to describe what Lakoff and Johnson (1999) refer to as an "empirically responsible" moral philosophy.[9] Reason is embodied and the means by which reason is accomplished are metaphorical. An embodied, cognitive science recognizes that the human conceptual system is directly connected to and enabled by our physical perceptual, imaging, and sensorimotor systems. The concepts by which we frame our reality, therefore, are shaped by our embodied systems; the mind cannot be separate and distinct from the body. Base-level concepts are the primary level at which we engage the reality of our environments and, therefore, are the primary concepts used in the optimal framing of, and reasoning about, everyday life. Rational inferences are primarily instances of sensorimotor inference grounded in subjective experience and judgments. Truth and knowledge are the result of understanding emerging from ideas framed in terms of the primarily unconscious conceptual systems using experientially grounded reasoning structures. Abstract reasoning allows us to project beyond our base level experience, and occurs when we apply conceptual metaphors that facilitate our application of sensorimotor inference to, for example, prototypes, discussed later as models or standard examples exhibiting the essential features of a class or group.

Next, we consider the implications of "empirically responsible" moral philosophy. Morality is seen as enhancing human well being and includes such ideas as justice, fairness, compassion, virtue, tolerance, freedom, and rights. An extensive metaphorical mapping system enables us to conceive, reason about, and communicate moral ideas though a range of basic metaphors. Morality's source domain is our experiences lived by and through our physical bodies manifested as social interactions. Our key defining moral concepts appear to be limited to no more than two dozen. Table 9.1 provides examples of several of these source domains in terms of the bipolar examples of well being and ill being.

Looking at examples of ordinary language may help to demonstrate the power and pervasiveness of metaphors. Consider wealth and its relationship to well being. At a literal level most people consider having enough wealth to live comfortably better than being impoverished. But the equation of well being and wealth occurs metaphorically as well. A man can be considered rich in his friends and family. To increase well being is a gain and a decrease in well being is a loss or cost. A good reputation is highly valued; people count their blessings. We say of certain intangibles that they are priceless, even as we invoke the money-based concept of price. Later we will discuss morality as a form of double-entry accounting.

TABLE 9.1
**Bi-Polar Dimensions of the Source Domains for Metaphors
of Morality (characterizations of well being and ill being)**

Characterizations of well being/virtue	Characterizations of ill being/sin
Pure	Contaminated
Strong	Weak
Healthy	Sick
In control	Dominated
Freedom	Slavery
Wealth	Impoverished
Socially connected	Isolated
Protected	Vulnerable
Cared about	Ignored
In the light	In the dark
Upright	Unable to stand
Balanced	Off balanced
Nurtured	Neglected

A second example centers on health. Colloquially people say "when you have your health you have everything," and the underlying, explicit premise is that being healthy is better than being sick. We go on to metaphorically conceive of immorality as disease or a state of unhealthiness; immoral behavior is a contagion that can spread out of control. If someone commits an act we consider extremely evil, we may describe the perpetrator as "sick," or succumbing to unhealthy drives. Someone who is evil poisons the atmosphere. Our undesirable physical experiences of illness become metaphorically linked with our disapproval of behavior or personalities we consider unethical. Moral strength (a metaphor based on physical vigor) makes it possible to confront and overcome evil. Again, we see that our normatively laden language is thoroughly imbued with metaphors.

Moral Metaphor Systems and the Example of Accounting

Lakoff and Johnson (1999) claim that the *moral accounting* metaphor is one of the dominant means by which we understand moral interactions, obligations, and responsibilities. This metaphor system combines the metaphor of well being as wealth, a category indicated in Table 9.1, with other metaphors and accounting schemes to provide a complex and powerful context for moral reasoning. Some examples of phrases that reflect the metaphorical nexus are: "profiting from experience, having a rich life, investing in happiness, gaining from one's experience" and, on the loss side "wasting one's life' or 'losing one's integrity". Using metaphors, we map the attributes of wealth onto the state and process of being moral. Our moral well being is seen as a valuable commodity, something we can have more or less of, and that can be earned, deserved, or lost. The accumulation and connecting of such metaphorical structures constitute the representations we employ in reasoning.

Lakoff and Johnson (1999) claim that one key pattern called the object event-structure metaphor shapes most of our moral metaphor systems. In the object event-structure metaphor, the source domain is objects or the transfer of objects. Within the moral accounting metaphor system, we use objects (possessions), the acquisition or loss (motion in, motion out) of objects, and the direction of causality (giving, taking). Morality is conceptualized in terms of a financial transaction, and the effect is conceptualized as a change in a stock of well being. When two people interact, we metaphorically conceive of this event as an accounting transaction, with each transferring an effect to the other. An effect that enhances well being is a gain; one that degrades well being is a loss. In a moral accounting system, metaphorical accounts reflect the results of these transactions.

Moral bookkeeping, a metaphor of commodity transactions, allows us to track and compare the balances in the moral accounts. While not designating individual transactions as good or bad, the moral accounting metaphor system allows and enables us to have a structure with which we reason and discuss ethics, with an emphasis on obligations and justice. Lakoff and Johnson (1999, pp. 293–298) illustrate how the moral accounting system, in conjunction with other metaphors, can be used in framing and evaluating moral issues.

For instance, double-entry bookkeeping arithmetic is applied to the moral accounts; a credit entry in the accounts entails an equal debit entry. Justice is attained when the increases in well being equal the decreases in well being. The morality of the financial markets is applied in that there is an imperative to balance the accounts and pay one's debts. Reciprocity, in turn, is based on two moral accounting principles. First, a moral act is one that results in an increase in well being, and a negative act is one that decreases the well being of another. Increasing another's well being results in a moral credit due from them and decreasing another's well being creates a moral debt to them. Second, because there is a moral imperative to pay one's debts, not to do so is immoral.

Applying moral accounting arithmetic, when X does Y harm, Y is given something of negative value (a loss of wealth) and correspondingly had something of positive value (well being—wealth) taken away. In response Y's options are to either do something equally harmful to X or to do nothing. The two principles of moral accounting mentioned above offer Y a difficult choice. If Y carries out an act of equal negative value against X, then by the first principle, Y's act is an immoral one but by the second principle Y's action is moral. If Y takes no action, under the first principle Y has acted morally by avoiding harm, but Y has acted immorally under the second principal because the perpetrator X has not been held accountable. One principle must be given priority over the other. The morality of absolute goodness would privilege the first principle, and the morality of retribution would privilege the second principle.[10]

To use a current significant ethical issue, justifying the death penalty would be based on the morality of restoring society's moral accounts. Opposing the death penalty would be based on the principle that taking any life is immoral because doing so decreases that person's well being. The two metaphorical framings of the death penalty indicate that there is no absolute rule that determines one's beliefs regarding capital punishment. *Our attitudes vary with the metaphors we use to frame ethical issues.*

The moral accounting system provides criteria by which to identify an honorable person. An honorable person is one who pays his moral debts and does not allow moral debt to accumulate. Honor is conceptualized as social capital that is received for keeping one's moral books up to date and in balance. Dishonor is the accumulation of unpaid moral debt. Respect comes from the ability to be counted on to maintain a balanced set of moral books. Within the context of moral accounting, one can make restitution by paying back something of equal positive moral value to someone on whom you have inflicted some negative moral value (harm). There are many more applications and elaborations possible within the moral accounting system.

A THEORY OF EMBODIED MORAL REASONING

In this section, we summarize the central ideas of embodied moral reasoning and consider the implications of this proposed new conceptualization of morality and moral reasoning for moral understanding. Traditional theories of morality claim to provide Moral Law that enables us to do *the* right thing in a given situation. Yet, these theories do so only in rather uninteresting, indisputable situations. As such, these traditional theories are not very helpful when one is faced with real life situations that present conflicting obligations or do not fit the prototypical specifications (Johnson, 1993, pp. 188–189; Jonsen & Toulmin, 1988). Given the complexity and turbulence and rapidly changing nature of the business environment, students are unlikely to face situations that fit neatly into the parameters of traditional theory. However, the new, embodied conceptualization we describe does not provide universal moral laws either. So, upon what basis do we claim that an embodied theory of moral reasoning is superior to the more traditional theories? We believe that helping students to develop and exercise their moral imagination will help enable them to deal with the complexities they are likely to face.

The purpose of a theory of morality is to provide moral understanding. To do so, the theory should provide insights into the nature of moral problems, moral reasoning, and humans as moral agents, increasing our moral understanding and, thus, increasing the likelihood of acting more intelligently in a given situation. Lakoff and Johnson (1999) identify the basic elements of moral understanding as: prototypes, situational framing, metaphors, and narrative. Next, we review how our knowledge of these elements affects the way we understand moral reasoning. We believe that helping students develop and extend their moral imaginations will better enable them to face the complexities of the business world.

Prototypes

Described earlier, prototypes are models or standard examples exhibiting the essential features of a class or group. For many classes (particularly of ethically laden situations) there are members possessing the primary criteria associated with membership; such members serve as prototypes. There are other, noncentral members or situations that can be related to the class prototype through extension from the core. Johnson (1993) argues that if our basic moral concepts have prototypical structures, then moral judgment cannot consist of finding necessary and sufficient features of moral laws associated with a given situation because the moral law(s) do not map directly onto the majority of cases.[11] The rules do not provide the necessary guidance for their imaginative extension to nonprototypical cases, which tend to predominate. However, Johnson claims, the work in cognitive science concerning prototypes and their imaginative extension to nonprototypical cases can be applied in helping make intelligent moral decisions. In fact, he argues that prototypes provide the basis for moral principles because principles are typically abstractions derived from cultural prototypes and can be properly applied only relative to the prototype.

Prototypes provide the focal construct in moral experience and moral development.[12] Because of our social, physical, cultural, and cognitive limitations and nature, certain types of experiences may acquire special importance. Churchland (1989) suggests that these prototypical experiences are not the application of abstract concepts or laws but result instead from lived experiences.[13] For example, a concept of justice emerges out of the framing of prototypical situations where distributions of benefits were perceived as fair or unfair. The schemas we associate with situational prototypes contain not only rational elements but also affective dimensions that provide the motivation and energy for action. The meaning, focus, force, and development of a given prototype depends on the narrative context within which it is embedded, suggesting that a prototype applied within different narratives may motivate different actions.

Moral development occurs as we transform prototypes while applying them to unique life situations. To facilitate moral development, prototypes must be malleable and flexible, allowing us to imaginatively extend our moral categories as we mature and face increasingly complex situational contexts. Moral imagination is the process by which we extrapolate from prototypical concepts to nonprototypical life situations, all within the context of an embodied mind. Our primary imaginative mode is metaphor and through its application we create more complex and integrated prototypical representations.

Framing

Situations within which action is contemplated do not come with *the* proper, objective description implicitly presumed by traditional philosophical theories of morality. We understand very little about a social situation until we define its context. That is, using various imaginative structures we specify the background within which the present circumstance is suspended. By virtue of having to do so, we define the "reality" we simultaneously seek and shape our ethical decisions. Johnson (1993) refers to this process as framing. The most common (and possibly the only) frames are believed to be semantic and therefore facilitated by linguistic devices such as metaphor and certain prototypical representations. Johnson summarizes the implications of framing for understanding the nature of moral reasoning as follows:

> Knowing about the precise nature of the particular frames we inherit from our moral tradition and apply to situations is absolutely essential, if we are to be at all aware of the prejudgments we bring to situations. Knowing that there will always be multiple frames of any situation is also necessary, if we are to appreciate the nonabsolute character of our moral understanding. Not to know these things about ourselves is morally irresponsible. (Johnson, 1993, p. 192)

Metaphor

As we noted previously, many of our moral concepts are defined metaphorically. The frames we use in making sense of moral concepts and situations are constructed by metaphorical extrapolation of lived experiences.[14] Thus, we gain moral understanding as we apply metaphorical concepts to frame a situation, and use imagining to extrapolate from prototypes to evaluate new situations.[15] Metaphor is the primary device for extending the prototypical representations of moral principles to the novel and ambiguous cases. Learning is another area facilitated by metaphorical extrapolation. When we learn from experience, we extrapolate previous experiences into the current situation, which is possible because of the "imaginative flexibility" of the metaphorical device.

Narrative

We conceive of life as a sustained narrative. As we live this narrative, we develop our moral sensitivity, an ability to make subtle discriminations of character and moral salience, and empathy for others.[16] We must recognize the narratives inherited from the culture in which we live as well as those that we construct in our own lives. We must recognize a central role of narrative structuring of experience, and the particular narratives that make up different moral traditions. From these we undertake our own moral explorations in the narrative construction of our lives. Next, we consider the implications of this kind of moral imagination in teaching business ethics.

APPLYING MORAL IMAGINATION TO THE ETHICS CLASSROOM

The preceding material is dense, complicated, and contrary to traditional conceptualizations of moral reasoning. So, why are we arguing that the fundamental assumptions underlying traditional ethics are not relevant to resolving realistic moral dilemmas, and that a way we commonly teach ethics is at best irrelevant and at worst fundamentally flawed? What difference does accepting moral imagination as a key component in moral reasoning make in the way we live and teach ethics? A theory of morality should be a theory of moral understanding, not a theory of moral laws. Moral understanding is to a large extent the result of exercising moral imagination. To be morally astute requires that we understand the imaginative nature of human reason and its associated conceptual structures, including prototypes, framing, metaphors as well as the use of narratives. We need to investigate what these imaginative structures are, how they work, and the implications for the nature of moral understanding. We must give up the illusions of foundationalist values and of extreme moral subjectivism. We must also give up the idea that moral reasoning is the algorithmic application of a set of pre-articulated, universal rules to specific action situations. As faculty we must discern through detailed study what our metaphorical structures illuminate and what they obscure. From an enhanced understanding of ethically-related metaphorical structures, we gain insights into what might be changeable, how to facilitate the changes, and the implications of the changes for who we are and how we affect others.

Operationally, we must help students develop their moral imagination by honing their powers of discrimination, encouraging them to envision new possibilities, and to creatively consider the implications of the imaginative structures. Our primary task is refining our perceptions of character and situations, not learning how to apply moral laws. One step towards developing one's moral imagination means developing empathic imagination in order to enhance moral sensitivity. We should allow and encourage students to put themselves in the other's place (Werhane, 1999), to question their values and ideals from various perspectives, imaginatively encounter others' experiences, and imaginatively create alternative approaches to moral issues. In an increasingly globalized world where students can expect to more frequently interact with people of other cultures and countries, moral sensitivity becomes more important. The precepts of philosophical idealism can be easily interpreted by others as self-referenced, culture-centric, or even imperialistic.

Werhane emphasizes the constraining force of social roles and sees moral imagination as the means to eliminate those constraints. Werhane discusses the Challenger disaster and the narrow set of responsibilities that NASA scientists and managers saw their roles as entailing. Werhane (1999) and Hoivik (2004) recommend that moral imagination requires students to:

1. Begin with the particular (a position endorsed by Jonsen and Toulmin, (1988);
2. Disengage from their own biases;
3. Ground themselves in the "theoretically viable and actualizable" (Werhane, 1999, p. 101);
4. Ensure their ideas have a "normative or prescriptive character" (Werhane, 1999, p. 101).

While Johnson and Lakoff would probably have no quarrel with these recommendations, their own analysis implies a more thorough-going re-examination of classroom practices. Unfortunately, however, this is the area in which they provide the least guidance. Johnson says that we should not make ethics simply one more module in the business school curriculum. Instead "ethics pervades *every aspect of business*" (Johnson, 1993, p. 253). We should not treat ethics as technical problems because "Moral problems are often the ends themselves, about what we ought to choose and pursue" (Johnson, 1993, p. 253). Johnson and Lakoff see moral imagination as more than placing one's self outside of one's role as an employee or manager or scientist. Their conception is far deeper and more complex than that. For them moral imagination is the frame from which and by which we are able to reason ethically. We must explore and articulate our use of moral metaphor; we must also acknowledge the power and ubiquity of moral metaphors. The "invisible hand" of Adam Smith (2000/1776) is mentioned only once in a lengthy tome, yet that phrase is repeated endlessly and serves as a root metaphor for major social initiatives. Students must be guided through a process of introspection that examines their own level of adherence to metaphors and how metaphors shape and structure and enable their moral understandings. For instance, *The Invisible Heart* (Folbre, 2001) could serve as a text that would provide an alternative, complementary metaphor to the invisible hand, helping students and faculty to examine their existing metaphor structures and explore the implications of revising or expanding their moral metaphor structures. The invisible hand metaphor has unfortunately been used to invoke a crude sort of social Darwinism; people routinely rely on images of the strongest surviving and rising to the top, i.e., becoming more wealthy. Again, the underlying image is that the healthiest, strongest, most fit are the ones who do and should succeed in business. Folbre's book points out that the structure of business rests upon an invisible social structure of care, concern, and community, typically provided gratis or for low wages. While the activities of care-giving, child-rearing, nursing infirm relatives, and many other caring services are essential to society, they are not seen as central to the business arena (where only the fit survive). Folbre cleverly relies on a health metaphor herself. Hearts are a critical organ, essential to life, while a person could survive without a hand.

By considering the metaphorical structures of our moral understanding, we can gain insights into what metaphors we use in defining basic moral concepts and how these metaphors are organized and structured. By gaining a more complete understanding of our metaphorical structures we enhance our self understanding as to our values, what they presuppose, and the implications for our actions. "The structures of imagination are part of what is shared when we understand one another and are able to communicate within a community, (Johnson, 1987, p. 172). By comparing alternative metaphorical structures, we can also investigate the possibilities of common moral values evidenced across cultures arising out of our universal (or widely shared) sensorimotor and social experiences. Conversely, comparisons across metaphorical representations can indicate where and why individuals and groups of people vary in their moral values and their application. Without resorting to ethical relativism, one can still explore the alternative approaches and interpretations people of various cultures place on shared, universal experiences (Johnson, 1993; Hauser 2006). If moral understanding is metaphorically constructed and structured, then by specifying these structures, we can consider likely outcomes as well as the most promising avenues for bringing about change that would result in different moral understandings.

NOTES

1. Generally, these theories of moral reasoning are predicated on the presumption there are fundamental principles, whose justification does not derive from other beliefs and upon which other beliefs are derived and justified.
2. This reflects the mind-body dualism assumed in the traditional philosophical perspectives.
3. Note that we comfortably make this inference about SUVs even though they did not exist in 1958 and could not have been included in the set referred to when the rule was written.
4. This section draws heavily from Johnson (1993, chapter 8).
5. Note that literal description/representation is not metaphorical.
6. Lakoff and Johnson (1999) claim that any psychology or philosophy that presumes the faculty of reason exists independently of our body is false.
7. The discussion of basic level categories that follows is drawn from Lakoff and Johnson (1999, pp. 26–30).
8. Lakoff and Johnson (1999, p. 57) speculate that there may be at least several hundred such universal primary metaphors.
9. The discussion follows closely from Lakoff and Johnson (1999, pp. 553–557).
10. Lakoff and Johnson (1999) differentiate retribution from revenge based on the actor's legitimate authority. Revenge occurs when the books are balanced by someone who does not have legitimate authority.
11. Moral laws appear to be valid for the prototypical cases precisely because they are formulated to fit the central members of the category. However, Johnson suggests that most of the moral situations we face are not prototypical cases, and therefore the moral laws do not work very well.
12. See Johnson (1993, pp. 190–192).
13. Examples include fairness of distribution, property ownership, unprovoked cruelty, and breach of promise (Churchland, 1989).
14. Examples include cause, action, well-being, purpose, state, duty, right and freedom.
15. Johnson (1993) argues that because of the metaphorical grounding of moral concepts, we will seldom during moral deliberations be able to apply literal, univocal concepts to action states. Thus, this key tenet of Moral Law theories cannot be justified.
16. We may also develop moral insensitivity if our imagining structures are inflexible and narrow.

REFERENCES

Arrow, K. (1950). A difficulty in the concept of social welfare. *Journal of Political Economy, 58*, 328–346.

Bartlett, D. (2003). Management and business ethics: A critique and integration of ethical decision-making models. *British Journal of Management, 14*, 223–235.

Churchland, P. (1989). *A neurocomputational perspective: The nature of mind and the structure of science.* Boston, MA: MIT Press.

Derry, R., & Green, R. M. (1989). Ethical theory in business ethics: A critical assessment. *Journal of Business Ethics, 8*, 521–533.

Flyvbjerg, B. (2001). *Making social science matter.* Cambridge, UK: Cambridge University Press.

Folbre, N. (2001). *The invisible heart: Economics and family values.* New York, NY: The New Press.

Hart, H. L. A. (1958). Positivism and the separation of law and morals. *Harvard Law Review, 71*, 593–629.

Hauser, M. (2006). Moral minds: How nature designed our universal sense of right and wrong. New York, NY: Ecco.

Hoivik, H. v. W. (2004). The concept of moral imagination – an inspiration for writing and using case histories in business ethics? *Journal of Business Ethics Education, 1*, 31–44.

Johnson, M. (1987). *The body in the mind.* Chicago, IL: University of Chicago Press.

Johnson, M. (1993). *Moral imagination: Implications of cognitive science for ethics.* Chicago, IL: University of Chicago Press.

Jonsen, A. R., & Toulmin, S. (1988). *The abuse of casuistry: A history of moral reasoning.* Berkeley, CA: University of California Press.

Lakoff, G. (1996). *Moral politics.* Chicago, IL: University of Chicago Press.

Lakoff, G., & Johnson, M. (1999). *Philosophy in the flesh.* New York, NY: Basic Books.

Langenderfer, H. Q., & Rockness, J. W. (1989). Integrating ethics into the accounting curriculum: Issues, problems, and solutions. *Issues in Accounting Education, 4*, 58–69.

Macdonald, J. E., & Beck-Dudley, C. L. (1994). Are deontology and teleology mutually exclusive? *Journal of Business Ethics, 13*, 615–623.

Rorty, R. (2006). Is philosophy relevant to applied ethics? *Business Ethics Quarterly, 16*, 369–380.

Smith, A. (2000). *The wealth of nations.* E. Cannan (Ed.) New York, NY: The Modern Library. (Original work published 1776).

Werhane, P. H. (1999). *Moral imagination and management decision-making.* New York, NY: Oxford University Press.

Whitbeck, C. (1998). *Ethics in engineering practice and research.* Cambridge, UK: Cambridge University Press.

CHAPTER 10

TOWARD AN ETHICAL SENSE OF SELF FOR BUSINESS EDUCATION

Diane L. Swanson
Kansas State University

Peter Dahler-Larsen
University of Southern Denmark

ABSTRACT

In this chapter we describe how economic utility has endured long past its usefulness as an image of self that gets projected onto managers and business organizations. We compare this self-as-utility to other images as a backdrop for advocating that a new sense of self be envisioned for ethical business education.

INTRODUCTION

The idea that business exists to serve society is central to business ethics. Advocates of business responsibility do not deny that corporations have an economic role in society; they simply hold that this role should be tem-

Advancing Business Ethics Education, pages 191–220

pered by a concern for other social needs. Yet such calls for corporate citizenship have not coalesced into a coherent perspective for business education. Instead, ideological debates mar the discussions, particularly in North America where arguments have intensified along with a growing awareness of corporate power (Carroll, 1998).

The dispute typically pits those who want business to assume a mantle of citizenship against those who intimate that for business to go beyond a narrow pursuit of self interest amounts to corporate socialism (Friedman, 1962; 1970).[1] The latter group may be winning the day, given that most U. S. business schools have not reformulated their curriculum to put ethics at the core, even in the aftermath of recent corporate scandals (Adler, 2002; Swanson, 2004; Vidaver-Cohen, 2004). In our opinion, this resistance is fueled by a sense of self associated with economic utility theory. Our main thesis is that this formulation has been reified into an image that lags advances in theory and practice and undermines the notion that corporations and their agents have ethical responsibilities to society. The problem is particularly acute in business schools where economic-related coursework tends to promote decision making that is individualistic, opportunistic, and indifferent to the needs of others (Cohen & Holder-Webb, 2006; Ghoshal, 2003; Ravenscroft & Williams, 2004). That only one third of accredited U. S. business schools offer a separate course in business ethics (Willen, 2004), and presumably fewer require one, is not helping matters.

We approach this dilemma with a four-part research strategy aimed at discovering a sense of self for business education that is broadly compatible with other-regarding ethics. We do so by first describing utility's metamorphosis into a representation of self that accompanied the rise of commercialism in Europe. Second, we analyze some implications of this self-as-utility for business in society. Third, we compare utility with other theoretic representations of self, classified as moral collectivism, bureaucratic management, social engineering, holism, reflexivity, and dialogic. Fourth, we exhibit these perspectives longitudinally as a backdrop for discussing some implications for business education, stressing that it will be difficult if not impossible to deliver ethics coherently in the business curriculum absent a conscious and conspicuous reformulation of self.

First, we must provide a caveat. This chapter focuses on a particular problem of self as an image that implies a context, state of being, and mode of action simultaneously (see Albert, Ashforth, & Dutton, 2000 for the self as a proxy for these dimensions). Because the object of inquiry is image cast by theory, we do not deal with managers or corporations as agents of social action per se. For example, we do not delve into organizational behavior or address individuals psychologically in terms of conduct, traits, motives, skills, values, neuroses, complexes, and so on. Also, as a matter of scope, we make no attempt to deal with the vast literature that places traditional concepts of self under suspicion, such as the writings of Freud, Marx, Nietzsche, and their exponents. Even so, our view is influenced by a dominant theme of 20th century philosophy, which is that the self is difficult to construe absent traditional religious explanations (Mannheim, 1936; Roderick, 1986). Likewise, we trace the image of self invoked in the secular realm of business to the rise of commercialism in Europe when the economic actor was (theoretically) separated from the sacred realm of community and defined narrowly in terms of utility. Finally, we argue that a new sense of self needs to be conveyed in business education, especially since ethics requires a deliberate consideration of the needs of others, which self-as-utility cannot accommodate well.

THE IMAGE OF SELF-AS-UTILITY

Self… must be treated as a construction that, so to speak, proceeds from the outside in as well as from the inside out, from culture to mind as well as from mind to culture

—Bruner, 1990, p. 108

Narrow Self Interest

The idea of narrow economic self-interest emerged around the time of the Commercial Revolution in Europe when a formerly powerless merchant class challenged the divine rights of kings to regulate feudal economies (Ferguson, 1950). Although the rise of the merchant class was by no means sudden or uniform, its overall push was for a more egalitarian order to replace the prerogative of kings to carry out God's immanent plan. Yet because certain philosophers feared that the new order would bring about chaos and conflict by upsetting the stability of social structure dictated by feudalism, they eventually seized upon the "invisible hand" of markets as a mechanism for claiming that the public interest could be aligned with that of an emerging business class (Hirschman, 1981; Sahlins, 1976). Progress was acclaimed as business was ideologically released from the traditional ideals and restraints of moral community, while the individual economic actor was granted unprecedented autonomy and freedom of choice (Etzioni, 1988). Despite this change, continuity with medieval thought was preserved in that the architects of the new order simply substituted an invisible hand in markets for unseen intervention from god (see Beck, 1932). In short, a sacred force was reformulated as secular (Nelson, 2001).

Eventually, the individual was factored into the new order as a choice maker driven by egoistic self-interest, mathematically modeled as utility or the habitual pursuit of pleasure and avoidance of pain (Ferguson, 1950).

Classical economists adopted this idea and extrapolated it into the law of supply and demand, predicting that markets fueled by such narrow self-interest would tend to yield socially optimal outcomes (Lekachman, 1976). The logic was that autonomous individuals motivated by pleasure-seeking would make market-based exchanges of reciprocal advantage that would culminate in the greatest quantity of human satisfaction in terms of economic efficiency. In this way, narrow self-interest and the greatest good became inextricably linked, the former modeled as choice understood to be interdependent, measurable, and cumulative across individuals (Hausman & McPherson, 1996).

This ideology became so entrenched that when neoclassical economists later supplanted cardinal utility with ordinal rankings they retained the basic tenets of hedonistic self-interest. By then the model had become an *ideal type* theory of economics (Gilpin, 1987), construed as mechanical or automated in the sense that its logic, drawn from a mathematical formulation of utility, was generalized to the fixed, inexorable ends of economic efficiency. As the paradigm matured, efficient outcomes were separated from the moral issues of equitable distribution of income and wealth (Hausman & McPherson, 1996; Redman, 1994). The tradition continues to this day as a separation of factual analysis from moral prescription, which legitimizes business as an amoral force in society (West, 1993). This imprimatur of amorality foreshadowed utility's metamorphoses from theory to image.

From Theory to Image

Again, this chapter does not deal with social action. Rather, we are interested in how theories implicate certain images of self, just as abstract systems of thought reflect and influence how humans construe reality (Berger & Luckmann, 1966; Luckmann, 1983; Ferraro, Pfeffer, & Sutton, 2005). These implications are particularly forceful when fundamental questions of "Who am I?" and "How do I relate to my surroundings?" are at stake. By suggesting answers to these questions, the self becomes a proxy for a state of being, perspective on action, and context for identity all at once (Albert et al., 2000). Theoretical perspectives that function in this way transmit an influence that transcends pure logic (Berger & Luckmann, 1966), sometimes becoming self-fulfilling (Ferraro et al., 2005). As powerful symbols of cultural knowledge, they can morph into metaphors that span levels of analysis. When projected onto whole organizations and organizational fields they form images of collective personhood with far reaching consequences (Albert et al., 2000; Czarniawska, 1997; Gioia, 1998; Illich, 1972; McSwite, 2001; Meyer, Boli, & Thomas, 1994; Morgan, 1997).

Similarly, economic utility functions as a distinct psychology of consciousness that catapults egoistic self-interest into an ideology that rationalizes institutional economic growth at the expense of widespread ecological problems, declining morality, and a deteriorating sense of society (Bauman, 1993; Castoriadis, 1982; Loevinger, 1987). In the process, self-interest becomes a working metaphor for abdicating responsibility to community (Aram, 1993; Scott & Hart, 1979; Swanson, 1999). Yet this rationalization may be winding down as a grand narrative of modernity (Lyotard, 1979). While elaborating on the fall of grand narratives is beyond the scope of this chapter, we propose that utility has endured far past its usefulness as an image of self, especially since the economic paradigm drawn from it is mostly silent on the undesirable effects of corporate power (Etzioni, 1988; Frederick, 1987; Ravenscroft & Williams, 2004; Swanson, 1996). We contend that this silence helps perpetuate a sense of amoral management and egocentric corporate control, discussed next.

Amoral management. The inability to come to grips with corporate power is consistent with the belief that managers need not deliberate over their obligations to community. Instead, the contemporary version of neoclassical economics holds that social control as the law, public policy, and ethical custom will rectify any adverse impacts of managerial decisions over time (Friedman, 1962; 1970). So goes the mechanical paradigm's division of private and public realms internalized as modern consciousness (Berger, Berger, & Kellner, 1973). But it is a problematic view that fails to acknowledge institutional arrangements whereby corporations influence their own social control by lobbying Congress and carrying out other forms of political advocacy (Frederick, 1987; Jacobs, 1999). Clearly, corporations wield immense social power. An economic theory that elevates narrow self-interest while ignoring this power implies that managers have impunity from the consequences of their actions, even if they carry out dehumanizing practices (Arendt, 1964; Ashforth, 1994) or pursue personal greed to the detriment of their firm's best interests (Englander & Kaufman, 2004). In other words, self-as-utility implicitly rationalizes amoral management. It also contaminates the stakeholder model with the logic of egocentric corporate control.

Egocentric corporate control. The stakeholder model depicts the corporation in the center of a network of constituents, including customers, suppliers, government regulators, the media, and social activists (Freeman, 1984). This illustration can easily be employed to suggest that managers should attend to those stakeholders ranked highest in terms of their ability to cooperate with or threaten the organization (see Savage, Nix, Whitehead, & Blair, 1991). This strategic use of the stakeholder model bears a strong albeit unintended affiliation with self-as-utility. The kinship is fivefold. One, portraying the firm as a focal point in a managerial span of control recalls the egocentrism of utility. Two, pursuing opportunities and avoiding threats parallels utility construed as seeking pleasure and foregoing pain. Three, prioritizing stakeholder interests is methodologically consistent with the ranking of utility in conventional economic theory. Since these rankings are intended to be interdependent and cumulative, the connotation is that stakeholder interests can escalate into collective action that obstructs corporate goals. In short, the threat of social control is implied.

This goes to the fourth commonality between self-as-utility and the strategic use of the stakeholder model: both can be interpreted to suggest that social control or pressure from society is a restraint or inconvenience rather than an opportunity to align managerial and corporate interests with community needs. The corollary is that managers should minimize the threat of social control by co-opting or accommodating the most important stakeholders. By extension, those stakeholders lacking influence, including future generations and the natural environment, can be overlooked, warded off, marginalized, or exploited. Ironically, this stance detracts from formulating policies that might preclude the need for social control in the first place (Swanson, 1999).

Finally, the fifth affinity between self-as-utility and the strategic use of the stakeholder model is that the latter easily functions as a vehicle for the amoral management implied by the former. Paradoxically, firm-centric managers can be cast as socially responsible if they co-opt or accommodate the most influential stakeholders while ignoring, warding off, or marginalizing others. The contamination of utility is so complete that when corporations take the interests of marginal stakeholders into account, their actions can easily be viewed as discretionary or paternalistic. It is as if feudal lords descend from their manors to help the poor serfs. This condescension belies contemporary ideals of corporate citizenship and reminds us that the Commercial Revolution did not completely discard habits of medieval thought, just as organizational theory that grants managers unexamined hierarchical privilege and power has not discarded the feudal mentality of kings (Schein, 1989).

Twilight of Self-As-Utility?

Metaphorically, the self-as-utility sees another human superficially as a reflection of its own narrow interests (Etzioni, 1988). Similarly the stakeholder model functions as a conduit for this perspective when it is used to convey organizations as vehicles for amoral management and egocentric corporate control. Admittedly, this image is not unambiguous, since the stakeholder model can also be used to represent the medieval gestalt that economic activity is interwoven into a web of community life. Even so, the strategic use of the stakeholder model resonates with social science that devalues social bonds, elevates some humans at the expense of others, and endorses their manipulation for gain (see Carr & Zanetti, 1999; Derrida. 1976; Laing, 1959). In this respect, managers are equivalent to game strategists when they view stakeholders as mere threats or opportunities (see Smirich & Stubbart, 1985).

Ironically, utility may contain the seeds of its own demise. Myopic managers and egocentrically controlling corporations cannot adapt well to fast-changing, uncertain, and complex environments. As such, they risk poor economic performance (Cohen & Prusak, 2001; Scott & Hart, 1979; Swanson, 1999). Moreover, reducing stakeholders to objects of manipulative control is out of sync with the spirit of freedom that helped rationalize utility in the first place. Another apparent contradiction is that corporate advertisements meant to communicate a spirit of harmony between business and society are at odds with the commingling of amoral management and egocentric control traceable to utility (Cheney, 1991; Schultz, Hatch, & Larsen, 2000). That utility is undermined by its own logic is not particularly surprising, since internal contractions are characteristic of absolutist ideologies that culminate into oppressively unproductive views of society (Popper, 1945). Given this situation, it is important to discover a sense of self for business education that foregoes amoral management and egocentric corporate control in favor of a more other-regarding ethical posture toward society. We begin this search next.

SEARCHING FOR A SELF FOR BUSINESS IN SOCIETY

The modern, self-sufficient scientific cosmology has not even succeeded in providing plausible answers to the human quest for a subjectively meaningful location of the self in the universe

—Luckmann, 1983, p. 4

The Method

We have cast utility in the twilight of its usefulness not as an exercise in nihilism but rather to set the stage for discovering a self befitting ethical business education. Since self simultaneously conveys a state of being, perspective on action, and context for identity, it lends itself to versatile methods of analysis (Albert et al., 2000). We leverage this potentiality by classifying the self according to three complementary methods. The first is a variation of Sennett's (1978) technique of postholing, which amounts to a sampling of phenomena as moments in time. Accordingly, we draw images of self from select theoretical perspectives relevant to business in society, classifying them in terms of an interpretive principle, climate of thought, historical ascendancy, and defining problem for self, starting with utility in Table 10.1. Second, in Table 10.2 we analyze these classifications in a typology according to other dimensions of logic. Taken together, the taxonomy and typology (Tables 10.1 and 10.2) convey distinctive elements and suppositions that can be analyzed more concretely. This construction is an important step in our search, since most theoretical perspectives or schools of thought convey unexamined images and metaphors (Scott, 1992), including those related to self (Mead, 1934). Finally, our third classification, Figure 10.1, is a longitudinal exhibition of insights gleaned from our sample, from which we induce implications for business education.

This three-part method is potentially powerful. Since images span levels of analysis, our examination can yield insights into how representations of managers, business organizations, and society pertain to one another. Moreover, our method is sound in that typologies are commonly used to demarcate new theoretical territory, which is what we are trying to achieve. That said, we acknowledge that classification systems essentially convey habits of thought, not universal or eternal truths (Richardson, 1990). Guided by this understanding, our typology (Table 10.2) delineates logic that we trace to climates of thought vis-à-vis the taxonomy (Table 10.1) as a backdrop for understanding some lessons implied (Figure 10.1). Our hope is that this method sheds some light on a sense of self appropriate for business education in the 21st century.

Classifying Self Types

To reiterate, Table 10.1 classifies images of self according to a) an interpretive principle, b) climate of thought, c) historical ascendancy, and d) defining problem for self. The resulting nomenclatures are utility, moral collectivism, bureaucratic management, social engineering, holism, reflexivity, and dialogic.

It is important to note that this sample does not rule out the existence of other self types, just as taxonomy of flora does not preclude the discovery of new varieties (Bailey, 1994). Furthermore, as reflections of theory these images are neither mutually exclusive nor strictly linear. Some overlap or exist synchronically in our classifications. For instance, as we note later, amoral control is compatible with representations of both utility and bureaucratic management. Additionally, as the discussion of Table 10.2 will demonstrate, some selves convey logic aimed at the certainty of predetermined or pre-fixed goals while others exhibit more receptivity toward

TABLE 10.1
Taxonomy of Images of Self Relevant to Business in Society

| | | Images drawn from theories | | | | | |
| | | System views | | | | Emerging views | |
Descriptors		Utility	Moral collectivism	Bureaucratic management	Social Engineering	Holism	Reflexivity	Dialogic
Interpretive principle		Freedom to satisfy individual interests	The need for duty to others in community	Efficacy of professionally managed organizations	Efficacy of widespread controls	Systems are unknowable	Doubt in self and systems	Knowledge is relative to a variety of viewpoints
Climate of Thought		Mechanical economics	Moral community	Scientific management	Forecast economics	Complexity theory	Post-modern skepticism	Post-modern discovery
Historical Ascendancy		1800s	Early twentieth century	1930s–1950s	1960s–1970s	1970s–1980s	End of century	End of century
Defining problem for self		Individual no longer embedded in moral community	Dichotomy between the individual and moral community	Loss of individual freedom to bureaucratic control	Loss of individual freedom to system control	Loss of autonomy and faith in social engineering	Loss of ego-defined self-mastery	Loss of absolute certainty

TABLE 10.2
Typology of Key Dimensions Related to Images of Self

		Accent on		
		Self or focal firm	Others in community	General systems
Accent on certainty	High	(1) **Utility and Bureaucratic management** (Amoral control of stakeholders)	(2) **Moral collectivism** (Duty according to pre-established rules)	(3) **Social engineering** (Widespread controls)
	Low	(4) **Reflexivity** (Doubt rather than control)	(5) **Dialogic** (Relationship instead of rules)	(6) **Holism** (Recognition of patterns instead of the assumption of perfect knowledge)

uncertainty. Overlaps notwithstanding, the groupings are distinct enough for comparative analysis, consistent with our goal of distinguishing historical influences in order to break new ground in our search.

Utility. Although economic self interest is commonly associated with the writings of Adam Smith, this association is overly drawn. After all, Smith penned *The Theory of Moral Sentiments* in 1753 (1976/1753) before he wrote his more famous treatise *The Wealth of Nations in* 1776 (1937/1776). Nevertheless, Smith's broader view of morality in the former has been given short shrift while his treatise on laissez-faire markets in the latter is often invoked as a glorification of narrow self-interest (Collins, 1990; Zafirovski, 1998). Discussed previously, the stakeholder model transmits this misinterpretation when it is used to promote the egocentric interests of a singular focal firm instead of the broader needs of community. We have traced this problem to the formulation of utility as self-focused autonomous pleasure seeking, which functions as a poor theoretical foundation for understanding business's role in society (Etzioni, 1988). Moreover, utility theory has taken on mechanical overtones because this pursuit of self interest is presumed to yield desirable social outcomes automatically, as conveyed by the popular metaphor of the invisible hand. Shown in Table 10.1, a defining problem for the self is that the individual is no longer seen as embedded in a moral community that shapes its own collective meaning.

Moral collectivism. Emile Durkheim (1961, trans.) attempted to refashion duty into a response to utility by holding that individuals must exert discipline over their egocentric impulses and drives (Giddens, 1972). Oth-

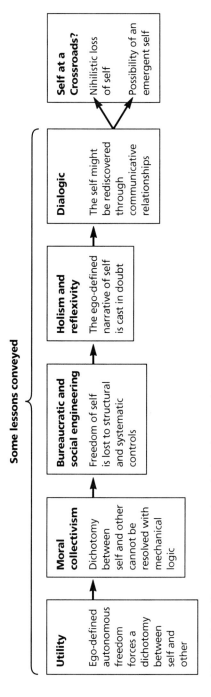

Figure 10.1. Longitudinal display of select images of self.

erwise, a cult of self-interest would justify transient, superficial relationships and unsavory conduct, rendering economics a public danger (Nisbet, 1966). Although this version of moral collectivism gained some prominence in the early 20th century, it did not usurp utility. Instead, the former was marred by a different use of mechanical logic. That is, Durkheim used rationality to place individuals beyond the bounds of community to determine a priori the rules that would apply equally to all (Giddens, 1972). Utility was turned on its head, so to speak, as the atomized individual was portrayed as an unnecessary abstraction and society was assumed to be the root and object of all morality. This subjugation rendered the reconciliation of the individual with society an intractable problem of logic that has dogged theories of moral community ever since (Etzioni, 1988; Selznick, 1992). In the final analysis, both utility and moral collectivism embody logic that tends to force a dichotomy between the interests of the individual and community.

Bureaucratic management. In tandem with the development of a theoretical tension between the individual and moral community, the logic of formal organization gained adherents. Proponents included Frederick Taylor (1947) who formulated rules of efficient production based on scientific management and Henri Fayol (1949) who devised principles for effective administration. Independent of these efforts, Max Weber (1946) developed a theory of bureaucracy that depicted formal organizations as iron cages or rational systems that catapulted knowledge toward pre-specified goals (Scott, 1992). Workers in this system were to be controlled by impersonal rules that subordinated their freedom to policies dictated by their superiors along chain of command structures. Weber's prediction that the mechanical aspects of formal organizations would have long lasting impacts on human consciousness came true when a coolly detached view of amoral control was internalized as professional management (Berger et al., 1973). Although proponents of Durkheim tried to apply moral collectivism to organizations, their view was never reconciled with formal bureaucratic logic, as the two schools of thought and the images drawn from them diverge too sharply (Scott, 1992). A defining problem for the self is a loss of freedom to bureaucratic control, as illustrated in Table 10.1.

Social engineering. The social engineering of the 1960s involved faith that professional experts could solve large-scale problems, a belief reinforced by the development of highly abstract mathematical models by which economists claimed to be able to forecast and engineer whole economies (Lekachman, 1976; Wilber & Harrison, 1978). In the process, John Maynard Keynes' (1936) assertion that optimal social outcomes are not preordained but require intervening fiscal and monetary policies was revitalized (Lekachman, 1976). As proof of this view, economists pointed to the unreliable business and consumer spending that marked the Depression of the 1930s, during which time Keynes had proposed that increased government expenditures could be magnified in overall spending to ameliorate low levels of national output and high unemployment. Decades later, the premise that whole economies could be engineered or finely tuned came to depend on valid forecasting techniques. Although laudable (and somewhat successful), the ascent of social engineering vis-à-vis forecast economics presaged a self that must yield to the impersonal machinations of experts. Keynes himself invoked this image when he observed that any person picked at random on the street could rightly claim to be a victim of some economist's misguided notions (Galbraith, 1959). The specter of all-pervasive control from faceless experts cast such a pall on freedom and autonomy that by the mid-1960s mechanical economics was a vision strangely out of sync with the fundamental tenets of Western society (Lekachman, 1976). In terms of imagery, social engineering represented yet another loss of individual freedom, this time to widespread system controls.

Holism. The instability associated with inflation and fluctuating interest rates and balances of trade in the 1970s could be seen as evidence that professional economists could not forecast environmental factors, much less control them (Lekachman, 1976; Redman, 1994). Whereas the architects of a philosophy for commercialism once feared that market economies would degenerate into social mayhem, the specter centuries later was that of economies spinning out of the control of professional experts. As social engineering became less defensible, a new gestalt emerged to challenge longstanding patterns of mechanistic thought. Gregory Bateson (1972; 1979) cast this view universally by conceptualizing the Mind as the nexus of all biological, ecological, and cultural interactions, asserting that mundane human intelligence could not possibly grasp the Mind's underlying regulating properties, much less control them. Put differently, just as a monitor cannot overview its own controls, the whole of the Mind cannot be reported in any subset of it. Not that holism denies the possibility of discrimination, as when higher order species' immune systems differentiate between self and non-self for survival. However, this ability is necessarily limited because the selective interaction of living systems with their environments obscures much of reality. A case in point is that blind fish in deep oceans are unable to have an overview of the totality of their environment. Even so, as a subset of Mind they can discern patterns that affect their existence, such as decreases in water temperature. Similarly, the best humans can strive for is the recognition of patterns in their environments (Bateson, 1979; Swanson, 2000).

Holism situates the self in unknowable interactive systems in which mechanical attempts at control can trigger substantial margins of error. The rub is that Western culture is prone to such errors, given its fetish for autonomy, instrumental calculus, and rational mastery. The worst-case scenario is that humans, playing god and not realizing that their knowledge is imperfect will destroy the very environment upon which they depend (Bateson, 1972). This view points to two key implications for the self. One, the myth of self-autonomy or free-standing individualism is stuck another blow. Second, a loss of faith in social engineering is underscored.

Reflexivity. The systems view of holism, which casts certainty as an illusion, coincides with the skepticism of reflexivity. According to Ulrich Beck (1994), a major exponent of this view, doubt is replacing faith in the grand narratives of progress, including the automated logic of laissez-faire economics. The efficacy of social engineering is especially in doubt, as it is increasingly difficult to find experts who agree with one another on anything. Moreover, the very notion of the self is rendered erratic in the face of massive, unprecedented reconfigurations in family life, education, work, politics, and international relationships (Feldman, 1998; Gergen, 1991; Giddens, 1994). Faced with such uncertainty, the self is subjected to therapeutic psychology which reconstructs personal bibliographies en masse. In this climate of skepticism toward the assumption of progress, one of the hallmarks of postmodern thought (see, e.g., Marcuse, 1964), the self faces a loss of ego-defined self-mastery, as indicated in Table 10.1.

Dialogic. Whereas the logic of utility and moral collectivism tends to force a dichotomy between the interests of self and others, bureaucratic management and social engineering subject the self to widespread controls. Subsequently, holism reveals the fallacies of such controls while reflexivity casts the self as steeped in uncertainty and doubt. Given this progression of images, the dialogic self can be seen as a response to the mechanical patterns of thought inherent in utility, moral collectivism, bureaucratic management, and social engineering. Specifically, dialogue foregoes a belief in the certainty of outcomes in favor of searching for consensus shaped by different viewpoints openly expressed (Calton & Payne, 2003; Isaacs, 1999). As Table 10.1 indicates, this exploration can yield relative knowledge shaped by the nature of the conversations at hand. Instead of taking social relations as pre-ordained (a la feudalism), manipulated (utility), subject to pre-determined rules (moral collectivism), or controlled en masse (bureaucratic management and social engineering), the dialogic self takes its cues from holism and reflectivity, attempting to discover the nature of complexity in relationships without any pretense of certainty or ego-mastery. In this way, the dialogic self image harkens to postmodernism, which accounts for social experience from multiple perspectives of discourse and practice, rather than assume a larger cumulative enterprise committed to the inference of general principles (Agger, 1991). Hence, as indicated in Table 10.1, the dialogic self embodies a loss of absolute certainty.

The implication of this iconic image is profound. For when the self is purged of the interior excesses of rationality, then new types of mutual relationships become theoretically possible (McNamee & Gergen, 1999). From this point of view, the dialogic self appears to be an important sign-post that the mechanical paradigm has indeed run its course.

Comparing Self Types

Table 10.2 is a typology of dimensions related to the self according to the a) degree of certainty implied for b) self (or focal firm), others in community, and general systems.

According to this schema, an accent on predetermined goals is common to the mechanical logic of utility, bureaucratic management, moral collectivism, and social engineering. That amoral control is congruent with self-as-utility and bureaucratic management is exemplified by the view, discussed earlier, that corporate managers should strategically manipulate stakeholders (cell 1). By comparison, social engineering implies an even wider scope of systems control (cell 3) whereas collectivism prescribes predetermined rules that govern a community of others (cell 2). In other words, control in the service of certainty is reflected in all three categories. In contrast, the remaining cells accommodate uncertainty better in that reflexivity conveys a self that must doubt rather than control (cell 4), while dialogue forgoes predetermined rules to appreciate the vagueness endemic in relationships with others (cell 5). Finally, the logic of holism takes uncertainty to be so pervasive that attempts to control systems will likely miss their mark, perhaps fatally. Consequently, it favors an ability to recognize patterns instead of assuming that knowledge is perfect enough for rational control (cell 6). In sum, these latter images reject mechanical control over predetermined outcomes conveyed by the former three images (cells 1, 2 and 3).

IMPLICATIONS FOR ETHICAL BUSINESS EDUCATION

The self is never given and is always in the process of transformation
—Kofman & Senge, 1993, cited in Brown, 1996, p. 98

While our analysis has many implications for business education, we will concentrate on the need to recast the self as an image that can be broadly compatible with other-regarding ethics. In the process, we acknowledge that we do not resolve the problem of self completely, as further advances will need to come from educators who are convinced of the worthiness of this project. Meanwhile, we will point to some areas ripe for change.

Recasting the Self

Figure 10.1 is a longitudinal display of the iconic self at a crossroads of sorts. We view business education at a similar fork in the road. On the one hand, disenchantment with mechanical logic and an ego-defined narrative of self portends nihilism or loss of meaning. On the other, ideology liberated from the burden of impossible control suggests an epiphany of self. By this we do not mean that a transcendental, ego-less self is on the horizon, but rather one defined by the open-ended logic and mutuality of relationships incarnate in the dialogic self. Of course, neither path is preordained. A third prospect is the status quo, which is that the logic of utility will continue to muddle and polarize the debate about business's role in society, pitting those who view business narrowly as a vehicle for self-interest against those who envision the institution more broadly. A fourth possibility is that the yearning for God's immanent plan that once marked feudal economies will morph into a quest to revive the divinity lost to commercialism. Indeed, this impulse may already be manifesting as a concern for spirituality expressed in some circles of management, which is perhaps yet another sign that the mechanical paradigm has lost steam. For when current ideology does not sufficiently address the human experience, people tend to look back to try to recapture the comforting certainty of earlier beliefs (Ayres, 1944; Frederick, 1987).[2]

We caution against looking back with nostalgia, forward with nihilism, or muddling through with confusing polarization. Rather, business education should convey the prospect of a self subject to fresh interpretation. To begin, we suggest explaining to students the cataclysmic lose of certainty implied when economic activity was partitioned from a divinely protected community. Examining this historical development would be more productive than rushing into predictable classroom discussions about business's role in society polarized between narrow self interest and broader community needs. As part of this project, educators should expose the mechanical fixation on pre-determined outcomes inherent in the logic of utility, moral collectivism, bureaucratic management, and social engineering while describing the more recent thought patterns of holism, reflexivity, and dialogue. The point is for pedagogy to take on a more open-ended quality so that students may engage in a mode of discovery rather than learning to parrot unexamined orthodoxy.

Along the way, students could grapple with the idea of the self seeking reintegration into community without blindly accepting the dichotomy between self- and other-interest forced by the uneasy co-existence of utility and moral collectivism. Students engaged in such deliberation are bound to grasp that a self based on ego-driven manipulation and control is not compatible with the respect for others called for by ethical perspectives, including deontology, justice, rights, and the ethics of care (see Beauchamp & Bowie, 1993). Absent such conscious reexamination, it will be difficult if not impossible for ethics to be delivered coherently in business education, as latent contradictions will undermine the effort. Recasting the self as emergent and subject to fresh interpretations would constitute a more fruitful approach.

Re-envisioning Management's Image

Critics have castigated business schools for perpetuating the behavior evidenced by the most recent outburst of corporate scandals (Benner, 2002; Fisher & Swanson, 2005; Ghoshal, 2003; Gioia, 2002; Ravenscroft & Williams, 2004; Swanson & Frederick, 2003). The problem is fueled by utility, which conflates narrow self interest with mechanical rationality, even though empirical evidence to validate such conflagration is scarce to nonexistent (Cohen & Holder-Webb, 2006; see also Shearer, 2002). When combined with other modes of mechanistic thinking, the resulting specter of control-seeking amorality not only is antithetical to ethics based on a concern for others, but also flies in the face of the mindset required to recognize and factor unexpected, novel information into decision making (Waddock, 2001). Clearly, a new image for management is needed that sheds a myopic emphasis on the certainty of prefixed goals associated with mechanical logic. Along these lines James March comments:

> To say that we make decisions now in terms of goals that will only be knowable later is nonsensical—as long as we accept the basic framework of the theory of choice and its presumptions of pre-existent goals. As we challenge the dogma of pre-existent goals, we will be forced to reexamine some of our most precious prejudices (March, 1982, p. 75, cited in Sarasvathy, 2001).

A danger of current prejudices is that a fetish for control creates a blind spot that keeps scholars incapable of envisioning a new view (Schein, 1989). A sense of ego mastery only makes matters worse (Bateson, 1972; 1979; Swanson, 1996). In contrast, holism, reflexivity, and dialogue point to decision-making that consciously strives to be aware of the flow of events and the need to discriminate among emerging patterns by exhibiting receptivity and humility in lieu of questing for certainty, manipulation, and control. In other words, management should be re-envisioned as a process of open-ended discovery instead of cast as rationalized amoral control. The point is to encourage students to deal with uncertainty and complexity by helping them quest for an embodiment of self that can incorporate all relevant information in decision making, especially that which concerns the welfare of others a la business ethics.

The dialogic self is particularly relevant to such imaging and imagining. After all, important information about complex business environments resides in stakeholders as their stories, espoused values, and perceived realities. Business students need to envision managers as engaging in open-ended and mutually sustaining conversations that illuminate these realities (Frederick & Weber, 1987). This is especially true for managing in global environments where cultural norms and values vary widely and emerging technologies redefine the very nature of markets (Sarasvathy, 2001). Under such conditions, the utility-inspired myth that mechanical, equilibrating forces can automatically guide business to desirable preconceived ends is incredibly naïve, as holism and reflexivity convey.

Re-envisioning Corporate Image

It will be challenging for business educators to facilitate a new image of corporations. After all, the influence of mechanistic utility is still strong, even though its logic took hold long before the advent of the large-scale organizations that process information stochastically and nonsensically in structures where technology and cultural arrangements exist uneasily (Frederick, 2006; Lindblom, 1977; March, 1982; Wilber & Harrison, 1978). To complicate matters, cultural perspectives meant to buffer organizations from the cult of individualism can unintentionally promote monolithically self-referenced and autonomous collectives of heroes, rituals, values, and shared purposes (Feldman, 1998; Smircich & Calas, 1987). This irony recalls the fallacy of collectivism, discussed earlier, except that the organization gets substituted for society as the source and object of morality (Dahler-Larsen, 1994; Ray, 1986). The resulting image of monolithic organizations that repress a variety of views portends a distrust of outsiders that makes doing business in diverse environments difficult if not impossible (Brown & Starkey, 2000). This dysfunctional image is compounded by the propensity of organizations to mimic or replicate one another symbolically (Feldman & March, 1981; Powell & DiMaggio, 1991). The resulting specter of whole organizational fields talking but not listening does not suggest an ability to respond well to community needs (Schwartz, 1991; Swanson, 1996).

Nor is the image of monolithically self-referenced organizations that manipulate their stakeholders a valid touchstone for business ethics education. Alternatively, if educators advance the views of holism, reflexivity, and dialogue, then students might be able to envision the stakeholder model as a rallying point for corporate citizenship instead of a conduit for amoral management and egocentric corporate control. Indeed, it may be that the stakeholder model has failed to achieve theoretical status precisely because monolithic cultures and egocentric control are such dubious moral platforms for business in society. Along these lines, we suspect that decentering the corporation from its stable focal point in the stakeholder model may provide new vistas for business education. After all, insights drawn from holism, reflexivity, and dialogue suggest that business relationships are far too complex to be portrayed as fixed points in networks. Rather, they are best understood as interacting nonlinear systems having unpredictable futures and indeterminate outcomes (Frederick, 1998; 2006).

Reconsidering the Business Curriculum

Coming to terms with the implications of such indeterminacy for ethics education is no easy matter. Take trust, for instance. Under conditions of complexity and uncertainty, it is problematic to view trust as statically vested in organizational promises that are continually redefined by plant closings, product recalls, layoffs, deregulation, private-public partnerships, changing job descriptions, and burgeoning multinational business (Cohen & Prusak, 2001). One way to deal with this ethical cul de sac is to explore trust as embedded in ongoing, truthful dialogues with stakeholders instead of attached to preset goals that deny the complex, interdependent, and dynamic effects of decisions that spill across organizational boundaries (Isaacs, 1999). As part of this exploration, students should be exposed to organizational methods designed to provide feedback on the quality of stakeholder relationships (see Beck, 1994) while encouraged to understand that such organizational innovations may be only loosely coupled to behavior (see Weick, 1976). For instance, a public display of conversing with stakeholders may function merely as a subterfuge for hypocritical control and superficial impression management (Brunsson, 1989; Isaac, 1999). This possibility underscores the need for instructors to expose amoral egocentrism in theory so that truly informed discussions of ethics can take place. Along these lines, coursework should also reveal the pitfalls of bureaucratic management where hierarchy distorts information along chain of command structures, rendering organizations slow to respond to novel information, including stakeholder interests (Broms & Gahmberg, 1983; Halal, 1994). Moreover, the inadequacies of perspectives that force decision makers to choose between narrow self interest and the needs of others should be reviewed in light of complex organizational and cultural realities.

Not that the logic of utility and moral collectivism should be completely discarded. Utility can be useful as a tool for weighing costs and benefits and a compass for keeping important goals like efficiency and profit in sight. Needless to say, such instrumental decision-making is germane to practical management (Frederick, 1995). Moreover, moral collectivism rightly conveys that corporations should attend to the needs of their host environments. Nevertheless, the excesses of utility, moral collectivism, and other forms of mechanistic thinking have survived long past their usefulness as dominant images of business in society, dampening coherent business ethics education in the process. This situation has occurred mostly by default, since business schools as a whole have not challenged the supremacy of narrow self interest and mechanistic thinking that shaped their curriculum from the start (Ferraro et al., 2005; Frederick, 2006; Ghoshal, 2003; Hoaas & Wilcox, 1995). The antidote is to require coursework that does, but not merely as a few add-ons. Essentially, a conscious re-evaluation of the whole curriculum is called for (Frederick, 2006; Ravenscroft & Williams, 2004; Vidaver-Cohen, 2004; Waddock, 2004).

In our view, such re-evaluation would involve putting images into perspective so that educators could identify the circumstances under which they lag advances in theory and practice. One approach would be to use Boulding's (1956; cited in Pondy & Mitroff, 1979) classification of nine images, each representing a system of unique properties that incorporate attributes of previous levels for dealing with complexity as reference points for understanding the pictures of management and corporations that get imparted to students:

- *Level 9*—Systems of unspecified complexity where images of systems are left open-ended to incorporate advances in thought.
- *Level 8*—Multi-cephalous systems with several brains, as in a social organization of people acting in concert to create shared order, history, value systems or civilization in its richest most complex form.
- *Level 7*—Symbol processing systems involving complex consciousness of image constructed according to shared assumptions of language.
- *Level 6*—Internal image systems imply detailed *awareness* of the environment via information receptors organized as knowledge structure.
- *Level 5*—Blueprinted growth systems, such as oak acorns and chicken eggs produce "seeds" containing the pre-program for their development.
- *Level 4*—Open systems maintain internal differentiation by adopting the orderliness of their external environment.

- *Level 3*—Control systems describe the regulation of systems seeking a prescribed target, such as socially engineered economics, heat seeking missiles and thermostats.
- *Level 2*—Clockworks represent dynamic properties of frameworks, such as the business cycles of *laissez faire* economics.
- *Level 1*—Frameworks are static representations of complexity, such as a chart of human anatomy or a system of cataloging. (Boulding, 1956, pp. 200–207)

Using these categories as touchstones, instructors could point to level 1 to remind students that some models are merely static representations of complexity and, therefore, are not to be accepted without critical analysis. This can set the stage for healthy skepticism and independent thinking. That done, images drawn from theory can be described relatively in terms of Boulding's levels, beginning with the clockwork or mechanistic properties of feudalism and utility-defined economics (level 2), the control aspects of utility, bureaucratic management, and social engineering (level 3), and the fallacies of cultural collectives that internalize only a limited understanding of their wider environment (level 4), replicating themselves institutionally based on such narrow precepts (level 5). In a more progressive vein, students could be encouraged to explore personal and organizational sensors of reflexivity (level 6), awareness based on language or dialogue (level 7), the possibility of shared community building (level 8), and unspecified complexity vis-à-vis holism (level 9) that transcends narrower replications of past programming or patterns of thought (level 6). This analysis is open-ended by design in that the ninth level augurs the unknown, just as Figure 10.1 points to imagery that can incorporate future advances in thought. By suggesting this approach, we do not mean to imply that the levels cannot be used for other purposes or that they fit our analysis like a glove. Our point is that tacitly held images should be subjected to critical analysis, keeping in mind that no single theoretical perspective gives a perfect, all-purpose point of view (Morgan, 1997).

A curriculum guided by such analysis would emphasize tools of dialogue in the context of global environments where information can be assigned various meanings due to cultural relativism and differences in shared language, histories, and values. By extension, coursework would be shifted away from narrow technical material to broader knowledge drawn from the liberal arts and the natural, social, and behavioral sciences. For instance, students faced with global complexities would be trained in tools of cultural anthropology that illuminate social norms and mores different from their own. In the process, they may discover that the independent construal of self common in Western cultures differs from the more interdependent, relational accounts found in other settings (Markus &

Kitayama, 1991). Coursework in language and conflict management skills would follow, augmented by on-the-job internships that expose students to the complexities of decision making that classroom-based education is ill equipped to simulate (Mintzberg, 2004).

Along the way, mechanical rationality would be de-emphasized in favor of understanding business and society in terms of complexity theory. As Frederick (2006) observes, corporate and community relations are coevolving nonlinear systems in which the civic role of business is a moving target, subject to an infinite variety of values at work on the interface between firms and their environments. Narrow mechanistic rationality cannot capture this interplay as well as complexity theory, which sees continuous transformation and emergent order as a natural state of affairs (Morgan, 1997). Notably, complexity theory can address the variety of values relevant to business, including a quest for managerial power that, along with organizational expansionist tendencies, can greatly diminish and degrade the life prospects of stakeholders and the natural environment (Frederick, 2006). It is important to confront the implications of such expansionist power seeking, especially given our earlier observation that economic utility has become an ideology of narrow self interest that rationalizes habitual economic growth at the expense of widespread ecological problems. Absent alternative images, students easily get the message that abdication of responsibility to community is the desired or normal state of affairs, just as the fiction of the isolated, self sufficient individual has led theorists to lose sight of the role of society and the symbiotic connection between the individual and group (Mannheim, 1936).

Waddock (2004) sums up the need for change by asserting that corporate—centric courses must become society-centric or even nature-centric with disciplinary specializations yielding to an integrated approach to business's role in society that can accommodate constant, complex change. Although the business curriculum needs to be revamped along these lines, we realize that such a re-haul is unlikely in the near future. Therefore, a more immediate tactic is the requirement of at least one course that can help students grapple with a sense of self befitting a society-regarding ethics in the context of environmental complexities. Such course can help offset the amoral subtext of utility and other forms of mechanistic thinking inherent in the curriculum and serve as a fulcrum for integrating ethical analysis across other courses over time (Swanson, 2004; Swanson & Frederick, 2003). After all, some evidence suggests that business students want more ethics education (Aspen Initiative for Social Innovation through Business [AISIB], 2002; Driscoll & Finn, 2005) and many if not most business school deans want to comply (Evans & Marcal, 2005; see also Evans & Weiss, chapter 3). Moreover, a preponderance of respondents to a *Wall Street Journal online* poll voted for ethics courses to be required of all MBA students (*Wall Street Journal online*, 2004). Yet, as indicated previously, only one third of accredited business schools offer an ethics course (Willen, 2004) and presumably fewer require one. Moreover, many have downsized ethics courses, even in the aftermath of corporate scandals (Kelly, 2002). This development is particularly disheartening in light of findings that normative myopia or the inability to factor ethics and values into decision making gets worse as students advance through the business school curriculum (AISIB 2002; Orlitzky, Swanson, & Quartermaine, 2006). In our view, this dubious track record is partly an artifact of utility and other mechanistic thought patterns that promote narrowly amoral images of self in the minds of students. There is no reason to accept this status quo, given indications that ethics and other behaviorally based skills can be taught and learned (Bebeau, 1994; Rest, 1986; Rynes, Trank, Lawson, & Ilies, 2003).

In the final analysis, a certain kind of society is possible because the individuals in it carry around in their heads some sort of picture of that society (Mannheim, 1936). Therefore, it is important that educators examine the images of self that get projected onto the business and society relationship and conveyed to students. Ideally, the projection should be constructively society-regarding, forward looking, and able to handle complexity instead of self-focused, atavistic, and myopically resistant to change. Our claim is not that we have found a complete reformulation of the self, but rather that we have charted its feasibility.

CONCLUDING REMARKS

We have compared the self-as-utility to other representations of self as a backdrop for proposing that business schools stop promoting outdated images in favor of more forward looking orientations. Our main contention is that self-as-utility keeps a society-regarding ethics at bay while perpetuating normative myopia and an inability to grapple with complexity in the minds of students. As an antidote, we have suggested that business educators expose the excesses of utility and other forms of mechanistic thinking while helping students search for a sense of self that can accommodate the needs of others in communities and organizational environments marked by uncertainty and complexity. In the short run, this means requiring at least one ethics course in which such issues can be raised and examined. In the long run, it means revamping the whole business curriculum. For us, the latter endeavor is the next horizon for advancing business ethics education.

NOTES

1. Actually, Friedman's (1962; 1970) stance against corporate social responsi-
    bility is moral to the extent that it is based on the rights of private property
    holders. Specifically, his position is that managers have a very strict moral
    duty to the owners or shareholders that preclude consideration of other
    stakeholders, except as a means to the assumed ends of shareholders (i.e.,
    wealth maximization) (Phillips, 2003). Our point is that this position is eas-
    ily interpreted as a rationalization for amoral decision making because it
    downplays the need for managers to intentionally adopt a broader sense of
    responsibility towards community. Friedman himself encourages this inter-
    pretation by implying that there is no need for corporate social responsibil-
    ity per se, since the actions of managers are already restrained by standards
    of public policy, the law, and ethical custom. This view, which takes
    restraints to decision making or social control as a given, does not encour-
    age a conscious deliberation of ethics on the part of corporate decision
    makers that would preclude the need for the law and ethical custom to
    assert themselves as default mechanisms of social control (Swanson, 1999).

2. Many of these quests to include spirituality in business are indeed forward-
    looking and devoid of rigid dogma associated with past thought patterns.
    For examples of such forward looking thinking, see Giacalone and Jurk-
    iewicz (2003) and chapter eight by Calton, Payne, and Waddock in this book.

REFERENCES

Adler, P. S. (2002). Corporate scandals: It's time for reflection in business schools.
    Academy of Management Executive, 16, 148–149.

Agger, B. (1991). Critical theory, poststructuralism, postmodernism: Their socio-
    logical relevance. *Annual Review of Sociology, 17,* 105–131.

Albert, S., Ashforth, B., & Dutton, J. (2000). Organizational identity and identifica-
    tion: Charting new waters and building new bridges. *Academy of Management
    Review, 25,* 13–17.

Aram, J. (1993). *Presumed superior.* Englewood Cliffs, NJ: Prentice Hall.

Arendt, H. (1964). *Eichmann in Jerusalem: A report on the banality of evil.* New York:
    Schocken.

Ashforth, B. (1994). Petty tyranny in organizations. *Human Relations, 47,* 755–777.

Aspen Initiative for Social Innovation through Business (AISIB). (2002, May). Where
    will they lead? MBA student attitudes about business & society. New York: Aspen
    ISIB. Accessed June 1, 2002, http: //aspeninstitute.org/isib/pdfs/sas.pdf.

Ayres, C. (1944). *The theory of economic progress.* Chapel Hill: University of North
    Carolina Press.

Bailey, K. D. (1994). Typologies and taxonomies. An introduction to classification
    techniques. *Sage University Paper Series: Quantitative Applications in the Social Sci-
    ences, 7(102),* 1–16.

Bateson, G. (1972). *Steps to an ecology of mind.* New York: Ballantine Books.

Bateson, G. (1979). *Mind and nature.* Bantham Books: New York.

Bauman, Z. (1993). *Postmodern ethics.* Oxford: Blackwell.

Beauchamp, T. L., & Bowie, N. E. (1993). *Ethical theory and business.* Englewood Cliffs, NJ: Prentice Hall.

Bebeau, M. (1994). Influencing the moral dimensions of dental practice. In J. R. Rest & D. Narvaez (Eds.), *Moral development in the professions* (pp.121–146), Hillsdale, NJ: Lawrence Erlbaum Associates.

Beck, C. L. (1932). *The heavenly city of the eighteenth-century philosophers.* New Haven: Yale University Press.

Beck, U. (1994). The reinvention of politics: Towards a theory of reflexive modernization. In U. Beck, A. Giddens & S. Lash (Eds.). *Reflexive modernization* (pp. 1–55). Stanford: Stanford University Press.

Benner, J. (2002, November 14). MBA accreditation body resists professors' call for required ethics course. *AFX Global Ethics Monitor Online.* Accessed November 14, 2002, http: //www.globalethicmonitor.com/afx-eth/homepage_summary.html.

Berger, P., Berger, B., & Kellner, H. (1973). *The homeless mind.* New York: Vintage Books.

Berger, P. L., & Luckmann, T. (1966). *The social construction of reality: A treatise in the sociology of knowledge.* New York: Doubleday.

Boulding, K. (1956). General systems theory—The skeleton of science. *Management Science, 2,* 197–208.

Broms, H., & Gahmberg, H. (1983). Communication to self in organizations and cultures. *Administrative Science Quarterly, 28,* 482–495.

Brown, D. (1996). The essences of the Fifth Discipline: Or where does Senge stand to view the world? *System Research, 13*(2), 91–107.

Brown, D., & Starkey, K. (2000). Organizational identity and learning: A pscychodynamic perspective. *Academy of Management Review, 25,* 102–120.

Bruner, J. (1990). *Acts of meaning.* Cambridge, Mass: Harvard University Press.

Brunsson, N. (1989). *The organization of hypocrisy, talk, decisions and actions in organizations.* Chichester, UK: Wiley.

Calton, J. M., & Payne, S. L. (2003). Coping with paradox: Multistakeholder learning dialogue as a pluralist sensemaking process for addressing messy problems. *Business & Society, 42,* 7–42.

Carr, A., & Zanetti, L. (1999). Metatheorizing the dialectic of self and other. *American Behavioral Scientist, 43,* 324–345.

Carroll, A. (1998). The four faces of corporate citizenship. *Business and Society Review, 100*(1), 1–7.

Castoriadis, C. (1982). The crisis of Western societies. *Telos, 53,* 17–28.

Cheney, G. (1991). The corporate person (re)presents itself. In E. L. Toth & R. L. Heath (Eds.). *Rhetorical and critical approaches to public relations* (pp. 165–183). Hillsdale NJ: Lawrence Erlbaum Associates.

Collins, D. (1990). Adam Smith's social contract: The proper role of individual liberty and government intervention in 18th century society. *Business & Professional Ethics Journal, 7,* 119–146.

Cohen, D., & Prusak, L. (2001). *In good company: How social capital makes organizations work.* Boston: Harvard Business School Press.

Cohen, J. R., & Holder-Webb, L. L. (2006). Rethinking the influence of agency theory in the accounting academy. *Issues in Accounting Education, 21,* 17–30.

Czarniawska, B. (1997). *Narrating the organization: Dramas of institutional identity.* Chicago: The University of Chicago Press.

Dahler-Larsen, P. (1994). Corporate culture and morality: Durkheim-inspired reflections on the limits of corporate culture. *Journal of Management Studies, 31,* 1–18.

Derrida, J. (1976). *Speech and phenomenon.* Evanston IL: Northwestern University Press.

Driscoll, C., & Finn, J. (2005). Integrating ethics into business education: Exploring discrepancies and variability among professors and students. *Journal of Business Ethics Education, 2,* 51–70.

Durkheim, E. (1961 trans.) *Moral education.* New York: The Free Press.

Englander, E., & Kaufman, A. (2004). The End of managerial ideology: From corporate social responsibility to corporate social indifference. *Business History Conference, 5,* 404–450.

Etzioni, E. (1988). *The moral dimension: Toward a new economics.* New York: Free Press.

Evans, F. J., & Marcal, L. E. (2005). Educating for ethics: Business deans' perspectives. *Business and Society Review, 110,* 233–248.

Fayol, H. (1949 trans.). *General and industrial management.* London: Pitman.

Feldman, M., & March, J. (1981). Information in organizations as signal and symbol. *Administrative Science Quarterly, 26,* 171–184.

Feldman, S. (1998). Playing with the pieces: Deconstruction and the loss of moral culture. *Journal of Management Studies, 35,* 59–79.

Ferguson, J. M. (1950) *Landmarks of economic thought.* New York: Longmans, Green and Co., Inc.

Ferraro, F., Pfeffer, J, & Sutton, R. I. (2005). Economics language and assumptions: How theories can become self-fulfilling. *Academy of Management Review, 30,* 8–24.

Fisher, D. G., & Swanson, D. L. (2005). A call to strengthen proposed NASBA ethics requirements: A three-step formula. *Compliance & Ethics, 2*(3), 36–38.

Frederick, W. C. (1987). Theories of corporate social performance. In S. P. Sethi & C. Falbe (Eds.), *Business and society: Dimensions of conflict and cooperation* (pp. 142–161). New York: Lexington Books.

Frederick, W. C. (1995). *Values, nature and culture in the American corporation.* New York: Oxford Press.

Frederick, W. C. (1998). Creatures, corporations, communities, chaos, complexity. *Business & Society, 37,* 358–389.

Frederick, W. C. (2006). *Corporation be good! The story of corporate social responsibility.* Indianapolis: Dog Ear Publishing.

Frederick, W. C., & Weber, J. (1987). The values of corporate managers and their critics. In W. C. Frederick & L. E. Preston (Eds.), *Research in corporate social performance and policy* (Vol. 9, pp. 131–152). Greenwich, CT: JAI Press.

Freeman, R. E. (1984). *Strategic management: A stakeholder approach.* Boston: Pitman/Ballinger.

Friedman, M. (1962). *Capitalism and freedom.* Chicago: University of Chicago Press.

Friedman, M. (1970, September 30). The social responsibility of business is to increase profits. *New York Times Magazine,* 122–126.

Galbraith, J. K. (1959). *The affluent society.* New York: Mentor Book.

Gergen, K. (1991). *The saturated self.* New York: Harper & Collins.

Ghoshal, S. (2003). B schools share the blame for Enron. *Business Ethics, 17,* 4.

Giacalone, R. A., & Jurkiewicz, C. L. (2003). Toward a science of workplace spirituality. In R. A. Giacalone. & C. L. Jurkiewicz, (Eds.), *Handbook of workplace spirituality and organizational performance* (pp. 3–28). Armonk, NY: M. E. Sharpe.

Giddens, A. (Ed.). (1972). *Emile Durkheim: Selected writings.* London: Cambridge University Press.

Giddens, A. (1994). Modernitetens konsekvenser. [*The consequences of modernity.*] Copenhagen: Hans Reitzel.

Gilpin, R. (1987). *The political economy of international relations.* Princeton, NJ: Princeton University Press.

Gioia, D. A. (1998). From individual to organizational identity. In Whetten, D. A. & P. C. Godfrey (Eds.), *Identity in Organizations: Building Theory through Conversations* (pp. 17–32). Thousand Oaks, CA: Sage.

Gioia, D. A. (2002). Business education's role in the crisis of corporate confidence. *Academy of Management Executive, 16,* 142–144.

Halal, W. H. (1994). From hierarchy to enterprise: Internal markets are the new foundation of management. *Academy of Management Executive, 8*(4), 69–83.

Hausman, D. M., & McPherson, M. S. (1996). *Economic analysis and moral philosophy.* New York: Cambridge University Press.

Hirschman, A. (1981). *Essays in trespassing: Economics to politics and beyond.* New York: Cambridge Press.

Hoaas, D. J., & Wilcox, D. C. (1995). The academic coverage of business ethics: Does economics measure up? *American Journal of Economics and Sociology, 54,* 289–303.

Illich, I. (1972). *DeSchooling society.* New York: Harper & Row, Harrow Books.

Isaacs. W. (1999) *Dialogue and the art of thinking together.* New York: Currency-Doubleday.

Jacobs, D. C. (1999). *Business lobbies and the power structure in America: Evidence and arguments.* Wesport, CT: Quorum Books.

Kelly, M. (2002). It's a heckuva time to be dropping business ethics courses. *Business Ethics. 16*(5 & 6*)*, 17–18.

Keynes, J. M. (1936). *The general theory of employment, interest and money.* New York: Harcourt, Brace & Company.

Kofman, F., & Senge, P. (1993). Communities of commitment: The heart of learning organizations. *Organizational Dynamics, 22*(2), 5–23.

Laing, R. D. (1959). *The divided self.* London: Tavistock Publication.

Lekachman, R. (1976). *Economists at bay: Why the experts will never solve your problems.* New York: McGraw-Hill.

Lindblom, C. E. (1977). *Politics and markets.* New York: Basic Books.

Loevinger, J. (1987). *Paradigms of personality.* New York: W. H. Freeman and Company.

Luckmann, T. (1983). *Life-world and social realities.* London: Heinemann Educational Books Ltd.

Lyotard, J. F. (1979). *Viden og det postmoderne samfund ("La condition postmoderne").* Århus: Sjakalen.

Mannheim, K. (1936). *Ideology and utopia.* USA: International Library of Psychology, Philosophy and Scientific Method.

March, J. G. (1982). The technology of foolishness. In J. G. March & J. P. Olsen (Eds.), *Ambiguity and choice in organizations* (pp. 69–81). Bergen, Norway: Universitetsforlaget.

Marcus, H. R., & Kitayama, S. (1991). Culture and the self: Implications for cognition, emotion, and motivation. *Psychological Review, 98,* 224–253.

Marcuse, H. (1964). *One-dimensional man.* Boston: Beacon Press.

McNamee, S., & Gergen, K. J. (1999). *Relation responsibility: Resources for sustainable dialogue.* Thousand Oaks, CA: Sage.

McSwite, O. C. (2001). The university as Hollywood: A "High concept" for century 21. *Organization, 8,* 417–424.

Mead, G. H. (1934). *Mind, self and society.* Chicago: University of Chicago Press.

Meyer, J.W., Boli, J., & Thomas, G.M. (1994). Ontology and rationalization in the Western cultural account. In W. R. Scott & J. W. Meyer (Eds.), *Institutional environments and organizations* (pp. 9–27). Thousand Oaks, CA: Sage.

Mintzberg, H. (2004). *Managers not MBAs.* San Francisco: Berrett-Koehler.

Morgan, G. (1997). *Images of organizations.* Thousand Oaks, California: Sage.

Nelson, R. H. (2001). *Economics as religion: From Samuelson to Chicago and beyond.* University Park, PA: The Pennsylvania State University Press.

Nisbet, R. A. (1966). *The sociological tradition.* London: Heinemann.

Orlitzky, M., Swanson, D. L., & Quartermaine, L.-K. (2006). Normative myopia, executives' personality, and preference for pay dispersion: Toward implications for corporate social performance. Business & Society, 45, 149–177.

Phillips, R. (2003). *Stakeholder theory and organizational ethics.* San Francisco, CA: Berrett-Koehler.

Pondy, L., & Mitroff, I. (1979). Beyond open system models of communication. In B. Staw (Ed.), *Research in organizational behavior* (Vol.1, pp. 3–39). Greenwich, CT: JAI Press.

Popper, K. R. (1945). *The open society and its enemies.* Princeton: Princeton University Press.

Powell, W. W., & DiMaggio, P. (Eds.). (1991). *The new institutionalism in organizational analysis.* Chicago: University of Chicago Press.

Ravenscroft, S., & Williams, P. F. (2004).Conference address: Considering accounting education in the USA post-Enron. *Accounting Education 13*(Supplement 1), 7–23.

Ray, C.A. (1986). Corporate culture: The last frontier of control? *Journal of Management Studies, 23,* 287–298

Redman, D. (1994). Karl Popper's theory of science and econometrics: The rise and decline of social engineering. *Journal of Economic Issues, 28,* 67–99.

Rest, J. (1986) *Moral development: Advances in research and theory.* New York, NY: Prager Press.

Richardson, L. (1990). *Writing strategies.* Thousand Oaks, CA: Sage.

Roderick, R. (1986). *Habermas and the foundations of critical theory.* London: Macmillan.

Rynes, S. L., Trank, C. Q., Lawson, A. M., & Ilies, R. (2003). Behavioral coursework in business education: Growing evidence of a legitimacy crisis. *Academy of Management Learning & Education, 2,* 269–283.

Sahlins, M. (1976). *Culture and practical reason.* Chicago: Aldine.

Sarasvathy, S. D. (2001). Causation and effectuation: Toward a theoretical shift from economic inevitability to entrepreneurial Contingency. *Academy of Management Review, 26,* 243–263.

Savage, G. T., Nix, T. W., Whitehead, C. J., & Blair, J. D. (1991). Strategies for assessing and managing organizational stakeholders. *Academy of Management Executive, 5*(2), 61–75.

Schein, E. (1989). Reassessing the "divine rights" of managers. *Sloan Management Review, Winter,* 63–68.

Schultz, M., Hatch, M. J., & Larsen, M. H. (Eds.). (2000). *The expressive organization: Linking identity, reputation, and the corporate brand.* Oxford: Oxford University Press.

Schwartz, H. (1991). Narcissistic process and corporate decay: The case of General Motors. *Business Ethics Quarterly, 1,* 249–268.

Scott, W. G., & Hart, D. K. (1979). *Organizational America.* Boston: Houghton Mifflin.

Scott, W. R. (1992). *Organizations: Rational, natural and open systems.* Englewood Cliffs, NJ: Prentice-Hall.

Selznick, P. (1992). *The moral commonwealth: Social theory and the promise of community.* Berkeley: University of California Press.

Sennett, R. (1978). *The fall of public man.* New York: Vintage Books.

Shearer, T. (2002). Ethics and accountability: From the for-itself to the for-the other. *Accounting, Organizations and Society, 27,* 541–573.

Smircich, L., & Calas, M. (1987). Organizational culture: A critical assessment. In F. M. Jablin, L. Putnam, K. Roberts, & L. Porter (Eds.), *Handbook of organizational communication* (pp. 228–263). Newbury Park, CA: Sage.

Smirich, L., & Stubbart, C. (1985). Strategic management in an enacted world. *Academy of Management Review, 10,* 724–736.

Smith, A. (1937/1776). *The wealth of nations.* New York: Random House, Modern Library.

Smith, A. (1976/1753). *The theory of moral sentiments.* Indianapolis, IN: Liberty Classics.

Swanson, D. L. (1996). Neoclassical economic theory, executive control, and organizational outcomes. *Human Relations, 49,* 735–756.

Swanson, D. L. (1999). Toward an integrative theory of business and society: A research strategy for corporate social performance. *Academy of Management Review, 24,* 506–521.

Swanson, D. L. (2000). Codetermination: A business and government partnership in procedural safety for ecological sustainability. *Systems Research and Behavioral Science, 1,* 527–542.

Swanson, D. L. (2004). The buck stops here: Why universities must reclaim business ethics education. In D. Reed & R. Wellen (Eds.), Special Issue on Universities and Corporate Responsibility, *Journal of Academic Ethics, 2,* 43–61.

Swanson, D. L., & Frederick, W. C. (2003). Are business schools silent partners in corporate crime? *Journal of Corporate Citizenship, 9,* 24–27.

Taylor, F. W. (1947). *The principles of scientific management.* New York: Harper.

Vidaver-Cohen, D. (2004). Fish starts to rot from head: The role of business schools in curriculum planning for ethics. *Journal of Business Ethics Education, 1,* 213–238.

Waddock, S. (2001). *Leading corporate citizens.* Boston: McGraw-Hill Irwin.

Waddock, S. (2004). Hollow men at the helm. *BizEd, 3*(5), 24–29.

Wall Street Journal online (2004, September 23). Question of the day: How much emphasis should M.B. A. programs place on business ethics? Accessed September 23, 2004, http://discussions.wsj.com/wsjvoices'messages.

Weber, M. (1946, trans.). *The theory of social and economic organization.* Gencoe: IL: Free Press.

Weick, K.,E. (1976). Educational organization as loosely coupled system. *Administrative Science Quarterly, 21*, 1–19.

West, R. (1993). Jurisprudence and Gender. In D. K. Weisberg (Ed.). *Feminist Legal Theory: Foundations* (pp. 206–223). Philadelphia, PA: Temple University Press.

Wilber, C. K., & Harrison, R. S. (1978). The methodological basis of institutional economics: Pattern model, storytelling, and holism. *Journal of Economic Issues, 12*, 61–89.

Willen, L. (2004, March 8). Kellogg denies guilt as B-Schools evade alumni lapses. *Bloomberg Press Wire.* Accessed March 10, 2004, http://www.cba.k-state.edu/departments/ethics/docs/bloombergpress.htm.

Zafirovski, M. (1998). Socio-economic and rational choice theory: Specification of the relations. *The Journal of Socio-Economics, 27*, 165–205.

CHAPTER 11

A DECISION MAKING FRAMEWORK FOR BUSINESS ETHICS EDUCATION

O.C. Ferrell
University of New Mexico

Linda Ferrell
University of New Mexico

INTRODUCTION

Advancing business ethics education is one of the greatest challenges facing business leaders today. While business programs in higher education have traditionally linked teaching of functional areas such as accounting, finance, marketing, and management to the activities of practitioners, this has not occurred in the teaching of business ethics. The 2005 National Business Ethics Survey, conducted by the Ethics Resource Center, found that 86% of employee's organizations have a code of conduct, 69% have ethics training, and 26% of organizations have all the elements of a formal ethics program (Ethics Resource Center, n.d). There are many critics of business schools who suggest that we are not connected to what is happening in the development and implementation of business ethics in corpo-

Advancing Business Ethics Education, pages 221–241
Copyright © 2008 by Information Age Publishing
All rights of reproduction in any form reserved.

rate America. This is because there have been dramatic changes in requirements in the last five years. Both mandatory and expected core practices of businesses have been driven by the institutionalization of business ethics through public policy.

The Federal Sentencing Guidelines for Organizations (FSGO), which went into effect in 1991, with significant amendments in 2004, generally tie potential penalties for violations of the law to the quality of corporate ethics and compliance programs. The United States Sentencing Commission, which developed the guidelines, recommends strict and severe enforcement of existing regulations and statutory requirements, particularly in cases where companies have failed to take proactive actions to promote ethics and compliance. Judges, courts, and regulatory agencies look for evidence of a proactive commitment to ethics including the existence of strong compliance programs, evidence of voluntary disclosure of misconduct, and evidence of full cooperation in the investigation of misconduct. Failing to find such evidence, the commission recommends that judges enforce regulations and sentencing without any mitigation.

The requirements imposed by the Sarbanes–Oxley Act (SOX) are also significant for ethical planning. This legislation has created new requirements for accountability and ethical conduct as a result of the corporate financial scandals in recent years. The major provisions of SOX include criminal and civil penalties for noncompliance violations, certification of internal auditing by external auditors, and increased disclosure regarding all financial statements. In addition, the law mandates codes of ethics for senior financial officers and disclosure of audit committee financial experts. A survey of corporate boards found that it costs organizations an average of $16 million each per year to comply with regulations under SOX (Gurchiek, 2005).

In addition, the Department of Justice, through the Thompson Memo (Larry Thompson, memo to the United States Attorneys, 2003) advanced general principles to consider in cases involving corporate wrongdoing. This memo makes it clear that ethics and compliance programs are important to detect types of misconduct most likely to occur in a particular corporation's line of business. Without an effective ethics and compliance program to detect ethical and legal lapses, the firm should not be treated leniently. Also, the prosecutor generally has wide latitude in determining when, whom, and whether to prosecute violations of Federal law. United States Attorneys are directed that charging for even minor misconduct may be appropriate when the wrongdoing was pervasive by a large number of employees in a particular role, e.g., sales staff, procurement officers, or was condoned by upper management. Without an effective program to identify an isolated rogue employee involved in misconduct, there can be serious consequences associated with regulatory issues, enforcement, and sentencing (Brewer, Chandler, & Ferrell, 2006).

The 2004 amendment to the Federal Sentencing Guidelines for Organizations requires that a business's governing authority be well informed about its ethics program with respect to content, implementation, and effectiveness. This places the responsibility squarely on the shoulders of the firm's leadership, usually the board of directors. The board must ensure that there is a high-ranking manager accountable for the day-to-day operational oversight of the ethics program. The board must provide for adequate authority, resources, and access to the board or an appropriate subcommittee of the board. The board must ensure that there are confidential mechanisms available so that the organization's employees and agents may report or seek guidance about potential or actual misconduct without fear of retaliation. Finally, the board is required to oversee the discovery of risks and to design, implement, and modify approaches to deal with those risks. If board members do not understand the nature, purpose, and methods available to implement an ethics program, the firm is at risk of inadequate oversight in the event of ethical misconduct that escalates into a scandal (Brewer et al., 2006).

The purpose of our chapter is to encourage decision making in ethics education that can help bridge the gap between schools of business, business practice, and public policy. All three areas are discovering the importance and role of organizational ethics programs in restoring integrity and confidence in business. To accomplish this objective, we offer a general framework to consider in establishing a strategic plan for ethics education. Implementation of this framework can be customized to the mission and needs of the educational institution.

THE OPPORTUNITY TO ADVANCE BUSINESS ETHICS EDUCATION

There is significant opportunity and need to generate awareness and understanding of important decisions in teaching business ethics. Organizations of all types are increasingly concerned about the potential impact of unethical behavior on stakeholders and on their own profits and survival. Most professors are not trained in how to teach organizational ethics in their curriculum. In addition, there is a lack of teaching materials, frameworks, and the skill to integrate these materials into courses, such as accounting, marketing, finance, information systems, as well as all management topics. There is often a limited awareness of the importance of principles and values to be synchronized with technical skills and strategic decision making. Yet all management-related and professional employees have to make ethical decisions on a daily basis as they carry out their responsibilities. In addition, as they rise into management positions, they are responsible for providing oversight of other employees to ensure that an ethical organizational culture is developed. There has to be subject content competence and ethical values, developed simultaneously, to avoid unethical behavior and to create a high integrity culture. All aspects of this business ethics rest on principle-centered leadership, discussed later.

Business ethics has moved from the "back room to the board room" and to the classroom over the last five years. Business schools are being asked to do a better job in teaching business ethics to help prepare future managers and to achieve accreditation by our major accrediting bodies through the maintenance of standards and constant improvement. Most corporations are developing ethics programs and making business ethics a higher priority than in previous years. Some approaches to business ethics are excellent for exercises in intellectual reasoning, but do not deal with the actual ethical decision making situations that people in business organizations face. To focus only on personal moral reasoning and philosophical frameworks, without the foundations of organizational ethical decision making, leave students unprepared for their business careers. The decision making approach we describe prepares students and educators to understand the ethical dilemmas that students will face in their careers (Ferrell, Fraedrich, & Ferrell, 2008).

Every individual has unique personal values, and every organization has its own set of values and ethical policies. Business ethics must consider the organizational culture and interdependent relationships between the individual and other significant persons involved in organizational decision making while facing organizational pressures and day-to-day challenges in the competitive environment. Employees cannot make most business ethics decisions in a vacuum, outside of organizational codes, policies, supervision, and culture. Most employees and all managers are responsible not only for their own ethical decision making, but also the decisions of the coworkers and employees they supervise. Therefore, teaching business ethics as only an independent personal decision-making model fails to address the requirement that employees help develop, manage, and improve organizational ethics programs. Employees must know when to report and address critical issues observed in the workplace. Students must learn to fit into the ethical culture of their organization and be responsible for their own decisions as well as upholding organizational standards.

Of the components that guide the decisions, actions, and policies of organizations, personal values in ethical decision making are but one. The burden of ethical behavior relates to the organization's values and traditions, not just to the individuals who make the decisions and carry them out. A firm's ability to plan and implement ethical business standards depends in part on structuring resources and activities to achieve ethical objectives in an effective and efficient manner.

Many people believe that business ethics cannot be taught. They believe that personal ethics is the only driver of organizational ethics. Although professors may not teach ethics, we suggest that by studying business ethics, a person can improve ethical decision making by identifying ethical issues and recognizing the risks and approaches available to resolve them. An organization's reward system can reinforce appropriate behavior and help shape attitudes and beliefs about important issues. Schools of business need a strategic plan and assurance of learning to achieve success in teaching business ethics. Business ethics changes in corporate America must be linked to the practice of functional areas of business. Outsourcing the teaching of business ethics to areas such as philosophy may not always provide this linkage.

FRAMEWORKS AND DOMAINS
FOR TEACHING BUSINESS ETHICS

Business ethics initiatives within the school of business should start by understanding the key frameworks and disciplines that have heavily influenced and define its boundaries. The authors of the AACSB International's Ethics Education Task Force Report "Ethics Education in Business Schools" reflect upon these dominant areas which they believe represent the domain of business ethics in Colleges of Business: Responsibility of Business in Society, Ethical Leadership, Ethical Decision Making, and Corporate Governance. Each of these areas is driven by academic research in management, marketing, finance, business law, accounting, as well as legal mandates thrusting business ethics into the forefront for both educators and practitioners.[2] The following are considerations and frameworks relevant to thinking about each of these broad categories.

Stakeholder Perspective

A stakeholder perspective is an appropriate framework for teaching all four areas of business ethics as identified by AACSB International. Many professors teaching business ethics, business and society, or specialized ethics courses in marketing, accounting, and management use a stakeholder framework to see how agreement, collaborations, and even confrontations exist on an ethics issue. Stakeholders designate the individuals or groups that can directly or indirectly affect, or be affected by, a firm's activities (Freeman, 1984). Stakeholders can be viewed as both internal and external. Internal stakeholders include functional departments, employees, boards of directors, and managers. External stakeholders include interest groups, consumers, competitors, advertising agencies, and regulators (Miller & Lewis, 1991). A robust ethics education requires that the various relationships be identified and interests understood.

Students need to understand that stakeholders can be characterized as primary or secondary. Primary stakeholders are those whose continued participation is absolutely necessary for business survival; they consist of employees, customers, investors, suppliers, and shareholders that provide necessary infrastructure. Secondary stakeholders are not usually engaged in transactions with the business and are not essential for its survival; they include the media, trade associations, non-governmental organizations, along with other interest groups. Different pressures and priorities exist from primary and secondary stakeholders (Waddock, Bodwell, & Graves, 2002). Unhappy customers may be viewed with less urgency than negative press stories that can damage a business (Thomas, Schermerhorn, & Dienhart, 2004). Highly visible secondary stakeholders such as an interest group or the media may at times be viewed with greater concern than employees or customers. Remote stakeholders at the fringe of operations can exert pressure calling into question the firms' legitimacy and right to exist (Hart & Sharma, 2004). The three critical elements in assessing stakeholder influence are their power, legitimacy, and urgency of issues (Mitchell, Agle, & Wood, 1997). Understanding the dynamic interaction of these elements is crucial to students' education and stakeholder relationships.

Power has been defined as the ability to exercise one's will over others (Schaefer, 2002). Legitimacy relates to socially accepted and expected structures that help define whose concerns or claims really count and urgency captures the dynamics of the time-sensitive nature of stakeholder interactions (Mitchell et al., 1997). Power and legitimacy may be independent, but the urgency component sets the stage for dynamic interaction that focuses on addressing and resolving ethical issues.

Stakeholder shared ethical values and norms. Ethics-based instruction should point out that major stakeholders may have different needs, and a fine-grained approach may be needed to ascertain even differences within major stakeholder groups, such as customers, employees, suppliers, and investors (Harrison & Freeman, 1999). On the other hand, usually a certain number of individual stakeholders share similar ethical values and norms (Maignan & Ferrell, 2004). Some of them choose to join formal communities dedicated to better defining, and to advocating, these ethical values and norms.

Stakeholder issues in business. Business education conveys that stakeholder ethical values and norms apply to a variety of business issues such as sales practices, consumer rights, environmental protection, product safety, and proper information disclosure (Maignan & Ferrell, 2004). Noticeably, stakeholder values and norms concern both issues that do and do not affect stakeholders' own welfare. For example, consumers may worry not only about product safety, but also about child labor, an issue that does not impact them directly. Stakeholder issues are the concerns that stakeholders embrace about organizational activities and the residual impact.

Stakeholder pressures. As illustrated in Figure 11.1, various stakeholder communities are likely to exercise pressures on the organization and on each other in order to push forward their own ethical values and norms. Figure 11.1 further illustrates that, in spite of disparities across communities, stakeholders conform to broad and abstract norms that define acceptable behavior in society. Noticeably, each business has its own values and norms depicting desirable behaviors based on its corporate culture and operations. These organizational values and norms overlap with those of some stakeholder groups, especially with those of primary stakeholders since they are in the best position to exercise an influence on the organi-

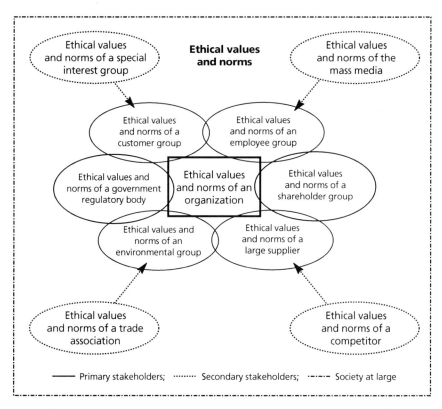

Figure 11.1. Interactions between organizational and stakeholder ethical values and norms. Adapted from Maignan, Ferrell and Ferrell (2005).

zation. Students should understand that stakeholder pressures create ethical issues.

Responsibility of Business in Society

The responsibility of business in society is one of the four major areas of coverage recommended by AACSB International. Social responsibility is the strategic focus taken by business for filling its economic, legal, ethical, and philanthropic responsibilities expected by its stakeholders (Thorne, Ferrell & Ferrell, 2008). All types of businesses can implement social responsibility initiatives to further their relationships with customers, employees, and the communities in which they operate. Although the efforts of large corporations usually receive the most attention, the actions of small business may have a greater impact on local communities. Business ethics, corporate volunteerism, compliance, corporate citizenship, and reputation management are all terms that are used to describe the social responsibility acts of business organizations. In most societies, business is granted a license to operate and the right to exist through a combination of social and legal mechanisms. Businesses are expected to pay taxes, abide by laws and regulations, treat employees fairly, follow through on contracts, protect the natural environment, meet warranty obligations, and adhere to many other legal and ethical standards. Companies that continually meet and exceed these standards are rewarded with customer satisfaction, customer loyalty, employee dedication, investor support, strong community relationships, supplier satisfaction and commitment, and the time and energy to continue focusing on business-related concerns. Firms that fail to meet relevant stakeholder expectations can face penalties, many of which divert their attention away from accomplishing core business objectives.

The success of social responsibility involves the extent to which a firm embraces the social responsibility philosophy and follows through with the implementation of initiatives. Social responsibility must be fully valued and championed by top managers who give it the same planning time, priority, and management attention as is given to other company initiatives. Social responsibility is not just an academic term; it involves action and measurement or the extent to which a firm embraces the philosophy of social responsibility and then follows through with implementing its initiatives. Social responsibility requires formal commitment, and a way of communicating the company's social responsibility philosophy and commitment. Courses in business and society recognize business as an important institution in society. In these courses, business and society should be addressed from an economic, legal, ethical, and philanthropic perspective, according to Archie Carroll's pyramid of social responsibility (Carroll, 1991).

Fundamentally, businesses have a responsibility to be economically viable so that they can provide a return on investment for their owners, create jobs for the community, and contribute goods and services to the economy. The economy is influenced by the ways in which organizations relate to their stakeholders, their customers, their employees, their suppliers, their competitors, the community, and even the natural environment. In conjunction with the goal to maintain profitability, companies are required to obey laws and regulations that specify responsible business conduct. Society enforces its expectations regarding the behavior of businesses through the legal system. If a business chooses to behave in a way that customers, special interest groups, or other businesses perceive as irresponsible, these groups may ask their elected representatives to draft legislation to regulate the firm's behavior, or they can use civil litigation to make the firm play by the rules. Civil litigation is the major device for resolving ethical disputes. If a firm or individual has been damaged by another party, they can use the court system to acquire restitution.

Organizations must also address their ethical responsibilities. Business ethics refers to the principles and standards that guide professional behavior in the world of business (e.g., right or wrong behavior within an organizational culture). These principles and standards are not determined by a philosophy textbook, but by stakeholders that interface with the company (e.g., customer, employees, suppliers, special interest groups, competitors, communities, etc.). The most important ethical principles have been codified into laws to require conduct that conforms to societal expectations. In addition, most firms operate in industries where professional associations have articulated best practice principles for appropriate conduct.

With financial success, organizations are capable of addressing their philanthropic responsibilities that promote human welfare and goodwill. Voluntary contributions of money, time and other resources help to contribute to communities and improve the quality of life for the business and its stakeholders. Although the philanthropic dimension may be voluntary, communities and society expect business to "give back" and help solve many of the social problems in our society. Business students can learn about the role of business in giving back through service learning projects and club activities in support of social causes.

Ethical Leadership

To move from just being an ethical person in everyday life experiences to being an ethical leader in a corporation requires an understanding of the ethical decision-making process. Leadership also requires an understanding of the firm's vision and values, as well as the challenges of responsibility and risk in achieving organizational objectives. AACSB International includes ethical leadership as a major element in business ethics education.

Lapses in ethical leadership do occur even in people who possess strong ethical character, especially if they view the organization's ethical culture as being outside of the realm of decision making that exists in the home, family, and community. This phenomenon has been observed in countless cases of so-called good community citizens engaging in ethical misconduct that sometimes lead to corporate ethical disasters. An ethical individual can be a cautious and conforming participant in a corporate culture that tolerates unethical conduct. Consider that many executives facing ethical disasters were viewed as outstanding community leaders in their personal lives, yet became embroiled in scandals at their companies.

In the long run, if a company's leader fails to satisfy stakeholders, he or she will not retain a leadership position. A leader must not only have the respect of stakeholders but must also provide a standard of ethical conduct to them. Archie Carroll (2003), University of Georgia business professor, crafted "7 habits of highly moral leaders" based on the idea of Stephen Covey's *The 7 Habits of Highly Effective People* (Covey, 1990). We have adapted Carroll's 7 Habits of Highly Moral Leaders to create our own "7 Habits of Strong Ethical Leaders" (Table 11.1). In particular, we believe that ethical leadership is based on holistic thinking that embraces the complex and challenging issues companies face on a daily basis. Ethical leaders need both knowledge and experience to make the right decision. Strong ethical leaders have both the courage and the most complete information to make decisions that will be the best in the long run. Strong ethical leaders must stick to their principles and, if necessary, be ready to leave the organization if its corporate governance system is so flawed that it is impossible to make the right choice.

TABLE 11.1
Habits of Strong Ethical Leaders

1. Ethical leaders have strong personal character.
2. Ethical leaders have a passion to "do right."
3. Ethical leaders are proactive.
4. Ethical leaders consider stakeholders interests.
5. Ethical leaders are role models for the organization's values.
6. Ethical leaders are transparent and actively involved in organizational decision making.
7. Ethical leaders are competent managers who take a holistic view of the firm's ethical culture.

Source: Adapted from Carroll (2003) in Ferrell, True, and Pelton (2003)

If leaders do not actively serve as role models for the organization's core values, then those values become nothing more than "lip service." Top management and coworkers perceived as leaders are the primary influence on individual ethical behavior. Leaders whose decisions and actions are contrary to the firm's values send a signal that the firm's values are trivial or irrelevant. Firms such as Enron and WorldCom articulated core values that were only used as "window dressing." On the other hand, when leaders model the firm's core values at every turn, the results can be powerful.

Business ethics consulting companies are reacting to the mushrooming attention many firms are paying to business ethics, but most of this is driven by compliance initiatives required by SOX and the amendments to the FSGO. Very little of this new interest in business ethics is related to the emergence of ethical leadership at the top. There is more of a "scared rabbit" syndrome among top executives looking to dodge, hide, and protect themselves from the wolves—otherwise known as the SEC. Without a change of corporate culture, consulting companies will install ethics programs and nothing more, which might be equated to a minimalist burglar alarm system that organizational members learn to trigger when needed. Only through committed strong leadership that is implemented into strategic planning and effective corporate governance can effective ethical leadership be a driving force in creating an ethical organizational culture. The failure to address ethical leadership in business school courses can provide the impression that this important part of business ethics is not the responsibility of management. Teaching ethical leadership reinforces the importance of creating an ethical culture and helps to counter the myth of responsibility only for one's own ethical decisions.

Ethical Decision Making

In teaching business ethics it is necessary to understand how people make business ethics decisions. This area of understanding relates to AACSB International's ethical decision making dimension. Within the context of an organization, there is an ethical component to business decisions and this decision may be influenced by the organization, the specific situation, or pressure exerted by coworkers. Figure 11.2 illustrates a model of ethical decision making in an organizational environment. External stakeholder interests, concerns or dilemmas help trigger ethical issue intensity. Organizational culture (internal stakeholders) and individual moral philosophies and values influence the recognition of ethical issues and business ethics decisions.

The decisions or outcomes are evaluated by both internal and external stakeholders. Although it is impossible to describe precisely how or why an

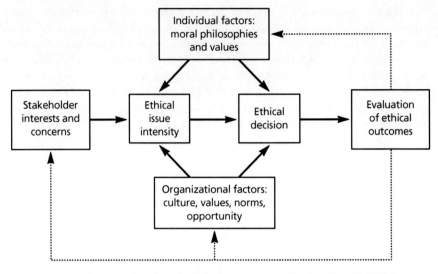

Figure 11.2.   Organizational Ethical Decision Making Model. Ferrell (2005).

individual or a work group may make a specific decision, we can generalize about average or typical behavior patterns within organizations.

First, as previously discussed, organizations can identify the importance of stakeholders and stakeholder issues and gather information to respond to significant individuals, groups, and communities. Next, in the decision-making process, managers should identify the importance or relevance of a perceived issue— i.e., the intensity of the issue (Jones, 1991). The intensity of a particular issue is likely to vary over time and among individuals and is influenced by the organizational culture, values and norms; the special characteristics of the situation, and the personal pressures weighing on the decision. Personal moral development and philosophy, organizational culture, and coworkers determine why different people perceive issues with varying intensity (Robin, Reidenbach, & Forrest, 1996).

Perhaps one of the greatest challenges facing the study of business ethics involves the role of individuals and their values. Although most of us would like to place the primary responsibility for decisions with individuals, years of research point to the primacy of organizational factors in determining ethical decisions at work (Ferrell, 2005). However, as shown in Figure 11.2, individual factors are obviously important in the evaluation and resolution of ethical issues, and familiarity with theoretical frameworks from the field of moral philosophy is helpful in determining ethical decision making in business (Murphy, Laczniak, Bowie, & Klein, 2005). Two significant factors in business ethics are an individual's personal moral philosophy and stage of moral development. Through socialization, individuals develop their own ethical pattern of behavior, including judgments about right or wrong actions. This socialization occurs from family, friends, business school education, religion, and other philosophical frameworks that an individual may embrace (Ferrell, 2007).

Research indicates that attitudes are prompted by complex interactions between individual and organizational member evaluations of an ethical issue. Of importance to understanding ethical decision making is that organizational members rely on context-specific attitudes rather than generalized or enduring attitudes (Cohen & Reed, 2006). This indicates that the organizational culture will be the major influence on ethical decision making in a business context. Ethical decisions are made in the context of social networks that influence ethical decision making.

Although individuals must make ethical choices, it is also true that they often make these decisions in committees, group meetings, and through discussion with colleagues. Ethical decisions in the workplace are guided by the organization's culture and the influence of others, such as coworkers, superiors, subordinates. In fact, more ethical misconduct is done to benefit organizational performance rather than to satisfy personal greed (Kelly, 2005).

The ethical climate of an organization is a significant element of organizational culture. Whereas a firm's overall culture establishes ideals that guide a wide range of behaviors for members of the organization, its ethical climate focuses specifically on issues of right and wrong. The ethical climate is the organization's character or conscience. Codes of conduct and ethics policies, top management's actions on ethical issues, the values and moral development and philosophies of coworkers, and the opportunity for misconduct all contribute to an organization's ethical climate. In fact, the ethical climate actually determines whether or not certain dilemmas are perceived as having an ethical intensity level that requires a decision.

Organizations can manage their culture and ethical climate by trying to hire employees whose values match their own. Some firms even measure potential employees' values during the hiring process and strive to choose individuals who "fit" within the ethical climate rather than those whose beliefs and values differ significantly. A poor "fit" can have very expensive ramifications for both organizations and employees. Beyond the potential for misconduct, a poor employee-organization ethical fit usually results in low job satisfactions, decreased performance, and higher turnover (Sims & Kroeck, 1994).

Ethics education should emphasize the importance of organizational culture and the influence of coworkers who may foster conditions that limit or permit misconduct. When these conditions provide rewards, such as financial gain, recognition, promotion, or simply the good feeling from a job well done, the opportunity for unethical conduct may be encouraged or discouraged based on ethical climate. For example, a company policy that does not provide for punishment of employees who violate a rule (e.g., not to accept large gifts from a client) provides an opportunity for unethical behavior. Essentially, this lack of policy allows individuals to engage in such behavior without fear of consequences. Thus, organizational policies, processes, and other factors may contribute to the opportunity to act unethically.

Opportunity usually relates to employees' immediate job context—where they work, with whom they work, and the nature of the work. The specific work situation includes the motivational "carrots and sticks" that superiors can use to influence employee behavior. Pay raises, bonuses, and public recognition are carrots, or positive reinforcement, whereas reprimands, pay penalties, demotions, and even firings act as sticks, or negative reinforcement. For example, a salesperson that is publicly recognized and given a large bonus for making a valuable sale that he obtained through unethical tactics will probably be motivated to use unethical sales tactics in the future, even if such behavior goes against his personal value system. Indeed, research by Bellizzi and Hasty (2003) has shown that there is a general tendency to discipline top sales performers more leniently than poor sales performers for engaging in identical forms of unethical selling behavior. Neither a company policy stating that the behavior in question was unacceptable nor a repeated pattern of unethical behavior offset the general tendency to favor the top sales performers. A superior sales record appears to induce more lenient forms of discipline despite managerial actions that are specifically instituted to produce more equal forms of discipline. Based on their research, Bellizzi and Hasty concluded that an opportunity exists for top sales performers to be more unethical than poor sales performers.

Figure 11.2 can help students put ethical decision making in business context and see how the process fits together. Once students begin to understand that good ethics is linked to organizational performance they see why it is necessary to have organizational ethics and compliance programs. Also, students begin to see the personal costs including reputation damage from misconduct. Ethics education needs to eradicate the myth that there is a tradeoff between ethics and profits in a business. Important thought leaders such as Ip and Whitehouse (2006) and Peter Drucker (1974) often discuss the tradeoffs between responsibility to society and profits. This balance of profits and responsibility takes on a new dimension when analyzed from a stakeholder framework.

Corporate Governance

Corporate governance is a formal system of accountability and control for organizational decisions and resources. Accountability relates to how well the content of workplace decisions is aligned with a firm's stated strategic direction. Control involves the process of auditing and improving organizational decisions and actions. The philosophy that a board or firm holds regarding accountability and control directly affects how corporate governance works. The major categories to consider in corporate governance discussions include the SOX, FSGO and 2004 amendments, shareholder rights, executive compensation, mergers and acquisitions, composition and structures of boards of directors, auditing and control, risk management, and CEO selection and executive succession plans. These issues normally involve strategic-level decisions and actions taken by boards of directors, business owners, executives, and other people with high levels of authority and accountability. The FSGO 2004 amendments hold the board of directors responsible not only for financial audits, but for ethics programs and monitoring systems in the organization. Through the SEC and the Sentencing Commission, corporate governance is continually refined and regulated. All of this legislation attempts to get companies to act responsibly and create effective ethics programs.

AACSB International has emphasized corporate governance as a major requirement in business ethics education and conducts a yearly conference on Ethics and Governance. Most businesses and many courses taught in colleges of business operate under the belief that the purpose of business is to maximize profits for the shareholders. In 1919, the Michigan Supreme court in the case of *Dodge v. Ford Motor Co.* ruled that a business exists for the profit of shareholders, and the board of directors should focus on that objective. On the other hand, the stakeholder model places the board of directors in the control position to balance the interests and conflicts of the various constituencies. External control of the corporation includes not only government regulations but also key stakeholders such as employees, consumers, and communities, who exert pressures for responsible conduct. The FSGO provides incentives for developing an ethical culture and efforts to prevent misconduct. SOX legislation holds top officers and the board of directors legally responsible for accurate financial reporting (Thorne et al., 2008).

Students need to recognize that failure to balance stakeholder interests can result in a failure to maximize shareholders' wealth. Wal-Mart may be failing to maximize the growth of its market value because investors are concerned about its ability to manage stakeholder interests. Wal-Mart's shareholders have seen almost no stock growth over the past few years as it battles employees, communities, and special-interest groups over ethical issues. Most firms are moving toward a balanced stakeholder model, as they see that this approach will sustain the relationships necessary for long-term success.

Officer compensation packages challenge directors, especially those on the board who are not independent. Directors have the opportunity to vote for others' compensation in return for their own increased compensation, a situation rife with conflicts of interest. Opportunities to know about the investments, business ventures, and stock market information create issues that could violate the duty of loyalty. Insider trading of a firm's stock is subject to very specific rules, and violations can result in serious punishment.

The development of a stakeholder orientation should interface with the corporation's governance structure. Corporate governance is also part of a firm's corporate culture that establishes integrity of all relationships. A governance system that does not provide checks and balances creates opportunities for top managers to put their own self-interests before those of important stakeholders.

Members of a company's board of directors assume responsibility for the firm's resources and legal and ethical compliance. The board appoints top executive officers and is responsible for providing oversight of their performance. For public corporations, boards of directors hold the ultimate responsibility for their firms' ethical culture and legal compliance.

Changes in technology, consumer activism, government attention, and other factors have raised questions about such issues as executive pay, risk and control, accountability, strategic directions, shareholder rights, and other decisions made for the organization.

Accountability for organizational decisions and resources begins with a strategic mission and vision that informs all levels of employees and stakeholders. From this strategic direction, it is possible to account for and assess decisions made on behalf of the organization. Thus, corporate governance is about the process and content of decision making in business organizations. Students need to understand this important area because key responsibilities for business ethics are embedded in these decisions. Finance and accounting students need to understand the importance of establishing internal controls and the role of values in principal-centered decisions. All students need to know the role and purpose of corporate governance, especially in a post-SOX business environment.

THE IMPORTANCE OF ADVANCING BUSINESS ETHICS TO EDUCATORS AND PRACTITIONERS

It can be seen that students need to develop a holistic understanding of how ethical decisions are made in an organizational context. They need to appreciate the many reasons to develop the most effective organizational ethics and compliance programs and to develop an ethical culture. Organizations face significant threats from ethical misconduct and illegal behavior from employees and managers. Well-meaning managers often devise schemes that appear legal, but are so ethically flawed they result in scandals and legal issues. There is a need to identify potential risks and uncover the existence of activities or events that relate to misconduct. There must be a plan and infrastructure to determine what is happening and deal with it as soon as possible rather than covering up, ignoring, and assuming that no one will ever find out about ethical and legal lapses. There is a need to discover, disclose, expose, and resolve issues as they occur. All firms have misconduct and discovering and dealing with these events is the only effective way to be successful in today's complex regulatory system. The existence of plaintiff friendly civil litigation can destroy reputation and draw intense scrutiny to a company.

Ethics programs should be regularly assessed or audited to determine their effectiveness. In particular, it is useful to focus on the key factors that influence how ethical decisions are made, including organizational culture, peers, superiors, and formal systems of reward and punishment. Students, as future business managers, need to enter the workplace with ethics skills already in hand. Unless students understand the nature and risks of ethical decision making in an organization, they could fail to understand their responsibility in developing oversight and maintaining standards. If students believe that ethics is just a personal decision, then they could engage in complacency when unethical behavior is observed.

What are the rewards of ethics and compliance? An Open Compliance Ethics Group study indicates that among companies with an ethics program in place for ten years or more, none has experienced damage to their reputation in the last five years (Brewer et al. 2006). The U.S. Sentencing Commission reports no firm with an effective ethics and compliance program was sentenced between 2000 and 2005 (Desio 2006). Communication by the firm's leadership helps keep the firm on its ethical course, and these executives must ensure that the ethical climate is consistent with the company's overall mission and objectives. Developing a values-based orientation fosters a system that provides a core of ideals such as respect, honesty, trust, and responsibility. In a values-centered program, employees become more open, are willing to deliver necessary information to supervisors, and generally begin to feel comfortable about how to make decisions in situations where there are no defined rules.

To advance business ethics education, students need to understand the dangers of emphasizing legal compliance at the expense of developing an ethical corporate conscience. Training, educating, and motivating employees to act in ways consistent with both legal requirements and ethical expectations is at the core of planning to prevent and manage misconduct. Companies themselves do much to establish the values, the culture, and the expectations for conduct that employees hold about daily life within the firm. This is achieved explicitly thorough codes of conduct and statements of values/ethics documented in organizational communication. This is also accomplished implicitly through dress codes, anecdotes about company heroes and villains, treatment of customer complaints, treatment of employee complaints, how meetings are conducted, and the manner in which behaviors and accomplishments get rewarded and recognized compared with those behaviors criticized, ignored, or punished. In fact, ethical leadership and ethical culture of the organization are key considerations in any potential legal conflict that an organization faces (Brewer et al., 2006).

Managers cannot motivate employees or coordinate their efforts without effective communication about values, standards, and expectations. Communication is important in providing guidance for ethical standards and activities that provide integration between the functional areas of the business. No program can be implemented without complete understanding of its objectives and employee cooperation to make it work. While most managers and employees don't have "ethics" in their job title, everyone is ultimately accountable.

Advancing business ethics education requires a strategic plan for integrating the kind of knowledge and frameworks we have discussed into both undergraduate and graduate programs. AACSB International leaves these important decisions up to each business school while sponsoring or co-sponsoring Teaching Business Ethics Conferences in 2004, 2005, and 2006. On the other hand, many business ethics advocates do not believe that there has been enough leadership and support for business ethics education. (Swanson & Frederick, 2005) Most business school professors know little about this dynamic area and how it relates to the functional courses that they teach. Without powerful internal advocates and a strategic plan for business ethics content coverage from a holistic perspective, most business schools will fail to adequately address this important part of business education. Simply asking faculty if they teach business ethics is not enough to provide assurance that important subject matter has been covered.

Deans need to become leaders and provide resources and support to advance business ethics education within their schools. Sending key support faculty to Teaching Business Ethics Conferences, as well as special tracks and sessions at academic conferences that address this topic, can create informed faculty to support initiatives.

The business community is waiting for business schools to provide informed graduates that can appreciate and support their ethics and compliance initiatives. Graduates need to embrace and provide leadership for principal-centered decision making and ultimately leadership. Students must understand that they are responsible for more than just their own decisions. The vast majority of business schools do not require courses in business ethics or business and society. The time for discovery, advancement and application is now!

NOTES

1. Some of the material in this manuscript has been adapted from "What Your Mother Never Taught You: How to Teach Business Ethics", "Current Developments in Managing Organizational Ethics and Compliance Initiatives", and "Developing a Framework for a College of Business: Business Ethics Initiative" by O.C. Ferrell and Linda Ferrell. See unpublished white papers at the E-Ethics Center, www.e-businessethics.com.

2. The Association to Advance Collegiate Schools of Business (AACSB) is the international accrediting body for colleges of business. Its Ethics Education Task Force Report was designed to outline key areas for colleges of business to consider in developing business ethics in its curriculum. For information, go to http://www.aacsb.edu/resource_centers/ethicsedu/default.asp.

REFERENCES

AACSB International website, (n.d.). Report from AACSB International Ethics Education Task Force, accessed April 24, 2007, http://www.aacsb.edu/resource_centers/ethicsedu/default.asp, ,

Bellizzi, J. A., & Hasty, R. W. (2003). Supervising unethical sales force behavior: How strong is the tendency to treat top sales performers leniently? *Journal of Business Ethics, 43*, 337–351.

Brewer, L., Chandler, R., & Ferrell, O. C. (2006). *Managing risks for corporate integrity: How to survive an ethical misconduct disaster.* Mason, OH: Thomson/Texere.

Carroll, A. B. (1991, July/August). The pyramid of corporate social responsibility: Toward the moral management of organizational stakeholders. *Business Horizons, 42*, 39–48.

Carroll A. B, (2003). Ethical leadership: From moral managers to moral leaders. In O. C. Ferrell, S. True, & L. Pelton, (Eds.), *Rights, relationships and responsibilities* (pp. 7–17), Vol. 1. Kennesaw, GA: Kennesaw State University.

Cohen, J. B., & Reed II, A. (2006). A multiple pathway anchoring and adjustment (MPAA) model of attitude generation and recruitment. *Journal of Consumer Research, 33*, 1–15.

Covey, S. R. (1990). *The 7 habits of highly effective people* (1st ed.). NY: Free Press.

Desio, P, (2006.) United States Sentencing Commission, Presentation at the Ethics and Compliance Officers Association Meeting San Antonio, Texas

Drucker, P. (1974). *Management: Tasks, responsibilities, practices.* NY: Harper & Row.

E-Ethics Center (n.d.). Retrieved April 26, 2007, www.e-businessethics.com.

Ethics Resource Center (n.d). National Business Ethics Survey. *How employees view ethics in their organizations 1994–2005* (pp.12, 13, 56). Retrieved April 26, 2007, http://www.ethics.org.

Federal sentencing guidelines for organizations (2004), United States Sentencing Commission.

Ferrell, O. C. (2005). A framework for understanding organizational ethics. In R. A. Peterson & O. C. Ferrell (Eds), *Business ethics: New challenges for business schools and corporate leaders* (pp. 3–17). Armonk, NY: M.E. Sharpe.

Ferrell, O. C. (2007). Nature and scope of marketing ethics. In G. Gundlach, L. Block, & W. Wilkie (Eds), *Explorations of marketing in society* (pp. 858–952). Mason, OH: Texere/Thomson South-Western.

Ferrell, O. C., Fraedrich, J., & Ferrell, L. (2008). *Business ethics: Ethical decision making and cases* (7th ed.). NY: Houghton Mifflin Company.

Freeman, R. E. (1984). *Strategic management: A stakeholder approach.* Boston, MA: Pitman.

Gurchiek, K, (2005, January), Sarbanes-Oxley compliance costs rising, *HR Magazine,* Accessed May 9, 2007, http://findarticles.com/p/articles/mi_m3495/is_1_50/ai_n8699080

Harrison, J. S., & Freeman, R. E. (1999). Stakeholders, social responsibility, and performance: Empirical evidence and theoretical perspectives. *Academy of Management Journal, 42*(5), 479–485.

Hart, S. L., & Sharma, S. (2004). Engaging fringe stakeholders for competitive imagination. *Academy of Management Executive, 18*(1), 7–18.

Ip, G., & Whitehouse M. (2006, November 17). How Milton Friedman changed economics, policy and markets. *Wall Street Journal,* A1.

Jones, T. M. (1991). Ethical decision making by individuals in organizations: An issue-contingent model. *Academy of Management Review, 16,* 366–395.

Kelly M. (2005, Summer). The ethics revolution, *Business Ethics, 19,* 6.

Maignan, I., & Ferrell, O.C. (2004). Corporate social responsibility and marketing: An integrative framework. *Journal of the Academy of Marketing Science, 32*(1), 23–19.

Maignan, I., Ferrell, O. C., & Ferrell, L. (2005). A stakeholder model for implementing social responsibility in marketing. *European Journal of Marketing, 39*(9/10), 956–977.

Miller, R. L., & Lewis, W. F. (1991). A stakeholder approach to marketing management using the value exchange models. *European Journal of Marketing, 25*(8), 55–68.

Mitchell, R. K., Agle, B. R., & Wood, D. J. (1997). Toward a theory of stakeholder identification and salience: Defining the principle of who and what really counts. *Academy of Management Review, 22*(4), 853–886.

Murphy, P. E., Laczniak, G. R., Bowie, N. E., & Klein, T. A. (2005). *Ethical marketing.* Upper Saddle River, NJ: Pearson Prentice-Hall.

Robin, D. P., Reidenbach, R. E., & Forrest, P. J. (1996). The perceived importance of an ethical issue as an influence on the ethical decision-making of ad managers. *Journal of Business Research, 35,* 17–29.

Schaefer, R. T. (2002). *Sociology: A brief introduction* (4th ed). Boston, MA: McGraw Hill.

Sims, R. L., & Kroeck, K. G. (1994).The influence of ethical fit on employee satisfaction, commitment and turnover. *Journal of Business Ethics, 13,* 939–947.

Swanson, D. L., & Frederick, W. C. (2005). Denial and leadership in business ethics education. In R. A. Peterson & O. C. Ferrell (Eds.), *Business ethics: New challenges for business schools and corporate leaders* (pp. 222–240). Armonk, NY: M.E. Sharpe.

Thomas, T., Schermerhorn, J. R., & Dienhart, J. W. (2004). Strategic leadership of ethical behavior in business. *Academy of Management Executive, 18*(2), 56–66.

Thompson, L. (2003, January 20). *Memo to the United States Attorneys.* Retrieved January 21, 2008, from http://www.usdoj.gov/dag/cftf/corporate_guidelines.htm.

Thorne, D. M., Ferrell, O. C., & Ferrell, L. (2008). *Business and society: A strategic approach to social responsibility* (3rd ed.). Boston, MA: Houghton Mifflin.

Waddock, S. A., Bodwell, C., & Graves, S. B. (2002). Responsibility: The new business imperative. *Academy of Management Executive, 16*(2), 132–149.

CHAPTER 12

CREATING ENVIRONMENTAL CHANGE THROUGH BUSINESS ETHICS AND SOCIETY COURSES

Denis Collins
Edgewood College

ABSTRACT

This chapter explores how to improve the environmental performance of local organizations through MBA and undergraduate Management and Business & Society course assignments. Edgewood College MBA students apply "The Natural Step" framework to their organizations' operations and initiate changes that improve their environmental performance. Undergraduate Business & Society students research and implement campus energy efficiency techniques, manage a campus-wide Eco-Olympics, and publish case studies that showcase local environmentally friendly business practices. These environmental service-learning activities have contributed to fostering a Business School and college culture that embraces environmental innovations. Students want to make a difference and these projects enable them to do so. Materials are provided to assist professors in implementing these class projects.

Advancing Business Ethics Education, pages 243–263
Copyright © 2008 by Information Age Publishing
All rights of reproduction in any form reserved.

REQUIRING ENVIRONMENTAL MANAGEMENT CHANGES

Professors have an obligation to not only convey information to students, but also empower students to apply the knowledge being learned in a meaningful manner and examine the impact of the applied knowledge on relevant stakeholders, including present and future employers. Organizations are dynamic, not static; they are clay to be shaped, not concrete. Our students typically earn, or already have, positions of authority and influence their organization's evolutionary progress. Students can more intentionally experience their ability to influence organizational events and relationships while studying at higher education institutions, in partnership with professors who guide them to sources of knowledge and serve as coaches for hands-on change experiences.

The recently revised version of Bloom's learning taxonomy begins with students remembering information as the most basic form of education and then progressing through understanding, applying, analyzing, evaluating and creating new ideas (Anderson & Krathwohl, 2001). The higher stages of learning are often the basis of education within professional programs, including Business. Accounting, Finance, and Marketing professors convey state-of-the-art knowledge and expect students to either implement the knowledge or encourage others in their organization to do so. Applying what they learn, and analyzing and evaluating the results, deepen a student's understanding of the concepts being taught. If students do a good job, they not only receive a good grade in class, but they might also receive a highly desired job offer or promotion.

Similarly, I organize my Management and Business & Society courses around Bloom's learning taxonomy by designing MBA and undergraduate class projects aimed at improving the environmental performance of a student's employer or the college. I choose "environmental" change, rather than some other change topic, because of the serious threat of global warming (Gore, 2006) and the increasing managerial receptivity to improving environmental practices (Hawken, Lovins & Lovins, 2000; McDonough & Braungart, 2002). The project offers students an opportunity to provide immediate "value added" and "make a difference" in their organizations as a result of enrolling in the class. Students study project management and organizational change, apply these concepts in the spirit of continuous improvement to generate new knowledge, and then critique what they experience. From this perspective, a class of twenty students can provide business professors an opportunity to improve the management of twenty organizations. This is particularly the case if the student is in a part-time MBA program, an adult taking evening undergraduate courses to move up the corporate ladder, or a traditional undergraduate working part-time evenings or weekends.

My concern about "imposing" environmental change on organizations, a potential misuse of professorial authority, has evolved over time. My Management and Business & Society courses have always had a significant amount of service-learning and experiential activities (Collins, 1996, 2006). I want my students to be more socially aware by the end of the semester. We study, debate, and experience enough controversy so that students who lean left politically have a better understanding of those who lean right politically, and vice versa. My students serve food at a soup kitchen, visit a religious organization unlike their own, share their beliefs about the purpose of life, work on consulting projects for nonprofit organizations and small businesses, and compare the ethics and business practices of their own organizations to "best practices." Refusing to participate in any of these activities, including serving food at a soup kitchen, negatively impacts their grade.

Requiring new experiences, such as taking a field trip, is a long-accepted pedagogical tool. Requiring that students make their organizations more ethical, however, is very contentious. My students assess their organization's ethical integrity, brainstorm how their organizations can expand their social responsibilities, and develop action plans for improving their organization's ethics training, but I do not require that they implement any of their suggestions. Organizations are complex institutions on their unique evolutionary paths. The terms "ethics" and "social responsibility" are accompanied by a lot of moral baggage that can alienate managers. Managers do not want to be accused of being unethical or socially irresponsible. Ethics is at the heart of organizational operations, a well-fortified area that is defensively protected by upper-level managers. Instead, I am content with planting seeds in the minds of students that I hope yield fruit.

However, I have found managers to be much more receptive to improving environmental performance. Unlike ethics, environmental management practices are usually treated on par with concepts such as GAAP practices, investment strategies, or marketing analysis. Environmental management is considered a tool or technique, rather than the heart of the matter. In addition, I do not require that a specific practice be implemented. Instead, each student determines the next appropriate step in his or her organization's continuous improvement path and then initiates the change.

Whereas asking managers to improve their organization's ethics training is likely to result in an "Are you saying that we're unethical?" response, asking managers to improve their organization's environmental performance is equivalent to asking managers to improve their organization's investment strategy—something worthy of further discussion. Importantly, environmental management discussions can open the door to ethics discussions. But this highly desired outcome is not a required outcome.

The remainder of this chapter describes four environmental change projects. The first is an MBA project where students apply an environmental framework to assess their organizational operations and initiate change. The second project is the same assignment applied to the college by undergraduate students. The third project is a residence hall "Eco Olympics" managed by undergraduate students. The fourth project requires students to research local environmentally friendly business practices, write the results up as case studies, and publish the results in the local media. I also provide suggestions on how to manage the class and student teams, and discuss how these environmental change class projects have influenced other campus activities.

THE MBA ENVIRONMENTAL CHANGE PROJECT

Edgewood College is a small, liberal arts college in Madison, Wisconsin, with approximately 1,500 undergraduate students and 1,000 graduate students. Edgewood College has a core group of faculty members committed to greening the campus, the curriculum, the local community, and the organizations our graduates will help manage in the future. Many of these activities have stemmed from individual efforts by professors associated with our Environmental Studies Department.

Shortly after my arrival at Edgewood, I was invited to join the Environmental Studies Department, a group of interdisciplinary scholars and teachers whose cross-listed courses serve as the foundation for the Environmental Studies minor. The more I interacted with this unique group of faculty, the more I integrated environmental issues into my business courses.

The "Organizational Behavior and Development" MBA course meets for nine class sessions, one night a week, for three hours, and is offered every semester. For the Spring 2005 semester, I introduced a lecture on "The Natural Step" (TNS), a framework for conceptualizing an organization's environmental impacts. The students, who tend to be middle-level managers at local companies, calculate their own ecological footprint (see Table 12.1) and then conduct an environmental analysis of their company's operations. TNS, developed by Swedish scientists during the 1980s and 1990s, is a four-step analytical process that provides a common philosophy, language and approach for improving an organization's relationship with the natural environment (Nattrass & Altomare, 1999). In January 2006, the city of Madison adopted TNS as an analytical framework for city decision-makers, creating a conceptual bridge between the college, city government, and the organizations employing my students.

The students focus on the first three of the four-step TNS analysis:

- Step 1: *Reduce wasteful dependence on fossil fuels, underground metals, and minerals.* We are removing too many substances from the Earth's

TABLE 12.1
Calculating Your Ecological Footprint

How many people are in your household? _____

Car energy use:

  Vehicle 1:

    _____ Miles driven per month/year (circle one)

    _____ Miles per gallon for vehicle *or* is it: small/medium/large-truck (circle one)

  Vehicle 2:

    _____ Miles driven per month/year (circle one)

    _____ Miles per gallon for vehicle *or* is it: small/medium/large-truck (circle one)

Air travel:

  _____ Miles traveled by airplane per month/year (circle one)

Electricity use:

  _____ Kwh per month/year (circle one)

Home heating:

  Natural gas: _____ Therms per year

  Or oil: _____ Gallons per year

  Or propane: _____ Gallons per Year

Submit information into ecofootprint calculator at: www.nativeenergy.com/safeclimate
_calculator.htm.

crust. Substitute minerals that are abundant in nature for scarce minerals, and use all mined materials efficiently.

- Step 2: *Reduce wasteful dependence on chemicals and unnatural substances.* We are producing too many synthetic compounds that are difficult for nature to breakdown. Substitute natural substances that are abundant, or chemical compounds that breakdown easily in nature, for synthetic compounds, and use all compounds produced by society efficiently.

- Step 3: *Reduce encroachment on nature (land, water and wildlife).* We are increasingly interrupting the natural flow of ecosystems. Draw on resources from only well managed eco-systems, use them efficiently and minimize the manipulation of nature.

- Step 4: *Meet human needs fairly and efficiently.* Human needs are not being met on a worldwide basis. Use all our resources efficiently, fairly and responsibly so that the needs of all stakeholders—customers, staff, neighbors, people in other parts of the world, and people who are not yet born—stand the best chance of being met.

The first three TNS steps provides the basis for their environmental change project and accompanying paper submitted at the end of the semester (see Table 12.2). The fourth step does not lend itself well for student analysis because it is more of a socio-political statement than an environmental management practice. Based on their TNS analysis, students

TABLE 12.2
Making a Difference Environmental Change Report

1. *Cover page:* Creative title, name of organization, authors, date, class name, professor's name.
2. *Table of contents:* List major subheadings and page numbers in report
3. *Executive summary:* Summarize all the key information contained in this report that your boss (or senior manager) should know all on one page; be clear and inclusive, and don't be preachy. This *is not* an introduction to the paper. It may be the only page a busy executive reads so it must contain all the relevant findings regarding the environmental audit, your change recommendation, obstacles to implementation, and the outcome of your efforts. [1 page—and do not exceed 1 page]
4. *The Natural Step Environmental Audit:* Evaluate your organization's environmental performance using the first three Natural Step objectives: a) reduce wasteful dependence on fossil fuels, underground metals, and minerals, b) reduce wasteful dependence on chemicals and unnatural substances, and c) reduce encroachment on nature, particularly regarding energy use, water use, air, material resources, food, land, transportation, and building dynamics. Complete the chart below and then, in paragraph form, discuss your satisfaction or dissatisfaction with each step. If possible, collect relevant data. [2 pages]

	Environmental strengths	Potential environmental improvement areas
Fossil fuel and mineral use analysis		
Chemical and unnatural substance analysis		
Encroachment on nature analysis (land, water, wildlife)		

5. *Screening table:* Develop a screening table for three strategies that address an important potential environmental improvement area. Evaluate the strategies using the following three categories: cost, effectiveness, can accomplish this semester. Use a 1–5 scale with "5" representing the best value in each category: low cost, high effectiveness, high likelihood of accomplishing this semester.

   Use the screening table analysis to pick a "low-hanging fruit" solution (something relatively easy to change), and explain your choice in paragraph format.

   To increase likelihood of success, you should be able to empirically demonstrate that your strategic solution will either reduce costs (i.e., decrease amount of payments for landfill disposal), increase revenue (i.e., attract new business), or increase employee productivity (i.e., improve morale).

6. *Lewin Force-Field Analysis:* Develop a force-field organizational change chart for your change recommendation, similar to the example below. List the forces against change first, and then explain how to overcome that particular change obstacle, including data if needed. Discuss the prioritization of the obstacles; which obstacle is the most problematic and why? [1–2 pages]

Current state (environmental problem):	Future state (environmental goal):
(2) force to overcome the change obstacle ➡	➡ (1) Forces against change

7. *Action plan:* Given your recommended solution and anticipated obstacles, develop an "action plan" for accomplishing the solution and overcoming the obstacles. More succinctly clarify: a) The *problem* you are correcting, b) the *goal,* c) the *strategy* you will pursue, and d) how you will *measure* success. Refer to your strategic solution as a "pilot project" and keep the parameters reasonable.

   To increase likelihood of success, you should be able to empirically demonstrate that your solution will either reduce costs (i.e., decrease amount of payments for landfill disposal), increase revenue (i.e., attract new business), or increase employee productivity (i.e., improve morale).

8. *Meeting with change agent:* Prior to change agent meeting, obtain relevant cost or survey data that supports the change you will be recommending. Assume that the change agent is interested in the change (particularly its cost savings or revenue generation). Begin the meeting by praising the change agent and/or organization's environmental accomplishments and educate the change agent about the cost savings, revenue generation, or employee morale impacts. The change agent should become your ally, and vice-versa. Exhibit the attitude that you want to make the change agent look good by implementing your recommended change. This is not about you, it is about the change agent and your company.

   Discuss the dynamics of your meeting with the organizational change agent responsible for the area involving your change recommendation. Explain [1–2 pages]:

   (a) What is the change agent's power base?
   (b) Is change agent a blue, green, brown or red personality and how did this impact the communication style you used?
   (c) What social tactics did you use to influence the change agent?
   (d) How did you try to motivate the change agent—apply MBO, equity theory, etc.?
   (e) How did you communicate with the change agent—how did you encode and transmit the message?
   (f) The context of your meeting with the change agent—where did you meet, what was on the agenda, how did the meeting go?
   (g) What was the change agent's response to the data you provided?

9. *Outcome:* What was the result of the meeting? Did the change take place? How much success did you have? What would you do differently to achieve greater success? [1–2 pages]

10. *Change experience reflection:* Summary of primary lessons learned as a result of doing this project, including lessons learned about yourself. [1 page]

conduct an environmental audit that highlights organizational strengths and weaknesses. They then provide three strategies for addressing a particular environmental improvement area and evaluate each of the recommended strategies in terms of cost, effectiveness, and length of time it would take to implement the change. The ideal choice, referred to as a "low-hanging fruit," is one that has low costs, high effectiveness, and high likelihood of being accomplished during the semester.

After the change recommendation is selected, students must gather empirical evidence demonstrating how the strategic solution will either reduce costs, increase revenue, or increase productivity, arguments managers typically find more persuasive than "do the right thing." Next, students conduct a Lewin force-field analysis that lists all the probable obstacles and strategies for overcoming each obstacle (Brager & Holloway, 1992). All this information serves as the basis for an action plan, which is presented to the organization's change agent for approval, modification, or rejection.

If the change agent rejects the student's recommendation, the student must negotiate alternative strategic recommendations for improving the organization's environmental performance. The change agent may have some other environmental change item on his/her "to do" list that the student can champion. After initiating the environmental change process and, hopefully, implementing the change, students analyze their environmental change experience in terms of key concepts discussed in class, such as power bases, communication styles, social tactics, motivation techniques, and meeting context.

Below is a list of some of the environmental changes MBA students implemented in their organizations:

- Recycling and reducing the use of computer paper
- Providing healthier vending machine food options
- Installing energy efficient lighting and motion sensors
- Eliminating hazardous chemical use in a research lab
- Conserving energy by turning off computers at the end of the day
- Donating excess hospital supplies to developing nations
- Developing a ride share program

UNDERGRADUATES APPLYING "TNS" TO EDGEWOOD COLLEGE

I began teaching at Edgewood College during the Fall of 2002, after having taught at two other universities the previous twelve years. Service learning, where students apply textbook knowledge in the local community and then reflect on their experience, has always played an important role in my courses (Collins, 1996, 2006). For my Edgewood College undergraduate "Social Responsibility in Business" class, offered every semester, I formed a partnership with the Boys & Girls Club of Dane County. Student teams have created a program guide for potential members, a hiring manual for administrators, a training manual for new employees, a recycling curriculum for members, and catalogued donated books for their library, among other accomplishments.

I was very pleased with the service-learning projects, yet wanted to take advantage of a unique opportunity to integrate business student learning with their peers in the natural sciences. I shifted our project focus inward during the Spring 2005 semester and designed several campus-based environmental projects. My business students read campus ecological research reports written by natural science students, studied the results, considered the management implications, and then implemented, in partnership with college administrators, some of the organizational changes suggested by the natural science majors.

Their accomplishments that semester included:

- Implementing a recycling program for a residence hall
- Decreasing electricity use in a residence hall
- Reducing the amount of paper printed by students in the computer labs
- Selling reusable mugs in the cafeteria and advertising discounts available for using mugs instead of Styrofoam coffee cups
- Relocating smoking receptacles further from the entrance of buildings

The following semester, Fall 2005, the business students directly applied TNS analysis to college operations. Each student chose a low-hanging fruit and they formed teams based on common concerns. Their final projects included:

- Implementing a more efficient classroom wastebasket recycling program
- Developing a database of local food sources for the cafeteria
- Marketing the cafeteria's reusable mug policy
- Creating a website for the Environmental Studies program
- Reducing electricity use in a residence hall
- Reduced heat use in a classroom building

ECO-OLYMPICS

In November 2005, I represented Edgewood College at a sustainable campuses conference sponsored by the Environmental Protection Agency. One of the sessions included a presentation about Duke University's Eco-Olympics, where campus residence halls compete against each other to reduce energy, waste, and water consumption (www.duke.edu/web/ESC/2005-10-31Eco-olympics.html). Students earn points for conservation and by attending events pertaining to environmental education and impact reduction. The residence hall with the highest score at the end of the Eco-Olympics earns a prize, such as a Ben & Jerry's ice cream party. This seemed a logical next step in the evolution of my environmental service-learning project.

During the Spring 2006 semester, the 24 students enrolled in the undergraduate "Social Responsibility in Business" course managed an Eco-Olympics among the five residence halls on the Edgewood College campus. I integrated the project goals into the course learning objectives by establishing direct links with knowledge content and skill development. By managing the Eco-Olympics students would:

1. Learn how to reduce the amount of heat, water and electricity consumed within a building.
2. Learn how to increase awareness of environmental impacts among members of an organization.
3. Learn how to motivate others to change their behaviors.
4. Develop project management skills.
5. Develop team management skills.

We formed seven teams in class, each with three or four students. Five of the teams were assigned to our five residence halls, one team per building. These teams met with residence hall directors and assistants to develop a plan that would generate the highest level of student resident participation. The teams performed an environmental audit of the residence hall, developed suggestions for changing resident energy consumption behaviors, and encouraged resident hall students to participate in other environmental activities associated with the Eco-Olympics.

The remaining two teams performed support activities. One team was responsible for organizing a campus talk given by the CEO of an environmentally friendly business, sponsoring an environmental movie shown in the student center, and conducting a fair trade coffee taste test. The student cafeteria sold regular coffee but not fair trade coffee, which provides higher income to the coffee bean growers (Talbot, 2004), because the cafeteria manager believed that fair trade coffee did not taste as well as regular coffee. Most of the taste test participants preferred the unmarked fair trade coffee. Fair trade coffee became available in the cafeteria during the Fall 2006 semester and a student team advertised its virtues over regular coffee.

The seventh team was responsible for obtaining donations from local businesses for prizes, publicizing the Eco-Olympics on campus, and managing an Environmental Ethics Bowl where residence hall teams compete against each other in analyzing environmental case studies.

The Environmental Ethics Bowl is a derivation of the national Ethics Bowl, initiated by Professor Robert Ladenson of the Illinois Institute of Technology in 1993, and held in conjunction with the Association for Practical and Professional Ethics' annual February meeting (Borrego, 2004; Ladenson, 2001). Student teams analyze and debate an ethical issue and are then evaluated by a panel of judges based on their intelligibility, depth, focus, and judgment. We obtained six one-page environmental cases used in previous Ethics Bowls and distributed them to teams representing each residence hall. The largest residence hall sponsored two teams so that there would be an even number of teams pairing off against each other. Each team was given two cases, one to present and one to rebut. The format for the Environmental Ethics Bowl, a two-hour event for six residence hall teams, appears in Table 12.3.

The movie, talk, fair trade coffee taste test and Environmental Ethics Bowl raised environmental awareness on campus. But the primary purpose of the Eco-Olympics was to change the energy consumption behaviors of students living in the college's five residence halls.

TABLE 12.3
Environmental Ethics Bowl Contest Format

1. The Environmental Ethics Bowl facilitator introduces the two teams and the judges, reads the case to the audience, and then poses a question about the key ethical issue in the case to Team A—3 minutes
2. Team A answers the case question—4 minutes
3. Team B meets to develop a rebuttal to Team A's arguments—1 minute
4. Team B provides a rebuttal—2 minutes
5. Team A meets to develop a response to Team B's rebuttal—1 minute
6. Team A responds to the rebuttal—3 minutes
7. The judges each ask Team A questions about what's already been stated or other ethical issues associated with the case—3 minutes
8. Judges evaluate the performance of Team A and Team B using the scorecard criteria—3 minutes
9. The Environmental Ethics Bowl facilitator reads the second case to the audience, and then poses a question about the key ethical issue in the case to Team B—3 minutes
10. Team B answers the case question—4 minutes
11. Team A meets to develop a rebuttal to Team B's arguments—1 minute
12. Team A provides a rebuttal—2 minutes
13. Team B meets to develop a response to Team A's rebuttal—1 minute
14. Team B responds to the rebuttal—3 minutes
15. The judges each ask Team B questions about what's already been stated or other ethical issues associated with the case—3 minutes
16. Judges evaluate the performance of Team B and Team A using the scorecard criteria, the team with the most points is announced the winner—3 minutes

---

For each residence hall, I obtained baseline calculations for heat, water, and electricity consumption for the month prior to the Eco-Olympics. I calculated a baseline water measure by reading the water meter in each residence hall on January 15 and February 15. I calculated heat and electricity consumption based on local utility bills for the same 30-day time period.

On February 23, resident hall students were formally challenged to reduce these monthly baseline calculations prior to April 20, Earth Day. Each of the five Eco-Olympics teams organized a campaign to educate students in their assigned residence hall about energy consumption and conservation recommendations. They posted flyers, held informational meetings in the resident hall, and motivated residents to participate in the environmental activities.

On April 20, I read the water meters to determine how much water was consumed during the two month Eco-Olympics and obtained the utility bills for each residence hall to determine electricity and heat consumption. The residence hall that achieved the greatest percentage decrease in each category won a prize and was awarded a plaque. Residence halls also won prizes and plaques for having the greatest percentage of residents participating in the other Eco-Olympic events (attending the environmental movie, attending the environmental talk, and participating in the fair trade coffee taste test) and for winning the Environmental Ethics Bowl. The residence hall that won the most Eco-Olympic events was crowned the grand prize champion and awarded a Ben & Jerry's ice cream social.

During the two-month Eco-Olympics, the resident halls, on average, reduced:

- Water consumption by 54%, with the winning residence hall reducing water consumption by 57% (280 gallons per resident)
- Electricity consumption by 4.2%, with the winning residence hall reducing electricity consumption by 10.4% (40 kwh per resident)
- Heat consumption by 17.0%, with the winning residence hall reducing heat consumption by 22.4% (6 therms per resident)

How do these impressive energy consumption reductions compare to the same three-month period the year prior to the Eco-Olympics? I compared the 2006 contest energy calculations with the same four month time period in 2005, to create a control group comparison. For the parallel time period in 2005, electricity consumption declined on average by 5.5% (compared to 4.2% for 2006) and heat consumption declined on average by 19.1% (compared to 17.0% for 2006). Water consumption for the parallel 2005 time period cannot be determined because water meters are not read on a monthly basis. Energy reductions were less, not greater, during the Eco-Olympics year. This disappointing finding requires additional research. Energy consumption reductions in 2005 could have been greater than the

2006 Eco-Olympics year because of weather patterns, the length of winter break, when Spring break occurs, or a host of other factors.

There were several other complications related to obtaining reliable comparative measures for the contest—two residence halls shared the same water meter, one residence hall's heat consumption was unavailable, one residence hall has classrooms, and one residence hall has a cafeteria.

One thing is very clear. Residence hall students were educated by their peers about environmental issues and energy conservation techniques, an essential learning objective. The greatest increased awareness about environmental issues, however, occurred among the students enrolled in the class who taught resident hall students about environmental issues and energy conservation techniques and motivated them to change behaviors.

At the end of the Eco-Olympics, each student team submitted a "Making a Difference" project paper (Table 12.4) that included the team's original

---

TABLE 12.4
Making a Difference Eco-Olympics Project Report

1. *Cover page*: Creative title, authors, date, class name, professor's name
2. *Table of contents*: List major subheadings and page numbers in report
3. *Executive summary*: Summarize the information contained in this report. This *is not* an introduction to the paper. Instead, it should clearly and concisely summarize the details regarding who, what, when, where, and why, along with what was accomplished, and information demonstrating that the goal was achieved (or not achieved). This may be the only page an executive might read, so if key information is omitted then the executive will not know what you did or accomplished. Avoid jargon and vague generalities. [Never more than 1 page]
4. *Environmental issue*: What issue did the team address? Why? [1 paragraph]
5. *Action plan*: Describe your initial plan to accomplish your goals. Who was going to do what, when, where, and why? Then create a Lewin Force-Field Analysis organizational change chart as shown below. First, list the forces against change (given your initial plan, these are your obstacles you expected to have to deal with, the things you thought might go wrong). Then for each obstacle, describe how your group thought it might overcome the obstacle. [1–2 pages]

Current state (environmental problem): students insensitive to environmental issues		Future state (environmental goal): students become good environmental agents
(2) Force to overcome change obstacle	**(1) Forces against change**	
How will you overcome student apathy?	Students are apathetic	
How will you overcome obstacle #2? (etc.)	Anticipated obstacle #2 (etc.)	

TABLE 12.4
Making a Difference Eco-Olympics Project Report (continued)

6. *Implementation experience and results*: What was your experience implementing your plan. Who did what, when, where, and why? What unanticipated obstacles happened and what did you do about them? Tell stories about what actually happened, including items in your Task Activity Time Log (Appendix A). What results did you accomplish? Provide actual data when appropriate. [1–2 pages]

7. *Team performance reflections*: Taking a step back, what did the team do right and wrong? What would you do differently if you were to start this project all over again? [1 page]

8. *Organization and course concept reflections*: Taking a step back, what are the team's thoughts about current environmental management practices at Edgewood College? Comment on insights from your course readings on ethics and the Hawken, Lovins & Lovins book that might be relevant to your experience. What dilemmas did you encounter in trying to change institutional and human behavior? Why does it take so long for institutions and people to adopt environmentally friendly ways of being? [1–2 pages]

9. *Appendix A*: Task Activity Time Log—Dated diary documenting what each team member did on each work day using the table below. End with summary of how much time each team member put into the project.

Date	Task activity (short one sentence description stating who did what on which date; longer detailed activity explanations should appear in text under action plan or implementation experience)	Person (people) doing task	Amount of time to do task
Summary of amount of time per student:		**Student #1:**	Total amount of time
		Student #2:	Total amount of time

10. *Appendix B*: Summary of each person's primary lessons learned as a result of doing this team project, including lessons learned about yourself. [1 page per team member]

11. *Appendix C*: Any other relevant information associated with the project, such as a copy of survey or flyer. Explain why the information is relevant.

action plan for obtaining their unique goal, a Lewin force-field analysis stating initial obstacles (such as student apathy), strategies for overcoming those obstacles, implementation details, actual results, and lessons learned from the experience.

CASE STUDIES ON LOCAL ENVIRONMENTALLY
FRIENDLY BUSINESSES

Madison, Wisconsin is home to many progressive businesses engaged in socially responsible activities, including environmental management. In the Spring of 2004, I offered an elective course titled "Ethical Business Practices in Madison" with the purpose of creating a database of local socially responsible business practices. For two consecutive semesters students researched socially responsible business practices, interviewed company managers, and wrote case studies about the companies they researched. Students also researched companies that went beyond the call of duty in serving at-risk kids, and, in partnership with the Samaritan Counseling Center, we chose winners for a newly created Good Samaritan award.

For the Fall 2005 semester, I more narrowly defined social responsibility in terms of environmentally friendly business practices. Whereas I team taught the first three class renditions with the former mayor of Madison, I now elicited assistance from the Executive Director of Sustain Dane, a nonprofit organization that networks with business leaders and environmental activists who seek to transform Dane County into an environmentally sustainable community.

Sustain Dane's Executive Director was interested in showcasing several environmentally friendly businesses on his organization's website (www.sustaindane.org). We developed a list of eight companies in different industries known for being environmentally friendly. The students researched the companies, interviewed their managers and environmental activists, and composed case studies documenting each company's environmentally friendly practices.

We intended to initiate a dialogue in class where management representatives from each of the participating companies could share their "best practice." Unfortunately, only one company representative was able to attend due to a snowstorm that particular day.

As an alternative, we decided to initiate a dialogue by publicizing their ecological activities in the local media. *Madison Magazine*, an influential local monthly magazine, agreed to publish an article describing the environmentally friendly practices at three companies the students researched (Collins & Eannelli, 2006). We chose companies that addressed different aspects of environmental management—training, processes, and mission. Madison Cutting Die (MCD) trains its managers in The Natural Step framework, which is then applied to company operations. Best Cleaners is the first drycleaner in Wisconsin to exclusively use a technology that results in zero hazardous waste. Cascade Asset Management collects and resells computer and electronics parts rather than dumping them in landfills. We plan on inviting these environmental business leaders to campus for further dialogue and networking.

MANAGING THE CLASS AND STUDENT TEAMS

It is essential that the class projects be tightly linked to the curriculum. The key to service learning is the linkage between the "service" and the "learning." The "Social Responsibility in Business" class meets for 75 minutes, twice a week, for 15 weeks, a total of 30 class sessions. Approximately 40 percent of the semester is related to the service-learning project. In preparation for the project, I teach four class sessions on environmental problems and public policy solutions, innovative environmental management techniques, TNS analysis, and project management.

Prior to the project management class session, I distribute a list of service-learning project options and each student ranks order his or her top three choices. I create the 3 or 4 member teams informed by student preferences—maximizing the number the students who get to work on their highest preference—and diversity factors (gender, race, major, clique).

During the project management class session, in addition to creating a time-management plan for completing the project assignment, student teams discuss their responses to a "Team Role Survey" (see Table 12.5), which clarifies the skills and duties needed for different roles a student can fulfill on a team, and review a "Peer Evaluation Form" (see Table 12.6) that they have to submit at the completion of the project to inform my grading process (Marcic, Seltzer & Vaill, 2001). I assign the project paper a grade and all team members receive that grade unless the peer evaluation forms suggest that one member should earn a higher grade for exemplary performance, or a lower grade for inadequate performance.

Students also earn project points based on their performance during team meetings (see Table 12.7). They earn points for being prepared for the meeting, attending the meeting, and being a constructive participant during the meeting. At the end of each team meeting, those in attendance summarize what the team accomplished during the meeting, describe what each member must do in preparation for the next team meeting, and provide an agenda for the next team meeting. Students complete the team meeting form as a group, sign it, and submit it to me at the conclusion of the meeting.

The teams typically meet once a week during a regularly scheduled class session for seven or eight consecutive weeks. Many Edgewood College undergraduate students take 18 credits a semester and work 30 hours a week at a part-time job. It is nearly impossible for them to meet outside the regularly scheduled class time. We do not meet as a class during these working sessions, although I am always available in my office for consultation. The teams can meet anywhere they want to make progress on their projects—in the classroom, computer lab, library, an administrator's office,

TABLE 12.5
Team Role Survey

Your name: _____

Circle the answer that most closely resembles your attitude for each of the following 5 statements using the following 1–5 Scale. The more honest you are the more helpful the information you will receive.

    1 = Very low; 2 = Somewhat low; 3 = Neutral; 4 = Somewhat high; 5 = Very High

How interested are you in . . .

1. being a team leader (whose role is to get team members involved in activities and keep the team on track)?	1	2	3	4	5
2. completing forms and other records for the team?	1	2	3	4	5
3. taking the role of encouraging others in your team to participate?	1	2	3	4	5
4. taking the role of checking other members' understanding of the problem the team is solving?	1	2	3	4	5

Role	Skills/duties	Examples of comments
1. Leader	• Direct team's activities to ensure all parts of assignment are completed on time • Direct team members to stay on task and fulfill roles • Encourage team dialogue about its process	• "We're getting off topic and we only have 10 minutes left!" • "We still need to come up with a plan." • "Team member B, are you happy with the way we are all participating?"
2. Recorder	• Complete all team materials • Provide copies of information for absent team member	• "Our performance to date is as follows . . ." • "Does everyone agree with what I wrote down?"
3. Encourager of participation	• Encourage all team members to participate in discussions • Make sure no team member dominates discussions • Ask for team opinions	• "Team member C, what is your opinion on this?" • "Everyone tell me your opinion and I'll write it on the board for us to discuss."
4. Checker of understanding	• Develop method to check everyone's understanding before team meeting ends • Make sure each member can verbalize the reasoning behind the team's decisions	• "Team member A, please repeat what our solution is." • "Team member C, please summarize why we decided to pursue the first option."

etc. The teams can also meet at a time other than the scheduled class session time, if that is what is needed to accomplish their goal.

    The "Team Meeting Assessment" form provides essential feedback about the team's project management progress. I intervene when the submitted form suggests that a particular team member is performing inadequately, the reported work accomplished or work to be accomplished appears misdirected or inadequate, or the team requests my intervention. I meet with each team for 10 minutes during their fourth group meeting to review their progress and future plans.

TABLE 12.6
Peer Evaluation Form

Your name: _____

Please evaluate yourself and each group member in a fair and accurate manner. Your ratings will be kept *anonymous*. Take your time and provide a useful and complete evaluation.

1. *Point allocation*—below, rate yourself and your team members using a zero to four point scale (4 = superior, 3 = adequate, 2 = average, 1 = poor, and 0 = no contribution).

Team member names:	You	Person #1	Person #2	Person #3
Organizational ability				
Cooperativeness				
Originality or creativity of ideas contributed				
Functional contribution—analysis and recommendations				
Dependability				
Quantity of work contributed				
Quality of work contributed				
Total points				

2. *Percent allocation*—below, rate yourself and your team members using the following 80% to 120% scale:

120%: This team member performed a lot more than everyone else
100%: This team member performed the same as everyone else
80% (or less): This team member performed a lot less than everyone else

Team member names (including yourself)	120%, 100% or 80% using scale above
_____	_____
_____	_____
_____	_____
_____	_____

Please provide comments on back explaining your evaluation

TABLE 12.7
Team Meeting Assessment

The team project is worth 200 points—80 points for your performance during team meetings and 120 points for the quality of the final product.

You must meet as a team an equivalent of 8 class sessions to work on your team project. Each working session is worth 10 points. After each team meeting please Xerox this page, insert the points representing each team member's effort for the work session, have each person in attendance sign the sheet, and then give it to me at my office or slide it under my door. Please be honest in your assessments.

Date:

Team members	Name	Name	Name	Name
1. Work session preparation: Fulfilled expected work tasks due—Point scale: 0 (none), 1 (little), 2 (half), 3 (a lot), or 4 (all)				
2. Work session attendance—Point scale: 0 (missed it), 1 (some); 2 (most), 3 (attended all of it)				
3. Was a constructive participant during work session—Point scale: 0 (no), 1 (a little), 2 (most of the time), 3 (all the time)				
Total points earned by each team member				

What did team members do during the 75 minutes set aside to work on the project?

What will team members do before the next team meeting?

What will team members do during the next 75 minutes set aside to work on the project?

OTHER CAMPUS INITIATIVES

The class projects described in this chapter have contributed to fostering a culture in the Business School and campus-wide that embraces environmental innovations. We have received recognition both on campus and in the local community for these efforts. During the Summer of 2005, I became chairperson of a "Green Campus Task Force" whose purpose is to more directly engage students, faculty and staff in developing an environmentally sustainable living and learning community on campus. First year accomplishments include the creation of an Environmental Indicator Report that will serve as an annual benchmark. The criteria—hazardous waste and waste minimization, solid waste materials and recycling, energy use, and water use—are those recommended by the Campus Consortium for Environmental Excellence (www.c2e2.org), which is developing a national database.

In 2006, Edgewood College received Green Tier certification from Wisconsin's Department of Natural Resources (DNR). Green Tier is a new state-wide innovative environmental initiative that recognizes and rewards superior environmental performance (www.dnr.state.wi.us/org/caer/cea/environmental). Green Tier companies must develop a functionally equivalent Environmental Management System (EMS) in accordance to ISO 14001 that includes an environmental policy, environmental planning, environmental implementation and operations, environmental measurement and corrective action, and management review for continuous improvement. Edgewood College is the first college or university in Wisconsin to obtain Green Tier status.

As these events unfold, differentiating ourselves as an environmental leader in Madison and southern Wisconsin took on greater strategic importance in the college's identity. Administrators became even more committed to LEED (Leadership in Energy and Environmental Design) certification for a new residence hall under construction (www.usgbc.org). We obtained Kresge Foundation and Focus on Energy grants to offset some of the planning and documentation costs associated with the LEED certification process. The building will have solar panels to heat water and rain gardens for irrigation, and all construction resources will come from within a 500 mile radius to benefit local businesses. High-level administrative discussions about LEED certification inspired a meeting with executives of the local energy utility, Madison Gas & Electric, to explore win-win partnership opportunities between the two organizations.

Mohandas Gandhi eloquently noted that "You should be the change you want to see in the world." Only then does the messenger gain legitimacy. By establishing ourselves as an environmental leader, Edgewood College has greater legitimacy in helping local businesses adopt more sustainable environmental practices.

Rather than just telling our students how businesses have to become more environmentally friendly, Business Ethics & Society professors are in a unique position to implement environmental change within local businesses through our courses. The TNS environmental change audits, Eco-Olympics, and case studies on environmentally friendly business practices are just a few of many possibilities in this evolving process.

REFERENCES

Anderson, L. W., & Krathwohl, D. R. (Eds.). (2001). *A taxonomy for learning, teaching, and assessing: A revision of Bloom's taxonomy of educational objectives.* New York: Longman.

Borrego, A. M. (2004, March 5). Ethics bowls exercise students' moral muscles. *Chronicle of Higher Education, 50,* A31.

Brager, G., & Holloway, S. (1992). Assessing prospects for organizational change: The uses of force field analysis, *Administration in Social Work, 16,* 15–28.

Collins, D. (1996). Serving the homeless and low-income communities through business & society/business ethics class projects: The University of Wisconsin-Madison plan, *Journal of Business Ethics, 15,* 67–85.

Collins, D. (2006). Taking business ethics seriously: Best practices in teaching and integrating business ethics within a business program. In R. DeFillippi & C. Wankel (Eds.), *New visions of graduate management education.* (pp. 319–349). Greenwich, CT: Information Age Publishing.

Collins, D., & Eannelli, K. (2006, July). Get more green by going green. *Madison Magazine,* 89–96.

Gore, A. (2006). *An inconvenient truth.* New York: Rodale Books.

Hawken, P., Lovins, A., & Lovins, L.H. (2000). *Natural capitalism: Creating the next industrial revolution.* New York: Back Bay Books.

Ladenson, R. F. (2001). The educational significance of the ethics bowl. *Teaching Ethics, 1,* 63–78.

Marcic, D., Seltzer, J., & Vaill, P. (2001). *Organizational behavior: Experiences and cases, Sixth Edition.* Cincinnati, Ohio: South-Western College Publishing.

McDonough, W., & Braungart, M. (2002). *Cradle to cradle: Remaking the way we make things.* New York: North Point Press.

Nattrass, B., & Altomare, M. (1999). *The natural step for business: Wealth, ecology and the evolutionary corporation.* British Columbia, Canada: New Society Publishers.

Talbot, J. M. (2004). *Grounds for agreement: The political economy of the coffee commodity chain.* Lanham, Maryland: Rowman and Littlefield.

CHAPTER 13

EDUCATING MANAGERS FOR GLOBAL BUSINESS CITIZENSHIP

Donna J. Wood
University of Northern Iowa

Jeanne M. Logsdon
University of New Mexico

ABSTRACT

The alphabet soup of social responsibility and ethics is already daunting—B&S, BE, CSR, CSP, CC[1]—and yet we believe that a new concept is needed—global business citizenship (GBC). Many of our publications over the last few years have focused on developing the theoretical, historical, conceptual, and empirical underpinnings for GBC, and the culmination (at this writing) is the recent book we coauthored with colleagues Patsy G. Lewellyn and Kim Davenport: *Global Business Citizenship: A Transformative Framework for Ethics and Sustainable Capitalism.*

In this chapter, which is informed by our recent book, we will first briefly overview the problems with other conceptualizations of ethics and social responsibility. We will then review the theory and conceptual development of GBC's operating model. Next we illustrate how to teach GBC through readily

Advancing Business Ethics Education, pages 265–283
Copyright © 2008 by Information Age Publishing

available cases and related web research, and in this context, we'll discuss some of the challenges that arise when using a global perspective to teach business ethics and social responsibility.

AN INTRODUCTION TO GLOBAL BUSINESS CITIZENSHIP

One of the core unresolved issues in the development of the corporate social responsibility (CSR) concept is that of *place* as a domain that in part defines what corporate responsibilities are, and to whom they are owed. When the concept first became popular in the 1960s in the United States, it was easy enough to define CSR in terms of a business firm's obligations to *society*. These obligations were typically assumed to involve the appropriate use of business's inordinate economic, social, and political power to help solve pressing social problems such as institutional racism, poverty, and urban decay.

This way of defining CSR became obsolete with the onset of rapid globalization. International trade had been part of the world commercial picture for millennia, but it was not until the combination of instantaneous satellite and cable communications, internet data capacity, and the crumbling of the former Soviet Union and its nexus of nations, that globalization really took off.

Globalization is perhaps the most challenging development of modern times, and it has certainly presented an enormous challenge to proponents of CSR. Globalization has pushed the stark economic contrasts of poor and rich nations to center stage. It has weakened governments without creating a replacement institution to look out for the public good, and it has exposed the corruption and militarism of many developing-nation governments. It has revealed both the astonishing successes and the devastating excesses of capitalist business. And it has laid bare the startling cultural differences in custom and belief that characterize the nations and peoples of the world.

Most of the nay-sayers in the globalization discourse are frightened or furious about the current visible abuses of human beings and the earth itself in the service of financial capital. They believe that globalization leads inevitably to giant corporations that assume the powers of government and then use those powers to further their own ends rather than the public good. Given all that we have learned about global business in the last 25 years or so, it is not surprising that this view is so prevalent.

Our view, though, is different; and it is not a view that unduly praises the corporation and its capitalist environment. We believe that globalization can yield the very best that capitalism has to offer—rapid innovation, technological progress, rising quality of life, more choices for all, equal opportunity to share in society's benefits, and equal protection from its harms. And most importantly, following decades of study of the political, legal, social, and ethical environments of business, we are convinced that *it will be businesses themselves that lead the way to a new negotiated order, a widely accepted set of standards on human rights, labor conditions, the environment, corruption, and economic development.*

We are not arguing that this *should* happen; we are arguing that it *will* happen. Indeed, the evidence is all around us that it *is* happening.

However, the important practices that are emerging globally require a powerful new conceptualization of management and organizational responsibilities. The two leading contenders, corporate social responsibility and corporate citizenship, have already been tainted by narrow usage and ideological overtones. We therefore offer the concept and theory of global business citizenship (GBC) to this end. Wood, Logsdon, Lewellyn, and Davenport (2006) define a global business citizen as follows: "*A global business citizen is a business enterprise (and its managers) that responsibly exercises its rights and implements its duties to individuals, stakeholders, and societies within and across national and cultural borders*" (p. 4).

THE GLOBAL BUSINESS CITIZENSHIP PROCESS

Table 13.1 shows the conceptual origins of the four steps in the GBC process, derived from the theoretical argument developed in Wood and Logsdon (2002), Logsdon and Wood (2002), and numerous subsequent publications.

TABLE 13.1
Developing the GBC Steps from Strategy and Moral Certainty

Degree of ethical certainty	Multi-domestic approach to strategy	Globally integrated approach to strategy
High: principles—a limited number of basic universal rules.	(Ethical relativism)	**Step 1:** code of conduct
Moderate: consistent norms—acceptable local variations.	**Step 2:** local implementation	(Ethical imperialism)
Low: incompatible norms—norms that are incompletely governed or ungoverned by, or appear to be in conflict with, principles.	**Step 3:** problem analysis and experimentation	**Step 4:** systematic and systemic learning

Source: Adapted from Logsdon & Wood, 2002.

A Hybrid Approach to Ethical Strategy

These four steps of the GBC process emerge from a theoretical analysis described in more depth elsewhere.[2] Briefly, the GBC process involves taking a hybrid approach to strategy that blends the multi-domestic ("when in Rome") and globally integrated ("everywhere the same") approaches, because companies face varying degrees of ethical certainty across times and places. "Ethical certainty" is a concept that addresses the degree to which company values and principles match up with behaviors, practices, and customs in a particular locale or across sites.

The GBC process, as shown in Table 13.1, takes into account the fact that some conditions of ethical certainty require a company to take an absolute and uniform policy, whereas other situations demand responsiveness and adaptability. For example, it is illogical to take a multi-domestic approach under conditions of high ethical certainty. This results in ethical relativism, when a company adopts different ethical principles for different cultures, providing the company with no firm moral basis. And, taking a headquarters approach by imposing a single way of doing things on all cultures even when local cultural variations do not conflict with principles is equally illogical and disrespectful as well. Neither strict relativism nor imperialism has a place in global business citizenship.[3]

We need to point out that the model shown in Table 13.1 is not meant to suggest, for example, that a code of conduct is needed only in conditions of high ethical certainty, or that systematic and systemic learning is valuable only in conditions of low ethical certainty. The four GBC steps that emerge represent the *ideal* GBC process under varying conditions of ethical certainty. Because the company *needs* high ethical certainty in terms of its enacted ethical principles and values, it makes sense to take a globally integrated approach to formulating a code of conduct. Because the company *needs* to implement the code respectfully in all relevant cultures, it makes sense to take a multi-domestic approach to local implementation, assessing whether seemingly different local practices actually conform to or violate the principles. For the same reason, when the company encounters conflicts, gaps, or uncertainties in ethical principles and behaviors, it *needs* to undertake deeper analysis to steer a respectful and effective ethical course. And finally, because there are so many variations in and interpretations of human practice, the company *needs* to systematize what it learns about ethics implementation so that the overall turbulence of global ethics is reduced to manageable proportions. The steps shown in the cells of Table 13.1, then, represent a coordinated approach, a logical sequence of steps that companies need to be willing to take in order to deal with the array of ethical certainties (or uncertainties) that they will face.

In brief, global business citizenship is a set of policies and practices that allow a business organization to identify principles of ethical management and apply them concretely and respectfully. The GBC process requires:

1. A set of *values and universal ethical principles* embedded in the corporate code of conduct and policies;

2. *Implementation* of these values and principles throughout the company's operations, with reasonable local variations that do not conflict with principles;

3. *Analysis and experimentation* to deal with problems of fit, conflicts, contradictions, and normative voids; and

4. *Systematic processes* to organize and communicate the results of implementation and experiments to facilitate learning within the organization and outside it.

Elaborating on the Four Steps of Global Business Citizenship

Each step of the GBC process offers opportunities for companies to learn how to implement a global ethics approach, and each offers pitfalls as well. A fuller explanation of each step follows.

Step 1—Code of Conduct. As a first step toward global business citizenship, the company accepts a small set of basic universal principles that govern its conduct wherever it operates. The Global Compact's Ten Principles, for example, represent widely accepted and justifiable norms of business conduct. Principles, then, are used to inform the company's code of conduct, which serves as the company's guidance system. GBC guidance systems require alignment between "talk" and "walk."

Codes provide specific guidance for situations that organizational members will typically encounter. A useful code of conduct will cover normal business functions and operations (e.g., design, marketing, distribution, employee practices) and will also deal with situations that are specific to the firm or its industry (e.g., hazardous wastes in oil refining). The code and its underlying principles will be reflected in the firm's manuals of standard operating procedures or organizational routines as well, so that all employees—not just top management—can be clear and consistent about the organization's duties to stakeholders.[4]

Step 2—Local Implementation. Managers are expected to implement the company's code of conduct in all the various locations where the company does business. This is not always difficult. In many cases, there will be few or no conflicts or gaps between the code's guidelines and local customs, cultural norms, or national standards because the company's values, code of conduct, and corporate policies have been well designed. Thus, local variations in practice can be accepted.

However, managers must be conscientious in making these judgments. They must be aware of the problems that may arise by arbitrarily applying the company code in cases where customs or local standards are in conflict with it. Or, there may be unintended consequences from implementing the code that will create problems for stakeholders or ethical dilemmas for the company that were simply not addressed in the code itself. Engaging in stakeholder dialogue and being open to feedback about code implementation are important sources of information to responsible managers about whether the company's actions are effective and acceptable. If problems surface, managers should be prepared to move to Step 3.

Step 3—Problem Analysis and Experimentation. Cases in which company codes of conduct cannot easily be applied require more attention. These cases may include situations where unintended negative consequences become apparent, or where local custom diverges substantially from the code, or where local practice is based on values or norms that conflict with the company's core ethical principles. In such cases, local managers need to analyze how these differences can be resolved in ways that do not violate basic principles.

It may be that managers can experiment to find a reasonable way to accommodate local customs and still be consistent with company standards. In other cases, the manager may resolve conflict by supporting the company's code and will need to communicate clearly and respectfully to local stakeholders and others the reasons why this decision has been made. Or, the local manager may need to communicate to headquarters about why a company policy should not be applied and some alternative action is better in this case. Understanding the ethical principles at stake is crucial in articulating these reasons, as is having a solid relationship with key stakeholders.

Step 4—Systematic and Systemic Learning. This is the essential last step in GBC implementation. Initial local implementation (Step 2) as well as problem analysis and experimentation (Step 3) will best serve the human enterprise and the organization's purposes when the company institutes feedback loops and learns systematically from its experiences. *Systematic* learning involves grasping the structural and normative similarities and differences among the various situations the company encounters in its many locations, extracting the essence of these experiences, and providing models or exemplars of what works and what doesn't work in terms of adapting and experimenting with implementation of principles. It also involves altering the guidelines of the code itself when it becomes apparent that certain aspects of the code cannot reasonably be implemented.

Finally, a GBC company will also engage in *systemic* learning, sharing its experiences with other companies so that mistakes need not be magnified and best practices can be widespread. For example, the Global Compact's "Communications on Progress" website (see Table 13.2) provides a forum for companies to share their examples of implementation successes and problems and to learn from the experiences of other companies.

Global business citizenship, we argue, is the right way for managers and companies to steer their own courses through these rocky shoals of globalization. Global business citizenship is a path to sustainable capitalism, bringing innovation and wealth creation to all.

TABLE 13.2
Websites for Student Research

Amnesty International	www.amnesty.org
Business for Social Responsibility	www.bsr.org
Church World Service	www.churchworldservice.org
Council of Institutional Investors	www.cii.org
Global Compact	www.unglobalcompact.org
Global Reporting Initiative	www.globalreporting.org
Heifer International	www.heifer.org
Human Rights Watch	www.hrw.org
Institute for Social and Ethical Accountability (ISEA)	www.accountability.org.uk
Investor Responsibility Research Center	www.irrc.org
Millennium Development Goals	www.un.org/millenniumgoals/
	www.developmentgoals.org
	www.undp.org/mdg/
	www.unmilleniumproject.org
SIGMA Project	www.projectsigma.com
SustainAbility	www.sustainability.com
The Gap's first social report	www.gapinc.com/social_resp/social_resp.htm
The Prince of Wales International Business Leaders Forum	www.iblf.org/CSR/csrwebassist.nsf/content/f1b2b3a4.html
Transparency International	www.transparency.org
UNICEF	www.unicef.org
World Health Organization	www.who.int/en/
World Trade Organization	www.wto.org

Note: Websites do change, so ask students to find the appropriate site if the one listed is no longer in service.

CHALLENGES OF TEACHING GLOBAL
BUSINESS CITIZENSHIP

Using the concept of global business citizenship in the classroom is ener-
gizing and enlightening for students and professor alike, but it has its challenges. As a way to overview the "how" of GBC teaching, it is useful to
review the barriers and sources of resistance to GBC in the classroom and
to discuss how we try to overcome them with students. For the most part we
are talking here about undergraduates and MBA students—students in
their teens and twenties. Executive education classes are another story and,
maybe not surprisingly, not nearly as hard a sell as the younger students
can be. Practicing managers have sufficient experience to know that ethics
awareness is desirable, and they want to learn how to bring such awareness
into their practice. In our experience, they are more likely to understand
the negative as well as positive consequences of business operations and to
accept a measure of responsibility with respect to those negative outcomes.

Challenge #1: Students' Ignorance about Global Business
and Other Cultures

It is normal for younger students to be relatively uninformed about the
realities of global business and cultures beyond their own. Isn't that after
all one of the functions of a college education? We find in our classrooms
that the most effective devices for broadening students' perspectives in a
hurry are *video* and *web research*. Our students are web-savvy and TV-raised.
We have to reach them where they already live. If they can see the faces,
hear the voices, and experience the milieu of other cultures, they can
begin to cultivate the empathy and understanding that is essential for ethical, responsible global business practice.

There are now a number of good video resources that can be used in
conjunction with GBC teaching. "Battle of the Titans," for example, is an
hour-long film from the late 1990s that examines globalization from the
point of view of Texans whose boot factory is closing, Puerto Ricans who
are happily getting the new jobs, Egyptian workers in a sewing factory,
Nigerians both rich and poor, Indonesian country girls brought to the city
to be kitchen workers, and French fishermen who are out of work because
of imported products from low-wage countries.

"The Women's Bank of Bangladesh," another hour-long film, is a fasci-
nating portrayal of how the Grameen Bank operates. Much of it is subtitled
and students tend to find it boring, so this is a film to be used in small
doses, interspersed with discussion, lecture, presentations, or other devices
to keep students' attention.

The feature film, "The Corporation," has some good material in it and is accompanied by a book.[5] This DVD offers, among other things, some decent business history, interviews with stockbrokers and Wall Street traders, a bit of corporation law, a discussion of property rights, overviews of several well-known business disasters, and several clips of Ray Anderson, founder and CEO of Interface, Inc., talking about environmental responsibility.

CNBC offers a two-hour DVD called "The Age of Wal-Mart," and there are smashing new videos on child labor, including the just-released "Stolen Childhoods." The PBS website offers Frontline videos on various topics concerning business ethics or business and society.

"Enron: The Smartest Guys in the Room" can captivate an audience for a full two hours. It's amazing to see and hear Jeff Skilling, Ken Lay, Andy Fastow, and others talking up Enron stock even as the company is crashing and burning.

On the positive side, Heifer International, the Heifer Project people, have recently released a DVD that shows how developing-world people have benefited from the animals provided by Heifer. Clips are available in 4-minute, 12-minute, and 30-minute segments, offering something of value for every audience and every classroom need.

Some of the old stand-bys of business & society/business ethics teaching are also useful in broadening students' global perspectives. In particular, the Merck-Mectizan video from Business Enterprise Trust/HBS Press and the Dateline NBC tape on H.B. Fuller in Honduras, called "Sticking to Promises," are very helpful in getting students to see the many faces of globalization.

Web-based research is a hit with students. Because they already spend a great deal of time on the web, students are amenable to formal web-research assignments. There is an extraordinary variety of resources available for teaching global business citizenship. Students may be asked to research and present on topics such as the Millennium Development Goals, AIDS/HIV in Africa, the consequences of NAFTA, or the EU's political problems. They can look into corporate websites to see social responsibility and environmental reports along with mission/vision/values statements, and then they can go to the library's bibliographic databases and the web's search engines to discover the rest of the story. Students can find out about sweatshops, social reporting, national corruption, human rights-oriented groups, the Kyoto Protocol, Exxon Valdez, global warming, the chemical industry's Responsible Care program, and literally thousands of other topics related to business ethics or business and society.

We are often amazed at the other great websites that our students find that we had yet to locate. Nevertheless, Table 13.2 presents a few of the sites that we like.

Challenge #2: How Can Businesses Be "Citizens"?

Some astute questioner is bound to raise this issue fairly early in the discussion of GBC. Our earlier work on GBC took this question seriously, and following an analysis of several variations on citizenship, concluded that businesses could be thought of as secondary citizens, serving human needs and interests, if one adopts an organizational-level perspective and a universalist rights-and-duties position on what it means to be a citizen. (See Wood & Logsdon, 2002, for a more extensive analysis.)

The question could be addressed through student research and class presentations. We steer students to Aristotle's ideas on the duties of a citizen; let them discover that early citizenship created obligations to the nation-state in exchange for certain protections, and that "rights" were a later addition to the citizen's bundle of benefits. We have them read T. H. Marshall (1950) on the expansion of rights through British history. We let them review basic U.S. civics and discover what citizenship means in America today, and then ask them to compare those ideas with citizenship rights and duties in, say, Rwanda, Myanmar, Brazil, or Poland.

A challenge to our contention that businesses can be thought of as citizens is found in works such as Matten, Crane, and Chapple (2003), Matten and Crane (2005), and Moon, Crane, and Matten (2005), who argue that globalization has pushed businesses into the vacuum left by declining government power. We don't have any quarrel with that position. We do, however, think it is important to frame the discussion in terms that are more evocative of negotiation and voluntarism than of government's coercive power, so we prefer to think of businesses as "citizens of the world," even though businesses are indeed beginning to fill many of the former functions of government.

Challenge #3: Comparing GBC to CSR and CC

Corporate social responsibility (CSR) has been a formal and regular part of business education since the late 1970s, and the concept, of course, originated much earlier. Because the two concepts have similarities, the question might well arise, how is CSR different from GBC? In short, GBC is a coherent way of thinking about social responsibility and ethics within *and across* national and cultural borders. CSR suffers, by contrast, because of its typical emphasis on single-society responsibility and its difficulty in dealing with cross-border issues.

We suggest initiating a discussion of the American right's initiative to change the American political consciousness via think-tank research, political activism, control of the media, and so on. One can find good background information on this movement, and it might be an eye-opener for students who believe that life has always been exactly as it is for them at this moment. The point of such a discussion would be to show how CSR has been tainted by the right as a "socialist" or "Marxist" concept, "anti-American" and "anti-business," and even "immoral." Such language does make it difficult to conduct a rational debate about business's social responsibilities!

Another concept, corporate citizenship (CC), achieved popularity in the 1990s, and may also need to be distinguished from GBC. Although some scholars and managers use CC simply as a replacement term for the broad-based and fundamentally ethical CSR, most instead define CC as a company's voluntary philanthropy and other feel-good interactions with local communities. There's nothing wrong with voluntarism, one can point out, except that if societies depend on voluntarism to accomplish desperately needed tasks, then those tasks may or may not get done. And, there's no way to hold companies accountable for their voluntarism; they don't owe it and don't have to do it, so communities have no grounds for demanding that their rights be upheld. Corporate citizenship is a valued part of GBC, but alone, it is simply too weak to carry ethics and responsibility across borders and cultures.

Challenge #4: Resistance from the Finance-Model Ideologues

Frankly, we have stopped arguing with the finance ideologues because they aren't listening, and we suggest that others consider this route too. Scholars are willing to consider new ideas, especially if they make sense and appear to work; ideologues are not willing. Enough said?

OK, maybe a better defense than this is called for. Maybe students are not ideologues, but are merely uninformed. One can point out that the idea that business's only responsibility is to make a profit for investors is a relatively new way of seeing the corporation in society, and that ideas are the products of people, not immutable natural laws. One can point out that it seems clear that saying "See? The market works!" after a major corporate disaster is not an adequate response to the human suffering that was caused. One can make the argument that the smart business leaders work for a more stable, predictable environment, and that involves behaving responsibly.

There's another approach, quite different, that can be even more effective. When challenged by the finance/economics view of the firm, simply acknowledge it as "one view." Then point out that the beauty of a college education is that different courses offer different points of view, so that students can reach their own conclusions about what the world is like and what their role in that world should be. This approach sidesteps the challenge, but invites students to open their minds to another perspective without the threat of having to abandon what seems to be the preferred view of corporations in business schools.

Challenge #5: The Cultural Relativism Problem

Students are often reluctant to engage in rigorous moral analysis. Often their reluctance comes from an emerging sense of cultural and ethical relativism that is common to the college experience but does not allow them to admit that there are limits to acceptable human behavior.

We try to tackle this problem first by teaching the pitfalls of ethical relativism. Ultimately, there *is* no firm moral ground if any culture is right about anything, and then even atrocities can be accepted as "normal" if they routinely happen within a culture. Then, through exercises and class discussions, we lead students to see that there are values they themselves hold that they would not be willing to compromise, in spite of another culture's strong beliefs or practices. Then, examining life in business organizations helps students to realize that firms too can hold values they are not willing to compromise.

The appropriate place of cultural relativism becomes clearer when we present and discuss case examples of how companies try to adapt their practices to respect local custom *and* abide by big-ticket principles. In fact, GBC is ideally suited for helping students to put relativism in its proper role as an adaptive mechanism. For example, students learn that if a company values global child labor prohibitions, it cannot hire 7-year-olds anywhere it operates, but it might be able to hire 14-year-olds (the U.N.'s minimum standard) if such hiring is legal, makes sense for the company, and does not exploit the young workers.

Challenge #6: GBC Looks Farther Ahead Than Most Students Like

The big picture of GBC envisions a world where the vast differences in wealth and well-being among the world's peoples have moderated and where every person on earth has not only a degree of physical, food, water, and health security, but also access to the opportunities provided by education and occupation. This can be hard for students to grasp.

Honestly, it is difficult for most of us to imagine what the global business environment might be like in 50 years. And a failure to imagine long-term can cause people, especially young and impressionable students, to abandon worthy projects and goals because they seem hopelessly out of reach.

To meet this challenge, we don't start with the big picture, but end there. In class we try not to emphasize the long-term view until students have had a chance to build up their awareness and understanding of the global environment, its opportunities and threats. So, we start with the faces and voices, as we discussed with respect to Challenge #1, and then move to the problems and issues—poverty, pollution, clean water shortages, exploitation of cheap labor, corrupt governments—by way of on-the-ground examples, followed by statistics and big trends. Next, we let students get a look at the many company-based and collaborative experiments that are already happening to try to alleviate poverty, provide educational and economic opportunity, and so on. The Global Compact website (see Table 13.2) is a wonderful source of such experiments. Finally, we introduce the Millennium Development Goals, an ambitious initiative to halve—and ultimately end—poverty and lack of opportunity worldwide by the year 2015. We start small, end with the big picture. Many more students "get it" than otherwise would.

Challenge #7: Nice Theory, But Will It Work?

We don't spend much time in the classroom going over the theory that underlies GBC. We always provide all the references, of course, and students who are motivated and interested can follow up. Most students, however, learn better from cases and examples than from the logical presentation of theory, so we quickly survey the GBC concept and move right into case teaching, using examples from the Global Compact website, company materials from members of Business for Social Responsibility (see Table 13.2), and a wide variety of readily available web-based resources.

Here's a partial list of the cases we have already researched and can include in classes. The cases are available in our book, *Global Business Citizenship*:

1. *EDF: Normal Business Practice.* French power company EDF is collaborating with several other companies and organizations to bring solar energy to Mali.
2. *Hindustan Sanitaryware: Design for Water Conservation.* Hindustan produces toilets that use minimal water to flush, saving water, meeting ISO standards, and serving as supplier of choice for European and American multinationals locating in India.
3. *Bouygues Telecom: Office Waste Sorting.* Employees are asked to devise the most satisfactory way to meet office waste recycling requirements.

4. *Bernard Michaud: Quality Control in Beekeeping.* Training in quality honey production practices in the developing world builds new cottage industries that can command premium pricing.

5. *Aarhus United: A Little Nut and A Big Problem.* Gathering shea nuts in Burkina Faso does not involve child slavery, but the company grasps the depth of poverty among its gatherers and searches for a way to help.

6. *Connor & Associates: One Step at a Time.* They make it look easy: find a child in a supplier factory? Send her to school and promise her a job on completion. But the ease of implementation is built on rigorous policies and practices.

7. *Compliance and Local Adaptation: Beauty Essential Co., Ltd.* This Thai clothing manufacturer initiated process improvements to meet SA 8000 requirements on labor conditions, and discovered unexpected efficiencies and worker motivation.

8. *Compliance, Conflicts, and Tool Development: Royal Dutch Shell.* Working with a template from the Danish Institute for Human Rights (DIHR), Shell developed a data-gathering and assessment instrument to be used country by country to identify the most likely human rights violations and the ease with which guidelines could be adopted and implemented.

9. *Experiment in Monitoring and Transparency: The Gap.* Stung by global criticism of child and forced labor in its supply chain, this company partnered with several NGOs to map its supplier landscape and to produce a detailed and informative social report, complete with next-step objectives.

10. *Interface, Inc.'s Sustainability Reporting.* Encouraging all companies to climb "Mount Sustainability" is Ray Anderson's mission, and his company is leading the way toward manufacturing design for net zero environmental impact.

As any case-writer knows, the information one gets from a company does not necessarily tell the whole story. It is very instructive for students to take the small caselets from the Global Compact website, for example, and google for more of the story. They have to learn how to recognize issues and topics, assess sources, compare bits of information, put together timetables, develop a way to deal with conflicting information, and so on—all the skills of research that will stand them in such good stead throughout their lives.

Here's one example of what they will discover. The Bouygues Telecom case on the Global Compact website describes the company's experiments in recycling office wastes. They decided to try out three different methods and let the employees decide, and eventually a suitable recycling method was indeed chosen. What the Global Compact case does not contain, however, is some vital information on environmental pressures. Ten years earlier (!), the French Parliament had passed a law requiring that by 2004, no waste that was recyclable could be put into French landfills. Bouygues Telecom's experiments then, although commendable, were certainly not voluntary. Nevertheless, they asked their employees to find the best way to implement requirements, giving ownership of the ultimate solution to the people who would have to make it work.

When students discover environmental pressures such as excessive or incompetent regulation, turbulent political shifts, uncontrollable stakeholder movements, and so on, they can become overwhelmed and disillusioned about global social responsibility. This gives us an opportunity to help them understand the dynamic interplay between environment and behavior at the organizational level. It's just another step along the way to helping students develop a richer understanding of the world and its peoples, problems, and opportunities.

SOME PRACTICAL TIPS FOR TEACHING GLOBAL BUSINESS CITIZENSHIP

Given the challenges we have outlined above, here are some of our most useful do's and don'ts for teaching global business citizenship and corporate social responsibility across borders.

DO:

- Use a loose framework: preferably a stakeholder approach, perhaps combined with the structural principles from Wood's (1991) corporate social performance model. The stakeholder perspective is generally very accessible to students, and Wood's structural principles of CSR provide a way of understanding how responsibilities will vary at the individual, organizational, and institutional levels of analysis.
- Emphasize CSR as standard operating procedure, not as add-ons or free-standing programs. Charitable giving and voluntarism dominate the CSR landscape at present, and there are many wonderful examples out there. But it's important to stress that charity and voluntarism don't change an organization's structure, culture, and processes, and such change is the key to a truly responsible business organization.
- Focus on what's happening in the real world with respect to stakeholder engagement, accountability, social investing, Global Compact, Business for Social Responsibility, the Kyoto agreements, and so on. Students can make presentations on the various topics, organizations,

or events, or they could produce one-page fact sheets that accumulate into toolkits or handbooks for GBC learning and practice.

- Use *lots* of cases of many types: short, long, company- or industry-based, sole efforts and collaborations, issue- or decision-focused, good news, disasters, struggling projects and experiments.
- Be sure to build lots of real examples into any lectures you do.
- Point out that GBC practices often have strategic or competitive advantage benefits to companies.
- Make it clear that ethics-based GBC practices may need to be done whether there's a profit advantage or not. We may not always know what's right in a given situation, but it's not always hard to decide that something is just plain wrong.
- Make extensive use of web resources, the business press, and your local newspapers. Today's students are wonderfully proficient at using the web, so use their skills and help them learn about both good and suspicious sources and evidence.

Here's our short list of what not to do.
DON'T:

- Argue too much with Milton Friedman's *New York Times Magazine* article. It's *so* passé. If you really want to make the argument, use *Capitalism and Freedom* (1962) instead. Friedman makes an extensive, if flawed, case for a libertarian philosophy. Students may have read some Ayn Rand, and that's a useful connection to make if you want to illuminate Friedman's position.
- Make a big deal of the "pros and cons" as Keith Davis had to do in his 1973 article on CSR in the *Academy of Management Journal* (Davis, 1973). The field is past it, and so is business practice.
- Assume that GBC is philanthropy and community relations.
- Assume that GBC and ethics are identical. They're partially overlapping concepts.
- Assume that GBC will look the same all over the world.
- Let students get away with thinking that GBC is about image and superficial public relations.
- Require old-fashioned term papers. They're too easily bought or traded, and even if students actually do them, you might find them heavily plagiarized from websites, which many students don't believe is stealing. We think that this just defeats the purpose of a business & society/business ethics class.

CONCLUSION

Teaching business & society/business ethics is even more fun today than it was 25 years ago ... and potentially more dangerous, too. Companies are more sophisticated, and they're doing a lot more, but some are not necessarily ready to give up the "flavor of the month" approach to social responsibility. There's a great deal more information available than there used to be. Global stakeholders have made a huge difference in how companies think about and deal with social responsibility, and students need to know about them. And globalization is proceeding, whether we like it or not, making it all the more important for managers to get the message of social responsibility.

We think it matters enormously that current and future business leaders and managers understand the processes of globalization and the crucial role they themselves play in shaping its directions and consequences. We offer you the concept and teaching tools of global business citizenship to help with this crucial task.

ADDITIONAL RESOURCES

The Global Compact website, www.unglobalcompact.org, mentioned in Table 13.2, is highlighted here as an invaluable source of information on how companies around the world are working to implement the Global Compact's ten principles covering labor rights, human rights, environmental protection, and corruption.

Raising the Bar: Creating Value with the United Nations Global Compact, edited by Claude Fussler, Cramer, and van der Vegt (2004) and published by Greenleaf Press, is chock-full of data, cases, and sources on CSR-related efforts of all types around the world. It's a resource book you should definitely have if you plan to teach global business citizenship.

There are several books out on Grameen Bank and the micro-lending movement, including *Banker to the Poor* by Grameen founder Muhammad Yunus and Alan Jolis (2001), *The Price of a Dream* by David Bornstein (1996), and *Give Us Credit* by Alex Counts (1996). In 2006, Yunus and Grameen Bank were awarded the globe's highest honor—the Nobel Peace Prize—for their faithful and hugely successful attention to providing economic opportunity to the world's poorest people.

S. Prakash Sethi's 2003 book on multinational corporate codes is a good resource: *Setting Global Standards: Guidelines for Creating Codes of Conduct in Multinational Corporations.*

Our new book, *Global Business Citizenship* (Wood, Logsdon, Lewellyn, and Davenport, 2006), is a comprehensive, affordable guide to corporate social responsibility and ethics in multinationals, with a more detailed articulation of the challenges of global business, the theory and process of GBC, global stakeholder pressures, and lots of good examples and cases. At ten chapters, the book is suitable as a supplement to a regular textbook or as the primary text for 10-week course.

There are many other great sources of information on global business ethics and social responsibility. Let your students help you find them!

NOTES

1. B&S, BE, CSR, CSP, CC—The acronyms stand for business and society, business ethics, corporate social responsibility, corporate social performance, and corporate citizenship.
2. For a fuller treatment of the steps in the GBC process, see Logsdon and Wood (2002); Wood and Logsdon (2002); and Logsdon (2004). Additional conceptual development for GBC is found in Logsdon and Wood (2003), Wood and Logsdon (2003a; 2003b), Queiroz and Wood (2003), and Wood (2004).
3. Also see Donaldson (1989) and Donaldson and Dunfee (1999).
4. For analysis of the GBC attributes of corporate codes of conduct, see Logsdon and Wood (2005).
5. Frankly, we find the accompanying book to be a disappointment, but the author is a newcomer to business & society/business ethics and has discovered it as a topic but not as a scholarly field.

REFERENCES

Bornstein, D. (1996). *The price of a dream: The story of the Grameen Bank and the idea that is helping the poor to change their lives.* New York: Simon & Schuster.

Counts, A. (1996). *Give us credit.* New York: Times Books.

Davis, K. (1973). The case for and against business assumption of social responsibilities. *Academy of Management Journal, 16*(2), 312–322.

Donaldson, T. (1989). *The ethics of international business.* New York: Oxford University Press.

Donaldson, T., & Dunfee, T. W. (1999). *Ties that bind: A social contracts approach to business ethics.* Cambridge, MA: Harvard Business School Press.

Friedman, M. (1962). *Capitalism and freedom.* Chicago: University of Chicago Press.

Fussler, C., Cramer, A., & van der Vegt, S. (Eds.). (2004). *Raising the bar: Creating value with the United Nations Global Compact.* Sheffield, UK: Greenleaf Publishing.

Logsdon, J. M. (2004, Spring). Global business citizenship and the natural environment. *Business & Society Review, 109*(1), 67–87.

Logsdon, J. M., Davenport, K. S., Lewellyn, P. G., & Wood, D. J. (2005, March). Teaching global business citizenship. *Proceedings of the International Association for Business & Society,* Sonoma, CA.

Logsdon, J. M., & Wood, D. J. (2002). Business citizenship: From domestic to global level of analysis. *Business Ethics Quarterly, 12*(2), 155–187.

Logsdon, J. M., & Wood, D. J. (2002, June). Global business citizenship: Operationalizing integrated social contracts theory. *International Association for Business and Society Proceedings,* Victoria, British Columbia, Canada.

Logsdon, J. M., & Wood, D. J. (2003). Implementing global business citizenship: Multi-level motivations and an initial research agenda. In J. Hooker & P. Madsen (Eds.), *International corporate responsibility: Exploring the issues* (pp. 423–446). Pittsburgh: Carnegie Mellon University Press.

Logsdon, J. M., & Wood, D. J. (2005). Global business citizenship and voluntary codes of ethical conduct. *Journal of Business Ethics, 59*(1–2), 55–67.

Marshall, T. H. (1950). Citizenship and social class, and other essays. Cambridge: Cambridge University Press.

Matten, D., & Crane, A. (2005). Corporate citizenship: Toward an extended theoretical conceptualization. *Academy of Management Review, 30*(1), 166–179.

Matten, D., Crane, A., & Chapple, W. (2003). Behind the mask: Revealing the true face of corporate citizenship. *Journal of Business Ethics, 45*(1–2), 109–120.

Moon, J., Crane, A., & Matten, D. (2005) Can corporations be citizens? Corporate citizenship as a metaphor for business participation in society. *Business Ethics Quarterly, 15*(3), 429–453.

Queiroz, A., & Wood, D. J. (2003, June). In search of theory: Global standards of business conduct. *International Association for Business and Society Proceedings,* Rotterdam, The Netherlands.

Sethi, S. P. (2003). *Setting global standards: Guidelines for creating codes of conduct in multinational corporations.* Hoboken, NJ: John Wiley.

Wood, D. J. (1991). Corporate social performance revisited. *Academy of Management Review, 16*(4), 691–718.

Wood, D. J. (Ed.). (2004). Global business citizenship. A special issue of *Business & Society Review, 109*(1).

Wood, D. J., & Logsdon, J. M. (2001). Theorizing business citizenship. In J. Andriof, & M. McIntosh (Eds.), *Perspectives on Corporate Citizenship* (pp. 83–103). London: Greenleaf.

Wood, D. J., & Logsdon, J. M. (2002). Business citizenship: From individuals to organizations. In E. Freeman & S. Venkataraman (Eds.), *Ethics and Entrepreneurship: The Ruffin Series, 3,* 59–94, Charlottesville, VA: Philosophy Documentation Center.

Wood, D. J., & Logsdon, J. M. (2003a, June). Global business citizenship: Evaluation & transparency in organization-environment relations. Paper presented at the annual meeting of the European Business Ethics Network, Oslo, Norway.

Wood, D. J., & Logsdon, J. M. (2003b, June). Global business citizenship: Applications to human rights & environment. *International Association for Business and Society Proceedings,* Rotterdam, The Netherlands.

Wood, D. J., Logsdon, J. M., Lewellyn, P. G. & Davenport, K. (2006). *Global business citizenship: A transformative framework for ethics and sustainable capitalism.* New York: M.E. Sharpe Publishers.

Yunus, M., & Jolis, A. (2001). *Banker to the poor: The autobiography of Muhammed Yunus.* New York: Cambridge University Press.

CHAPTER 14

EDUCATING STUDENTS IN CORPORATE GOVERNANCE AND ETHICS

Archie Carroll
University of Georgia

Ann Buchholtz
University of Georgia

INTRODUCTION

Before the collapse of Enron, once the seventh largest company in the U.S., analysts were lauding the improvements in corporate governance that had been made as a result of pressure from institutional investors, such as more independent directors and more directors who owned stock in the company (Byrne, 2000). After Enron went bankrupt, with WorldCom and Global Crossing following closely behind, a host of firms began restating their earnings, leaving investors wondering what went wrong and where could they place their trust. The comment of former U.S. Securities and Exchange Commission (SEC) Chairman William McDonough reflected the seriousness of the situation, "I firmly do believe that the whole American system of life, government and the management of our economy were

Advancing Business Ethics Education, pages 285–304
Copyright © 2008 by Information Age Publishing
All rights of reproduction in any form reserved.

in jeopardy as the American people were losing faith in the system" (Toedt-man, 2003, p. 1). Clearly, the checks and balances that were put in place to govern corporations had failed (Monks & Minow, 2004). This served to underscore the importance of corporate governance and ethics as a topic for business education.

By looking at the aftermath of these corporate meltdowns, students are better able to understand not only the benefits of good corporate governance but also the tremendous toll that poor corporate governance can take. With billions of dollars in shareholder wealth gone, thousands of jobs lost, and countless lives ruined, the ethical implications are clear. We begin our lessons in ethics and corporate governance by making students aware of the extent of the fallout from the corporate scandals. This provides students with a sense of the economic and the human cost of inattention to the governance of the corporation. The movie "Enron: The Smartest Guys in the Room" (available on DVD) provides a riveting account of the downfall of Enron. If time will permit, this movie would provide students with a clear overview of the Enron scandal and its aftermath. Be aware that there are brief scenes of nudity in the movie which may not be appropriate for certain audiences. An alternative to watching the movie is to assign students the book on which it is based (McLean & Elkind, 2003).

Our discussion of teaching corporate governance is structured around Chapter 19 "Owner Stakeholders and Corporate Governance" of our text-book *Business and Society: Ethics and Stakeholder Management* (Carroll & Buch-holtz, 2006). Portions of this chapter are derived from the book. In this chapter, as well as in our book, we approach corporate governance from the Anglo-Saxon perspective. The size constraints of a chapter preclude in-depth analysis of the range of governance models in the world. However, we do alert the students to other models so that they can place this discussion in context.

We begin our discussion by linking the concept of legitimacy to corporate governance. We then provide a brief discussion of corporate governance systems around the world, followed by a more in-depth explanation of the structure of Anglo-Saxon corporate governance. We then present the concept of agency problems and the role of the board in their mitigation. Issues surrounding compensation, the market for corporate control, and board member liability are discussed in this context. Finally, we move to the topic of improving corporate governance. We cover the Sarbanes-Oxley Act (SOX), changes in the board of directors, and the rise of shareholder involvement as ways in which corporate governance is being reworked to mitigate the problems that led to Enron and its aftermath. We briefly mention several other initiatives companies have made on their own to be ethical towards other stakeholders.

THE ROLE OF LEGITIMACY IN CORPORATE GOVERNANCE

For students to understand the concept of corporate governance, they need to understand the idea of legitimacy. While students may find legitimacy to be somewhat abstract, it is vital in that it helps explain the importance of the relative roles of a corporation's charter, shareholders, board of directors, management, and employees. These are all important components of the modern corporate governance system.

Organizations are considered to be legitimate if their activities are compatible with society's norms (Epstein & Votaw, 1978). Thus legitimacy is a condition that exists when there is congruence between the organization's activities and society's expectations. While, legitimacy is a condition, *legitimation* is a dynamic process by which business seeks to perpetuate its acceptance. The dynamic process aspect should be emphasized because the expectations of society change, and so business must change to remain legitimate. For students to fully understand the concept of legitimacy, it should be presented at both the micro, or company, level and the macro, or business institution, level.

At the *micro level of legitimacy*, we refer to individual business firms achieving and maintaining legitimacy by acting in a way that is consistent with societal expectations. According to Epstein and Votaw (1978), companies have different ways to approach this. When a company's practices don't match society's norms, they can either change their practices to match society or try to change society's norms to match the company's practices. It can be useful to have students try to think of examples of this occurring in business. In 2002, the pharmaceutical industry developed a new ethics code that banned the more lavish gifts, trips and dinners given to doctors because those began to take on the aura of a bribe. Pharmaceutical companies responded by switching to more modest lunches (still worth millions of dollars). This is one of many examples of companies changing themselves to fit society's expectations.

When discussing firms that change to imitate other firms, students may wonder whether companies are simply following best practices because they have been shown to work well rather than imitating other firms in an effort to enhance their legitimacy. Westphal and Zajac (1994) examined announcements of long term incentive plans (LTIPs) and found that 21 to 45% of firms never implemented the plans they said they would put in place. They then analyzed stock market reactions to the adoption of LTIPs and found that the stock market responded favorably to LTIP adoption whether or not the firm subsequently put the plan in place (Westphal & Zajac, 1998).

Examples of companies trying to change the expectations of society to fit their practices are a bit more difficult to find because it is more difficult for companies to do. Encouraging society to adopt use of new technologies can be the source of examples of this. Amazon.com was successful at changing the way people buy goods when it began marketing through the Internet. Other examples could come from the banking industry when it convinced customers to begin using ATMs and to bank online.

Finally, an organization may seek to enhance its legitimacy at the micro level by becoming identified with other organizations, people, values, or symbols that are considered highly legitimate by society (Epstein & Votaw, 1978). This can occur in a variety of ways. National ad campaigns often include famous spokespersons to give the company's products or services credibility. Celebrities, former politicians, and other famous people are often appointed to managerial positions or board directorships. Even at the local level, star athletes, football coaches, and other well known and respected people may be asked to endorse a company's products by sitting on the board or appearing in commercials.

The *macro level of legitimacy* refers to the corporate system—the totality of business enterprises. Prior to the Enron debacle, it was difficult to talk about the legitimacy of business in pragmatic terms at this level. However the wave of corporate meltdowns that ensued after Enron, threatened the macro level legitimacy of the business enterprise. This level of legitimacy is vital to business because the entire existence, acceptance, and form of business as an institution are at stake. Nearly a quarter century before Enron fell, William Dill warned that business's social (or societal) legitimacy was a fragile thing (Dill, 1978):

> Business has evolved by initiative and experiment. It never had an overwhelmingly clear endorsement as a social institution. The idea of allowing individuals to joust with one another in pursuit of personal profit was an exciting and romantic one when it was first proposed as a way of correcting other problems in society; but over time, its ugly side and potential for abuse became apparent. (p. 11)

With quite a bit of the excitement and romanticism long since worn off, business must accept that it has a fragile mandate. The legitimacy of business is subject to constant ratification. Business has no inherent right to exist—It exists solely because society has given it that right (Dill, 1978). Once students understand this point, it may be useful to discuss the book or the movie made from the book, *The Corporation* (Bakan, 2004). The premise of the book and movie is that corporations have status as legal persons and so we should examine the kind of person the corporation is.

It may be helpful for students to compare the micro view of legitimacy with the macro view. They should soon see that, although specific business organizations try to perpetuate their own legitimacy, they are rarely concerned with the corporate or business system as a whole. While trade and industry groups will, on occasion, concern themselves with the overall legitimacy of business enterprise, they take pains to not interfere in the workings of individual businesses. The gap this leaves is exemplified by the Enron and WorldCom scandals wherein the actions of individual businesses threatened the legitimacy of business as a whole. This is unfortunate because the spectrum of powerful issues regarding business conduct clearly indicates that institutional introspection is needed if business is to survive and prosper. If business is to continue to justify its right to exist, the question of legitimacy and its operational ramifications must be remembered.

AN OVERVIEW OF CORPORATE GOVERNANCE

The word *governance* comes from the Greek word for steering (Corporate America's woes, continued, 2002). Shareholders and other stakeholders count on boards to steer the company in the proper direction. For business to maintain its fragile mandate, it must be governed in a way that maintains its legitimacy in the eyes of the public. *Corporate governance* refers to the method by which a firm is being governed, directed, administered, or controlled and to the goals for which it is being governed. Countries around the world differ in the ways in which they handle corporate governance; however, the differences are diminishing as governance practices converge. It may be useful for students to generate a list of the reasons why corporate governance around the world is becoming more homogeneous.

Monks and Minow (2004) cite a variety of reasons for this convergence. First, private business is becoming accepted as the key source of wealth creation and job generation. Globalization in general is also a force for convergence; Global companies and global investors create pressure for more standardized governance mechanisms. The need businesses have for capital, and the demands of the investors who provide it, further prompt the convergence of international standards. Finally, international organizations such as the G8, the World Bank and the Organization for Economic Cooperation and Development (OECD) have contributed to convergence by calling for standards of best practice and by assisting countries, particularly those with emerging markets, in improving their corporate governance.

In spite of the general trend toward convergence, there remain factors that limit the extent to which governance systems resemble each other throughout the world. Countries still have different cultures and different values, and that creates differences in the way their corporations are governed (Monks & Minow, 2004). For example, both Japan and Germany are known for being countries that emphasize the stakeholder in comparison to the Anglo-Saxon model of shareholder primacy. For example, Japan is known for its *keiretsus* with insider relationships that maintain control of businesses up and down the value chain and across industries, while Germany is known for its system of *codetermination* that places an emphasis on employee participation. The challenges of a global marketplace have caused these countries to begin to adopt some of the aspects of the Anglo-Saxon model; however, the two countries remain unique in their perspectives on corporate governance (Jackson & Moerke, 2005). For students of ethics and governance, it is helpful to discuss the implications of the worldwide convergence to an Anglo-Saxon model. As Dore (2005) argues, this convergence also represents a shift in distributional outcomes—favoring the shareholder over the stakeholder. This raises ethical issues that can provide an opportunity not only to better understand the relationship of shareholders and stakeholders but also to explore the distributional justice implications of the shift.

The remainder of this chapter will discuss governance from the Anglo-Saxon perspective. This perspective is characterized by shareholder primacy, i.e., the interests of the shareholder come first. The corporation's four major groups (in descending order of authority) are the shareholders (owner/stakeholders), the board of directors, the managers, and the employees. Overarching these groups is the *charter* issued by the state, giving the corporation the right to exist and stipulating the basic terms of its existence. *Shareholders* are the owners of a corporation. As owners, they should have ultimate control over the corporation. This control is manifested primarily in the right to select the board of directors of the company. Generally, the degree of each shareholder's right is determined by the number of shares of stock owned. The individual who owns 100 shares of stock has considerably less ownership power than the large public pension fund that owns 10 million shares. Because there are too many shareholders to govern the firm effectively, they elect a smaller group, known as the *board of directors*, to oversee the managers and make sure they are representing the best interests of the shareholders. Subordinate to the board of directors is *management*—the group of individuals hired by the board to run the company and manage it on a daily basis. Along with the board, top management establishes overall policy. Middle- and lower-level managers carry out the policy and supervise the non-managerial *employees* who are hired by the company to perform the actual operational work.

Students are often confused by the relationship of the board to the CEO. Even business students sometimes think that the CEO hires and fires the board. While this may have been true in practice when CEOs became entrenched with rubber stamp boards, it is the opposite of the way it is set up to be. Beginning by asking students what the relationship is between the board and the CEO, and then seeing what misconceptions students may hold, is a good way to discern their current level of understanding of corporate governance. Understanding how much (or little) they know can be valuable in gearing the remainder of the course to their needs.

THE AGENCY PROBLEM—SEPARATION OF OWNERSHIP FROM CONTROL

The above description explains how corporate governance is supposed to work. It is designed to address the problems that can arise from the *separation of ownership from control*. In the pre-corporate period, owners managed their companies themselves and so there was no separation between ownership and control. Even as firms grew larger and other managers were hired, the owners often were on the scene to oversee operations. As the public corporation grew, however, stock ownership became widely dispersed, and a separation of ownership from control became the prevalent condition. Eventually no one or no one group owned enough shares to exercise control. In this situation, the most effective control that owners could exercise was the election of the board of directors to represent them and watch over management in their stead.

The problem with this evolution was that owners no longer held the power to protect their investments. Managers became more powerful as many shareholders considered themselves to be investors more than owners because an individual shareholder's stake in a firm is extremely small compared to the number of shares outstanding. The other factors that added to management's power were the corporate laws and traditions that gave the management group control over the *proxy process*—the method by which the shareholders elected boards of directors. As it evolved, it became easy for management groups to create boards of directors of like-minded executives who would simply collect their fees and defer to management on whatever it wanted. As a result, power, authority, and control began to flow upward from management rather than downward from the shareholders (owners). *Agency problems* developed when the interests of the shareholders were not aligned with the interests of the manager and the manager (who is simply a hired *agent* with the responsibility of representing the owner's best interest) began to pursue his or her own self-interest rather than the best interests of the shareholders.

It is useful for students to think through how and why agency problems can occur. Information asymmetry is one problem that develops because managers are at the business each day and they know what is happening. Owners on the other hand are distant from the action and, in most cases, their investments are not sufficient to merit the kind of information gathering and assessment that a larger level owner would do. It is the job of the board to reduce information asymmetry through their oversight of management.

The Board of Directors

As the preceding discussion indicates, there is a potential governance problem built into the corporate system because of the separation of ownership from control. The board of directors is put in place to oversee management on behalf of the shareholders—but are they succeeding? The answer seems to be both yes and no. Prior to the Enron scandal, James Heard, Vice-Chairman and former CEO of Institutional Shareholder Services, had seen many positive changes resulting from the pressures institutional investors imposed: more directors were independent, more directors owned stock in the company, and boards were more likely to demand change (Byrne, 2000). If that was true, and there is every reason to believe it was, then how could the corporate meltdowns have ensued? There is positive news about the behavior of corporate boards following Enron. In a 2003 survey of corporate directors, 75% of respondents said they were spending more time on board matters each month and 67% said full board meetings are now longer (Leinster, 2003).

If corporate governance has improved, are the problems now resolved? It may be useful to discuss with students whether they believe the problems are now resolved and, if not, why they believe they have reason to still be concerned. Asking them both before and after the more in-depth discussion on corporate governance can give them something to consider as they mull over the information presented. One thing should be clear to them; effective corporate governance is neither simple nor easily obtained.

Board Independence

One of the concerns most often expressed about boards of directors is that board members are controlled by CEOs and that they will simply provide rubber stamp approval to whatever the CEO does. This concern is the reason that the relative proportion of *outside directors and inside directors* has become an issue. Outside directors are independent from the firm and its top managers. In contrast, inside directors have some sort of ties to the firm. Sometimes they are top managers in the firm; other times, insiders are family members or others with close ties to the firm or the CEO. The concern is that inside directors will feel indebted to the CEO and, therefore, they may hesitate to speak out when necessary.

The problem is not just about finding honest board members. Even board members who want to act independently are unlikely to succeed in doing so. Bazerman, Loewenstein, and Moore (2002) cite a variety of studies that show that even the most honest and meticulous person is likely to distort information in ways that are self-serving and that benefit those with whom he or she has a relationship. For example, professional auditors given an auditing exercise with imaginary clients will still show favoritism toward the clients with whom the auditor has an (imaginary) relationship. This is an excellent and highly accessible reading to assign to students; it will give them a feel for the challenges inherent in finding effective oversight even when all the people involved are trying genuinely to do their best.

Board Interlocks

Another issue related to board independence is the extent of interlocks between corporate boards of directors. At the highest levels, there are connections between board members at different corporations. An entertaining website, www.theyrule.net, provides students with a chance to get a pictorial view of the nature of the interlocks. They can click on a particular company, find out who the directors are, and then determine to which companies each of these directors are attached. Students can also pick two companies and find a path that links them together through board members; the outcome is similar to that of the "seven degrees of separation" game. Students will soon find that it does not take long to generate a complex web of associations among major firms. Once students realize the extent of the interlocks in boards today, they can begin to discuss the implications that has for corporate governance. It may be necessary to prompt them with the information that a Korn/Ferry International Study found that there was a CEO/COO from another company on 86 percent of billion-dollar company boards (Monks & Minow, 2004). Students can then consider the tradeoff between the potential conflict of interest and expertise that a board member brings to the table.

Board Member Liability

The issue of board member liability came to the fore most recently with the Enron and WorldCom settlements in which board members were required to pay millions from their personal funds (Scannell & Langley, 2005). While this has happened before, it is typically reserved for the most egregious of cases (Lenckus, 2006). The Caremark case set the stage for directors' concerns about *personal liability*. Caremark, a home health care company, paid substantial civil and criminal fines for submitting false claims and making illegal payments to doctors and other health care providers. The Caremark board of directors was then sued for breach of fiduciary duties because the board members had failed in their responsibility to monitor effectively the Caremark employees who violated various state and federal laws. The Delaware Chancery Court ruled that it is the duty of the board of directors to ensure that a company has an effective reporting and monitoring system in place. If the board fails to do this, individual directors can be held personally liable for losses that are caused by their failure to meet appropriate standards (Monks & Minow, 2004).

The Issue of Compensation

CEO Compensation

The issue of executive pay was a lightning rod for the concern that managers place their own interests over those of their shareholders. Two issues are at the heart of the CEO pay controversy: a) the extent to which CEO pay is tied to firm performance, and b) the overall level of CEO pay. It can be difficult for students to grasp the issue of executive compensation because the numbers are so large. A website that helps give those numbers meaning is www.aflcio.org/paywatch. Visitors to the website can determine how many years they would have to work to earn the annual salary of a CEO in a given company, they can compare a given CEO's salary to that firm's performance, they can learn how to begin a campaign of shareholder activism, and they can play "Greed: The Executive Paywatch Board Game."

Executive Retirement Plans

Executive retirement packages once flew under the radar, with relatively little public notice of its excesses. Recently, however, details of some retirement packages have become public (Sweeney, 2003). Former General Electric Chairman and CEO Jack Welch's retirement package was disclosed during his divorce proceedings. The perks he enjoyed included country club memberships, wine and laundry services, luxurious housing and access to corporate jets. Also, the New York Stock Exchange awarded its former Chairman and CEO Richard Grasso a $139.5 million retirement package, in spite of moribund stocks and cost-cutting pressures. The public's frustration stems partly from the fact that these CEO retirement packages are very different from the retirement packages that most workers receive. Less than half of today's workers have retirement packages at all and those that do usually have the less lucrative defined contribution rather than the defined benefit plans (Sweeney, 2003). Students can find information on specific CEO retirement plans at www.aflcio.org/paywatch.

Outside Director Compensation

Paying board members is a relatively recent idea. Eighty years ago, it was illegal to pay nonexecutive board members. The logic was that because board members represented the shareholders, paying them out of the company's (i.e., shareholders') funds would be self-dealing (Colvin, 1997).

In 1992, board members typically spent 95 hours a year on the board; however, by 2000 that figure had nearly doubled to 173 hours. The average director received a 23 percent increase in pay for the 82 percent increase in time spent on the job ("The fading appeal of the boardroom," 2001). Not surprisingly, a 2003 survey by *Corporate Board Member* magazine found that 80% of board members felt directors should be paid more in light of the "added responsibility of recent board governance reforms" (What directors think study - 2003).

IMPROVING CORPORATE GOVERNANCE

From a teaching standpoint, providing students with some of the major actions, or best practices, for improving corporate governance is a logical follow-up to identifying and discussing the governance issues and their ethical implications. In response to governance issues, actions that have taken place include those initiated by government, by corporations themselves, and by the marketplace of stakeholders affected by corporate governance, especially shareholder groups.

In recent years, the most dramatic initiative of government to improve corporate governance has been the landmark legislation, the Sarbanes-Oxley Act of 2002 (SOX). This act is now considered to be a part of what has been termed the "Enron Effect." It was a specific government response to the fraud and criminal conduct exposed in the Enron scandal (Thomas, 2006). After discussing Sarbanes-Oxley, we then proceed to other efforts to improve corporate governance, which have been initiated by corporations themselves, and then by shareholders. First, changes are being made in the composition, structure, and functioning of boards of directors. Second, shareholders—on their own initiative or on the initiative of management or the board—have been assuming a more active role in governance. Each of these courses of action deserves closer examination.

Sarbanes–Oxley: A Major Government Response

Government regulations are passed when it is believed that the issues are of such magnitude that they cannot be left to management's own ethics or discretion to act. Such was the case in the aftermath of the Enron scandal of 2001 when the public was crying out for Congress to do something. On July 30, 2002, the *Accounting Reform and Investor Protection Act of 2002* was signed into law. Also known as the *Sarbanes-Oxley Act (SOX),* it amends the securities laws to provide better protection for investors in public companies by improving the financial reporting of companies.

According to the Senate Committee report, the issue of auditor independence is a core feature of the Sarbanes Oxley Act (Schlesinger, 2002). Some of the ways the Act endeavors to ensure auditor independence are by limiting the non-auditing services an auditor can provide, requiring auditing firms to rotate the auditors who work with a specific company, and making it unlawful for accounting firms to provide auditing services where conflicts of interest (as defined by the Act) exist.

In addition, the Act enhances financial disclosure with requirements such as the reporting of off-balance sheet transactions, the prohibiting of personal loans to executives and directors, and the requirement that auditors assess and report upon the internal controls employed by the company. Other key provisions include the requirement that audit committees have at least one financial expert, that CEOs and CFOs certify and be held responsible for financial representations of the company, and that whistle blowers are afforded protection. Corporations must also disclose whether they have adopted a code of ethics for senior financial officers and, if they haven't, provide an explanation for why they haven't (Schlesinger, 2002). The penalties for non-compliance with SOX are severe: A CEO or CFO who misrepresents company finances may be fined up to $1 million and imprisoned for up to 10 years. If that misrepresentation is willful the fine may go up to $5 million with up to 20 years imprisonment (Segal, 2002).

It is easy for students to think that SOX is a government initiated act with which they do not have to be familiar. But, it is important that business students, in particular, know the major features of the law because they will doubtless be living with it upon graduation and progression into their companies. While SOX has had its successes, it also has created difficulties for businesses as they try to comply. A good assignment here would be for students to do their own internet research on Sarbanes-Oxley, identifying its major features, its advantages and disadvantages, and the changes it has undergone. Ask the students to identify the five major aspects of the law that address issues with business ethics implications.

Corporate Initiatives: Changes in Boards of Directors

The most significant course of action taken by companies to improve corporate governance has been changes made in the structure and functioning of boards of directors. In the past decade or so, these changes have occurred because of the growing belief that CEOs and executive teams need to be made more accountable to shareholders and other stakeholders. To understand corporate governance, it is important that students understand these changes as well as other recommendations that have been set forth for improving board functioning.

Composition of the Board

Prior to the 1960s, boards were composed primarily of white, male inside directors. An inside director is a person who is also a member of the management team. It was not until the 1960s that pressure from Washington, Wall Street, and various stakeholder groups began to emphasize the concept of board diversity. Forty years later, their efforts had begun to pay off: 78 percent of U.S. board members were outsiders (The fading appeal of the boardroom, 2001). Of the S&P 500 companies, 93 percent had at least one woman director. Although most firms still only have one token woman director, the tide seems to be shifting: 21 percent of new board members were women, and 25 percent of the nation's largest companies had more than one female director (Gutner, 2001). Ethnic minorities are making inroads, too. Sixty percent of U.S. corporate boards now have ethnic minority directors, with African-Americans comprising 39 percent, Latinos comprising 12 percent, and Asians comprising 9 percent of the positions. The world seems to be awakening to the importance of diverse and independent boards. The problem is that good, experienced candidates are increasingly hard to find (Board diversity increases, 2000).

It is useful for students to research the challenges in building diverse and independent boards and to assess critically the efforts that have been made in that direction. Problems include the demand that outstrips the perceived supply and the resultant challenges in attraction and retention of board members. The increased demands on board members add another layer of complication. Today, advocates of strong, independent, and diverse boards have largely succeeded in convincing corporations of the importance of board composition. The difficulty now is in putting those recommendations into effect. A major ethical question remains: will these boards truly be independent of management in their judgments and decisions?

Use of Board Committees

Corporate boards divide themselves into committees to conduct their work. The *audit committee* is typically responsible for assessing the adequacy of internal control systems and the integrity of financial statements. The *nominating committee*, which should be composed of outside directors, or at least a majority of outside directors, has the responsibility of ensuring that competent, objective board members are selected. The *compensation committee* has the responsibility of evaluating executive performance and recommending terms and conditions of employment; this committee should be composed of outside directors. Finally, each board has a *public issues committee*, or *public policy committee*. Although it is recognized that most management structures have some sort of formal mechanism for responding to public or social issues, this area is important enough to warrant a board committee that would become sensitive to these issues, provide policy leadership, and monitor management's performance on these issues.

Students can usually identify with the work of committees by comparing it to their own committee work. Depending on the time allotted to corporate governance, it may be useful to have students study firm proxy statements to see who is on what committee. At the very least they should become aware of how SOX has changed the composition, structure and mandates of board committees.

Exercising Control Over CEOs

It has always been a major responsibility of board directors to monitor CEO performance and to get tough if the situation dictates. Historically, chief executives were protected from the axe that hit other employees when times got rough. Changes are now occurring that are resulting in CEOs being taken to task, or even fired, for reasons that heretofore did not create a stir in the boardroom. These changes are occurring because of the tough, competitive economic times; the rising vigilance of outside directors; and the increasing power of large institutional investors. CEOs are being replaced because shareholders are upset over underperformance, inflated compensation, and ethical transgressions.

Most students will not have much interest in the details of board structure and functioning; however, these are important components of corporate governance and are vital in discussions of business ethics. A useful exercise with respect to the firing of CEOs, a topic which the students might find very interesting, is to have them do research and identify five CEOs who have been fired in the past five years. Ask the students to identify the reasons why the CEOs were fired and to describe what the reasons had to do with effective corporate governance.

Ask the students to pay particular attention to CEOs who were accused of improperly conducting themselves or engaging in personal indiscretions. Have each student be prepared to describe what he or she found. In addition, ask the students whether CEOs ought to be fired for off-the-job personal behaviors, such as that experienced by CEO Harry Stonecipher, who was discharged at Boeing based on having an affair with an employee. Students will not find many examples similar to Stonecipher's in which the CEO was fired for such indiscretions. However, this number could change in the future as companies continue to infuse business ethics in their corporate cultures. Have the students debate both sides of this issue, drawing into the discussion the importance of stakeholder and leadership implications.

Stakeholder Responses: Increased Role of Shareholders

Prior to the 1980s, civil rights activists, consumer groups, and other social activist pressure groups insisted that companies embrace their causes. Today, companies increasingly understand the stakeholder perspective. However, it has created a new dilemma for companies as they deal with two broad types of shareholders, both of whom feel like neglected constituencies. First, there are the *traditional shareholder groups* that are primarily interested in the firm's financial performance. Examples of such groups include the large institutional investors, such as pension funds. Second, there are growing numbers of *social activist shareholders.* These groups are typically pressuring firms to adopt their desired postures on social causes, such as Third World employment practices, animal testing, affirmative action, and environmental protection.

Shareholder Initiatives for Greater Influence on Boards

These initiatives may be classified into three major, overlapping areas: a) the rise of shareholder activist groups, b) the filing of shareholder resolutions and activism at annual meetings, and c) the filing of shareholder lawsuits.

Rise of Shareholder Activist Groups.   One major reason that relations between management groups and shareholders have heated up is that shareholders have discovered the benefits of organizing and wielding power. *Shareholder activism* is not a new phenomenon. It goes back over 70 years to 1932, when Lewis Gilbert, then a young owner of 10 shares, was appalled by the absence of communication between New York-based Consolidated Gas Company's management and its owners. Supported by a family inheritance, Gilbert decided to quit his job as a newspaper reporter and "fight this silent dictatorship over other people's money." He resolved to devote himself "to the cause of the public shareholder" (Tainer, 1983, p. 2).

Shareholder activism came into its own in the early 1970s with Campaign GM, also known as the Campaign to Make General Motors Responsible (Tainer, 1983). A direct consequence of the success of Campaign GM was the growth of church activism. Church groups were the early mainstay of the corporate social responsibility movement and were among the first shareholder groups to adopt Campaign GM's strategy of raising social issues with corporations. Institutional investors (pension funds, church groups, foundations) now dominate the marketplace and thus wield considerable power because of their enormous stock holdings.

One of the best examples of an institutional investor that wields tremendous power with companies is CalPERS, the California Public Employees Retirement System, which manages pensions and health benefits for its members. Whereas the Interfaith Center on Corporate Responsibility (ICCR) seems to focus more on general social and ethical issues, CalPERS seems to focus more on the economic benefits of its members. Both of these shareholder activist groups are quite powerful, and when they speak, Corporate America listens.

From a teaching perspective, having the students analyze the web pages of ICCR at www.iccr.org and CalPERS at www.calpers.ca.gov will give them an excellent education concerning these two gigantic shareholder interest groups. Have the students extract and summarize useful information about the issues of interest to each of these two groups and have them identify some recent successes these activist groups have had with major employers.

Use of Shareholder Resolutions and Activism at Annual Meetings.   One of the major vehicles by which shareholder activist groups, such as ICCR, CalPERS, and others, communicate their concerns to management groups is through the filing of *shareholder resolutions,* or shareholder proposals. An example of such a resolution is, "The company should name women and minorities to the board of directors." To file a resolution, a shareholder or a shareholder group must obtain a stated number of signatures to require management to place the resolution on the proxy statement so that it can be voted on by all the shareholders. Resolutions that are defeated (fail to get majority votes) may be resubmitted provided that they meet certain SEC requirements for such resubmission.

From a teaching standpoint, the issues of shareholder resolutions and activities at annual meetings are best handled by letting students do web research on the most recent shareholder proposals filed and track news reports in the summer of events taking place at the most recent spring annual meetings. Students may find the latest shareholder resolutions at http://www.iccr.org/shareholder/proxy_book07/07statuschart.php.   Students may also be invited to discover "how to file a shareholder resolution" by going to the following web page: http://www.aflcio.org/corporate-watch/paywatch/what2do/w_howshare.cfm. This will give the students insights into the qualifications that must be met to file a resolution.

Filing of Shareholder Lawsuits.   Shareholder suits are easy to file but difficult to defend. One study estimated that 70 percent of the suits are settled out of court. Therefore, charges of corporate wrongdoing are seldom resolved. Quite often, these lawsuits are seen as legitimate protests by shareholders against management actions, and the threat of litigation does deter corporate misbehavior. From the company's viewpoint, however, such lawsuits are often seen as an expensive nuisance.

Congress sought to stem the growing tide of shareholder lawsuits in the mid-1990s by passing the *Private Securities Litigation Reform Act of 1995.* The law made it more difficult for shareholders to bring class-action lawsuits to federal court (Schatz & Clark, 1998). However, rather than stemming the tide of lawsuits, the act simply prompted shareholders to change their venue. Suits filed in federal court decreased, while suits filed in state courts increased. Also, by forcing class-action lawyers to improve their game, it prompted a new era of big lawsuits and larger settlements (A blazing summer, 2005). The Securities Litigation Uniform Standards Act of 1998 was designed to plug that loophole. It says that "Any covered class action brought into any state courts shall be removable to the federal district courts for the district in which the action is pending" (Securities litigation reform revisited, 1999). Because of the ethics and fraud scandals of the early 2000s, settlements in securities class action lawsuits escalated from around $5 billion in 2004 to $20 billion by 2005 (A blazing summer, 2005). It took lawyers a few years to get their cases together, but once done, they were very successful.

Sound corporate governance dictates that boards not only pay attention to shareholders but other stakeholders as well. Some of the recent board initiatives aimed at addressing stakeholder issues include management-level positions such as Ethics Officers being appointed, board training in business ethics, board diversity and independence, and evaluations of board members. As a teaching/learning exercise, have students discuss the possible ethical issues and conflicts that boards may experience within their own functioning as well as in their relationships with CEOs and management.

CONCLUSION

Recent events in corporate America have served to underscore the importance of good corporate governance. Although they are the firms' owners, shareholders are too diffuse and removed from the corporation to effectively monitor the activities of the corporation and its managers. For that reason they must rely on the board to represent their interests by advising and monitoring corporate management. To protect their interests and ascertain that corporate governance is effective, shareholders have grouped together to regain their ownership power. Institutional shareholders own sufficient blocks of stock to gain the ear of the firm's boards and executives. They have been using this access to effect change. To help understand the above events, students need to understand basic concepts of corporate governance to include the idea of business legitimacy and the agency issues created when management groups do not attend to the shareholders' best interests. Issues that arise in board functioning are replete with ethical aspects and dimensions. This includes the role of the board of directors, issues surrounding executive and board compensation, and retirement plans that often go unnoticed.

The topic of governance can sometimes seem a bit distant for students and so it is important to provide them with examples to which they can relate. A scandal took place during fall of 2006 that refocused attention on board of director dynamics—it is one that students are likely to find interesting while also learning more about the functioning of boards. The company was Hewlett-Packard (HP) and the issue had to do with the board chair becoming so obsessed with trying to root out the source of board leaks to the press that she ended up overseeing the spying of directors' telephone records. At this writing, the ethics, wisdom, and legality of this practice were still being debated, but it would be an excellent assignment for students to investigate and report on if they are interested in the ethics of board of directors' practices (Kaplan et al., 2006). It can be reported, however, that the board chair was forced to resign because of her role in the questionable invasion of the privacy of board members and the media.

There can be few topics more important in the teaching of business ethics than that of corporate governance. Students at all levels need to understand how corporations were intended to be governed, what mechanisms have worked and failed, and what steps are being taken by government (e.g., Sarbanes-Oxley), shareholder groups, and companies themselves. It requires initiatives on all these fronts to ensure that effective and ethical corporate governance takes place.

REFERENCES

Bakan, J. (2004). *The corporation: The pathological pursuit of profit and power.* New York: Free Press.

Bazerman, M. H., Loewenstein, G., & Moore, D. A. (2002). Why good accountants do bad audits. *Harvard Business Review, 80*(11), 96.

A blazing summer. (2005, August 11). *Economist,* 61–62.

Board diversity increases. (2000, January). *Association Management,* 25.

Byrne, J. A. (2000, January 24). The best and worst boards. *BusinessWeek,* 142.

Carroll, A., & Buchholtz, A. K. (2006). *Business and society: Ethics and stakeholder management* (6th Ed.). Mason, Ohio: Thomson Southwestern.

Colvin, G. (1997, February). Is the board too cushy? *Director,* 64–65.

Corporate America's woes, continued. (2002, November 28). *The Economist,* 59–61.

Dill, W. R. (Ed.). (1978). *Running the American corporation.* Englewood Cliffs, NJ: Prentice-Hall.

Dore, R. (2005). Deviant or different? Corporate governance in Japan and Germany. *Corporate Governance: An International Review, 13*(3), 437–446.

Epstein, E. M., & Votaw, S. D. (Eds.). (1978). *Rationality, legitimacy, responsibility: Search for new directions in business and society.* Santa Monica, CA: Goodyear Publishing Co.

The fading appeal of the boardroom. (2001, February 10). *The Economist, 67.*

Gutner, T. (2001, April 30). Wanted: More diverse directors. *Business Week,* 134.

Jackson, G., & Moerke, A. (2005). Continuity and change in corporate governance: Comparing Germany and Japan. *Corporate Governance: An International Review, 13:* 351–361.

Kaplan, D. A., Breslau, K., Stone, B., Joseph, N., McGinn, D., & Gordon, D. (2006). Suspicions and spies in Silicon Valley. (Cover story). *Newsweek, 148*(12), 40–47.

Leinster, C. (2003). Board meetings are taking longer. *Corporate Board Member, 6*(7), www.boardmember.com.

Lenckus, D. (2006). Directors focus on insurance after costly settlements. *Business Insurance, 40*(1), 12–12.

McLean, B., & Elkind, P. (2003). *The smartest guys in the room: The amazing rise and scandalous fall of Enron.* New York: Portfolio.

Monks, R. A. G., & Minow, N. (2004). *Corporate governance* (3rd. ed.). Malden, MA: Blackwell Publishing.

Scannell, K., & Langley, M. (2005). After Enron, WorldCom, directors display higher level of concern over their own legal liabilities. *Wall Street Journal - Eastern Edition, 245*(52), C1–C4.

Schatz, S. M., & Clark, D. J. (1998, June). Securities litigation. *International Financial Law Review,* 27.

Schlesinger, M. (2002, November/December). 2002 Sarbanes-Oxley Act *Business Entities,* 42–49.

Securities litigation reform revisited. (1999). *Journal of Accountancy, 187*(1), 20–21.

Segal, J. A. (2002, November). The joy of uncooking. *HR Magazine,* 52–57.

Sweeney, J. J. (2003, September 19). The foxes are still guarding the henhouse. *Los Angeles Times,* p. B13.

Tainer, L. (1983). *The origins of shareholder activism.* Washington, D.C.: Investor Responsibility Research Center.

Thomas, C. B. (2006, June 5). The Enron effect. *Time,* 34–35.

Toedtman, J. (2003, July 31). Lawmakers commemorate one-year anniversary of corporate governance legislation. *Knight-Ridder Tribune Business News,* 1.

Westphal, J. D., & Zajac, E. J. (1994). Substance and symbolism in CEOs' long-term incentive plans. *Administrative Science Quarterly, 39*(3), 367–390.

Westphal, J. D., & Zajac, E. J. (1998). The symbolic management of stockholders: Corporate governance reforms and shareholder reactions. *Administrative Science Quarterly, 43*(1), 127–153.

What directors think study (2003). *Corporate Board Member.* Retrieved July 19, 2006, www.boardmember.com

APPENDIX

Business Roundtable	www.businessweek.com
CALPERS	www.calpers.ca.gov
Citizen Works	www.citizenworks.org
Corporate Governance	www.corpgov.net
The Economist	www.economist.com
Investor Responsibility Research Center	www.irrc.org
Interfaith Center on Corporate Responsibility	www.iccr.org
Living Wage	www.livingwagecampaign.org
Martha Stewart	www.marthatalks.com
OMB Watch (citizen's group)	www.ombwatch.org
Pay Watch	www.aflcio.org/paywatch
Securities and Exchange Commission	www.sec.org
United for a Fair Economy	www.ufenet.org

CHAPTER 15

BEYOND AGENCY THEORY

Common Values for Accounting Ethics Education

Michael K. Shaub
Texas A&M University

Dann G. Fisher
Kansas State University

INTRODUCTION

Whenever discussions arise about the purposes of accounting ethics educa-tion, two very different questions come to the forefront: What *should* we do, and what *can* we do? Both discussions are important, and the normative discussion probably ought to precede the practical one. Practicality tends to lead to watered down recommendations that have little impact on accountants' ethics, reinforcing the idea that accounting ethics education is a fruitless pursuit. On the other hand, we risk alienating many who would willingly improve accounting ethics when we divorce the normative from the practical.

Advancing Business Ethics Education, pages 305–328
Copyright © 2008 by Information Age Publishing
All rights of reproduction in any form reserved.

Ethical decision-making can be represented as having three potential influential components: deontological (duty) considerations, ontological (virtue) considerations, and teleological (potential decision outcome) calculations (Jordan & Sternberg, 2006). In enlisting the contributions of those accounting professors who do not focus on ethics, we often ask them to include ethics as a component of their courses. Many who are willing are most comfortable dealing with teleological ethics, and prefer to shy away from discussions of duty or virtue. They are inclined to think that it is quite difficult to determine what accountants ought to do unless situations are straightforward or illegal, whether the behavior is based on duties or character. But avoiding these issues is not an option. The American Institute of CPAs' Code of Professional Conduct (2006) explicitly requires that CPAs consider their duties, and not just the potential consequences of unethical behavior. Moreover, the Code of Conduct sets forth a plethora of virtues (e.g., honesty, integrity, confidentiality) designed to influence and constrain the behavior of practicing accountants.

Despite the difficulties, an opportunity exists to enlist the efforts of a broader complement of faculty members by reframing the ethics issue. We call this "finding the subversive normative." Finding common values in the accounting profession has become more difficult over time. This trend parallels that in society as a whole, but in the accounting profession it has been driven by CPA firms' increasing profit orientation and changing culture as management consulting services became increasingly important to the practice (Zeff, 2003). Nevertheless, there are several values that are largely noncontroversial, or for which a compelling case can be made without much difficulty. These values unite the profession, their benefits are clear, and they have face validity.

The purpose of this chapter is to identify these values and to develop a strategy for implementing them in the accounting profession. This strategy begins with ethics education in the accounting degree programs that will produce new entrants to the profession. It continues in the culture and professional education provided by the accounting firms that groom these new entrants and prepare them for higher level positions in public accounting, industry, and government.

The next section of this chapter describes how agency theory has influenced accounting ethics education. We then identify three guiding values for the accounting profession that can potentially be inculcated in students and young professionals, and discuss the challenges involved in transmitting these values. This is followed by a strategy for enlisting the help of key professors in this endeavor. We then offer concluding thoughts.

AGENCY THEORY AND ACCOUNTING ETHICS EDUCATION

Prior to the 1970s, accounting academicians generally focused their efforts on normative theorizing and applied articles aimed at improving existing practice. A paradigm shift occurred in the late 1960s to quantitative research influenced by economic and finance methodology, a movement that many accounting academicians hoped would bring greater status within the broader academic community (Van Whye, 1994).

During the 1970s, accounting academicians were quick to embrace the agency theory model that was introduced in the finance literature by Jensen and Meckling (1976) because this model, with its simplifying assumptions of human behavior, is empirically testable (Cohen & Holder-Webb, 2006). In modeling principal-agent behavior, Jensen and Meckling (1976) presumed that all agents are driven strictly by self-interest. Toward this end, agents would shirk, misappropriate resources, and misrepresent their input without conscience (Noreen, 1988).

The assumption of self-interest is an empirically testable assertion that has not been directly tested in the accounting literature. Instead, the self-interest presumption was given a free pass into the accounting literature as part of Watts and Zimmerman's (1986) celebrated *Positive Accounting Theory*. Watts and Zimmerman asserted that managers choose accounting principles not because they best represent the underlying economic activity, but rather because they advance their own economic self-interest. Normative theories, in their view, are merely apologies used to support economic self-interested maneuverings. During the reign of positive theory, challenges to self-interest as the sole motive of business actors were conveniently swept aside as normative, and as such, inferior thinking. This left little room for a discussion of what accounting policy should be, let alone the ethics of the accounting policy choices managers were making.

Although modeling human behavior as self-interested might simplify the examination of "what is," repeatedly exposing students to such thinking may influence what they believe "ought to be." Accounting educators repeatedly, programmatically exposing students to a belief that everyone is self-interested legitimizes self-interested behavior and unwittingly promotes self-interest as a professional norm. Research suggests that students trained in this dark view of human nature do indeed become more self-interested (Marwell & Ames, 1981; Frank, Gilovich, & Regan, 1993; Ferraro, Pfeffer, & Sutton, 2005; Ghoshal, 2005).

The enduring legacy of agency theory, arguably the most popular theory employed by accounting researchers over the past three decades (Cohen & Holder-Webb, 2006), creates resistance to change in the quantity and quality of ethics coverage in the accounting curriculum. Doctoral granting schools provide the greatest remuneration within the accounting discipline (Plumlee, Kachelmeier, Madeo, Pratt, & Krull, 2006) while demanding that their faculty publish in the top-tier journals committed to the precepts of agency theory. By proselytizing our doctoral students in the dogma of agency theory and reserving space in the top journals for the work that this legacy begets, accounting faculty at doctoral granting institutions ensure that agency theory is not only self-fulfilling, but also self-supplying.

This theoretical reductionism may even be responsible for narrowing the skills of the professoriate. Plumlee et al. (2006) predict a dearth of faculty trained in anything other than financial accounting, read agency theory, an outcome that they posit stems from the perceived difficulty in publishing research conducted in specialized areas like audit or tax in the top-tier journals. Moreover, many of those who have come to the professoriate in the past couple of decades or who will soon enter the Academy have little or no professional accounting experience. Whereas earlier generations of academics were seeded with people with extensive experience in the profession, the attractiveness of academic salaries and lifestyles for accounting professors has led to younger entrants to doctoral programs. Many do not have undergraduate accounting degrees. They have been recruited to the professoriate because their backgrounds yield the skills needed to perform the quantitative research valued by the faculty at doctoral-granting institutions. We would expect then that these faculty will hold an allegiance to the egoistic presuppositions of agency theory learned in doctoral programs rather than to the traditional values of the profession, such as public trust, honesty, integrity, and objectivity.

The commitment to the precepts of agency theory makes wholesale change to the quantity and quality of ethics coverage in the accounting curriculum, such as has been proposed by the National Association of State Boards of Accountancy (NASBA, 2005), unlikely to succeed. The approach that we put forth here is more evolutionary than revolutionary. We propose three basic, guiding values for the accounting profession. Rather than forcing change on faculty who do not wish to change, we seek the commitment of influential faculty capable of and willing to change student perspectives of accounting professionalism. The remainder of the chapter describes our plan.

THREE GUIDING VALUES FOR THE ACCOUNTING PROFESSION

We propose three guiding values for the accounting profession:

1. Don't be stupid.
2. Tell the truth.
3. Find fraud and expose liars.

Don't be Stupid

This principle or value—don't be stupid—may be the most difficult of the three to persuade the accounting profession to adopt. On its face, this value seems silly, since no one embraces the idea of being stupid. But it requires, of course, an agreement about what it means to be stupid.

Most would agree that engaging in behavior that systematically harms you is stupid, whether you embrace agency theory or the Ten Commandments as your guiding principles. In fact, Jensen and Meckling (1976) view self-interested behavior as the ultimate rationality that is at the center of agency theory. Their later attempts to broaden the theory to include preferences other than money (Jensen & Meckling, 1994) and even nonrational behavior (Jensen, 1994) still put the individual's self-interest at the center of ethical decision-making. It may be couched in more noble terms, such as their contention that the central principle of agency theory is not to "steal all you can," but to recognize that because of agency costs, including monitoring costs, agreements are always in the best interests of parties in agency relationships because they can share the gains. Still, the driving appeal is to self-interest.

Sternberg (2002, 2003a), on the other hand, claims that egocentrism is one of the five fallacies of thinking that must be overcome in order for people to be wise. The other four fallacies—omnipotence, omniscience, invulnerability, and unrealistic optimism—have been at the heart of many of the problems encountered by the accounting profession in recent years. These will be discussed at length later in this chapter.

Whether egocentrism should be the central focus of moral reasoning (Jensen & Meckling, 1976) or whether it is one of the five fallacies of thinking that prevents people from being wise (Jordan & Sternberg, 2006) is an open question worthy of debate. It cannot be both simultaneously. Either egocentrism is a fallacy that causes harm, or it is the best way to insure the good.

A persuasive case must be made that purely self-interested behavior really is "stupid." The next section describes how self-interested behavior, along with evidences of the other four fallacies of thinking, have degraded outsiders' views of the business world and the accounting profession, inviting regulatory interventions such as the Sarbanes-Oxley Act. We view auditors' willingness to be susceptible to these fallacies as "stupid," though Sternberg (2005) would use the term "foolish."

Examples of the Five Fallacies of Thinking

According to Robert Sternberg (2002), the five fallacies of thinking are egocentrism, omnipotence, omniscience, invulnerability, and unrealistic optimism. In describing these, Sternberg (2005, p. 358) states, "Unsuccessful leaders often show certain stereotyped fallacies in their thinking. Consider five such flaws (Sternberg, 2003a, 2003b). They are found in almost all failed leaders, such as those at Enron, WorldCom, Arthur Andersen, Adelphia, and numerous other similar organizations.

Sternberg, a well-known psychologist and former president of the American Psychological Association, sees the transparent failures of the accounting profession and corporate leaders in recent years as classic examples of these five fallacies at work.

Because egocentrism, one of the five fallacies, is explicitly put forward by Jensen and Meckling (1994) as normative behavior, the discussion of egocentrism will be far more extensive than that of the other four fallacies. However, Jordan (2005, p. 174) found a significant positive correlation on measures of all five fallacies, indicating that they are interrelated.

Egocentrism.   In discussing egocentrism, Sternberg (2005, p. 358) asserts, "This fallacy occurs when successful leaders start to think that they are the only ones that matter, not the people who rely on them for leadership." It would be hard to think of a better example of this fallacy than Dennis Kozlowski, the former CEO of Tyco International (Sternberg, 2006). Although he spread the wealth to a few selected others, such as his administrative assistant and CFO Mark Swartz, Kozlowski's famous excesses, including the $2 million birthday party for his wife on the island of Sardinia and his company apartment complete with $6,000 gold shower curtain, made him a poster child for executive greed.

Jensen and Meckling (1976) clearly believe that agency theory, or at least its revised version, the Resourceful Evaluative Maximizing Model (REMM), is normative (Jensen & Meckling, 1994). Declaring that self-interest is what we ought to pursue, Jensen (1994, p. 10) states, "Even more importantly, this dualistic model will lead, I believe, to much more effective normative propositions, programs, and devices for helping people to avoid or minimize the non-rational, dysfunctional aspects of their behavior." Moreover, Jensen and Meckling (1994, p. 11) claim, "Because of its ability to explain such remarkable shifts in cultural values, REMM also provides the foundation for thinking about how to change corporate culture."

Jensen and Meckling (1994) claim that because self-interest defines the shifts in cultural values, REMM should be used to determine how people ought to behave in an organization. Jensen's (1994) clearest statement of REMM as normative occurs when he explains that people are not always resourceful evaluating maximizers in accordance with the REMM model because they seek to avoid pain:

> Clinical psychological records as well as everyday observations of family, organizational, and social action, abound with examples of humans engaging in

non-rational behavior. By non-rational I do not mean random or unexplainable, I mean dysfunctional or counterproductive behavior that systematically harms the individual. But this non-rational behavior can be modeled relatively simply, and recognizing these non-rational aspects of human beings does not mean that we have to give up the powerful predictive ability of REMM. Indeed, the two phenomenon (sic) can and do simultaneously exist, and their joint recognition converts REMM from a purely *positive* description of human behavior to a *normative* model that says this is how humans should behave. Consistent with the view, I believe the solutions suggested by the psychological and psychiatric professions are best interpreted as helping people learn to correct their "mistakes" in order to behave in more REMM-like ways. (Jensen, 1994, p. 7)

Jensen justifies the pursuit of self-interest by referring to Adam Smith's (1976, pp. 26–27) famous statement, "It is not from the benevolence of the butcher, the brewer, or the baker that we expect our dinner, but from their regard to their own interest." However, even Jensen recognizes that Adam Smith was a moral philosopher, not primarily an economist, and Smith made many statements that would indicate that he did not believe that egocentrism was normative. In fact, Smith had a clear idea of what the virtuous man *ought* to do in terms of self-interest, as expressed in *The Theory of Moral Sentiments*:

> To attain to this envied situation, the candidates for fortune too frequently abandon the paths of virtue; for unhappily, the road which leads to the one and that which leads to the other, lie sometimes in very opposite directions (Smith, 1966, p. 88)…The wise and virtuous man is at all times willing that his own private interest should be sacrificed to the public interest of his own particular order or society. (ibid, p. 346)

Adam Smith did believe that egocentrism was descriptive of the way people behaved, so much so that he did not believe that mutual stock companies could long survive (Smith, 1976). Except for the most repetitive tasks, he believed that distance and lack of supervision would doom these companies because of the egocentric nature of man. However, to conclude that Smith preferred egocentric behavior or thought that egocentrism was normative is entirely inaccurate.

Jensen and Meckling (1994, p. 11), on the other hand, take a purely consequentialist approach to morality, stating that "…cultural practices or values must adapt so as to approximate optimal behavior given the costs and benefits implied by the opportunity set." Customs, morals, and even religion evolve according to "…behavior patterns that reflect optimal response to the costs and benefits of various actions." The optimal new behaviors are accommodated "through experience, education, and death."

Values are a shell in Jensen and Meckling's REMM. It is not that one is honest, but rather that doing X makes one feel honest. One is allowed to value feeling honest and put it in the cost-benefit calculation, even as the highest-weighted component. But one is not necessarily honest.

Our assertion that Jensen and Meckling view values merely as a shell may seem to be a dramatic claim for us to make against agency theory until one considers that a fundamental assumption of agency theory and REMM is unlimited substitution—everyone will substitute freely one type of good for another, including readily sacrificing ethical values for other goods. Jensen and Meckling (1994, p. 15) claim, in comparing REMM with Maslow's (1943) hierarchy of needs (which does not explicitly provide for substitution, but claims that needs are satisfied in a particular order), "...individuals at any level of wealth are willing to sacrifice some amounts of any good for sufficiently large amounts of all other goods." Jensen and Meckling (1994, p. 5) state explicitly, "Goods can be anything from art objects to ethical norms." Thus, everyone will substitute their ethical norms for sufficient amounts of other goods under REMM (or agency theory), eliminating the possibility of holding to absolutes.

This is a cynical view of life, and it naturally hardens a culture taught to believe it. In the case of business ethics education, and more specifically accounting ethics education, it naturally hardens the financial professions and legitimizes motivations that continue to make headlines in the business press.

REMM allows raising the costs of behavior. But what reason can be given for raising those costs without values that involve more than simple calculations? Is it just that stealing makes us less efficient as a society, a company, a family? Is the final underlying value efficiency? There has to be at least one ultimate underlying value, whether it is pleasure maximization or something else. And is there any restraint if that one chosen value is, in the end, wrong or somehow self-defeating? Is it simply that in an evolutionary process you get whatever ought to survive as a set of values?

Jensen (1994) claims that altruism is actually self-interested behavior. This, of course, makes agency theory a tautology—whatever behavior a person engages in is what they prefer, whether it involves pure self-interest or altruism. We can tell what they prefer by what they do, but it is all self-interested. This outcome, however, is dependent upon Jensen equating self-interest with rationality and self-interest with acting upon one's preferences. To be self-interested is to have preferences directed toward one's own good. To be altruistic is to have preferences directed toward someone else's good. Note that Jensen has added the requirement that to be self-interested is to act on one's preferences, and to act on a preference reveals one's self-interest. But this is a circular fallacy.

Persons who are self-interested hold different preferences from those who are altruistic. Acting upon altruistic preferences reduces to self-interested behavior only if one equates rational choice as acting upon one's own interests rather than the interests of others. Yet, acting upon altruistic preferences may be every bit as rational as acting upon self-interested preferences. Preferences are rational if they are complete and transitive. Choices are rational if they are driven by preferences. The theory of rationality, however, does not place constraints on what a person prefers (Hausman & McPherson, 1996). Thus, a conflict does not exist between altruism and rationality nor is it imperative that altruism be linked with self-interest.

Jensen (1994, p. 5) answers his critics (such as Brennan, 1994) by saying that arguments for altruistic behavior imply that people are perfect agents for others, by which he means "…someone who makes decisions with no concern for his or her own preferences, but only for those of another, including an employer or principal." But being a perfect agent is not a requirement for altruism, nor does Brennan argue that it is. People do not need to be concerned *only* for others' interests in order to be altruistic; in other words, they are not required to ignore their own interests. Even the Golden Rule recognizes self-interest; the reference point for how to treat others is how *you* want to be treated.

Jensen (1994, pp. 7–8) admits that rationality is not complete as an explanation of behavior. He characterizes nonrational behavior as "…dysfunctional or counterproductive behavior that systematically harms the individual" and attributes this behavior to the desire to avoid pain. Surprisingly, he says, "These imperfections are not aberrations from normality, but rather an integral part of normality itself" while claiming that any non-REMM behavior has negative consequences, meaning that it is dysfunctional, or normatively bad. He even attributes "… the failure of the internal control systems that has led to the waste of hundreds of billions of dollars of resources and the failure of many of the crown jewels of corporate America over the last several decades …" to people's "reluctance to learn and adjust their behavior to better serve their own interests." Others would attribute these failures to aggressively self-interested behavior.

Missing from Jensen's discussion is any consideration of how morality constrains choices. Moral norms may compete with preferences rather than determine them. If one expands the definition of morality to be acting based on good reasons, then there is no conflict between morality and rationality (Hausman & McPherson, 1996). But once rationality is equated with self-interest, constraining one's preferences with moral norms is, by definition, irrational. Tying rationality to self-interest is a normative choice. If agency theory is the predominant "moral" theory taught in business school classrooms, we would expect to see behaviors that treat egocentrism not just as descriptive of business decision makers, but as normative for all rational individuals. And we do.

Omnipotence.   The second fallacy of thinking set out by Sternberg is omnipotence. According to Sternberg (2005, p. 359), "This fallacy occurs when leaders think they are all-powerful and can do whatever they want." For example, some leaders who have early success in a market believe that their market advantages are unassailable. Others will escalate their commitment (Staw, 1976) to a formerly winning strategy when the business begins to struggle because they have trouble picturing the company losing its advantage. This can lead to unethical behavior, as Street and Street (2006, p. 34) state:

> In as much (sic) as organizational decision makers entrapped in an escalation situation are likely to be sensitive to the economic costs of maintaining the current failing course of action, unethical options offering relief may provide practical appeal sufficient to induce such behavior.

This appears to have been the case at Enron. The company's stock price soared in 1999 and 2000 as the company produced both earnings and innovations. The company's leaders were regularly characterized in the business press as geniuses overseeing one of the world's best-run companies. But meeting the market's expectations became more difficult as Enron moved beyond being the market for natural gas trading into more "cutting edge" ideas for making markets. These ideas were largely failures and, along with major failed investments in India and elsewhere, left huge earnings gaps to fill.

Andrew Fastow was emboldened by his knowledge of structured financing to ask the board to trust him never to play both sides of a transaction, even though he controlled the special purpose entities set up to hide Enron's liabilities. His omnipotence at structuring deals that brought in many major banks as players made it appear that he could do no wrong, and that he had a right to siphon off profits from these transactions for himself and a few trusted associates. In a taped presentation to Merrill Lynch seeking investment in one of the special purpose entities included in the video, *The Smartest Guys in the Room*, a participant remarks that they cannot shoot holes in Fastow's presentation. Fastow smiles and says, "Good." At that moment, Fastow exudes a power, an omnipotence, which makes him seem invulnerable.

Another chilling example involves Robert Nardelli, the recently deposed CEO of Home Depot. At the company's annual meeting, which he convinced the board of directors not to attend, Nardelli restricted shareholders to one question and comments to one minute, a rule he enforced with large digital timers that triggered the microphones to be cut off (Grow, Foust, Thorton, Farzad, McGregor, Zegel, & Javers, 2007). When asked by one shareholder about conflicts of interest among the board of directors, Nardelli retorted, "This is not the forum in which to address these comments" (*New York Times On-line*, 2007).

Omniscience.   Omniscience "occurs when leaders think that they know everything, and lose sight of the limitations of their own knowledge" (Sternberg, 2005, p. 359). Omniscience is often linked to omnipotence, particularly in a profession such as accounting where knowledge advantages become economic advantages. Expertise has long been central to the profession, so much so that the fundamental requirement to be a certified public accountant has evolved over time to be the equivalent of a master's degree. Young accountants and auditors are promoted in their early years largely because they develop expertise that is valuable to their companies, their accounting firms, or their clients.

Many build on this process by pursuing an MBA at a top school, the way Andrew Fastow did. He had the intellectual horsepower and the academic pedigree, and he became part of the type of competitive environment at Enron that rewarded his ambition, particularly because of his close association with his mentor, CEO Jeffrey Skilling.

Skilling began to depend increasingly on Fastow to provide the schemes that would permit Enron to produce earnings. His omniscience about these issues was enough to convince the board that he could be allowed control of the special purpose entities because of their benefit in providing necessary financing, in spite of evidence that his actions were narrowly self-interested. And for Fastow, being smarter than those around him provided assurance that he could do what was necessary to keep the transactions from collapsing. All he needed to do was to keep the stock price up, since Enron shares were given to the special purpose entities to offset the liabilities they assumed.

Omniscience gives the impression that you can make a market for something that no one currently wants to buy, and that you can anticipate changes in the marketplace. The success of innovative companies such as Microsoft, Intel, Google, and Yahoo reinforce the idea that if a person is smart enough, success is inevitable. But wisdom requires recognizing the limitations of knowledge and our susceptibility to the omniscience fallacy.

Invulnerability.   Sternberg (2005) maintains that invulnerability occurs

...when leaders think they can get away with anything because they are too clever to be caught; and even if they are caught, they figure that they can get away with what they have done because of who they imagine themselves to be. (p. 359)

Overconfidence is most likely to be found in those who have historically had reasons to be confident about their success.

Hank Greenberg, the long-time chairman and CEO of AIG, had every reason to be overconfident about his prospects for remaining in that position for as long as he desired. He was universally recognized as one of the risk and insurance industry's most powerful leaders, an influential force not only in his own company but also in related companies run by family members, such as Marsh and McLennan. And his company had a history of uninterrupted success:

> For years, AIG's results were among the most predictable on Wall Street, even though its core business by nature was unpredictable... [I]t earned the adoration of shareholders by turning in quarter after quarter of double-digit growth in net income and steady improvement in other performance measures watched by Wall Street, including how much it put aside to pay future claims. Such results were the single-minded focus of the iron-fisted Mr. Greenberg as he transformed the company into a global conglomerate over the course of four decades. (McDonald, Solomon, & Francis, 2005, p. A7)

Yet after revelation of serial accounting misstatements over the years that forced multiple delays in the filing of its 2004 10-K, Greenberg was forced to resign as CEO. Some of the questionable transactions drew attention because they were apparently facilitated by General Re, a large reinsurance company that is a unit of Warren Buffett's Berkshire Hathaway.

Substantial evidence exists that overconfidence extends to auditors as well. Kennedy and Peecher (1997, pp. 280–281), for example, concluded, "We find that auditors are overconfident in assessments of their own and their subordinates' technical knowledge and that overestimates of subordinates' knowledge (optimism) increases as the knowledge gap between supervisors and subordinates increases." This is not a small problem, as overconfidence can lead to dysfunctional audit behaviors such as assigning auditors to tasks beyond their expertise, insufficient review of subordinates' workpapers, and inappropriate promotion. Auditors may also be overconfident about inherited hypotheses such as no significant change in an account from year to year, and thus rely too heavily on analytical procedures rather than doing additional audit testing (Glover, Prawitt, & Wilks, 2005).

At Enron, the corporate culture ensured that only those perceived to be the best of the best survived and moved to the top. It is not surprising that Andrew Fastow would have felt invulnerable in a setting where he was considered "the smartest guy in the room" and had explicit control over the structuring of special purpose entities, even convincing those above him to allow him to have ownership in them. Prentice (2004) offers this assessment of Fastow and WorldCom CEO Bernard Ebbers:

> One must suspect that the short-term gratification that Bernard Ebbers at WorldCom and Andrew Fastow at Enron enjoyed in the form of their fabulous if illicit remuneration outweighed in their minds the long-term risks of being caught (which may have been underappreciated due to overconfidence and overoptimism biases). (Prentice, 2004, p. 67)

Invulnerability is not limited to people doing evil because they believe they cannot be harmed. In the early part of this decade, the AICPA believed that its position in favor of providing extensive non-audit services to audit clients would prevail politically, even after the Enron debacle and the indictment of Arthur Andersen. Although the AICPA offered to give up providing two services to audit clients, financial information system design and implementation and outsourcing clients' internal audit functions (Aldhizer, Cashell, & Martin, 2003), it seemed unlikely that they would even have to go that far. But then the WorldCom story broke, and within about a month the president had signed the Sarbanes-Oxley Act banning a wide variety of same-client services.

Unrealistic Optimism.   Unrealistic optimism "occurs when leaders think they are so smart and effective that they can do whatever they want" (Sternberg, 2005, p. 358). Though optimism is generally a positive characteristic in leaders and managers, there is always the danger that overoptimism will cause an individual to ignore important evidence. And historic success can be a contributor to overoptimism. The cash flow that arises from a series of good decisions can mask previously bad decisions when the tide begins to turn against a company. Prentice (2004, p. 67), in summarizing the work of Langevoort (1997), states:

> ...that it is quite possible that in many cases of corporate disclosure fraud, the offending officers and directors were not consciously lying but instead were expressing honestly-held [sic], but irrationally optimistic views of their firms' conditions and prospects. (Prentice, 2004, p. 67)

Jeffrey Eischeid, former partner in charge of KPMG's Personal Financial Planning division testified that for all of their aggressive tax strategies, which no longer may be offered by the firm, they provided clients with "more likely than not" opinions, indicating that there was a greater than fifty percent chance that they would prevail if challenged by the Internal Revenue Service (Eischeid, 2003). According to a U. S. Department of Justice (2005) release announcing KPMG's agreement to pay $456 million to avoid prosecution as a firm,

> ...top leadership at KPMG made the decision to approve and participate in shelters and issue KPMG opinion letters despite significant warnings from

KPMG tax experts and others throughout the development of the shelters and at critical junctures that the shelters were close to frivolous and would not withstand IRS scrutiny.

KPMG's unrealistic optimism, which was in violation of Treasury Department Circular 230 (IRS, 2005) that governs tax practice, and may well have been in violation of the "realistic possibility" requirement of the AICPA's Statements on Standards for Tax Practice (AICPA, 2000), turned out to be very expensive.

The most effective way to address unrealistic optimism would be to predict it ahead of time, rather than seeing things in retrospect. The AICPA may still be suffering today from unrealistic optimism, hoping that the provisions of Sarbanes-Oxley will be rolled back with the retirement of both of the bill's namesakes from Congress. However, by the time any changes might take place, public companies will have implemented all of the law's requirements and put in place processes that yield some tangible benefits. It seems unlikely that companies that put in place stronger internal control structures or more accountable boards will decide to reverse course and dismantle this infrastructure. Many of these changes will likely come to be seen as best practices.

The Root Causes of the Five Fallacies.   At the root of the five fallacies of thinking is the failure to recognize the limits of expertise (Sternberg, 2005) and to recognize one's susceptibility to a loss of objectivity. The AICPA Code of Professional Conduct (AICPA, 2006) seeks to address the professional's "blind spots" in several ways. For example, "The principle of objectivity imposes the obligation to be impartial, *intellectually honest* [italics added], and free of conflicts of interest" (AICPA 2006, ET 55.01). This impartiality does not come naturally; people are naturally self-interested. Impartiality requires a commitment to adopting the perspective of a professional, as well as instituting objective processes that will help auditors to assess when slippage may have occurred.

Auditors must be aware of threats to their professionalism, particularly to their independence. They must also be aware of the potential to move from rational trust to emotional trust in their relationships with their clients. Auditors, over time, have the potential to become deeply interdependent with, and even deeply dependent on, their clients professionally (Shaub, 2004).

The Independence Standards Board (2001) recognized five primary threats to auditor independence against which accounting firms need to establish adequate safeguards. Self-interest threats generally arise when the auditor's financial interests are linked to the client. Self-review threats arise from auditors providing assurance on their own work. Advocacy threats to independence occur when auditors promote a client's position or opinion. Perceived or actual intimidation from clients may deter auditors from objectivity. Trust or familiarity threats exist when a close relationship makes the auditor too sympathetic to the client's interests.

In fact, all of these threats arise out of the pursuit of self-interest. Self-review was a problem prior to Sarbanes-Oxley because CPA firms pursued extensive consulting engagements with their audit clients. CPA firms advocating client positions are always seeking to further their self-interest in doing so, even when they are objective about an issue and agree with the client's position. Clients only intimidate CPA firms because it is in the CPA firm's self-interest to keep the client happy and because close relationships generate revenue streams for accounting firms. Yet all of these behaviors potentially undermine the auditors' objectivity about their client. The unrestrained pursuit of self-interest undermines auditors' objectivity and makes them susceptible to the five fallacies of thinking; being completely focused on self-interest makes auditors "stupid."

Tell the Truth

The second common value that should be readily embraced by the accounting profession is a commitment to tell the truth. This seems like an obvious obligation to most people outside the accounting profession, but the importance of telling the truth has not seemed self-evident within the profession. In fact, despite professional standards explicitly calling for it, the accounting profession is less committed to telling the truth than most of the public thinks.

The AICPA Code of Professional Conduct (2006) assigns CPAs three explicit duties that influence truth-telling—integrity, objectivity, and transparency. Together these build a strong case for a duty to maximize truth-telling.

Integrity is directly related to truth-telling. In fact, the relevant portion of the principles section of the AICPA Code of Professional Conduct (2006, ET 54.02) states that:

> Integrity requires a member to be, among other things, *honest and candid* [italics added] within the constraints of client confidentiality. Service and the public trust should not be subordinated to personal gain and advantage. Integrity can accommodate the inadvertent error and the *honest* [italics added] difference of opinion; it cannot accommodate deceit or subordination of principle.

Since this duty applies to all CPAs and not just to auditors, CPAs also have the duty to be honest and candid with one another. And for the auditor the need to be honest and candid is especially important because of the assigned role of preventing harm to the public. As is clear from rule 301 of the AICPA Code of Professional Conduct (2006), client confidentiality does not restrain an auditor from revealing violations of generally accepted accounting principles or generally accepted auditing standards.

Objectivity influences truth-telling as well. One must be clear thinking and impartial in order to be most likely to tell the truth. As stated earlier, the AICPA Code of Conduct (2006, ET 55.01) speaks of the duty of objectivity this way: "The principle of objectivity imposes the obligation to be impartial, *intellectually honest* [italics added], and free of conflicts of interest."

Finally, the AICPA Code's often-ignored duty of transparency is a clear call to maximize truth-telling, since it places equal responsibility on client CPAs and outside auditors to bring about this end. As the Code of Conduct (2006, ET 55.04) states:

> Members employed by others to prepare financial statements or to perform auditing, tax, or consulting services are charged with the same responsibility for objectivity as members in public practice and must be *scrupulous in their application of generally accepted accounting principles and candid in all their dealings with members in public practice* [italics added].

The terms "honest," "candid," and "intellectually honest" imply a strong duty to maximize truth-telling. But the ethical approach adopted by the profession has been to "not materially misstate" (Shaub, 2005). This has led to egregious behavior such as Andersen's well-documented decision to not require Enron to make an adjustment to its 1997 income statement that would have reduced earnings by 48 percent because the adjustment was "immaterial" (Brody, Lowe, & Pany, 2003).

Find Fraud and Expose Liars

The third common value that the accounting profession ought to embrace is a commitment to finding fraud and exposing liars. Finding fraud is made more challenging because of the inability of auditors to think creatively. Perhaps accounting programs largely produce those graduates who are able to conform to a particular professional image that is attractive to recruiters from professional services firms. These graduates are largely quite intelligent and well trained, but Sternberg (2001, p. 361) declares that, "beyond intelligence and other abilities, creativity appears to be in large part a decision...Some people use their intelligence to please the crowd, others to defy it." As accounting professors, we are rarely accused of preparing people who will "defy the crowd." We teach people to think alike, to hold to common principles. This is probably necessary in order to have standards against which we can judge aberrations such as fraud. But professors have been largely unsuccessful in inculcating in auditors the idea that dissent is an obligation of the profession.

The first step in preventing or detecting fraud is to allow for the possibility that it may actually exist. Suspicious behavior is behavior that is intended to prevent harm (Deutsch, 1962; Shaub, 1996). If auditors want to prevent harm to financial statement users, they must see professional skepticism as not only a neutral term, but also an obligation to dissent when indicators point to client information being misrepresented.

But to be successful at detecting and preventing fraud, auditors also need to develop creativity. Statement on Auditing Standards (SAS) 99 (AICPA, 2001), the U.S. fraud auditing standard, requires that auditors employ unpredictable auditing procedures. This standard was designed to counteract, in part, the history of auditors going to work for their clients and bringing with them historical knowledge about the audit firm's strategy for auditing the client. Though the Independence Standards Board identified this as a primary threat to auditor independence, its independence standard on employment by audit clients did not prohibit auditors from being employed by clients (Independence Standards Board, 2000). That restriction was left to the Sarbanes-Oxley Act (2002) to require a one-year "cooling off" period before auditors are allowed to assume critical financial roles with their clients. Apparently, the recently issued SAS 99 did not persuade Congress that auditors would be creative enough in developing unpredictable auditing procedures to protect the public.

Accounting professors have the opportunity to strategically build a commitment to truth-telling and finding fraud into the mindsets of their students. For example, students could benefit from additional exposure to forensic accounting techniques in their auditing courses. An increasing number of programs have added a forensic accounting or fraud examination course to their accounting curriculum since the Enron and World-Com scandals. Yet there has historically been some resistance to incorporating forensic techniques into mainstream audits because of the signal that it sends that auditors do not trust their clients.

This resistance arises, in part, because the auditing literature is ambiguous about the importance of professional skepticism. Though SAS 99 recognizes that professional skepticism is fundamental to the concept of due professional care, the AICPA's definition is less than forceful, indicating that skepticism "includes" a questioning mind. But the AICPA, and the accounting profession, stand alone in making skepticism a neutral term, involving neither trust nor distrust. Virtually any other use of the term "skeptic" involves challenging assumptions and calling into question assertions.

Only recently has the accounting profession sought to incorporate these concerns in auditing standards. Recent movement toward adopting a forensic approach as part of every financial statement audit is reflected in the recent Big 4 + 2 joint paper calling for a new approach to the audit (Global Capital Markets, 2006). Some see this as simply self-interested behavior intended to maximize audit fees and minimize auditor liability. Nevertheless, this call represents a significant shift in the thinking of the major audit firms.

To be professionally skeptical in an audit setting takes training and reinforcement. Yet Shaub and Lawrence (2002) provide cross-sectional evidence that aggressive skepticism that is present in new auditors is largely absent in the seniors that supervise them. This could be because these auditors learn to properly calibrate skepticism, becoming what Shaub and Lawrence call "measured skeptics," or watchdogs. But evidence exists that a number of these auditors become "conflicted skeptics," particularly if they are sanctioned by those in authority for expressing skepticism. Professors and accounting firm trainers can have a significant influence on young auditors' preparation for these types of situations. With the large accounting firms rethinking the audit approach, perhaps this is an ideal time for rethinking professional skepticism training in the accounting classroom and in auditor training classes. The next section describes an explicit strategy for enlisting a subset of accounting professors in changing the nature of accounting ethics education.

A STRATEGY FOR ENLISTING THE HELP OF KEY PROFESSORS

Most plans for changing accounting education include recommendations for how to teach ethics, and our approach is no exception. But perhaps even more important than adopting our three-pronged approach to teaching accounting ethics is our recognition that this effort in universities is doomed unless we enlist the commitment of key professors. Realistically, many professors will be resistant to a "back to the future" idea of reinvigorating professionalism in accounting by taking on more responsibility for not being stupid, telling the truth, finding fraud, and exposing liars. We have already established, for instance, that what we call "stupid" or lacking wisdom is seen by many professors as rational and even normative. It will be a long wait to convince them otherwise, and even the major scandals surrounding Sarbanes-Oxley have only served to modestly change consequentialist calculations of the effects of unethical behavior.

Enlisting the majority of professors to change students' perspectives is not mandatory, but engaging key professors in this endeavor is imperative.

By key professors, we mean the "moral movers" and those teaching critical courses.

The "moral movers" include professors that accounting majors look to for modeling the behavior of a professional. These are often professors with significant professional experience outside the classroom, who seem driven by something beyond simple technical competence. They embrace the idea that accounting, as a profession, takes seriously its responsibility for protecting the public interest. They communicate a sense of the profession's history and that there are qualities worth preserving over time. Often these professors express deep concern for student welfare and for the reputation of the business school generally and the accounting program specifically. Students naturally attach themselves to these professors, particularly those students who are concerned about what kind of person they will become when they enter the profession.

In identifying key professors, the question of agency theory as normative or positive will play a central role in what is communicated in the classroom. Key professors have the opportunity in the classroom to put forth a different model for what it is to be seen as an ethical accountant or auditor. But without their explicit commitment to change, the discussion of ethics will continue to be framed as an adaptation to agency relationships. It is no surprise, then, that an ethics requirement in the accounting curriculum, like the one put forth by the NASBA (2005), would be seen as a burdensome incurrence of costs that would reduce the number of accountants and auditors prepared for the marketplace. The argument (put forth by the American Institute of Certified Public Accountants and the American Accounting Association) is that the NASBA requirement would result in poorer quality audits, using standard economic assumptions that the regulatory burden of additional hours in the curriculum would cause students to shift into lower cost majors such as finance (Reckers, 2006). Of course, this model assumes away any benefit that might be derived from the fact that those self-selecting out of the accounting profession are the individuals who do not want to be bothered with taking ethics courses. This model also assumes that no one would be drawn to accounting as a major by the attractiveness of a profession committed to telling the truth and exposing liars, a self-selection bias that might increase the quality of the profession (Shaub, 2006).

Gaining support for our approach from professors who are teaching the critical courses in the curriculum is imperative. Certainly a strong case could be made for virtually any accounting course containing significant professionalism and ethics components. But the courses that seem to provide the initial links to the accounting profession for most students are intermediate accounting, managerial accounting, auditing, tax, and perhaps accounting information systems.

If the auditing professors, in particular, do not buy into our approach, it is unlikely that student exposure in the other courses will be sufficient to impart the perspective put forth here. Of all the CPA's roles, the audit is most clearly linked to the public interest; few would argue that the auditor has no responsibility to shareholders and investors. But if the auditing professor is alone in presenting this view of the profession, the importance and meaning will be overcome by the egoistic message prevalent in the rest of the curriculum, and students will be much less likely to adopt our new perspective.

The role of tax professionals has long been contrasted with the role of auditors because tax accountants are often seen as simply advocates for their clients. The Statements on Standards for Tax Service (AICPA, 2000), however, states that "In addition to a duty to the taxpayer, [the professional] has a duty to the tax system." Recent scandals linked to marketing tax shelters create new opportunities for tax professors to point out the limits of client advocacy and to emphasize the importance of tax CPAs' professionalism.

But perhaps the most critical courses are the intermediate financial and managerial accounting courses that prepare students for their roles in internal and external financial reporting. Professors in these courses have the opportunity to either emphasize or de-emphasize the importance of truth-telling in financial reporting. When accounting rules are viewed as arbitrary, truth-telling is undermined, although this can be offset somewhat by a commitment to maximizing disclosure. Professors who introduce reporting cases into these courses, particularly those with significant ethical implications, provide early opportunities for students to confront their professional roles.

CONCLUSION

The inculcation of agency theory as descriptive, and even normative, has a pervasive effect on young accountants' ethical perspectives. Agency theory as a meta-language is well established in business schools, and the presentation of an alternative model to ethical decision-making in accounting is likely to be resisted by accounting professors. But alternative approaches are not unprecedented, and a wealth of ethics literature in other business disciplines supports a position that people use approaches to ethical decision-making that incorporate duties, and not just consequences (e.g., Hunt & Vitell, 1986).

Many other models exist that could be used for teaching accounting ethics. One potentially attractive alternative ethical model to agency theory that is compatible with the approach that we have outlined here is Sternberg's call for wisdom, intelligence, and creativity (Sternberg, 2005). Intelligence and creativity without wisdom leave the accountant subject to the five fallacies of thinking, especially egocentrism. The key employees at Enron and WorldCom were intelligent and creative, but these energies were channeled by narrow self-interest. What might have restrained their behavior was a commitment to overcoming the fallacies of thinking that inhibit the development of wisdom. For that commitment to be internalized, it would likely need to have been a part of the culture, something almost impossible to envision in retrospect in those companies. But this is the kind of commitment that, when made by the board of directors and top management, permits the free flow of information upward within the organization. It becomes a learning organization, interested not only in trumpeting its successes, but also in being aware of its vulnerabilities.

Accounting professors can make it easier for these types of organizational environments to flourish by presenting a broader approach to ethical decision-making as normative. Agency theory is informative in describing the behavior of many, but when presented as normative, agency theory has the potential to become a self-fulfilling prophecy. And in a profession like accounting that relies on a commitment to others' interests to sustain itself as a profession, unrestrained self-interest has been and will continue to be a dangerous thing.

REFERENCES

Aldhizer, G., Cashell, J., & Martin, D. (2003). Internal audit outsourcing. *The CPA Journal, 73* (August), 38–42.

American Institute of Certified Public Accountants (AICPA). (2000). *Statements on Standards for Tax Service.* New York: AICPA.

American Institute of Certified Public Accountants (AICPA). (2001). *Statement on Auditing Standards No. 99.* New York: AICPA.

American Institute of Certified Public Accountants (AICPA). (2006). *Code of Professional Conduct.* Retrieved on May 17, 2007 from www.aicpa.org.

Brennan, M. J. (1994). Incentives, rationality, and society. *Journal of Applied Corporate Finance, 7*(Summer), 31–39.

Brody, R. G., Lowe, D. J., & Pany, K. (2003). Could $51 million be immaterial when Enron reports income of $105 million? *Accounting Horizons, 17*(2), 153–160.

Cohen, J. R., & Holder-Webb, L. L. (2006). Rethinking the influence of agency theory in the accounting academy. *Issues in Accounting Education, 21*(February), 17–30.

Deutsch, M. (1962). Cooperation and trust: Some notes. In M. R. Jones (Ed.), *Nebraska Symposium on Motivation* (pp. 275–319). Lincoln, NE: University of Nebraska Press.

Eischeid, J. (2003). Statement before the Senate permanent subcommittee on investigations. Retrieved May 17, 2007 from http://www.pbs.org/wgbh/pages/frontline/shows/tax/schemes/testimony.html.

Ferraro, F., Pfeffer, J., & Sutton, R. I. (2005). Economics language and assumptions: How theories can become self-fulfilling. *Academy of Management Review, 30*(1), 8–24.

Frank, R. H., Gilovich, T. D., & Regan, D. T. (1993). Does studying economics inhibit cooperation? *Journal of Economic Perspectives, 7*(Spring), 159–171.

Ghoshal, S. (2005). Bad management theories are destroying good management practices. *Academy of Management Learning & Education, 4*(1), 75–91.

Global capital markets and the global economy: A vision from the CEOs of the international audit networks. (2006). Retrieved May 17, 2007 from http://www.globalpublicpolicysymposium.com.

Glover, S., Prawitt, D., & Wilks, T. (2005). Why do auditors over-rely on weak analytical procedures? The role of outcome and precision. *Auditing: A Journal of Practice and Theory, 24*(Supp.), 197–220.

Grow, B., Foust, D., Thorton, E., Farzad, R., McGregor, J., Zegel, S., & Javers, E. (2007). Out at Home Depot. Retrieved January 26, 2007 from http://news.yahoo.com/s/bw/20070105/bs_bw/b4017001.

Hausman, D. M., & McPherson, M. S. (1996). *Economic analysis and moral philosophy.* New York, NY: Press Syndicate of the University of Cambridge Press.

Hunt, S., & Vitell, S..(1986). A general theory of marketing ethics. *Journal of Macromarketing, 6,* 5–16.

Independence Standards Board. (2000, July). *Independence standard no. 3: Employment with audit clients.* Retrieved January 18, 2008 from http://www.pcabus.org/Standards/Interim_Standards/Independence_Standards/ISB3.pdf

Independence Standards Board. (2001, July). *Staff report: A conceptual framework for auditor independence.* Retrieved January 18, 2008 from http://www.cfainstitute.org.centre/issues/comment/2001/01audit_indep.html

Internal Revenue Service (IRS). (2005). Treasury department circular 230: Regulations governing the practice of attorneys, certified public accountants, enrolled agents, enrolled actuaries, and appraisers before the Internal Revenue Service. Retrieved on May 17, 2007 from www.irs.gov/pub/irs-pdf/pcir230.pdf.

Jensen, M. (1994). Self-interest, altruism, incentives, and agency theory. *Journal of Applied Corporate Finance, 7*(Summer), 40–45.

Jensen, M. C., & Meckling, W. H. (1976). Theory of the firm: Managerial behavior, agency costs, and ownership structure. *Journal of Financial Economics, 3*(October), 305–360.

Jensen, M., & Meckling, W. (1994). The nature of man. *Journal of Applied Corporate Finance 7,* (Summer), 4–19.

Jordan, J. (2005). Business experience and moral awareness: When less may be more. Unpublished doctoral dissertation, Yale University.

Jordan, J., & Sternberg, R. (2006). Wisdom in organizations: A balance theory analysis. Unpublished manuscript, Dartmouth College.

Kennedy, J., & Peecher, M. (1997). Judging auditors' technical knowledge. *Journal of Accounting Research, 35*(2), 279–293.

Langevoort, D. (1997). Organized illusions: A behavioral theory of why corporations mislead stock market investors (and cause other social harms). *University of Pennsylvania Law Review, 146*(November), 101–172.

Marwell, G., & Ames, R. (1981). Econmists free ride. Does anyone else? Experiments on the provision of public goods. IV. *Journal of Public Economics, 15*,295–310.

Maslow, A. (1943). A theory of human motivation. *Psychological Review, 50*, 370–396.

McDonald, I., Solomon, D., & Francis, T. (2005, March 31). AIG admits "improper" accounting. *The Wall Street Journal*, A1, A7.

National Association of State Boards of Accountancy (NASBA). (2005). *Proposed revisions to the Uniform Accountancy Rules 5–1 and 5–2.* Retrieved May 17, 2007 from (http://www.nasba.org/NASBAfiles.nsf/Lookup/UAAEducationRules ExposureDraft/$file/UAA%20Education%20Rules%20Exposure%20Draft.pdf).

New York Times. (2007, January 4). Out with the old. Retrieved January 4, 2007 from http://www.nytimes.com/2007/01/04/opinion.

Noreen, E. (1988). The economics of ethics: A new perspective on agency theory. *Accounting, Organizations & Society, 13*(4), 359–369.

Plumlee, R. D., Kachelmeier, S. J., Madeo, S. A., Pratt, J. H., & Krull, G. (2006). Assessing the shortage of accounting faculty. *Issues in Accounting Education, 21*(May), 113–125.

Prentice, R. (2004). Teaching ethics, heuristics, and biases. *Journal of Business Ethics Education, 1*(1), 57–74.

Reckers, P. (2006). Perspectives on the proposal for a generally accepted accounting curriculum: A wake-up call for academics. *Issues in Accounting Education, 21*(1), 31–43.

Sarbanes-Oxley Act. (2002). Public Law 107-204. 107th Congress, 2nd session. Washington, DC: GPO.

Shaub, M. K. (1996). Trust and suspicion: The effects of situational and dispositional factors on auditors' trust of clients. *Behavioral Research in Accounting, 8*, 154–174.

Shaub, M. K. (2004). Trust as a threat to independence: Emotional trust, auditor-client interdependence, and their impact on professional skepticism. *Research on Professional Responsibility and Ethics in Accounting, 9*, 169–188.

Shaub, M. K. (2005). Materialism and materiality. *International Journal of Accounting, Auditing and Performance Evaluation, 2(4)*, 347–355.

Shaub, M. K. (2006). Give me the good and the bright. *The CPA Journal, 76*(February), 6, 8.

Shaub, M. K., & Lawrence, J. E. (2002). A taxonomy of auditors' professional skepticism. *Research on Accounting Ethics, 8*, 167–194.

Smith, A. (1966). *The theory of moral sentiments.* New York: Augustus M. Kelley.

Smith, A. (1976). *An inquiry into the nature and causes of the wealth of nations.* Oxford: Clarendon Press.

Staw, B. (1976). Knee-deep in the big muddy: A study of escalating commitment to a chosen course of action. *Organizational Behavior and Human Performance, 16*, 27–44.

Sternberg, R. (2001). What is the common thread of creativity? Its dialectical relation to intelligence and wisdom. *American Psychologist, 56*, (April), 360–362.

Sternberg, R. (2002). Successful intelligence: A new approach to leadership. In R. E. Riggio, S. E. Murphy, & F. J. Pirozzolo (Eds.), *Multiple Intelligences and Leadership* (pp. 9–28). Mahwah, NJ: Lawrence Erlbaum Associates.

Sternberg, R. (2003a). WICS: A model for leadership in organizations. *Academy of Management Learning and Education 2,* 386–401.

Sternberg, R. (2003b). *WICS: A theory of wisdom, intelligence and creativity synthesized.* New York: Cambridge University Press.

Sternberg, R. (2005). A model of educational leadership: Wisdom, intelligence, and creativity, synthesized. *International Journal of Leadership in Education, 8*(4), 347–364.

Sternberg, R. (2006, July). How could I be so stupid? *USA Today Magazine,* 70–72.

Street., M., & Street, V. L. (2006). The effects of escalating commitment on ethical decision-making. *Journal of Business Ethics, 64*(April), 343–356.

United States Department of Justice. (2005). KPMG to pay $456 million for criminal violations in relation to largest-ever tax shelter fraud case. Retrieved May 17, 2007 from http://www.usdoj.gov/opa/pr/2005/August/05_ag_433.html.

Van Whye, G. (1994). *The struggle for status: A history of accounting education.* New York: Garland Publishing.

Watts, R. L., & Zimmerman, J. L. (1986). *Positive accounting theory.* New Jersey: Prentice Hall.

Zeff, S. (2003). How the U.S. accounting profession got where it is today: Part II. *Accounting Horizons, 17*(December), 267–286.

CHAPTER 16

BUSINESS ETHICS AND SOCIAL RESPONSIBILITY IN THE HUMAN RESOURCE MANAGEMENT CURRICULUM

Marc Orlitzky
Nottingham University Business School

ABSTRACT

Human resource management (HRM) has an increasingly important role to play in enabling more socially responsible and responsive management. However, at present, employee issues are typically taught in a haphazard, piecemeal approach in introductory business ethics courses without a strong emphasis on the human resource (HR) functions that can support corporate social responsibility. To infuse HR ethics teaching with a clearer organization, this chapter presents possible teaching techniques in all of the four key functions of HRM: staffing, performance appraisal, compensation, and training and development. Hence, this chapter proposes a curriculum that addresses the key issues—identified by Orlitzky & Swanson (2006)—as part of a more socially responsible approach to HRM.

Advancing Business Ethics Education, pages 329–344

INTRODUCTION

In response to the public's growing insistence on corporate social and environmental responsibility, over 90 percent of large U.S. corporations now publish statements about their obligations to a wide range of stakeholders, according to a poll by Deloitte (DesJardins, 2006). This suggests that, at least in their words, most American companies do not endorse an exclusive focus on shareholder wealth maximization anymore. However, if corporate *actions* do not live up to the corporate rhetoric of "stakeholder management" or "dialogue," organizations' reputation and performance will be at stake because the public trust and confidence in corporate America will be undermined. Therefore, business school professors must switch attention to the effective *implementation* of business ethics and corporate responsibility in their teaching efforts.

The implementation of business ethics and social responsibility in organizations requires, among a myriad of other organizational adaptations, a clear focus on the human resource (HR) function (Orlitzky & Swanson, 2006). Employees at all levels must become involved in organizational efforts to bring about organizational cultures and structures that are supportive of social responsibility (Swanson, 1999). In general, social responsibility initiatives should aim to make organizations more responsive to stakeholders' concerns about social and environmental issues. Along these lines, many organizations are shifting from a reactive to a proactive and, in fact, increasingly interactive view of their stakeholders (Waddock, 2002). These strategic shifts require the cooperation and commitment of all employees, whose assistance is essential in strategy implementation. However, at the moment, the academic literature does not provide much in-depth guidance on the steps necessary to make human resource management (HRM) an integral component of organizations' social and environmental initiatives. In sum, HRM must become an integral element of the broader effort to make organizations more responsible citizens in society, and our teaching must reflect this new action-oriented emphasis as well.

This chapter explores the way in which ethics and social responsibility apply to all of the four functions of HRM: staffing, performance appraisal, compensation, and training and development. Furthermore, this chapter presents teaching techniques meant to illustrate the ethical issues related to these functions. To advance business ethics education, business ethics and social responsibility must be integratively taught in the context of all four functional areas of HRM. Like other business issues, HR decisions, policies, and programs raise a broad spectrum of normative questions, which HR directors and managers must be prepared to address in socially responsible ways. To that end, I provide a general suggestion for how business schools can deliver a curriculum that calls attention to these issues as well as some specific approaches to teaching and learning in this area.[1] These approaches are presented in the four functional areas of HRM in terms of some core issues identified by Orlitzky and Swanson (2006).

THE TEACHING OF ETHICS
AND SOCIAL RESPONSIBILITY IN HRM

In terms of the broader business school curriculum, it is essential that HRM students are exposed to the fundamentals of "Business, Ethics, and Society" before taking a discipline-specific HR ethics elective. In fact, my description of possible teaching approaches in HR ethics and social responsibility builds on this presumption of an existing stand-alone ethics course. A required stand-alone course in business ethics can impart the analytic tools for students' greater awareness of their own moral values as well as broader social issues (Swanson & Frederick, 2005). In this sense, it can serve as a springboard for the kind of elective HRM course described below. In other words, the proposed course presumes student awareness of various models of corporate responsibility and a working knowledge of a variety of moral frameworks, such as utilitarianism, deontology, virtue ethics, and ethics of care.

A Broadened Notion of Socially Responsible HRM

I propose that it is just as important to prepare employees for organizational opportunities to incorporate ethics *proactively* as it is for HR practitioners to redress ethical problems within organizations *reactively*. At this point, it is unclear how widespread ethical problems really are in today's American workplaces. Research by Danley and his colleagues showed that, in the mid-1990s at least, there was no widespread moral crisis in U.S. organizations (Danley, Harrick, Schaefer, Strickland, & Sullivan, 1996). In contrast to focusing on ethics as an external and internal control tool, proactive management may enable the type of ethical leadership required in today's organizations, which are typically caught in a large web of stakeholder pressures for socially responsible and responsive organizational initiatives (Paine, 2003). In this sense, morally aware HRM can make companies more responsible citizens in society and create the preconditions for improved social and financial performance (Solomon, 1985, 1999). This broadening of the entire HR function as proactive management for social responsibility is in line with proposals by prominent HRM researchers such as Ulrich (1998) and Rynes (2004).

But first, let us consider the double objectives of HR practitioners that must inform our teaching. On the one hand, HR directors and managers are required to serve the economic interests of the organization by designing HRM so that it enhances labor productivity and, ultimately, the organization's financial performance (Pfeffer, 1994, 1998). On the other hand, they have an obligation to look after employee interests. This in turn means that they need to be concerned with increasing employee job satisfaction, well-being, and the meaningfulness of work. Sometimes, these two objectives may point toward the same policies, programs, or organizational actions. At other times, they may be in tension. But it should be clear by now that the single-minded pursuit of a narrowly economic goal in HR managers' work would, in fact, be narrow-minded. Instead, today's HR directors and managers—especially if they aspire to work for large corporations—need a deeper understanding of the ethical issues that are outlined in this chapter.

At the same time, HR instructors and practitioners must realize that the consideration of ethics and social responsibility as strategic tools (for enhancing organizational economic performance) is not necessarily unethical (Husted & Allen, 2000). Rather, it may exemplify enlightened self-interest, which to some authors is the highest level of morality (see Locke, 2006; Rand, 1964). That is, behavior characterized by impeccable ethics and greater social responsibility may not only be prudent at the individual (employee) level of analysis (Solomon, 1999), but also at the organizational level of analysis, as some meta-analytic evidence has indicated (Orlitzky, forthcoming; Orlitzky & Benjamin, 2001; Orlitzky, Schmidt, & Rynes, 2003).[2] And so, the aforementioned double objectives of HRM ultimately point to a balanced consideration of economic and "humanistic" goals, which might not clash at all (Huselid, 1995; Pfeffer, 1998). More pointedly, HR practitioners have an obligation to make ethics and social responsibility work within a capitalist framework by recognizing the positive *moral* consequences of capitalist profit-seeking (Friedman, 2005; Hayek, 2001; Locke, 2006; Rand, 1967). Such an instrumental view of ethics and social responsibility does *not* imply that economic performance becomes the ultimate decision criterion to which the other dimensions of organizational performance are subordinated. Instead, it portends a balanced strategizing or a more thoughtful integration of market and nonmarket strategies (Baron, 2006).[3]

This chapter, with its emphasis on proactive HR management, does not cover those issues that comprise the traditional ethics curriculum fare. For instance, business ethics courses usually include discussions of such HR topics as downsizing, bribery, whistle blowing, comparable worth, employment at will, and other issues that, for the most part, manifest in the legal arena. However, in my view, such a legal focus often misses the point of effective ethics instruction, which is supposed to help future managers realize the synergies between successful business, ethics, and social responsibility (Solomon, 1985, 1994). Sometimes, there are tradeoffs, but we must not presume that these tradeoffs are inevitable. Furthermore, an emphasis on legal compliance tends to focus organizational efforts on moral mediocrity rather than excellence (Paine, 1994) and the proactive management of ethical issues discussed previously.

The following section will outline some teaching and learning techniques applicable to this enabling function of HRM in staffing, performance appraisal, compensation and other incentives, and training and development, respectively.

Staffing

For staffing to become more ethically and socially responsible, topics other than public policy and legal regulation (for example, equal employment, affirmative action, and discrimination in recruitment and selection) need to be explored. As Orlitzky and Swanson (2006) highlight, three such important staffing topics are a) the hiring of employees for cognitive moral development, b) more generally, an attention to new hires' personality traits, and c) a counterbalancing of any focused recruitment by a general promotion of employee diversity. Illuminating the nature of these three areas translates into an important learning objective in the teaching of the recruitment and selection aspects of staffing.

To cover the first two topics of hiring for moral development and personality factors, the instructor should start with an overview of Kohlberg's stages of cognitive moral development (Colby & Kohlberg, 1987), which are preconventional (punishment/obedience and instrumental orientations), conventional (interpersonal and law and order orientations), and postconventional (social contract and universal principles orientations). Because these stages affect managerial decision making (Weber, 1990), HR students should get a sense of the conceptual meaning of these stages of moral development. Arguably, one important aspect of the staffing function is to investigate individuals' moral fiber, which could be used to predict job applicants' integrity on the job. The importance of this aspect must be balanced with concerns about privacy when organizations try to measure job applicants' ethics.

After this introduction to the key issues, instructors should review the actual selection instruments used in today's organizations. In the measurement of job applicants' cognitive moral development (CMD), Standard Issue Scoring, the original technique proposed by Kohlberg (Colby & Kohlberg, 1987), has certain limitations. Although Kohlberg's open-ended interview technique was path-breaking, it necessitated extensive training for the interviewer and was time-consuming to administer (Treviño &

Weaver, 2003). In addition, it is unclear to what extent interviewers can factor out their own CMD in the assessment of others' CMD (Nisbett & Wilson, 1977) or whether verbalization in interview settings can tap tacit knowledge (Schweder, Mahapatra, & Miller, 1987). The classroom presentation of measures of CMD could conclude with two validated measures that seem most useful for organizations. One, in his Adapted Moral Judgment Interview, Weber (1990) improved on Kohlberg's measure by standard scoring individuals' responses to three hypothetical dilemmas. Two, Rest's (1979) Defining Issues Test (DIT) presents a reliable, validated, and useful multiple-choice alternative to the more time-consuming measures introduced before. More specifically, the DIT, including its updated version (i.e., the DIT2), measures respondents' moral schemas instead of Kohlberg's stages *per se* (Rest, Narvaez, Bebeau, & Thoma, 1999). Copies of these measures could be distributed to students and discussed. This discussion could include the possibility of using profession-specific DIT dilemmas (Rest & Narvaez, 1994).

After introducing the concept and possible measures of CMD, the instructor should address personality testing in an employee selection process, especially the empirically validated Five Factor Model of personality (Buss, 1989; Costa, Terracciano, & McCrae, 2001; Kreitler & Kreitler, 1990; McCrae & Costa, 1997). Recent research has found strong relationships between a) agreeableness and *normative myopia*, the latter defined as the managerial tendency to downplay social values and ethics in organizations (Swanson, 1999), and b) agreeableness and a managerial preference for small pay disparities between high and low earners within the organization (Orlitzky, Swanson, & Quartermaine, 2006; Swanson & Orlitzky, 2006). Agreeableness is a personality factor that describes the extent to which an individual is caring, trusting, and cooperative. After introducing these terms, the instructor should ask students for their characterizations of agreeable individuals' behaviors, concluding with an introduction of possible personality inventory measures of this trait (Barrick & Mount, 1991; Costa & McCrae, 1992; Goldberg, 1992). A caveat is that research in this area is preliminary and, therefore, agreeableness should not be considered the primary personality indicator of personal ethics. Even so, discussing this trait can signal the importance of measuring applicants' ethical inclinations. Thus, a good way to conclude this discussion is with a brief overview of research syntheses of integrity assessments in staffing, drawing, for example, on a study by Ones, Viswesvaran, and Schmidt (1993).

Mentioned previously, a focus on moral development and desirable personality traits should be balanced by an emphasis on the importance of diversity in organizations. Students should realize that, from a HR ethics perspective, it is never advisable to populate your organization with only one type of individual. Diversity typically allows for better problem solving

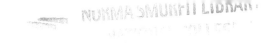

and decision making within organizations and, thus, may result in various financial benefits (Janis, 1982; Tsui & Gutek, 1999). Hence, it is vital that HR students appreciate both the instrumental benefits and moral imperative of workforce diversity. What follows are several exercises well suited for encouraging this realization:

1. Cases that motivate a deeper understanding of employee diversity—rather than a prescriptive emphasis on the legal environment—are assigned. These cases should make students question stereotypes and point out some organizational advantages presented by workforce diversity—both economic and social. Parts of Mary Gentile's (2003) HBSP eLearning Program *Managing Across Differences* is helpful in conveying the benefits of diversity, as is the Harvard case *Managing Diversity at Cityside Financial Services* (Ely & Vargas, 2006), and readings by Thomas and Ely (1996) and Mueller (1998).

2. Small groups are formed to explore cultural differences and prejudices. An experiential exercise that works well is included in the textbook *OB in Action* called "Who to Hire?" (Wohlberg, Gilmore, & Wolff, 1998). Students first rank diverse job applicants individually and subsequently, after team discussion, as a group. As part of this in-class exercise, students often are surprised to realize that cultural stereotypes often greatly affect their proposed hiring decisions and, in fact, might lead to a preference for employee homogeneity.

3. As a homework assignment after this bias-surfacing exercise, students are asked to come up with strategies to manage diversity. When discussing this homework assignment, students and the instructor might highlight the importance of *recognizing* and *appreciating* cultural differences. The alternative, namely any attempt to hide or diminish diversity, is shown to be counterproductive as far as social responsibility is concerned.

4. An optional last step of this exercise is a self-reflection assignment, in which students describe an episode of subtle discrimination in their own life and how they felt about differential treatment (because of their non-conformity with some dominant aspect of culture). In this expressive paper, students are asked to link their reflection to the aforementioned reading assignments and class exercises related to diversity.

The last two elements of this diversity appreciation exercise represent an adaptation of Irwin Siegel's (2000) exercise "Understanding Diversity and Difference," described in *Developing Adult Learners*. At the end of this exercise, the instructor could note that, according to some empirical evidence, training to combat managerial biases and stereotypes may promote greater diversity to only a limited extent. Instead, structural solutions, with clear responsibility assigned to diversity committees and staff positions, seem to be more effective in bringing about greater demographic diversity (Kalev, Dobbin, & Kelly, 2006).

Performance Appraisal

Any course in HRM ethics would also have to acknowledge the important role of performance appraisal in focusing employee efforts on ethics and social responsibility. At the same time, instructors need to convey that organizational values and principles related to ethics and social responsibility tend to be contingent on industry- or even firm-specific norms (Kabanoff, Waldersee, & Cohen, 1995; Victor & Cullen, 1987).

Besides that information, the overarching message in introducing this topic is that future managers must recognize that greater organizational integrity requires a broader performance focus than only financial criteria. One idea for conveying this message is to use Kaplan and Norton's (1992) Balanced Scorecard, which is a managerial tool that links operational, financial, learning, and customer-satisfaction performance measures. The relevant learning objective would be to add, more explicitly, ethical or social responsibility measures and apply this modified Balanced Scorecard to the performance appraisals of employees.

To help students realize how broader organizational performance indicators can affect more micro-level performance appraisal systems, instructors can proceed in one of two ways. They can draw on either a specific company, as a starting point, or a widely used organization-level standard of sustainability. If they choose the former, it will be important to use a company that specifies concrete values and principles, such as Merck, Johnson & Johnson, or Levi Strauss. If instructors choose the latter (which is my preference), they can refer to previous discussions of social responsibility and sustainability standards in the required foundational course in business ethics and distribute an overview of one the most widely used frameworks, the Global Reporting Initiative (GRI). The GRI is a widely used framework measuring an organization's commitment to, and implementation of, the triple bottom line (which includes indicators of financial, social, and environmental performance).[4] The instructor can then put students in small teams of three to four individuals and ask them to develop possible individual- or team-level performance indicators in line with the organization-level GRI. The point is *not* to come up with an ultimate or comprehensive list of performance criteria that steer employee motivation in the direction of greater social responsibility and ethics. Rather, the point is to encourage future managers' thinking about a more balanced, ethical, and comprehensive approach to performance appraisal *in the context of their organization or industry.* Of course, many, if not most,

GRI measures apply to the level of the workplace or strategic business unit and cannot be easily translated into performance measures at the employee level of analysis. Despite the difficulty of this exercise, students are likely to suggest participation in anti-corruption training, for example, or cost-effective safety improvements in products as possible indicators of employee performance.

Compensation and Other Incentives

One of the learning objectives in this third element of HR ethics is the establishment of a connection between reward systems and the aforementioned socially responsible performance appraisal. When dealing with working adults, the instructor could start by eliciting from them some information about their organizations' compensation practices: What performance dimensions do their organizations reward? What employee behaviors do their organizations incentivize? If the class consists of mainly younger students with limited work experience, the instructor could turn this descriptive question into a normative one: What types of employee behaviors, in their opinions, *should* organizations reward? To encourage everyone in the class to contribute their ideas, this important first step of the compensation exercise should typically occupy a good 15 to 20 minutes of class time.

As the next step in this exercise, the instructor should highlight the need for broadly based compensation systems that take into account employee performance along several dimensions. Here the discussion could shift from presenting incentives as a single-minded pursuit of financial performance goals to a broader frame that includes social and environmental performance indicators. For example, students might suggest that bonuses could be allocated to encourage employees to come up with constructive ideas for energy-saving techniques or other tactics useful for corporate greening. Their rationale might be that without some monetary incentives for non-economic performance, employees might fail to take corporate social and environmental responsibilities seriously. The case of Enron could be offered as an illustration of this kind of irresponsible behavior. After all, although Enron espoused, in top managers' rhetoric at least, various non-economic goals, Enron's compensation system was firmly centered on employees' economic contributions to the firm.

Yet, the discussion of the HR function of compensation cannot stop at the point of aligning monetary incentives with non-monetary goals. In fact, the instructor should offer several caveats at this point. First, purely monetary incentives might kill the kind of employee initiative and enjoyment that arises from assisting with social and environmental causes inside and outside the organization (Deci & Ryan, 1987). Second, the instructor should point out that there is a risk involved in making social and economic goals instrumental for higher monetary rewards. In economic downturns, in cases where firm financial support for these non-economic initiatives dry up, the incentivized behaviors might stop as well. Third, and arguably most important, the introduction of more incentives might lead to even more lopsided pay distributions within organizations. Large pay dispersions, for example in the form of tournament systems, can have worrisome side effects on employee morale, turnover, and even organizational performance, as demonstrated in empirical research (Bloom, 1999; Bloom & Michel, 2002; Shaw, Gupta, & Delery, 2002).[5] HR managers and directors must be careful not to design compensation systems with many dysfunctional side effects.

For students to recognize this third point, consider dividing the class into two organizations (with several sub-groups if the class size is over 14): one where highest-to-lowest income ratios do not exceed 10: 1, and one where these pay ratios approach the current average of 350: 1. Student teams are then asked to compile a list of pros and cons of these organizations characterized by their assigned pay ratios. After this discussion, the class is debriefed by comparing the students' ideas to facts drawn from the empirical literature. The students are then asked to address the problem of pronounced pay disparities by suggesting incentive systems for greater social or environmental performance. These suggestions might include social responsibility awards, ethics awards, or allowing employees to volunteer for community initiatives on company time (Roddick, 1991; Schwartz & Post, 2002). By the end of this discussion, students should realize that money might be less of a motivator for individuals at higher levels of cognitive moral development than individuals at lower levels of analysis. They should also realize the importance of tapping intrinsic motivation by expanding employee autonomy and choice for diverse ethics initiatives instead of trying to control employee behavior through extrinsic monetary rewards (Deci & Moller, 2005).

Training and Development

As mentioned before, desirable social performance and organizational ethics call for an interactive stakeholder approach (Calton & Lad, 1995; Waddock, 2002). Ideally, socially responsible and responsive organizations do not try to apply preconceived notions of "the good," but continuously consult with various stakeholder groups in the development of desirable social and environmental performance (Rasche & Esser, 2006). Thus, organizations should develop training and development (T&D) programs that promote the skills of effective stakeholder dialogues. As the first part of an exercise related to this HR function, students are asked to brainstorm possible goals of T&D programs in business ethics and social responsibility. As part of this brainstorming exercise, they should start with thinking about the individual skills necessary for organizational excellence in ethics and social responsibility. The qualities of effective stakeholder dialogue (outcome of part 1 of this exercise) may include interpersonal openness, tolerance, transparency, and the ability to treat others as equals (Pedersen, 2006). It is important for students to understand that to engage with a variety of stakeholders effectively, managers must be tolerant of a variety of stakeholder views and willing to share a lot of organizational information in joint decision making, in which no stakeholder group takes priority over all others. These qualities and goals are especially important for employees working in corporate affairs or communications departments. However, the contents of this last HR function are not only applicable to corporate affairs managers, but to almost anyone in today's business firms because increasingly boundary-spanning functions need to be performed by *all* managers (Burke, 1999).

As the second (and pivotal) point of this T&D exercise, students should be asked to develop possible workshops that might be helpful for the development of employee skills relevant for effective stakeholder dialogue, which is often characterized by cooperative inquiry (Reason, 2000). For students who have little background in the development of T&D programs, instructors would be well advised to rely on structured exercises that illustrate the required skills of effective boundary spanners. Several exercises on effective collaboration, dialogue, and receptive communication are in *The Fifth Discipline Fieldbook* (Senge, Kleiner, Roberts, Ross, & Smith, 1994). In addition, the HBS eLearning Program *Managing Difficult Conversations* is also helpful for developing some essential communication skills (Argyris, Senge, & Noonan, 2003). Whatever the specific T&D approach chosen by the students, instructors should conclude this discussion with a fairly consistent empirical finding: organizations that offer more T&D tend to perform better economically (Pfeffer, 1998).

CONCLUSION

This chapter has explored various ways in which the teaching of business ethics and social responsibility can be integrated with the four traditional HR functions of staffing, performance appraisal, compensation, and training & development. However, at this point, I would like to include a disclaimer or caveat about the tentative nature of my approach: Other instructors of HRM or ethics might see other linkages. In that sense, this chapter is only the start of a broader academic discussion, which will be necessary to bring about desirable change in HR education. This change could be facilitated not only by a separate course in HR ethics, but also by a module within a conventional HRM course. Regardless of the exact form of these curricular decisions, instructors ought to point out the linkages between all four HR functions and socially responsible management.

NOTES

1. In Orlitzky (forthcoming), I differentiate *corporate social responsibility* (CSR), *corporate social performance* (CSP), and *corporate citizenship* (CC) and explain my preference for the latter term.

2. Orlitzky and Benjamin (2001) won the 2001 Best Article Award given by the International Association for Business and Society (IABS) in association with *California Management Review.* Orlitzky, Schmidt, and Rynes (2003) won the 2004 Moskowitz award for outstanding quantitative research relevant to the social investment field. The sponsors of the Moskowitz Prize are Calvert Group, First Affirmative Financial Network, KLD Research & Analytics Inc., Nelson Capital Management, Rockefeller & Co., and Trillium Asset Management Corporation. The Moskowitz Prize is awarded each year to the research paper that best meets the following criteria: a) practical significance to practitioners of socially responsible investing; b) appropriateness and rigor of quantitative methods; and c) novelty of results. Both award-winning papers were based on my doctoral dissertation, which was completed in July 1998.

3. In the context of this self-reflective integration, instructors of ethics and social responsibility in HRM could question the term "human *resource*" for its potentially dehumanizing moral connotations. Southwest Airlines is an example of an organization that has abandoned the term "human resources" because of its negative connotations.

4. A good overview of GRI can be gleaned from the official GRI website: http://www.globalreporting.org/Home [last accessed on April 18, 2007].

5. In a tournament compensation system, an employee's pay depends on that employee's ranking relative to other employees. The prescription of relatively large pay differentials follows from agency theory, or the economic theory of incentives (Baron & Kreps, 1999).

REFERENCES

Argyris, C., Senge, P. M., & Noonan, B. (2003). *Managing difficult conversations [Interactive CD-ROM].* Cambridge, MA: Harvard Business School Publishing.

Baron, D. P. (2006). *Business and its environment* (5th ed.). Upper Saddle River, NJ: Prentice Hall.

Baron, J. N., & Kreps, D. M. (1999). *Strategic human resources: Frameworks for general managers.* New York: Wiley.

Barrick, M. R., & Mount, M. K. (1991). The Big Five personality dimensions and job performance: A meta-analysis. *Personnel Psychology, 44,* 1–26.

Bloom, M. (1999). The performance effects of pay dispersion on individuals and organizations. *Academy of Management Journal, 42,* 25–40.

Bloom, M., & Michel, J. G. (2002). The relationships among organizational context, pay dispersion, and managerial turnover. *Academy of Management Journal, 45,* 33–42.

Burke, E. M. (1999). *Corporate community relations: The principle of the neighbor of choice.* Greenwich, CT: Praeger.

Buss, A. H. (1989). Personality as traits. *American Psychologist, 44,* 1378–1388.

Calton, J. M., & Lad, L. J. (1995). Social contracting as a trust-building process of network governance. *Business Ethics Quarterly, 5,* 271–296.

Colby, A., & Kohlberg, L. (1987). *The measurement of moral judgment: Vol. 1. Theoretical foundations and research validations.* Cambridge, MA: Cambridge University Press.

Costa, P. T., Jr., & McCrae, R. R. (1992). *Revised NEO personality inventory (NEO-PI-R) and NEO five-factor (NEO-FFI) inventory professional manual.* Odessa, FL: Psychological Assessment Resources.

Costa, P. T., Jr., Terracciano, A., & McCrae, R. R. (2001). Gender differences in personality traits across cultures: Robust and surprising findings. *Journal of Personality and Social Psychology, 81*(2), 322–331.

Danley, J., Harrick, E., Schaefer, D., Strickland, D., & Sullivan, G. (1996). HR's view of ethics in the work place: Are the barbarians at the gate? *Journal of Business Ethics, 15*(3), 273–285.

Deci, E. L., & Moller, A. C. (2005). The concept of competence: A starting place for understanding intrinsic motivation and self-determined extrinsic motivation. In A. J. Elliot & C. S. Dweck (Eds.), *Handbook of competence and motivation* (pp. 579–597). New York: Guilford.

Deci, E. L., & Ryan, R. M. (1987). The support of autonomy and the control of behavior. *Journal of Personality and Social Psychology, 53,* 1024–1037.

DesJardins, J. R. (2006). *An introduction to business ethics* (2nd ed.). Boston, MA: McGraw-Hill.

Ely, R. J., & Vargas, I. (2006). *Managing diversity at Cityside Financial Services.* Cambridge, MA: Harvard Business School Publishing.

Friedman, B. M. (2005). *The moral consequences of economic growth.* New York: Knopf.

Gentile, M. (2003). *Managing across differences [Interactive CD-ROM].* Cambridge, MA: Harvard Business School Press.

Goldberg, L. R. (1992). The development of markers for the Big-Five factor structure. *Psychological Assessment, 4,* 26–42.

Hayek, F. A. (2001). *The road to serfdom.* London: Routledge.

Huselid, M. A. (1995). The impact of human resource management practices on turnover, productivity, and corporate financial performance. *Academy of Management Journal, 38,* 635–672.

Husted, B. W., & Allen, D. B. (2000). Is it ethical to use ethics as strategy? *Journal of Business Ethics, 27*(1/2), 21–31.

Janis, I. L. (1982). *Groupthink: Psychological studies of policy decisions and fiascoes.* Boston, MA: Houghton Mifflin.

Kabanoff, B., Waldersee, R., & Cohen, M. (1995). Espoused values and organizational change themes. *Academy of Management Journal, 38,* 1075–1104.

Kalev, A., Dobbin, F., & Kelly, E. (2006). Best practices or best guesses? Diversity management and the remediation of inequality. *American Sociological Review, 71*(4), 589–617.

Kaplan, R. S., & Norton, D. P. (1992). The Balanced Scorecard: Measures that drive performance. *Harvard Business Review, 69*(1), 71–79.

Kreitler, S., & Kreitler, H. (1990). *The cognitive foundations of personality traits.* New York: Plenum Press.

Locke, E. A. (2006). Business ethics: A way out of the morass. *Academy of Management Learning & Education, 5*(3), 324–332.

McCrae, R. R., & Costa, P. T., Jr. (1997). Personality trait structure as a human universal. *American Psychologist, 52*(509–516).

Mueller, K. P. (1998). *Diversity and the bottom line [Management Update].* Cambridge, MA: Harvard Business School Publishing.

Nisbett, R. E., & Wilson, T. D. (1977). Telling more than we can know: Verbal reports on mental processing. *Psychological Review, 84*(3), 231–259.

Ones, D. S., Viswesvaran, C., & Schmidt, F. L. (1993). Meta-analysis of integrity test validities: Findings and implications for personnel selection and theories of job performance. *Journal of Applied Psychology, 78*, 679–703.

Orlitzky, M. (forthcoming). Corporate social performance and financial performance: A research synthesis. In A. Crane, A. McWilliams, D. Matten, J. Moon, & D. Siegel (Eds.), *The Oxford Handbook of CSR.* Oxford, UK: Oxford University Press.

Orlitzky, M., & Benjamin, J. D. (2001). Corporate social performance and firm risk: A meta-analytic review. *Business & Society, 40*(4), 369–396.

Orlitzky, M., Schmidt, F. L., & Rynes, S. L. (2003). Corporate social and financial performance: A meta-analysis. *Organization Studies, 24*(3), 403–441.

Orlitzky, M., & Swanson, D. (2006). Socially responsible human resource management: Charting new territory. In J. R. Deckop (Ed.), *Human resource management ethics* (pp. 3–25). Greenwich, CT: Information Age Publishing.

Orlitzky, M., Swanson, D. L., & Quartermaine, L.-K. (2006). Normative myopia, executives' personality, and preference for pay dispersion: Toward implications for corporate social performance. *Business & Society, 45*(2), 149–177.

Paine, L. S. (1994). Managing for organizational integrity. *Harvard Business Review, 72*(2), 106–117.

Paine, L. S. (2003). *Value shift: Why companies must merge social and financial imperatives to achieve superior performance.* New York: McGraw-Hill.

Pedersen, E. R. (2006). Making corporate social responsibility (CSR) operable: How companies translate stakeholder dialogue into practice. *Business and Society Review, 111*(2), 137–163.

Pfeffer, J. (1994). *Competitive advantage through people: Unleashing the power of the workforce.* Boston, MA: Harvard Business School Press.

Pfeffer, J. (1998). *The human equation: Building profits by putting people first.* Boston, MA: Harvard Business School Press.

Rand, A. (1964). *The virtue of selfishness: A new concept of egoism.* New York: New American Library.

Rand, A. (1967). *Capitalism: The unknown ideal.* New York: Signet.

Rasche, A., & Esser, D. E. (2006). From stakeholder management to stakeholder accountability: Applying Habermasian discourse ethics to accountability research. *Journal of Business Ethics, 65*(3), 251–267.

Reason, P. (2000). Cooperative inquiry. In K. Taylor, C. Marienau & M. Fiddler (Eds.), *Developing adult learners* (pp. 85–89). San Francisco: Jossey-Bass.

Rest, J. (1979). *Development in judging moral issues.* Minneapolis, MN: University of Minnesota Press.

Rest, J., & Narvaez, D. (1994). *Moral development in the professions: Psychology and applied ethics.* Hillsdale, NJ: Erlbaum.

Rest, J., Narvaez, D., Bebeau, M. J., & Thoma, S. J. (1999). *Postconventional moral thinking: A neo-Kohlbergian approach.* Mahwah, NJ: Erlbaum.

Roddick, A. (1991). *Body and soul: Profits with principles.* New York: Crown.

Rynes, S. L. (2004). Where do we go from here? Imagining new roles for human resources. *Journal of Management Inquiry, 13*(3), 203–213.

Schwartz, R. H., & Post, F. R. (2002). The unexplored potential of hope to level the playing field: A multilevel perspective. *Journal of Business Ethics, 37*(2), 135–143.

Schweder, R. A., Mahapatra, M., & Miller, J. G. (1987). Culture and moral development. In J. Kagan & S. Lamb (Eds.), *The emergence of morality in small children* (pp. 1–83). Chicago: University of Chicago Press.

Senge, P. M., Kleiner, A., Roberts, C., Ross, R. B., & Smith, B. J. (1994). *The fifth discipline fieldbook: Strategies and tools for building a learning organization.* New York: Doubleday.

Shaw, J. D., Gupta, N., & Delery, J. E. (2002). Pay dispersion and workforce performance: Moderating effects of incentives and interdependence. *Strategic Management Journal, 23*(6), 491–512.

Siegel, I. (2000). Understanding diversity and difference. In K. Taylor, C. Marienau & M. Fiddler (Eds.), *Developing adult learners: Strategies for teachers and trainers* (pp. 232–233). San Francisco, CA: Jossey Bass.

Solomon, R. C. (1985). *It's good business.* New York: Atheneum.

Solomon, R. C. (1994). *The new world of business: Ethics and free enterprise in the 1990s.* Lanham, MD: Littlefield Adams.

Solomon, R. C. (1999). *A better way to think about business: How personal integrity leads to corporate success.* New York: Oxford University Press.

Swanson, D. L. (1999). Toward an integrative theory of business and society: A research strategy for corporate social performance. *Academy of Management Review, 24*, 506–521.

Swanson, D. L., & Frederick, W. C. (2005). Denial and leadership in business ethics education. In O. C. Ferrell & R. A. Peterson (Eds.), *Business ethics: The new challenge for business schools and corporate leaders* (pp. 222–240). New York: M. E. Sharpe.

Swanson, D. L., & Orlitzky, M. (2006). Executive preference for compensation structure and normative myopia: A business and society research project. In R. W. Kolb (Ed.), *The ethics of executive compensation* (pp. 13–31). Malden, MA: Blackwell.

Thomas, D. A., & Ely, R. J. (1996). Making differences matter. *Harvard Business Review, 74*(5), 79–90.

Treviño, L. K., & Weaver, G. R. (2003). *Managing ethics in business organizations: Social scientific perspectives.* Stanford, CA: Stanford University Press.

Tsui, A. S., & Gutek, B. A. (1999). *Demographic differences in organizations: Current research and future directions.* Lanham, MD: Lexington Books.

Ulrich, D. (1998). A new mandate for human resources. *Harvard Business Review, 76*(1), 124–134.

Victor, B., & Cullen, J. B. (1987). A theory and measure of ethical climate in organizations. In W. C. Frederick (Ed.), *Research in corporate social performance and policy* (Vol. 9, pp. 51–71). Greenwich, CT: JAI Press.

Waddock, S. A. (2002). *Leading corporate citizens: Vision, values, value added.* Boston, MA: McGraw-Hill.

Weber, J. (1990). Managers' moral reasoning: Assessing their responses to three moral dilemmas. *Human Relations, 43*(7), 687–702.

Wohlberg, J., Gilmore, G., & Wolff, S. (1998). *OB in action.* Boston: Houghton Mifflin.